THE NATURE OF HERITAGE

THE NATURE OF HERITAGE

THE NEW SOUTH AFRICA

LYNN MESKELL

A John Wiley & Sons, Ltd., Publication

Library of Congress Cataloging-in-Publication Data

Meskell, Lynn.
 The nature of heritage : the new South Africa / Lynn Meskell.
  p. cm.
 Includes bibliographical references and index.
 ISBN 978-0-470-67072-9 (hardcover : alk. paper) – ISBN 978-0-470-67071-2 (pbk. : alk. paper)
  1. Archaeology and Heritage–South Africa.   2. Ethnography–South Africa.   3. Cultural property–South Africa.   4. Post-apartheid era–South Africa.   5. National characteristics, South African.   6. Kruger National Park (South Africa)–History.   7. Kruger National Park (South Africa)–Antiquities.   8. South Africa–Race relations.   9. South Africa–Antiquities.   I. Title.
 GN656.M47 2012
 306.0968–dc23

                                                                                      2011015895

A catalogue record for this book is available from the British Library.

This book is published in the following electronic formats: ePDFs 9781118106624; Mobi 9781118106648; ePub 9781118106631

Set in 11/13 pt Dante by Toppan Best-set Premedia Limited
Printed and bound in Singapore by Fabulous Printers Pte Ltd

1   2012

For the people of Kruger National Park
past, present, and future

Contents

Acknowledgments   viii

Abbreviations   xiii

Introduction: Past Mastering in the New South Africa   1

1   Naturalizing Cultural Heritage   13

2   Making Heritage Pay in the Rainbow Nation   37

3   It's Mine, It's Yours: Excavating Park Histories   63

4   Why Biodiversity Trumps Culture   98

5   Archaeologies of Failure   125

6   Thulamela: The Donors, the Archaeologist, his Gold,
    and the Flood   149

7   Kruger is a Gold Rock: Parastatal and Private Visions
    of the Good   176

    Conclusions: Future Perfect   203

References   217

Index   248

Acknowledgments

This book, and indeed all my work in South Africa, was made possible by one incredible organization. I owe an enormous debt to the Andrew W. Mellon Foundation, specifically the committee for the New Directions Fellowship that enabled me to shift my research focus from the archaeology of ancient Egypt to contemporary South African heritage. Their faith in this project, and their additional program support to bring young South African scholars to Stanford University, has been unfailing. Particularly, I want to express my gratitude to Joseph Meisel, Harriet Zuckerman, and William Robertson for their years of generosity and guidance. Without them I would not have had the privilege of working in South Africa all these years and collaborating with so many talented young scholars in the Stanford–South Africa Heritage Exchange program. In addition, I am grateful for the generous support of the National Science Foundation, the Institute for Social and Economic Research and Policy (Columbia University), the Lang Fund (Stanford University), and the Clayman Institute (Stanford University).

My colleagues in South Africa have been inspirational and are the real reason why I was drawn to changing my research focus. The original invitation in 2002 by Martin Hall, Ben Smith and Geoff Blundell to lecture in South Africa had more impact than anyone could have envisaged. The National Research Foundation in South Africa kindly made that visit possible. Over the years the continued friendship, generosity, and intellectual insights from scholars at the University of the Witwatersrand has been invaluable, particularly Ben Smith, Geoff Blundell, Thembi Russell, Phil Bonner, and David Pearce. The transformative directions for heritage that Ben and Geoff have contributed through their work at the Rock Art Research Institute and Origins Center provided the key inspiration for my own work. They also facilitated my residency at Wits, thus cementing my commitment to the city of Johannesburg; they first introduced me to Kruger National Park and initiated me into the joys of biltong. Thembi Russell accompanied me on many of my fieldtrips to remote parts and braved spitting cobras, appalling roads, cultural villages, and my penchant for eating various antelopes. She taught me a great deal about being in South Africa and, from her critical vantage, its many potentials, not simply its problems. Martin Hall deserves special recognition as a mentor and friend whose pioneering research on the political economy of heritage in South Africa remains unsurpassed. This project owes an enormous debt to his unwavering intellectual presence.

Many people in South African National Parks deserve individual thanks for their time, enthusiasm, and support of the project. Without their contributions this book could not have been written. Edgar Neluvhalani and Sibongile Masuku Van Damme must be singled out for both inspiring and grounding my work, for their constancy and commitment, and their vision for a different South Africa. My life in Kruger was significantly enriched by living and working with Glynn Alard and Heidi Hansen, whose knowledge, patience, and good humor I can never fully repay. Thanyani Madzhuta has been there from the beginning and educated me about the history of Kruger and its communities inside and outside the fence. Among the many people who contributed to my fieldwork in and around Kruger are Emma Algotsson, Harry Biggs, Sue Eber, Mike English, Navashni Govender, Rina Grant, Patricia Khoza, Thembi Khoza, Leonard Luula, Sandra MacFadyen, Eric Makuleke, Patience Mdungasi, Bandile Mkhize, Precious Motubatse, Helen Mtheti, Danie Pienaar, Scott Ronaldson, Vanessa Strijdom, Randy Tanner, Raymond Travers, and Rene Travers. At Head Office in Pretoria I would like to thank Kevin Moore, Alexis Symonds, Johan Verhoof, and Rozena Waiget. From Mapungubwe National Park I would like to thank Paballo Mohofa, Cedric Sethlako, Allie Chauke, and Tzimingadzo Nemaheni.

I am deeply grateful to the elders and representatives of numerous communities around Kruger and Mapungubwe National Park, including the Makahane, Malatje, Machete, Vhangona, Lemba, Vhatwanamba and particularly Joseph Mkhabela and his family. Numerous residents in Musunda, Bende Mutale, Lilydale, Tshikuyu, Makushane, Welwerdiene, and Kliptown also shared their histories, time and ideas about heritage. In particular I want to acknowledge Joseph Endani, Alpheus Mapukumele, Freddie Mukosi Munzhelele, Alpheus Thomani Mudzanani, Bishop Malatji, Evans Malatji, Andries Makatikela, Andries Sihlangu, and the incomparable Philleos Machavi.

Other colleagues in South Africa who were generous with their time and research over the years include David Bunn, Jacklyn Cock, Gene Duiker, Amanda Esterhuysen, Simon Hall, Carolyn Hamilton, Nessa Leibhammer, David Lewis-Williams, Sibongile Masuku Van Damme, Clapperton Mavungha, David Morris, Cecilene Muller, Ndukuyakhe Ndlovu, Webber Ndoro, Sven Ouzman, John Parkington, Zarena Patel, Innocent Pikirayi, Steven Robbins, Collette Scheermeyer, Carmel Schrire, Alinah Segobye, Soul Shava, Nick Shepherd, and Leslie Witz. Les Carlisle and Lotus Khoza from AndBeyond, formerly Conservation Corporation Africa, have been generous with their time and support, introducing me to the people of Phinda, Bongani, and Ngala. Conrad de Rosner spent weeks each year with me in Bongani and Kruger, teaching me rock art recording, sharing new found sites and his knowledge of the Lowveld. His passion for South African heritage and the hospitality he extended to me and my colleagues was unstinting.

In the United States I want to thank my colleagues who have guided the project, Paulla Ebron, Miyako Inoue, James Ferguson, Liisa Malkki, Helen Stacy, Londa Scheibinger, and Jeff Kossef at Stanford and my former colleagues at Columbia in New York, Lila Abu Lughod, Sherry Ortner, Paige West, Nick Dirks, and Nan Rothschild. My current and former students have influenced my work more than they realize and have been gifted interlocutors, Lindsay Weiss, Erin Hasinoff, Karen Holmberg, Carrie Nakamura, Marisa Lazzari, Felipe Gaitan Amman, Rachel Ama-Asaa Engmann, Kathryn Lafrenz Samuels, Joshua Samuels, Trindad Rico, Madeleine Douglas, Corisande Fenwick, Alexandra Kelly, Helen Human, Maria Fernanda Escallon, and Claudia Luizza. I was very fortunate to have Lindsay Weiss work alongside me at Thulamela, accompany me on many interviews, and share her own expertise that has greatly enriched the project over the years. She was always more colleague than student and her intellectual dynamism can be seen in the better parts of my work. Rachel King deserves special mention not only for being a brilliant research assistant for this book, but for the summer of fieldwork we conducted together in Mapungubwe National Park in 2008.

I have benefitted enormously from discussions with scholars working on politics, rights and heritage in Australia, Steve Brown, Duncan Ivison, Ian Lilley, and Denis Byrne. In Spain I received an education from Felipe Criado, Alfredo Gonzalez-Ruibal, Ricardo Rodríguez, and students of the Laboratorio de Patrimonio in Santiago de Compostela. Over the years, aspects of this project were presented in Leiden, Uppsala, Ramallah, Paris, Johannesburg, Vancouver, Santiago de Compostela, Stockholm, Michigan, Bistol, Philadelphia, Gainesville, and Tucson, and I thank my hosts for providing such lively contexts for debate. Others who have offered their unique expertise and shared their writing include Anneli Ekblom, Chip Colwell-Chanthaphonh, Jean Comaroff, Diane Gifford-Gonzalez, Donald Moore, Paul Lane, Peter Pels, Peter Schmidt, Lucienne Thys-Senocak, and Ann Stoler. Denis Byrne, Martin Hall, Lindsay Weiss, and Erin Hasinoff bravely read the entire book and significantly improved it. Rosalie Robertson, my editor at Wiley-Blackwell, has my heartfelt gratitude for supporting the book and for working so hard to ensure its timely publication. At the press I also wish to acknowledge the ever-efficient Julia Kirk and the incomparable Felicity Marsh.

The book was written during my sabbatical in Oxford, Paris, and Istanbul. The glories of New College, Oxford provided a sublime place to write, thanks largely to Caroline Thomas, Michael Burden, David Parrott, Tamson Pietsch, the Warden, and other fellows. Oxford was also an inspirational place to think about South Africa thanks to the presence of William Beinart, Chris Gosden, Peter Mitchell, and Simon Pooley. During his visit to New College, Justice Albie Sachs encouraged me to write a positive account that did not draw hard lines or anger people in South Africa, though I have probably failed in that endeavor. As he says, the fact that South Africa is a country at all is one of the greatest stories of our times. During the year I also worked in Paris, enabling me to meet a new set of colleagues at UNESCO, and I thank Francesco Bandarin, Mechtild Rössler, Lazare Eloundou Assamo, Kishore Rao, and Nuria Sanz. And finally, I was lucky enough to finish the manuscript at the Research Center for Anatolian Civilizations in the company of Director Scott Redford and the fellows in Istanbul. My year abroad was made all the more special by the presence of Ian Hodder, who has lived with this project, travelled with me to Kruger, debated many of the ideas, read and undoubtedly strengthened any contribution this book might make. It is impossible to capture in words all the shared connections and experiences in a life joined by love, work, and fond similarity.

Finally, this book is dedicated to the people of Kruger National Park, past and present, to all those who lived upon its land, who inhabit its borders and remember its history, and those who are the custodians of its cultural and natural riches. Perhaps the final word should go to Albie Sachs, since he has so poignantly encapsulated South Africa's painful past and its amazing achievements after 1994: *We have many bad stories, and they need to be told, fearlessly, and again and again; as the saying goes, the beautiful people are not yet born. But I have lived at the heart of a truly wonderful story, seen it with my own eyes and felt it with my own heart, and will tell it to whoever is willing to listen.*

Lynn Meskell

Oxford, Paris, and Istanbul

The author and publisher gratefully acknowledge the permission granted to reproduce the copyright material in this book

Chapter 2
McGregor, J., and L. Schumaker. (2006). Heritage in Southern Africa: Imagining and marketing public culture and history. *Journal of Southern African Studies* 32: 649–65

Chapter 3
Carruthers, J. (1994). Dissecting the myth: Paul Kruger and the Kruger national park. *Journal of Southern African Studies* 20: 263–83

Every effort has been made to trace copyright holders and to obtain their permission for the use of copyright material. The publisher apologizes for any errors or omissions in the above list and would be grateful if notified of any corrections that should be incorporated in future reprints or editions of this book.

Abbreviations

ANC	African National Congress
ASAPA	Association of South African Professional Archaeologists
AU	African Union
BEE	Black Economic Empowerment
CBD	Convention on Biological Diversity
CBNRM	Community Based Natural Resource Management
CCA	Conservation Corporation Africa
COSATU	Congress of South African Trade Unions
CSR	Corporate Social Responsibility
DAC	Department of Arts and Culture
DANCED	Danish Cooperation for Environment and Development
DCA	Damage-Causing Animal
DEAT	Department of Environment and Tourism
DECCW	Department of Environment, Climate Change, and Water
ESI	Environmental Sustainability Index
FRELIMO	Frente de Libertação de Moçambique
GEAR	Growth, Employment, and Redistribution
GHF	Global Heritage Fund
GLTP	Great Limpopo Transfrontier Peace Park
ICOMOS	International Council on Monuments and Sites
ICCROM	International Centre for the Study of the Preservation and Restoration of Cultural Property
INGO	International Non-Governmental Organization
IUCN	International Union for the Conservation of Nature and Natural Resources
KZN	KwaZulu Natal
NEPAD	New Partnership for Africa's Development
NHC	National Heritage Council
NORAD	Norwegian Agency for Development Co-operation

Abbreviations

NSW	New South Wales
OAU	Organization of African Unity
RARI	Rock Art Research Institute
RENAMO	Resistência Nacional Moçambicana
SACP	South African Communist Party
SADC	Southern African Development Community
SADF	South African Defence Force
SAHRA	South African Heritage Resources Agency
SANParks	South African National Parks
SDI	Spatial Development Initiative
TPC	Threshold of Potential Concern
UNEP	United Nations Environment Program
UNESCO	United Nations Education Science and Cultural Organization
USAID	United States Agency for International Development
WMF	World Monuments Fund
WWF	World Wildlife Fund

Introduction

Past Mastering in the New South Africa

These deluded patterns of historical reflection and self-understanding are not natural, automatic, or necessarily beneficial to either rulers of ruled. Instead of reinflating imperial myths and instrumentalizing imperial history, I contend that frank exposure to the grim and brutal deaths of my country's colonial past should be made useful. (Paul Gilroy, *Postcolonial Melancholia*, 2005)

This is a book about past mastering, or the struggle to come to terms with the past. All heritage work essentially starts from the premise that the past is contested, conflictual, and multiply constituted. In that sense, the processing of history into heritage involves dealing with a negative legacy. I had been developing the idea of "negative heritage" after the events of 9/11 when archaeologists from the universities of Cape Town, the Western Cape, and the Witwatersrand kindly invited me to South Africa. My lectures dealt with the parallels that were being drawn between the destruction of the Bamiyan Buddhas in Afghanistan and the twin towers in New York City, where I then lived and taught. My long-term research interest has been the ways in which specific heritages are constructed and deployed at expedient political moments and how archaeological culture is mobilized in ideological struggles. What we were witnessing after 9/11 was a proliferation, or ramping up, of the visibility of cultural heritage in conflict situations where debate around culture and "civilization" was a tactic of hegemonic military power (Scham 2009).

In archaeology, discussions of heritage and conflict have been examined against the familiar backdrop of state-sanctioned programs of remembering or forgetting in Europe, typically Germany, where the continued efforts of past mastering are so central as to warrant the term Vergangenheitsbewältigung (Meskell 2002; Rosenfeld 2000). Significantly, strong ideological linkages existed between

The Nature of Heritage: The New South Africa, First Editon. Lynn Meskell.
© 2012 John Wiley & Sons, Inc. Published 2012 by Blackwell Publishing Ltd.

European fascism and Afrikaner nationalism in South Africa and found their material expression in the famous Voortrekker Monument outside Pretoria, a religio-nationalist mausoleum to the Great Trek (Coombes 2003). Apartheid South Africa effectively prolonged the precedents of colonial control, imbued it with religious morality, and established a society organized by race and privilege that persisted after all other African colonial regimes had been replaced by forms of majority rule (Hall 2005: 181). Like post-war Germany, South Africa today might be described as a post-conflict zone whose relationships with the past and sites of memory and trauma are being closely scrutinized. The nation's negative heritage is familiar from an international perspective, yet because democratic transition was so recent, one might apply the scholarly insights gleaned from post-conflict studies to an emergent situation. But most striking of all, developments in South Africa are compelling not because they *were* history but because they *are* unfolding in front of us.

In the weeks spent traveling and lecturing through South Africa I realized that instead of focusing on the well-documented past mastering of fascist Europe or contemporary examples from the Middle East, here was an opportunity to witness the forging of a nation only a decade after democracy. In that new crafting of nationhood, a proudly African past played a vital new role, revealed in the national motto and coat of arms, state medals and awards, in government speeches, the proliferation of museums and heritage sites, exhibitions and excavations, new school curricula, arts and crafts programs, and innumerable development initiatives. South Africa was "alive with possibility" as national marketing slogans suggested, and the past lay very much at the center of possible futures. It offered the perfect place to track the progress of the past from the dark days of apartheid repression to the future-geared nation of many colors, a Rainbow Nation no less. But more than its stated centrality, the past was imbued with seemingly therapeutic powers that claimed to heal the state and its citizens economically, socially, and spiritually. Recognition of the past would provide employment for previously disadvantaged South Africans through culture and tourism. It was broadcast in highway signage that read "Culture Creates Jobs" – albeit exclusively in English. The very constituents of people's embodied identities, their "race" and respective histories that once ensured their persecution and subordinate status, could now be transformed into capital. The past was more than an economic resource, however, it was the font of social and psychical uplift that would instantiate a sense of pride and empowerment that would literally heal the nation. Past deprivations were not allowed to sediment into the social bedrock of revenge and retribution, thanks to the enormous success of the Truth and Reconciliation Commission (TRC), the role of charismatic figures like Nelson Mandela and Desmond Tutu, and the general humanity or *ubuntu* of the South African people. The past would serve as therapeutic device, a guiding legacy for healing the nation and moving forward. There is always a sense of double time, where history is constantly refracted in the present and is a perpetual referent for future projections. These were some of the reasons I found the new nation so compelling for a new kind of study.

Studying South Africa's heritage at this particular historical moment called for a new suite of methodologies. At the outset I brought archaeologists, computer scientists, and heritage officers from Columbia University and South Africa together to conduct mapping and digital scanning of Thulamela (c.1440–1640), an Iron Age site in Kruger National Park that was held up as emblematic of South Africa's Rainbow Nation (Meskell 2007a).[1] We interviewed community representatives, South African archaeologists, and experts from South African National Parks (SANParks) about the history and significance of Thulamela. It was this ethnographic aspect of our research, the placing of the past and the new nation's attempts to balance cultural and natural assets, that proved most compelling. This discovery bound me to Kruger National Park, its history, its deep past, and its current refashioning under the new government. It later led to comparative fieldwork in Mapungubwe National Park, recently inscribed by the United Nations Education Science and Cultural Organization (UNESCO) in recognition of its archaeological heritage rather than its wilderness. Heritage initiatives were also emerging in the private sector, and I compared the role of cultural heritage and conservation at private lodges like Bongani, Phinda, and Ngala. A new nation needed new sites and new heritage programs, like those started by the Rock Art Research Institute in Johannesburg. This took me to different parts of the country from the Drakensberg rock art sites to townships like Kliptown to examine these new ventures and interview their participants. Archaeology, heritage, and ethnography would all need to come together if we were to understand developments as they unfolded.

For me, the most effective way to really understand the particular practices of past mastering in South Africa was to spend significant amounts of time on the ground, interviewing a diverse array of people, living in Kruger, and often working in tandem with the People and Conservation unit of SANParks. The summer months of 2003 to 2008 were spent in the field, and six months were spent in South Africa in 2005, funded through the Andrew W. Mellon Foundation. Thanks to their New Directions program I spent some 18 months retraining in sociocultural anthropology and familiarizing myself with the histories, politics, and social complexities of South Africa. There has been a growing lobby of ethnographers analyzing archaeological practices, sites, and landscapes, from various national, disciplinary, and political perspectives (Abu el-Haj 2001; Bartu 2000; Benavides 2005; Breglia 2006; Castañeda 1996; Scholze 2008; Wynn 2008). Hybrid studies in archaeology that embrace ethnographic approaches have also become mainstream (Byrne 2003; 2007; Ferguson and Colwell-Chanthaphonh 2006; Gonzalez-Ruibal 2006; Meskell 2009b; Weiss 2007). Archaeological research can only benefit from drawing upon a mosaic of methodologies that includes archaeological practice and museum or representational analysis as well as long-term involvement, participant observation, interviewing, and archival work.

While the research presented here takes advantage of diverse methodologies that I have termed "archaeological ethnography" (Meskell 2005a; 2007a; 2009c), it departs from prior studies in its wider attention to issues beyond archaeology and heritage. What began as a project of tracking the progress of archaeology after 10 years of democracy has necessarily come to embrace a much larger framing, including the fraught relationship between cultural and natural heritage, the primacy of biodiversity and global conservation, development and empowerment strategies, the sedimented legacies of racialized identities, and the differential impacts of state and private and non-governmental interventions in the new nation. The global imaginings of salvage, conservation, development, and the good are shot through with South African specificities and are impossible to embrace without critical scrutiny. The specters of colonialism, paternalism, or even tacit racism sometimes surface through the well-meaning efforts of aid, education, conservation, and uplift (Wainaina 2005; 2006). These are just some of the reasons why an archaeology of archaeology alone would not suffice.

There are three interwoven thematic strands within the text. The major theme to emerge from my work is that the protection of nature prefigures all discussions of the cultural past, its legislation, protection, presentation, access, and potential use. I argue that in the overlapping discourses of natural and cultural heritages and their legacies, cultural heritage has emerged as secondary. This shared history with nature in the ascendant can be traced through to the contemporary mobilization of biodiversity and conservation politics. While this is a global movement, South Africa offers an acute example of the dominance of nature over culture. The second theme is that of heritage as therapy, as a strategy for socio-economic empowerment and development in the particular social and governmental processes of post-apartheid South Africa. While there are resonances with other nations, the explicit modalities employed, the precise timing of the first democracy, the fallouts from the state's historic amnesia and its sometime inability to embrace ethnic difference, make the new South Africa a compelling case study. It is a classic example of the multivalent possibilities of negative heritage and of one nation's tactics for past mastering. My third concern is the relationship between state and private sectors and the partnerships that have arisen in the heritage sphere and the implications of those ventures in terms of therapeutic uplift and economic development strategies. These processes can be traced through both cultural and natural heritage domains, as the chapters devoted to Kruger National Park vividly demonstrate.

Culture and Nature in Kruger

My fieldwork was conducted primarily in Kruger National Park from 2004 to 2009, a nodal site in the history of South African heritage. Established in 1898, proclaimed in 1926, and named in honor of Boer president Paul Kruger, the park was a potent symbol of Afrikaner nationalism. It was first declared on the basis of its natural beauty and prevalence of game and is still known for its sightings of the Big 5 (lion, leopard, rhino, elephant, and buffalo). Today the park is some two million hectares of fenced land bordered by Zimbabwe to the north and Mozambique to the east. Since its beginnings as the Sabie Reserve (Carruthers 1995), successive wardens systematically evicted thousands of its indigenous inhabitants thus destroying their livelihoods. Those affected and many of their descendants continue to live along the park's borders and are exerting new claims for restitution. Studying heritage in Kruger National Park held a special attraction for a host of very different reasons: it was the jewel in the crown of African national parks, it was attempting to shed its brutal Afrikaner nationalist image, and a new African National Congress (ANC) black leadership encouraged black employment, participation, and visitation. For such an illustrious park, there has been a dearth of published ethnographic work; the reasons for this must be considered historic and political. Today the organization boasts successes in social transformation, and the park is much touted as a key driver for black economic empowerment and uplift. Yet Kruger continues to face enormous challenges resulting from its racist and repressive history, itself refracted in the impoverished conditions of those descendent communities forcibly removed and the specter of land claims and other forms of reparation.

Kruger was compelling for me as an archaeologist, being home to well over a thousand archaeological sites, dating from our early hominid ancestors to the recent past. Under the new dispensation, the long-ignored cultural past of the San and black South Africans could be finally showcased and appreciated.[2] In what follows I evaluate the state of the archaeological past in the park and the views of various stakeholders toward revitalizing ancestral and cultural sites, including resident scientific researchers, international scholars, and those evicted from the park. I argue that uncovering the African past has been precariously interpolated within an overarching focus on biodiversity conservation that developed in the early 1990s. Kruger serves as the perfect lens through which to examine the larger framings of nature-based tourism and conservation in South Africa and its accommodation of pressing social and historical inequities. The park is a parastatal agency, thus reflecting the tensions between state and non-state actors pertaining to economic growth and social inclusion in the arenas of employment, tourism, and conservation. Kruger's past and present is a study in socio-nature, an intercalation of seemingly separate and unacknowledged entities such as politics, economics, culture, science, nature, and ideology that have made and remade its landscape from prehistoric times onwards (Guattari 2000; Swyngedouw 1999). Struggles that arise within the history of the geography and social power geometries are therefore equally constitutive of the flux and dynamics of Kruger National Park as adaptive management policies, research strategies, or savannah heterogeneity.

Kruger neatly encompasses the three key concerns of the book and, given its legendary historical status and its current role as a Transfrontier Peace Park, it is timely that its history and future be reassessed. For these and other reasons – largely that people were so incredibly open to this research – I found Kruger captivating and feel very privileged to have been welcomed into the various communities. Over the years I have been based at Skukuza, Kruger's research station and main tourist hub. I had sustained interactions and interviews with park managers, research scientists and technicians, ecologists, service workers, rangers, heritage officers, and those forced from the park during previous regimes. Over a hundred formal, videoed interviews and hundreds more informal conversations form the basis of this research, along with archival analysis and participation in research meetings, conferences, and workshops. Together with heritage surveys, site monitoring, and participation in field projects, this forms a densely textured account of the place of the past in one of South Africa's most important and celebrated landscapes.

The questions that drove my early work in Kruger revolved around past mastering, specifically how might the depredations of colonial and apartheid eras be ameliorated? Given the erasures what did people know of their past in the park, specifically their ancestral sites? What was the role of archaeology and archaeologists in the programmatics of the new nation and how exactly would heritage pay? The idea that the poverty and fragility of life that I witnessed in communities on the western border could be addressed by a recuperation of the past seemed unlikely. Even the invidious notion of creating cultural villages and showcasing the imagined and ossified identities of the past for tourist revenues seemed impossible. How exactly could the archaeological past provide any form of therapeutic benefit, whether economic, social, or psychical? In many conversations it became clear that the category of heritage and dwelling upon the past were luxuries that people like myself could entertain. Certainly, almost every elder interviewed could recount stories from the past and, when pressed, shared their opinions on sites, archaeologists, and museums, but clearly these were not central concerns to them. Other imperatives occupied their thoughts and our conversations: compensation for the loss of their land and cattle, employment in the park for their families, developing international tourism in their villages, remuneration for destruction of their crops by animals escaping from Kruger, government aid, and the government making good on electoral promises. These concerns were repeated endlessly from the far north at Pafuri in the Limpopo province to the southern region around Mthetamusha in the province of Mpumalanga.

For my research to privilege the archaeological past and gloss over contemporary matters seemed disingenuous. If anything, it required reconfiguring so as to consider the broader category of history and interpolate something called "heritage" into more encompassing and compelling constructions of governmentality and environmentality (Agrawal 2005; Hayden 2003), biodiversity and conservation, development, and sustainability to prove more comprehensive. The very use of the word "heritage" raises a problem in South Africa because it enshrines all forms of contemporary culture and tribal configurations of music, art, dance, performance, and the like. Moreover, heritage in the form of historic sites and museums has been deemed the terrain of historians rather than archaeologists in both the eyes of the government and general public (Coombes 2003; Shepherd and Murray 2007). As prior scholarship reveals, archaeology owes its low status to the political profile of the discipline under apartheid, coupled with archaeologists' ambivalence and unwillingness to embrace the socio-political dimensionality of their work (Hall 1988; Shepherd 2002b; 2003), while historians have been traditionally more celebrated for their ethical engagements.

Many South African archaeologists are struggling to overturn this history of disengagement by fostering projects that incorporate heritage tourism, employment, and educational imperatives. Rock art specialists have worked with connected communities to develop sites such as Clanwilliam in the Cedarburg (Parkington 1999; Wurz and Merwe 2005), Wildebeest Kuil in Kimberly (Morris 2003; Weiss 2005; 2007), and Game Pass in the Drakensberg (Blundell 1996; 2004; Ndlovu 2009), as well as creating critical narratives for the new nation, as seen in the Origins Center at Wits University (Raman 2007). It is a time of circumscribed optimism, as numbers of black students enrolled in archaeology are inching upwards, new museums and interpretation centers are being built, there are openings in archaeology at the major institutions, donor and government funding continues, and dynamic interdisciplinary projects have recently been initiated (e.g., Bonner, Esterhuysen, and Jenkins 2007; Bonner, Esterhuysen, and Swanepoel 2009). In the public sphere, debate around heritage, monuments, and museums is not insignificant (Coombes 2003; McGregor and Schumaker 2006; Shepherd 2007), even if some popular discourse in the media remains tainted by outmoded ideas about race, identity, and historical events. Archaeology and heritage are finally becoming the subjects of vibrant public contestation rather than silence.

South Africa has come a long way in a very short time, and it is easy to overlook the vast steps forward in racial equality and social change, largely because the demands for housing, health, education, and basic services have not been met. The ANC itself has recognized that inequality has worsened in South Africa since they came to power. Poverty and unemployment are insoluble problems, particularly for those in townships and rural areas (Terreblanche 2003; van der Waal 2008: 64). Like other nations, the South African government outsources many of its basic operations, then buys them back as services in an all-pervasive service economy, including security, health, and housing (Comaroff and Comaroff 2009: 128). On billboards across the country the ANC boasts that over two million houses have been provided in seven years, and yet so many people continue to live in dire conditions. Crime and corruption are also rife (Comaroff and Comaroff 2006; Steinberg 2008). In writing about South Africa it is easy to forget the achievements and successes of the new nation after the thrill has gone (Farred 2004). The love affair the world had with the Rainbow Nation is certainly over, as the early promise of Mandela's era has irreparably faded in the wake of Jacob Zuma's populist presidency. New forms of racism, xenophobia, and ethnic tension have surfaced, and some of those struggles have clearly played out in understandings of the past and particular heritages. Most expectations and projections for the new nation were unrealistic, and like all failed attachments, many feel disappointed and disillusioned.

My own trajectory tells a similar tale of romantic ideals that South Africa's promotion of heritage could be sustained and beneficial for those who had suffered the worst kind of oppression and whose histories had been denied since the colonial era. Very quickly, however, the dream of "archaeology as therapy" receded in the wake of greater burdens and was replaced instead by hollow rhetoric and the penchant for workshop culture. Fanon was sadly right when he said that "those speeches seem like collections of dead words; those values which seemed to uplift the soul are revealed as worthless, simply because they have nothing to do with the concrete conflict in which the people is engaged" (2008: 14). As South Africans like to say, there are many "challenges." The global myth of the Rainbow Nation promised that democracy would usher in real change, but instead it has failed to address the old schisms around class and wealth. As an astute young colleague from Kruger opined, now there is equity without equality. The very legitimacy of liberal democracy relies on foundational narratives, as Wendy Brown (2001: 15) imputes, including equality, rights, and progress that, when challenged or exposed, produces another kind of political culture. South Africa may claim to be de-racialized, have one of the most advanced constitutions globally, and to be open for international business after decades of exclusion as a pariah state, but the new political culture has not ameliorated the "concrete conflict" that ordinary citizens face. The "age of hope" has given way to the new "age of despair" (Kagwanja 2008: xv). It is timely that we ask how these critical "challenges" produce other possibilities, sentiments, and historical accounts and examine how life is experienced amidst these broken narratives. In some way this book attempts to chart those developments as they pertain to the past in and around Kruger National Park.

While some accounts in this book chronicle certain failures, in terms of archaeology, heritage, and conservation, there are also positive stories and exemplary projects that potentially chart a way forward. South Africa has always positioned itself as a state of exception, but as the discussion underscores, heritage issues concerning identity claims, indigeneity, rights, access, and benefits are common to most settings today, irrespective of post-conflict or post-colonial status. The juggling of natural and cultural assets, the role of private–public partnerships, consultancies, and donor economies, the politics of international intervention, and the upsurge of interest in indigenous knowledge have become the hallmark of something called "global heritage," now being documented by a new generation of studies (e.g., Byrne 2007, Keitumetse 2009; Lafrenz Samuels 2009; Logan 2008; Logan and Reeves 2008; Lowenthal 2006; Meskell 2005e; Mortensen and Hollowell

2009; Segobye 2006; Weiss 2007). From this perspective, South Africa offers a critical distillation of global developments in political heritage, condensed into a decade or more, as a result of international and local efforts alike. Beyond the failed love affair, or therapy culture, the place of the past in South Africa is a salutary lesson in the promises and perils of heritage work.

Outline of the Book

In the chapters that follow I examine how heritage has been configured within the landscape of the new South Africa as primarily seen through its premier national park. Yet understanding the context of Kruger National Park requires a broader investigation into the histories and development of natural heritage and how thinking about nature and wilderness have indelibly shaped ideas about archaeological heritage and peopled landscapes. In the first chapter I chart those epistemic trajectories and intersections in thinking about natural and cultural sites, specifically around histories of enclosure and fortress conservation, aesthetic and moral values, and into our most recent formulations of biodiversity and sustainability. I argue that cultural heritage has often been "naturalized," taking its models from those developed to manage natural resources. From the outset these were international experiments that now have global currency, yet I also anchor them, where possible, in the context of South Africa. With its documented colonial history of exploration, conservation, and increasing segregation, South Africa is a particularly apposite location to consider emergent tensions between cultural heritage and nature preservation.

My second chapter provides a background to South African heritage, its particular history of racialization and the ever-present specter of tribalism. Here I demonstrate why South Africa is such a powerful site for heritage making, from the romanticism of the Rainbow Nation and African Renaissance rhetoric plied by politicians like Mandela and Mbeki to the rallying cries for reconciliation and restitution through a healing past. For the new democratic nation, looking forward first requires looking back. A material past, rather than material nature, would in fact provide "unity in diversity," as the national motto proclaimed in the now unspoken !Xam language, *!ke e: /xarra //ke* (Barnard 2003). Yet as the examples in this chapter demonstrate, since 1994 the state elided deep history in the public sphere beyond monumental facades and slogans, resulting in ethnic tensions, violent xenophobia, and a failure to combat issues of race and poverty. Culturalism supplanted racialism in the ANC's unstated political stance that has come to resemble that of their apartheid forebears. In the decade after apartheid's demise heritage has been liberalized, privatized, and increasingly naturalized. The politics of therapy and social cohesion have given way to stringent neoliberalism under the ANC: heritage must pay for itself rather than constitute the vehicle for empowerment and development.

The third chapter introduces the many histories of Kruger National Park, for so long silenced or sidelined under various political and managerial regimes. Forgetting both ancient and recent history has been a key strategy in denying African agency, but also the validity of new rights and claims, and has resulted in the ugly tensions now flaring over land reform, co-management, access, and benefit sharing. Remembering history and those who once lived in the park serves a twofold purpose. On the one hand, it reinstates the significance of San and black history, deemed necessary for the healing of a nation and the conciliatory process of moving forward. On the other, it forges good neighborliness in the present, creating new links between communities and conservationists, by admitting or even apologizing for the decades of dispossession and mistreatment. To date these processes of reparation have been slow to unfold, and many within park management still eschew both history and contemporary efforts of redress.

This leads into my fourth chapter, which describes Kruger National Park's new configuration as the nation's foremost site of biodiversity and wilderness. I argue here that in the early 1990s international biodiversity conventions occurred in tandem with the democratic transition in South Africa, thus providing a new vehicle to project the modern, neoliberal, international state to a welcoming global fraternity. The technocracy of SANParks entailed new management styles: economic liberalization, adaptive management, and resilience, minimum interference and sustainability, black economic empowerment and capacity building. Biodiversity values paralleled the social imperatives of an emerging African democracy, transformation, equity, efficiency, and growth. Yet the ANC management also struggled with the place of the African past after years of sedimented disinterest and racial discrimination. Romantic and outmoded notions of wilderness and *terra nullius* proved difficult to dislodge, undercutting both ancient heritage and living traditions. Acknowledging the vast needs of impoverished living communities on park borders also presented critical challenges to an organization that was itself undergoing transformation.

Chapter 5 focuses in on the place of archaeology in the park, looking at the afterlives of various sites. I describe the fallouts for Kruger and its numerous communities from failing to employ archaeologists and heritage experts across SANParks and instead allowing nature conservationists to manage heritage landscapes. Histories of occupation are negatively inflected, site infrastructure is poor, and archaeological management and preservation remains a low priority. The positioning of archaeology within SANParks is key, and, since there is little understanding that the discipline straddles both science and social science, it is not recognized as geography and ecology are. Moreover, its position within the People and Conservation unit that is devoted to outreach and community development projects renders cultural heritage a highly politicized undertaking separate from the mission of biodiversity conservation. The very reasons why African heritage was held up by the ANC as a mechanism for development and healing are the same reasons why heritage remains sidelined in Kruger: issues of race, equality, and acknowledgment of the past are unfinished projects. I employ the comparative example of Aboriginal heritage in Australian national parks to suggest that natural and cultural heritage can be successfully integrated.

The next chapter builds on these observations through a detailed case study of Thulamela, an Iron-Age hilltop site that gained enormous media and political attention in the mid-1990s. Cast as the first collaborative excavation between black and white South Africans, I unpack the many new processes and actors involved. Following the money enables us to see how the new South Africa called upon international NGOs and private sponsors to create neoliberal heritage that itself was supposed to benefit communities through extensive tourism and commodification. Tracking the archaeologists and their objects allows us to see how new desires for indigenous identities, political leverage, and individual celebrity wrested power from communities, alienated parks officials, and ultimately failed to produce new modes of heritage or reconciliation. Talking to community representatives reveals the place of black stakeholders then, and a decade later, and the priorities that were not captured in the race for a Rainbow-Nation heritage paradigm. This leads to a discussion of archaeology's role in South African history and where the current lines have been drawn since apartheid's end.

Chapter 7 looks more closely at issues of social justice raised by some communities that now buffer the park. From the perspective of recent histories, access to ancestral sites and natural resources, the vast majority of inhabitants on the fence line remain dissatisfied with the new Kruger administration. Whilst many acknowledge some appreciable changes accompanying the new dispensation, grievances run deep and have been voiced at state-mandated meetings calling for public participation in Kruger's management. This chapter describes those processes within the park and outside, raising again the highly racialized issue of land restitution, financial payouts, and other benefit sharing. Prompting from community representatives led me to explore more tangible benefits being offered by private conservation companies such as AndBeyond at their Phinda, Ngala, and Bongani lodges. Here I observed different possibilities for San and black heritage, incorporation of local tradition, natural resource access, and empowerment that is currently fraught in Kruger. Private–public partnerships, liberalization, and corporate social responsibility have reshaped conservation and heritage management since the ANC's adoption of its own self-styled structural adjustment.

The conclusion attempts to move beyond the struggles and failures of Kruger National Park that can be seen as endemic of the larger problems faced by South Africa after the initial thrill of the democratic handover. It recaps the major themes of the book and, in doing so, situates developments in South Africa within the wider global frame. Within that frame, I argue, cultural heritage is always future perfect and is increasingly employed as a vehicle for development and modernizing as well as reconciliation and uplift. Capitalizing culture today increasingly means that archaeologists have to work with and between international agencies like UNESCO, transnational projects, national governments, and indigenous groups while tackling questions of whether cultural heritage contributes to the emergent human rights, diversity, and sustainability, development and capacity building as well as human and global well being.

As outlined in this introduction, after the romance of peaceful transition has faded, post-apartheid South African heritage in the decade following the "age of hope" confronts inherited and novel challenges. The chapters that follow remind us that the legacy of racism remains and is further confounded by class and status inequities. Refusing to remember histories of difference and connection, I argue, can only lead to further fallbacks in the future. Regardless of our interest in material culture or material nature, there can be no heritage without history. Colonial and contemporary desires for pristine nature and people-free wilderness still mask underlying refusals to acknowledge indigenous presence, knowledge, and management. Conservation and heritage continue to operate as contested terrains. Taken together, culture and nature remain contentious ground for South Africans in the face of burgeoning appeals for recognition, for land and livelihood restitution, and for social justice. Archaeology and cultural heritage may have been minor players in these larger struggles, but we, as practitioners, can no longer ignore the much larger social and political landscapes within which we are entangled.

Notes

1   http://www.learn.columbia.edu/thulamela (accessed December 29, 2009).
2   Following Barnard (2007: 4–6) I use the term "San" to refer to a group of traditional hunter-gatherers or foragers who have also been called "Bushmen" or "Basarwa." The terms Bushmen and Barsarwa are not used here. I am aware that the term San has carried derogatory connotations in the past; I use the term without such intention. I chose to use "San" because this is the name preferred by most contemporary South African San groups and by the South African academy. I use the term Khoekhoe, meaning "people of the people," to refer to those people who traditionally herded cattle or sheep. They were once referred to as "Hottentots," but this is now widely regarded as offensive. As Barnard reminds us, there are objections to almost every generic term in use. By using two distinctive terms I do not seek to deny the demonstrated fact that there has been significant movement amongst and between San and the Khoekhoe groups in precolonial and colonial South Africa.

Chapter 1

Naturalizing Cultural Heritage

France has never believed in the notion of a pristine nature that has so confused the "defense of the environment" in other countries: what we call a "national park" is a rural ecosystem complete with post offices, well tended roads, highly subsidized cows and handsome villages. (Bruno Latour, *It's Development Stupid!* 2007)

In the attempt to hold nature still, as representation, uncanny effects are created and the alienation effect of the map becomes congenial. (Michael Taussig, *My Cocaine Museum,* 2004)

On my very first visit to South Africa my hosts enquired about the places and things I most wanted to see. Looking back now I recall that Kruger National Park came top of the list. So too did seeing herds of wildebeest, causing my colleagues understandable chagrin because I was mistakenly picturing the savannahs of East Africa. Significantly, and to my eternal embarrassment, I had omitted South Africa's archaeological sites. It was nature that had me entranced, particularly the idea of African wilderness, charismatic mammals, and safaris. In the years that followed, my research began to address that self-same subject making, asking why the desire for certain forms of nature might come at the expense of the cultural past? Why has the notion of wilderness achieved this privileged position and pro- tected nature entreated a global embrace, whereas human histories are perceived as particular, often factional, conflictual, and in need of reconciliation. Conducting research in national parks, home to many of South Africa's archaeological treas- ures, I began to question the tendencies towards isomorphism between natural and cultural heritage that were reflected in international declarations, national

The Nature of Heritage: The New South Africa, First Editon. Lynn Meskell.
© 2012 John Wiley & Sons, Inc. Published 2012 by Blackwell Publishing Ltd.

legislation, site management, and promotion. One major theme of this book is an exploration of the primacy of global imperatives surrounding natural heritage and why these are often overlaid onto archaeological heritage. Several historical strands of influential thinking from the Anglo-American tradition are thus outlined here as a necessary background to the chapters that follow. They draw together romantic and colonial sentiments that continue to have ramifications today in postcolonial contexts like South Africa. The other two themes of this book are also entwined in our understandings of past places: moral ideas about the value of heritage, whether derived from cultural or natural patrimony and, to a lesser degree, the role of public–private partnerships in their management. During my fieldwork in South Africa these matrices became evident, particularly in the political entanglement of natural and cultural heritage. Today ideas about conservation are sutured to development, diversity, and sustainable futures that have enchanted the global imagination.

Archaeologists would do well to investigate the intellectual traditions that have shaped ideas of cultural heritage through the lens of nature and conservation. Geographer David Lowenthal (2006) usefully draws attention to the comingling of natural and cultural heritage inheritances and asks what each domain might learn from the other. We typically deem archaeological and natural heritage distinct undertakings with very different modes of operation. This separation may be fitting in certain contexts, for example in Turkey (Thys-Senocak 2010) or Greece (Cengiz 2007), and is reflected in national ideologies and state managerial institutions (but see Catsadorakis 2007). However, cultural understandings of both categories vary, as do the implications of integrating heritages. An example there would be the spiritual inseparability of traditional Aboriginal culture and landscape in Australia (Byrne, Brayshaw, and Ireland 2001; Head 2002; Lilley and Williams 2005). Beginning in the 1990s there have been increasing moves toward integrating the preservation of culture and nature, globally spearheaded by UNESCO's influential Cultural Landscapes program (Rössler 2003). Tracing a genealogy of these interconnected heritage taxonomies would require a book-length treatment, yet it is important here briefly to outline some salient thinkers and historical trends that have been instrumental in forging ideas about heritage protection and our anxieties about occupation, rights of access, use, and loss. A suite of universalisms has emerged about the scarcity, non-renewability, and loss of natural heritage that pervades international legislation and monitoring, research, activism, and donor economies (Tsing 2005). We can no longer parse out natural heritage from the cultural sphere, ignore its dominance, or fail to address how tropes of nature's diversity, endangerment, and protection have irrevocably influenced our understanding of the cultural past.

In this chapter I argue that the legacies of enclosure, eviction, and salvage that developed around sites of natural value have indelibly informed our understanding and management of cultural places. Today nature-based narratives of diversity, sustainability, and community-based conservation have also permeated archaeological sensibilities. Archaeology has been reticent to acknowledge its intellectual debt to conservation, largely because of its willingness to hive off the material culture of dead societies rather than embed our practice in more living and contemporary concerns. Like geography and conservation science, archaeology was forged in a colonial crucible, when Europeans mapped and recorded the worthy remains (of aesthetic or scientific achievement) of cultures past before they disappeared or were destroyed. These material remains documented past lifeways and were considered vital in understandings of our own humanity. In the following sections I describe some historical strands of thought around natural heritage that have particular salience in the development of cultural heritage ideology and the fundamental ways in which we have come to devalue human presence in natural places.

South Africa offers a rich seam for exploring the development of protected natural heritage. Contemporary thinking about the environment, rather than an exclusive product of Western predicaments and philosophies, emerged as a direct response to the destructive social and ecological conditions of colonial rule in places like South Africa (Crosby 1986; Grove 1995: 486). During the 1600s at the Cape of Good Hope, colonial expansion and appropriation prompted a reevaluation of nature. Early botanical gardens were established and the task of locating Eden became a cultural preoccupation. At the heart of this relationship between people and nature were three concepts that can be traced back to the classical era: "the idea of a designed earth, the preoccupation with those environmental influences which affected the development of man and society and, lastly, the idea of man as a geographical agent" (Grove 1995: 24). South Africa, like other imperial colonies, later became a petri dish for studying the effects of famine, disease, the depletion of resources, and in reacting to these perceived threats, environmental policies were drafted between 1650 and 1850. Through the already international and inter-colonial channels among scientists, the sense of a global environmental crisis gained momentum. Here, the concept of nature as "that which we are not" also took root. Nature was considered external to humanity and so nature ceased to be fully "natural" as soon as human labor was applied to it (Soper 2000: 16). Ideas of conservation and progress thus came to rely upon the fundamental separation of humanity from nature (Igoe 2004: 77) in an ontology where nature was reified and human intervention predominantly vilified.

Of the many historical threads one might unravel in this history of intersection between natural heritage and a peopled past, I focus here on three that have particular relevance to my work in South Africa. The first two stem from the colonial era and can be traced through to the post-apartheid present. The first thread addresses the enclosure movement that began in England during the fifteenth century and was later exported to its colonies. Enclosure found full expression in fortress conservation (Brockington 2004), typically mobilized in the national parks of ex-colonies whether in Africa or North America. Enclosure, I argue, has also been adapted as a strategy for the protection of archaeological sites with the resultant fencing out of previous occupants and stakeholders. The second thread recalls the implicit moral judgments about particular natural and cultural sites that we deem worthy of salvage, on the basis of their representative, scientific, or aesthetic value. The third strand differs considerably in its predominantly modern constitution and reflects upon emergent global discourses that privilege diversity and sustainability. Unity in diversity was a concept first promulgated by Alexander von Humboldt to describe ecosystem functioning and was adopted in the new South Africa to reflect its multiethnic constituency. The concept has been similarly influential in articulating networks of cultural expression, conservation movements, and global pressures to enhance sustainability. Bolstered by UNESCO declarations and international development ventures, modern nations are being encouraged to draw from the legacies of nature and culture to forge possible futures.

Enclosures and Fortresses

Beginning in the fifteenth century a new capitalist order carved up the English medieval landscape, transforming common property systems of fields and pastures into private property, and this was accompanied by a system of fences and fines. The movement marked a new register of state intrusion into the lives of peasants, resulting in dispossession and new classificatory zones of wilderness and empty lands. Enclosure underscored existing inequalities around wealth, class, and ethnicity resulting in the displacement of rural communities. Enclosure, then, can be thought of as a legal measure or governmental regime as much as a physical one. Enclosure is still viewed negatively as a dominant topography that many have vigorously resisted in cultures of protest (Johnson 2008: 13–15). The Levellers, so named, according to some traditions, for their destruction of hedges, fought enclosure on a platform of equality and popular sovereignty and struggled against the familiar forces of repression, poverty, and land dispossession. They produced a remarkably modern *Agreement of the People* in 1649 (Winstanley 1945) and presaged modern environmental movements by asserting that the earth was a "common storehouse for all."

The seventeenth century was the preeminent period of English enclosures. At this time all land that could profitably be used was considered "agricultural land," with only a small proportion designated "waste land." The economic gains for landlords at this time were formidable, and in terms of the cash value of produce may have ranged from 50 to 100 percent. By 1760 at least 75 percent of land in England was already enclosed, though the percentage increase in economic output had declined somewhat. Conversely, the commons has steadily decreased from 1.7 million acres in 1873, to 1.1 million in 1958 (Wordie 1983: 501). Today England retains less than 1 million acres of common land of its total 32.5 million acres, the vast majority of which have been declared "areas of outstanding beauty" or sites of special scientific interest (SSSI).

Enclosure was ripe for export, particularly to British colonies where "productive" and "aesthetic" landscapes could be profitably parsed out from traditional land use. Indigenous groups at home or abroad, whether Native Americans or the Irish, were rendered uncivilized peoples without property, bounded lands, fences, or organized agriculture; these lacks supplied full justification for state or colonial appropriation. The British elite in the early 1800s likened the segregation and subjugation of their domestic foe to their imperial subjects, so that subduing Finchley Common and Hounslow Heath became as critical as controlling Malta and Egypt (Igoe 2004: 81). Peasants at home and abroad must be directed toward commercial agriculture rather than their traditional practices. Political moves to enclose land fundamentally changed rural and nomadic people's relationship with the land and their socio-economic situation, whether in England or East Africa. Parallels to modern-day structural adjustment programs have not gone unnoticed that similarly segregate, deprivilege, and displace the rural poor (Igoe 2004: 81). Large-scale farming replaced individual African agro-pastoralists and sport hunting sought to exclude indigenous hunting practices. The destruction of traditional hunting rights had a devastating effect on African culture, irrevocably changing diet, economic and social relations, and severing connections with the physical environment (Adams and McShane 1996: 32). At first native peoples were seen as too natural, too like nature. Soon this would be reversed and they would be perceived as threatening the balance of nature, hunting in unacceptable ways, and engaging in unsustainable practices (Adams 2003a: 35).

Enclosure in South Africa has been relatively understudied, but the coercive shift from indigenous communal tenure to private property gained momentum in the 1860s. British settlers were encouraged to recreate "home" and British notions of property by digging ditches or planting hedges. These actions were seen as improving the land, not only in terms of profit but as part of the civilizing mission (Beinart 2003: 47). The Fencing Acts of 1883 and 1910 were key in strengthening landowners control of the environment and of its commercial productivity. They also produced new categories of trespass and reordered rural social relations that saw Africans further disempowered (Chapter 3). As Van Sittert argues (2002: 95), before the British reformed the land system the boundaries of farms were undefined and permeable. Colonial administrators reissued grants on perpetual quitrent after accurate survey in an attempt to fix them on the surveyor's map. Buffer zones of crown land between neighbors gradually disappeared and farm boundaries became uniformly coterminous. This new form of territoriality served colonists well since enclosure facilitated the landed control of an indigenous majority with a minimum of effort (Van Sittert 2002: 98). Boundary demarcation accelerated dramatically from 1875 onwards. In the 1890s some 5000 square miles was surveyed and divided into 8000-acre divisions creating hundreds of farms marked by stone beacons and given exotic, worldly names (Stevenson-Hamilton

1929: 185). This created the first reliable map of the country and cast it in the nomenclature of European civility. There were no less than eight recognized categories of fence instigated as a wholesale means to control livestock disease, predators, and theft. Fences were also material measures to control shadow economies and severely delimit traditional lifeways. Enmity ensued with Africans either dispossessed or forced to pay for fencing through increases in hut tax.

Black South Africans were effectively being *fenced out* by enclosure and simultaneously *fenced in* by a new system of native reserves. In the Transvaal, the 1881 Pretoria Convention between British and Republican governments provided for a Native Lands Commission that demarcated boundaries for native reserves (Matthew 1915: 10). Those reserves comprised only 7 percent of South African land and could not accommodate the native population. From these laws, the 1887 Squatters Law developed and the Native Land Act of 1913, which prohibited blacks from buying or leasing land outside the reserves from whites. The foundations of apartheid segregation had been laid. The beginnings of "bad neighbourliness" that is bemoaned around Kruger can be traced to the aforementioned developments, coming as it did on the heels of drought, rinderpest, war, and the transition from farm labor to migrant labor (Van Sittert 2002: 112). Enclosure and fencing created new categories of "wandering natives" and "squatters" in Kruger National Park, and new designations of trespass, poaching, and other forms of criminality hinged upon changes in colonial topographies. And like much conservation and heritage rhetoric, enclosure was administered as a betterment strategy, a rehabilitation of the landscape from degradation, disease, and depredation, for which Africans were largely blamed and from which white settlers ultimately benefitted. As an early form of environmentality, enclosure and fencing separated commercial farming and conservation, it articulated productive and aesthetic domains, and further alienated black South Africans from their lands and lifeways.

This history of fencing and enclosure in South Africa heralded the creation of fortress reserves like Kruger, Kalahari Gemsbok, and Mountain Zebra national parks. The whole idea of a fenced park, according to Adams and McShane (1996: 56), signals our failure to balance human needs with those of nature. It exposes a mythical Western ideal of wild Africa that imagines a timeless barrier against both humans and nature; the land inside the fence shall endure, untainted by people, regardless of what happens beyond. Both culture and nature suffer as a result. From the 1930s the dominant policy of national parks has been preservation without human habitation (Brockington 2004), and sometimes without even the acknowledgement of historic occupation. Fictions of *terra nullius* (or empty lands) and unspoiled nature powered the broader vision of protected areas in the decades that followed. Fenced reserves seek to preserve a pristine wilderness that never existed, while circumscription endangers cultures that long ago successfully adapted to living with animals. The monolithic desire to save wildlife, regardless of the harm that effort might cause living communities, has led conservationists to idealize national parks as the ultimate moral good while eschewing the immorality of destroying human lifeways. Creating parks, even the newly conceived Great Limpopo Transfrontier Peace Park (GLTP), requires permanently removing communities that live on or near newly protected land. By fencing out people, real attempts at reconciliation or peace are sabotaged (Draper, Spierenburg, and Wels 2004; Rodgers 2009; Spierenburg, Steenkamp, and Wels 2008; Wolmer 2003). Connections to historic or ancestral sites and ongoing traditions are attenuated and cultural and natural heritages remain oppositional. Since the mid-1980s there has been a gradual expansion of protected areas that now cover 12 percent of the Earth's surface. Some of those participating countries have disallowed human occupation in more than 30 percent of their territory, making this a much more actively "conserved" world than ever before (Brockington 2009: 14).

Histories of enclosure have critically informed the desire for people-free landscapes and the evidential erasure of human activity, culminating in the ideal partition of either productive landscapes or aesthetic ones. Enclosure is still operational today (Vasudevan, McFarlane, and Jeffrey 2008), not only in conservation areas, but also in rural places like eMacambini in KwaZulu Natal. Attempts to deprive thousands of people of land through the commercial development of AmaZulu World by Ruwaad Holdings Dubai constitute a form of dispossession by accumulation (Harvey 2003). Commodification of the Zulu past, with statues of Shaka and promises of capital injection instead, threaten to displace thousands and destroy ancestral graves. Enclosure, gentrification, and other forms of dispossession by accumulation continue to re-order urban (Blomley 2008), rural (Donahue 2001) and protected areas (Spierenburg, Steenkamp, and Wels 2008), further compromising the poor and the commons alike. Enclosure refers not simply to the material force of fencing, but the imposition of an ideology that shapes and alienates territory so that the map, as Taussig (2004) so aptly describes, becomes congenial. In the context of Kruger, boundary lines created a pleasing prospect for generations of white South Africans while black communities were alienated and segregated from their sites and ancestral places.

The tenets and tactics of enclosure, I suggest, have also impacted our consideration of ancient sites, cultural landscapes, and heritage management. Matthew Johnson (1996; 2008) has described the British enclosure movement as critical for understanding systems of property and landscape that have infused national archaeological traditions. However, archaeologists have not considered the moral and material effects of exporting enclosure across the empire in the way anthropologist Jim Igoe (2004) has usefully done for conservation history (but see Giles and Finch 2008). Nor have archaeologists fully explored the concept of enclosure in concert with contemporary heritage management strategies that seek to separate and sever former occupants from ancestral territory (but see Byrne 2003; Segobye 2006). Archaeologists themselves are fence builders, cordoning off sites for protection as a regular feature of site management strategies internationally (Libsekal 2008; Lydon 2005).

Like conservationists, archaeologists have typically enjoyed the high moral ground of rescuing heritage for the future. However, unlike many of our colleagues in conservation science who feel embattled and consider that their agendas have been hijacked (Brockington and Igoe 2006: 425), archaeologists enjoy the professional benefits and kudos of collaborative projects and have rushed to adopt the mantra of community participation. Others have purported to practice "indigenous" archaeology whether apposite or not. According to Byrne, heritage practitioners promoting the community conservation approach want to believe it works; yet the vehemence of the positive spin often obscures the shallowness of its penetration (Byrne 2009: 87). The modalities of archaeological protection, the treatment of sites, and their occupants / custodians, have all been prefigured by the tenets of nature conservation from colonial times onwards. The Native American expulsion from Yellowstone starting in the 1800s (Keller and Turek 1998) must be seen as a pivotal episode since the conjunction of eviction, enclosure, erasure of history, and the invocation of *terra nullius* were exported worldwide as "the Yellowstone model." In 1926 it would influence South Africans lobbying for the establishment of Kruger National Park under the National Parks Bill: their proposal to the House of Assembly was that Kruger would be even larger than its American counterpart (Ramutsindela 2004: 23).

Since heritage conservation does not occupy the same register as nature conservation, it is difficult to quantify the land and livelihoods that have been sacrificed for the sake of archaeology globally. Protected heritage does not necessarily produce the degree of conservation refugees as protected nature nor occupy comparable physical territory. It has been estimated that the number of people displaced worldwide from traditional homelands over the past century for conservation is estimated to be close to 20 million, 14 million of them in Africa alone (Dowie 2009: xxi). Similar relationships exist today between many nations and their traditional communities who live amidst archaeological ruins, who sometimes continue traditional practices, and at other times make their living from heritage tourism and archaeological projects. Archaeologists have been slow to identify the victims of our own excavation and conservation efforts, since this detracts from our perceived good work of rescue, preservation, and uplift (Gonzalez-Ruibal 2009; Herzfeld 1991; 2006; 2009). Archaeologists have yet to calculate the global human scale of heritage dislocations or even its territorial extent. But the coercive removals of settlements to fulfill UNESCO requirements for Mahabodhi temple in India, around the Pyramids in Giza (Shetawy and El Khateeb 2009), in Luxor (Meskell 2005e; Mitchell 2002b), and in East Jerusalem (Abu el-Haj 2001; Greenberg 2009) are not insignificant. In the case of Luxor, the Egyptian government has systematically removed thousands of people from Gurna over the last century, many of whom were engaged in heritage tourism and have since been pressed into agricultural labor (Meskell 2005e; van der Spek 1998). Repeated attempts to relocate the Jordanian Bedouin from Petra (Massad 2001) and Wadi Rum (Brand

2001) were also conducted under the banner of national development and modernity.

Mirroring the discourse of fortress conservation, I argue that residents around cultural sites have been either evicted or persecuted because of these same embedded proximities and histories of access and utilization of sites that have now been recast as endangered places. Employing Brockington's (2004; West, Igoe, and Brockington 2006) thesis developed for nature conservation we can identify the epistemic shifts that enable these intercalations. First, people are viewed as encroaching and threatening the integrity of heritage sites. They are typically charged with misreading the past or being ignorant of its value, further providing grounds for their expulsion. Second, those communities are often positioned as interlopers rather than the "original" peoples who built or traditionally used such sites. They are rendered illegitimate and suspect, as are their claims. Third, and in a bizarre twist, international agencies often step in to assist these same local people after dislocation through development projects. The joint strategies of dislocation and development can be seen globally whether one studies South Africa, North Africa (Lafrenz Samuels 2009; 2010), Mexico (Breglia 2006), or the United States (Colwell-Chanthaphonh and Ferguson 2006). From this perspective, since valuable resources have been poured into heritage sites, foreign tourism revenues must be prioritized. Monuments are bearers of national pride and so heritage (whether natural or cultural) cannot be compromised by the presence of local people. Wilderness, pristine landscapes, and lost civilizations must be protected *from* humanity *for* all humanity, beyond the needs of a few individuals or communities. But like fortress conservation (Igoe 2004: 73), exclusionary heritage projects fall short of their promises and cannot guarantee the safety of sites without the very collaboration of local stakeholders that they have come to eschew.

Beauty and Duty

In this section I outline briefly the historical positions of critical Euro-American figures who have shaped moral sentiments about nature, its protection and value, and have ineluctably influenced our thinking about archaeological sites and their connected communities. A longer historical analysis of the philosophy of nature or attempts to write histories of nature lies beyond the scope of this work. My starting point here recalls the secularization of arts and sciences in the eighteenth century that prompted Western aesthetics to objectify nature through science and subjectify it through aesthetics. I argue that this history presages our current discussions around natural and cultural heritage and informs the tenets of our universal heritage body, UNESCO. Significance, value, preservation, and moral uplift are qualities that we now readily attach both to natural and cultural sites. So how did we move from the position of heritage as beauty to duty?

Illustrated in the writings of Rousseau and Goethe, the mid-eighteenth century witnessed a crescendo of self-proclaimed naturalism and social ferment that acquired moral overtones. Goethe claimed (1998: 21) that romantic landscapes reflected "a tranquil sense of the sublime in the form of the past, or what amounts to the same, of solitude, remoteness, seclusion." By the early 1800s concepts about human impacts on the environment were already taking shape in Europe. Influenced by Herder's liberalism, concern for moral progress, and his respect of foreign culture, Alexander von Humboldt argued that indigenous groups like Native Americans had suffered all manner of degradation through European destruction of their traditional lifeways. With a background in natural philosophy and botany, he criticized the destructions of forests, the brutality of European dominance, and the imposed hardships upon those who were forced to labor in the service of their colonial forebears. Nature, he asserted, was to be gently followed and improved, not plundered for the sake of wealth (Grove 1995: 368–9), famously quoting that "nature is perfect till man deforms it with care" (Humboldt 1850: x). Humboldt's writings are full of longing and nostalgia for both ancient people and landscapes, lamenting "the golden age that has ended. In this paradise of American jungles, as everywhere else, a long, sad experience has taught all living beings that gentleness is rarely linked to might" (Humboldt 2007: 66). Yet typical of his time, he described native peoples as friendly, tame, and peaceful, but also wild, lazy and indigent (Humboldt 2007: 79). Inspiring modern movements around the preservation of natural (and cultural) heritage, his views on the environment combined scientific knowledge and personal observations. Humboldt propounded the idea of "unity in diversity" and the inextricable connections between human and natural phenomena, the seminal idea of our linkage and responsibility that was later harnessed in modern ecological thought. Reflecting upon his voyage down the Amazon he became critical of human presence, arguing that "you get used to seeing man as not essential to the natural order . . . this view of a living nature where man is nothing is both odd and sad" (Humboldt 2007: 99). During his American visit many embraced Humboldt's cosmopolitan views as paralleling their own thesis of "Manifest Destiny" understood as the "free and democratic future of all humanity and of the United States as 'Nature's Nation'" (Buttimer 2006: viii). Given the romantic appeal of his writing and sketches on the tropics, Humboldt has been lastingly influential on our ideas of landscapes, diversity, and conservation.

Romanticism sanctified "both nature and antiquity, promoting their protection against not only decay and dissolution but from improvidence and iconoclasm" (Lowenthal 2006: 81). Romanticism, however, had its own internal differences that were largely wrought by the massive upheavals of society and thought between 1790 and 1815. The French Revolution, the Napoleonic Wars, and the Industrial Revolution all fashioned a sense of the past that was remote and irrecoverable, while the rise of nationalism evoked new attachments to archaeological monuments as collective symbols. Writers including Rousseau, Goethe, Wordsworth, and Scott celebrated the landscapes and antiquities of the past and entrenched the veneration of both cultural and natural heritage (Lowenthal 2006: 81). Landscape architects like Humphrey Repton and Capability Brown created genteel landscapes replete with fabricated fallen monuments and follies. At the same time romanticism revered the "brutishness" of wild places as mysterious and a source of wonder and moral instruction (Adams 2005: 103). Heritage was perceived as a conduit for connecting us with the past and edifying our future.

North American figures such as Ralph Waldo Emerson and Henry David Thoreau took the aesthetics of nature in a different direction and combined it with developments in the natural sciences. In the 1860s George Perkins Marsh sparked controversy by submitting that humans were the major threat to nature and its fundamental harmony (Carlson 2008: 212; Lowenthal 2000). Environmental optimism continued unchecked, however, while reverence for wild nature gained ground, thus illustrating the bifurcation between productive and aesthetic environments. Yosemite National Park commissioner Frederick Olmstead asserted that the power of nature to affect people was an index of their civilization and cultivated taste (Igoe 2004: 89). Nature was thus set aside for the educated white classes and further detached from its indigenous stewards. Influential American naturalists John Muir and John Burroughs continued with this position in which wild nature was privileged and human intrusion was vilified (Carlson and Lintott 2008). Influential environmentalists like Aldo Leopold appealed to biocentric ethics in claiming the inherent value of "wilderness" and rare species, with native species being prized over invasive and exotic varieties (Caldicott 2008: 111). His famous "land ethic" can be encapsulated in the dictum that "a thing is right when it tends to preserve the integrity, stability, and beauty of the biotic community. It is wrong when it tends otherwise" (Leopold 1949: 224–5). The rampant conquest of nature in the early nineteenth century was replaced by concerns over nature's collapse (Lowenthal 1997) and, from the later twentieth century, was characterized by the widespread acceptance of human agency in nature's degradation and its potential salvation.

The moral economy of nature has continued to strengthen under modernity, contrasted, as it has effectively been with the evils of industrialization, commercialism, commodification, labor, and resource depletion. Popular ecological thinking turns on the idea that nature exists in pristine opposition to human culture, and that across Africa wild nature is concomitantly devalued in proportion to human involvement. Goodin's (1991) "green theory of value," posits that value is accrued through natural processes rather than by "artificial" human ones. Interdisciplinary scholarship in geography, biology, and ecology is attempting to challenge the popular arguments of deep ecology and its anti-anthropocentrism (De Jonge 2004; Kareiva *et al.* 2007). It is a truism that human impact on the environment in modern times has been devastating. Environmental and climate change summits, the inexorable marketing of green lifestyles, and globally coordinated rock concerts are just some of the responses. Judgments about human impacts have also been projected across time and space and include everyone from our prehistoric ancestors to indigenous peoples today. People are part of nature, as many scholars have argued (Hannigan 2006; Zimmerer and Bassett 2003), yet that view and its practical implications have not always filtered down to those who manage conservation areas. Indeed what are the grounds for valuing environments less for their anthropogenic histories? Conservation biologists might reply "ecosystem services" facing such a proposition, arguing that all natural assets are negatively impacted by human presence. Yet ecosystem services are themselves defined around people: they describe the range of provisioning and regulating, cultural and supporting ecosystem functions that support people (Gibson *et al.* 2008: 180). Thompson (2008: 260) argues that science cannot provide us with the foundation for making these evaluations and there is no reason for preferring one development of our evolutionary heritage to another. Rather, she claims it is the "aesthetic" approach to valuing nature that offers an argument for the protection and preservation of certain things and environments (Thompson 2008: 265). Nature's intrinsic value is not a non-anthropocentric value, and we need not dismiss human agency or the history of intercalation between the human and nonhuman.

Significantly for heritage purposes, the aesthetic value of nature has been transferred to the cultural realm, where the purity of material remains are often considered to be threatened by the impositions of human access, resource use, potential employment, economic benefit, or commodification. Like wild places, the archaeological past should only be lightly improved or shored up. Past places must resist the impacts of contemporary peoples who are viewed as predominantly destructive and self-interested. Lowenthal is correct that "scientific experts continue to view nature as superior to culture, the alterations of humanity as inferior to the previous untouched fundament" (2006: 87). The tenets of conservation have subsequently been accepted on a global scale and permeated well beyond discussions of the environment, to archaeological remains that are, ironically, human creations in the first instance. The historical conjuncture between natural and cultural heritages has had an inescapable and potentially detrimental impact, particularly for indigenous groups and those with felt connections to place. These are often the very communities that have suffered persecution or expulsion at the hands of preservationists. Beginning in North America, the first steps toward site protection were initiated with Roosevelt's 1901 Forest Service, followed by the 1906 Antiquities Act. The act gave the American president discretion to protect "historic landmarks, historic and prehistoric structures" that were situated upon lands owned or controlled by the government and also to create reserves. This act also recognized that "significance" is tantamount to "historical, scenic and/or scientific values." The first sites nominated were the Grand Canyon, Death Valley, and Joshua Tree National Park (McGimsey and Davis 1984). Natural places such as these are overlain with cultural significance that cannot be neatly disaggregated, and this tension continues to be problematic in US environmental policy (King

1998). Natural resources and places provided the model for the paradigm of non-renewability and uniqueness, thereby necessitating protection from human affairs.

The 1972 UNESCO Convention Concerning the Protection of the World Cultural and Natural Heritage forged perhaps the most important and overt conjoining of the two heritages. UNESCO is the international organization par excellence for cultural heritage, yet it has recently focused increased attention upon biodiversity and protected areas in conjunction with the International Union for the Conservation of Nature and Natural Resources (IUCN) and other powerful ancillary organizations like the World Wildlife Fund (WWF), the Nature Conservancy and countless NGOs whose mission is protecting nature. The IUCN was founded in 1948 by Julian Huxley and now includes over 1000 agencies and 10,000 experts globally. This is in stark contrast to UNESCO's smaller cultural offshoots, such as the International Council on Monuments and Sites (ICOMOS) and the International Centre for the Study of the Preservation and Restoration of Cultural Property (ICCROM). For UNESCO, cultural heritage consists of monuments or sites of outstanding universal value from the perspective of history, art, or science. Similarly, natural sites are deemed to be areas of outstanding universal value from the vantage of science, conservation, or aesthetics. The organization's singular mandate is "to take the appropriate legal, scientific, technical, administrative and financial measures necessary for the identification, protection, conservation, presentation and rehabilitation of this heritage" (UNESCO 1972). We might consider here that the two heritages may be incommensurate in some contexts and the conflation elides the social construction and value systems inherent to each. Such compounding further depicts the role of archaeologists as good conservationists (literally saving the planet). However, the global salvage mission that UNESCO and others such as Conservation International and the WWF promote has attracted criticism because of their support of nation-state domination and of policies that devalue humanity and endorse commercialism and because of their failure to incorporate indigenous heritage perspectives. Today heritage is increasingly part of an international agenda that both participates in and is critical of globalization and global politics.

Underpinning UNESCO is a suite of judgments resting on the presumed universals of beauty, scientific knowledge, and representativeness (Ericksen 2009). The World Heritage List of 890 properties includes 689 cultural, 176 natural, and 25 mixed from 148 state parties. These have accumulated over the duration of the organization's history. However, a closer examination of those newly listed "cultural" sites for post-1994 South Africa, such as Mapungubwe Cultural Landscape (a national park run by SANParks) and the Richtersveld Cultural and Botanical Landscape (a national park run by SANParks) highlights that cultural heritage has also come to stand for nature. Cruikshank (2005: 251) has similarly drawn attention to the politics of "natural" designations in Canada that devalue human presence and historic traditions. Her findings at the Glacier Bay world heritage site document the decisive rift for First Nations custodians whose cultural practices and subsistence patterns were imperiled by the stroke of a pen. The domination of "natural" sites occurs largely in Australia, Brazil, and on the African continent, contrasting with Europe, where the declared sites are indisputably cultural, including palaces, historic centers, churches, and archaeological sites. While the work of UNESCO is about saving sites and the majority of its patrimony is cultural, in 2010 its focus seems squarely upon sustainability, biodiversity, risk and disaster, marine and forest conservation, and cultural landscapes.[1] Despite the dual mandate representing cultural and natural heritage, UNESCO's central interest is moving toward landscape, climate, environment, and biodiversity. UNESCO's Help Save Sites donation page directs you straight to an image of a panda (the symbol of the WWF),[2] while climate change dominates their program news and publications (UNESCO 2009). One could position these integrated developments as reflecting positive steps toward acknowledging socio-nature (Swyngedouw 1999) and regard them as demonstrating that finally nature's social shaping is being recognized. However, in expanding the enormity of nature in crisis, biodiversity and climate change have become hegemonic and the peopled aspects of place have become further eroded.

Diversity, Sustainability and Future Generations

The most recent set of convergences for natural and cultural heritage stem from global debate around biodiversity, sustainability and endangerment originating in the early 1990s. In this section I discuss the implications for archaeology and natural sites together through discourse and developments spanning little more than two decades. Every day we are surrounded by ever-increasing calls for action, donation, restraint, and mindfulness about the environment and natural resources. It is not surprising, then, that cultural agencies have adopted the same affective mantras: vanishing heritage, destructive development, threats from visitation, and loss of integrity.[3] Rather, it is the scale and proliferation of these ancillary effects and our reticence to disentangle these borrowed prescriptions that I find striking. No one could deny our global environmental precariousness or the credibility of scientific predictions. So severe is our crisis that influential propositions like Weisman's *The World Without Us* (2007) now proffer extremist fantasies where humanity disappears from the planet and natural diversity prevails, thus celebrating our own demise (Chakrabarty 2009; Zizek 2010). In what follows I am concerned that human agency is typically cast as deleterious and that this model has been readily embraced within cultural heritage discourse.

Recalling Humboldt's legacy, I turn first to the prioritization of diversity in natural and cultural arenas. Material nature (West 2006: 164) is powerfully connected to arguments of human livelihoods and survival, genetic capital, and human adaptation in the face of global change. Banking on biodiversity thus entails bringing together social movements and capital knowledge within a transnational assemblage of organizations, actors, knowledges, endangered species, and genes (Escobar 2008: 14). It is difficult to challenge the premise that our own future biological success is premised on the management of nature rather than upon the management of a material past. Biodiversity then leverages weightier claims than archaeological heritage. A radical and complementary view, though, might posit that unless we come to terms with cultural difference, historic trajectories, and genealogies of oppression, our survival as a species also looks rather grim. New exigencies and pieties around global ecological responsibility and species survival fuse in the largely accepted tenets of one-worldism. Bruno Latour (2004b: 462) problematizes this singular view of the globe, critiquing the "first modernity" dream of an already existing common sphere. In the cultural field many practitioners assert that preserving material heritage is a universal good and therefore constitutes global patrimony. The quotidian and centrifugal efforts by metropolitan museums to house the world's treasures (Appiah 2006; Cuno 2008), wresting them from local and national stakeholders, is one damaging result of that position. Heritage studies are just touching on those domains, their cosmopolitan constitution, and the tensions between global and local ethical positions (see papers in Meskell 2009a; Mortensen and Hollowell 2009).

There have been notable efforts to incorporate culture within the locus of biodiversity. The United Nations Environment Program (UNEP) produced *Cultural and Spiritual Dimensions of Biodiversity* (Posey 1999), which incorporates ancient spiritual attitudes to diverse nature and ecology-based worldviews, but then moves quickly into an ecocentrism that configures nature as central and cultural contributions secondary. Culture is understood as the traditional practices that shape biodiversity, indigenous ecological information, and attempts to safeguard intangible knowledge, language loss, and knowledge transmission. Ecological citizenship and ecosystem resilience is paramount, while people and the cultural practices that have maintained the diversity are discussed only after descriptions of plants and animals (West 2006: 164). Culture is transposed into the "culture of sustainability" because "cultural diversity should be regarded as a powerful guarantee of biodiversity" (UNESCO & UNEP 2002: 7). Biodiversity thus enlists cultural diversity for support, especially in the face of the acknowledged failures of development since the 1970s. UNESCO suggests that both diversities, biological and cultural, are mutually reinforcing and interdependent. During the 2002 UNESCO summit held in Johannesburg the familiar elements of both mystical ecology and governmentality emerged: Indigenous stewards "live in harmony with nature . . . [and their] traditional spiritual values often serve to prevent overexploitation of resources" (UNESCO & UNEP 2002: 14). Cultural diversity has intrinsic potentials "as a source of innovation, creativity and exchange," which points to its asset standing and market value from the balanced scorecard approach. Biodiversity "does not pose any theoretical difficulty" in their view, yet UNESCO has lately admitted that "cultural diversity" rests on the problematic tension between diversity and universality (Droit 2005: 201). Respect for diverse cultural traditions and ways of being is central, yet we should not imply that all people have to maintain some measure of ethnic difference or live in cultural stasis to be valued. Linguistic and legal anthropologists have critiqued the green metaphor of endangered language and culture since both are always already in a dialectics of formation and dissolution, porous and only relatively stable (Coombe 2003: 279). Levi-Strauss (1963) famously remarked that diversity is less a function of the isolation of groups than of the relationships that bind them together. We might do well to be wary of any modus operandi in which individuals and communities are commensurate with animals and environments.

It is not often the case that anthropologists, much less archaeologists, are involved in such high-level global discussions. In Johannesburg Arjun Appadurai (2002) contributed to the UNESCO/UNEP roundtable and nuanced the debate in forceful ways by emphasizing cultural needs and goods. Appadurai argues that diversity must also extend to the political realm, necessitating a maximum diversity of moral visions, not simply organisms or identities. Given mounting anxieties surrounding renewable resources, he imputes that there are no more vital "renewable resources than our children, our dreams and aspirations, our talents and imagination, in short, other than our humanity itself" (2002: 49). Indigenous communities have been exceptional trustees of the biodiversity of their own environments, rather than people that need to be coerced into protectionism. Quoting Wally Serote, South African poet and CEO of Freedom Park, Appadurai charges that for more than half of the world's population, biodiversity and environmental sustainability seem to be cruel jokes, mere circuses for the elite. Linking back to his own politicized scholarship (1990; 1991; 1996), he posits that natural and cultural diversity might offer the best counterpoint to the ideological and technological uniformity resulting from unrestrained market-driven globalization. While market logics seem to dominate global relationships, we must be mindful of the tensions between environmental concerns, market concerns, and development concerns. And while cultural diversity should be fundamentally connected to questions of law, ethics, and freedom, the forces of global consumerism have made it difficult for many societies to maintain their cultural dignity. The eco-environmental drive for diversity can result in the perilous panoply of products, slogans, and lifestyles that are geared to foreign tourism and consumption. Proliferating tribal villages in South Africa, "primitive" performances, and the presentation of groups like the San are troubling examples that are discussed in the next chapter. These initiatives are far from harmless or uplifting, since many living cultures are being forced to redesign themselves for the entertainment of visitors instead of exploring their own forms of cultural creativity (Appadurai 2002: 19). Appadurai echoes the concerns of others working in archaeology and heritage (Breglia 2006; Byrne 2009; Hall 2005; Hall and Bombardella 2005; Rassool and Witz 1996; Segobye 2006) and flags the potential of shared expertise, where cultural and natural sites, knowledges, and legacies might be considered evenly, exposing the differences rather than assuming simplistic convergences.

Diversity affords goods and services that have been embraced by development agencies, corporations, and transnational organizations. UNESCO has employed the language of cultural diversity through its Convention on the Protection and Promotion of Cultural Expressions (UNESCO 2005) and is keen to ensure free trade and the free flow of information. Reduced to its commodity base, diverse culture must be made freely available for public sector interventions into the market economy. Minorities and indigenous groups who might benefit from their own traditional expressions are often considered secondary (Coombe 2005: 41–2). It is instructive to see how this rhetoric is taken up in South Africa. The highly influential former Minister for Arts and Culture, Dr Z. Pallo Jordan (2007), claims that the term "cultural diversity is a concept that undergirds certain intangible, yet very important human rights. Indeed it is enshrined in our own constitution along with recognition of the right of freedom of expression." Given how cultural difference was deployed under apartheid, Jordan further states that,

> Our South African experience demonstrates the dangers that can lurk behind misguided attempts to seal-off cultural communities from each other like silos of different grains. The Verwoerdian nightmare of "separate development" was built on such absurd assumptions. Colonial conquest, the commercialization of agriculture, industrialization and a host of other factors having thrown African, White, Coloured and Asian together in one society, the notion that this historic omelet could somehow be unscrambled was bound to result in tragedy . . . But our country's past abounds in experiences that warn against the converse attitude. Intolerance towards cultural diversity can be as destructive a force, resulting in forced "assimilation," cultural denigration, racial chauvinism, racial oppression and cultural aggression. (2007)

The notion of cultural diversity for its own sake has taken root since the concept of biodiversity achieved global recognition and force. As the foregoing speech exemplifies, there are real dilemmas implicit in simply overlaying diversity onto the sphere of cultural heritage. There are other dangers in South Africa in the aggressive marketing of cultural and ethnic difference, especially where cultural and natural heritages are combined for commercial purposes. Culture gets naturalized in this process, but nature remains primary. Nature sets the stage, allowing for the possibility of thriving "tribal cultures" while voyeuristic onlookers remain enthralled by indigenous people's preservation of beauty and diversity in a colorful, feathered, beaded sort of way. In South Africa, as I will go on to describe, the decoupling of nature and indigenous culture still remains difficult in the diverse realms of cultural villages, rock art projects, nature-based development, and tourism. Visiting San rock art sites depicting exotic game in national parks while viewing their living counterparts in a "safari" setting, troublingly reinforces the position of San as natural subjects (or as extinct in many narratives, see Kuper

2003: 393) and therefore closer to the bush and wildlife (Cock 2007: 138; Meskell and Weiss 2006, Robins 2001, Weiss 2007). We ignore the genealogies and conflations of nature and culture at our own peril, but more seriously at the expense of those individuals who have already suffered grave historical injustice.

From our colleagues working to stem the tide of diversity loss and extinction, heritage agencies have borrowed language of loss and destruction. Coupled with the unfortunate tropes of civilization and barbarism, the Global Heritage Fund's (GHF) worldwide mission is to "work to save the last remaining cultural heritage sites in developing countries. Each year, we lose more of these ancient Cradles of Civilizations to destruction, unplanned development, looting, vandalism, and neglect."[4] A trend across heritage NGOs and UNESCO alike is the centrality of environmental crisis. Imperiled monuments watch-listed by the WMF (started in 1996) were clearly modeled on the IUCN's Red List of Threatened Species™ (started in 1994). Here too conservation agencies have increasingly naturalized and absorbed culture instrumentally. Conservation International has translated human communities into "Cultural Services" as part of an ecosystem services model. People are part of the ecological equation only in how they relate to natural resources rather than as entities in themselves (see also Bamford 2007). Communities are factors in regards to the management of ecotourism in Madagascar, in providing a buffer for forests in Kenya, deferring developers in Venezuelan protected areas or deploying traditional practices of taboo to safeguard natural resources in Fiji.[5] By naturalizing culture as an endangered object, natural scientists can then select data that effectively conflate their own environmental and social agendas (Cruikshank 2005: 256; Raffles 2002). Culture and communities now have some visibility in nature conservation agencies, but they are typically rendered as either one aspect of ecosystem services or as partners who are supporting the goals of international organizations, potentially above their own local needs. I suggest that there has been a trend in cultural heritage organizations toward prioritizing ecological and climatic risk that has displaced cultural heritage and its immediate stakeholders. In both contexts culture has increasingly been framed as subservient or instrumental to environmental crisis and management.

Heritage is always disappearing, and the fear of this loss drives the heritage industry. Against the backdrop of risk culture (Beck 1995, 2009) we have welcomed the global profusion of sites, parks, museums, archives, interpretive centers, and digital heritage. National summits on cultural heritage and risk are multiplying. ICOMOS has launched a series of international conferences around archaeological heritage management and climate change in the twenty-first century. In 2007 the European Parliament in Strasbourg exhibited *Archaeology and Climate Change: Heritage Under Threat*. The environmental message has permeated organizations like English Heritage as well as popular presentations of archaeology by Tony Robinson's *Man on Earth* series on UK Channel 4 in 2009 (which incidentally mirrors David Attenborough's *Life on Earth* series). Risk registers are prepared for individual countries that identify threatened heritage places, monuments, and sites. They present typical case studies and trends and share suggestions for solving individual or global threats to our cultural heritage.[6] From polar heritage to the Pacific, archaeological sites that are deemed valuable are in a state of emergency (see also Layton, Stone, and Thomas 2001). Archaeological heritage, as we have understood it from a specifically modern, Judeo-Christian perspective, largely inhabits a risk category because of its material fragilities (Holmberg in press). Of course, this would not be the same if we adhered to a Buddhist or Australian Aboriginal heritage ethic, for example (Byrne 1991; 2007; 2009; Hasinoff 2009; Herzfeld 2003), with the caveat that these positions are never monolithic either. Whatever the perspective, a tenuous logic presumes that cultural materials can be regarded as equivalent to a species or an ecosystem.

Global ecological health and global heritage have come to inhabit a shared moral ethos (Lowenthal 2006: 85), albeit not a comparable urgency. In view of scale, it might seem unthinkable to compare the global exigencies of environmental protection and cultural heritage, yet there is a shared history that extends back to UNESCO's 1972 convention. Starting in 1959, UNESCO's efforts to save Egyptian monuments before completion of the Aswan Dam (Droit 2005) was the first instance of massive international mobilization around cultural sites. Conversely, the recent threat to archaeology and local people from the Merowe Dam went almost unnoticed. UNESCO reports that the 26 international safeguarding projects it has launched since its establishment have cost close to $US1 billion.[7] Member states pay a compulsory contribution of US$7 million every two years to the World Heritage Fund (Bandarin 2007: 22). If we take a single conservation agency, like the WWF, they have invested over US$1.165 billion in more than 11 000 projects since 1985.[8] In the first half of the twentieth century archaeology captured an elite international imagination, whereas in recent decades the seismic shifts toward nature conservation, risk, extinction and climate change have triumphed (Beck 1995; Clark 2002). I would thus take issue with Lowenthal's view (2006: 84) that cultural heritage encourages more empathy than its natural counterpart or that humans respond more easily to relics and rise to their defense.

Ecological services promise to deliver returns while cultural benefits have proved difficult to quantify. That perceived difference is reflected in the vast global capital conservation agencies like WWF (5 million members globally) and the Nature Conservancy (over one million members) have to distribute, as compared to heritage bodies like the WMF or GHF. In 2008 WMF spent some $12.4 million on projects, a decade earlier their working budget was $3.4 million.[9] Heritage budgets are paltry in comparison to the millions wielded by donor agencies or philanthrocapitalists like Bill Gates who focus on environmental issues. Conservation organizations are some of the largest NGOs in the world, employing tens of thousands of people, controlling billions of dollars and mobilizing international projects and influence (Brockington 2009: 15). Their global concerns and rallying of resources inhabit a different order of things, unquestionably.

Extensive media coverage, philanthropic efforts, and celebrity support have also been effectively harnessed around nature. Preservation of cultural heritage or archaeological objects cannot come close to matching this, although there is no reason why the return of the Parthenon marbles or saving sites in Afghanistan should not enlist millionaires or celebrities.

The concept of biodiversity is part of a larger set of processes that are changing the way we understand and engage not just with nature (Escobar 2008: 143) but also with culture. I have argued that these imperatives influence our thinking about the past, specifically the ways we currently reconfigure heritage value around diversity, or inventory cultural sites, create at-risk categories or link climate change with preservation (Addison 2007; Arantes 2007; UNESCO 2009). Diversity also magnetizes the virtues of sustainability and the promise of rewards for future generations. Sustainability is commonly defined as development that meets the needs of the present without compromising future generations' ability to meet theirs. The gravity of these interconnections and their potentially disastrous ramifications was made clear by the 1987 Brundtland Commission and the Earth Summit in Rio de Janeiro in 1992, then encapsulated in the 1994 statement by the Union of Concerned Scientists.[10] The Millennium Ecosystem Assessment went on to report that 60 percent of the earth's ecosystem services are degraded by human activity (Link 2006). Critics charge that the rhetoric of sustainable development relies on flawed logics: the anthropocentric notion that the earth's value is instrumental and utilitarian; that conserving nature is dependent on generating economic capital; and that it perpetuates political and socio-economic structural inequalities (Golliher 1999: 447). From its base in ecology, the sustainability lobby has relied heavily on diversity and renewability, but is beginning to incorporate human rights, economic justice, and peace building.

Sustainability has entered the global lexicon rapidly and dissonantly. Everything now must be sustainable, including our housing, lifestyles, corporate structures, economic growth, museums, and even heritage sites. An entire issue of *Museums and Social Issues* in 2006 was devoted to the museum's role in fostering cultural sustainability. Heritage practitioners are beginning to engage the tenets of sustainability because they offer linkages between local and global scales and bridge past and future, the socio-economic and the environmental (Brattli 2009; Candelaria 2005; Helmy and Cooper 2002; Rico 2007; Tomalin, Simpson, and Bingeman 2000; Wurz and Merwe 2005). A parallel interest has emerged in studying ancient societies that practiced "sustainable" lifeways (Erickson 2003). Archaeologist Charles Redman, who directs the School of Sustainability at Arizona State University, and his colleagues examine ancient human impacts on the environment in an effort to understand long-term resilience and sustainable landscapes. Other developments include the Sustainable Preservation Initiative, an NGO with links to UCLA and the Archaeological Institute of America, whose self-proclaimed "mantra is Saving Sites by Transforming Lives." Perceived threats include disappearing heritage, economic crisis, unsustainable preservation, war and looting, and general loss. Their solutions call for "extreme" tourism, a digital SWAT team to virtually map sites, and a global network of experts.[11] The proliferation of such NGOs fostered by academics and others is intriguing, although tangible solutions and working-case studies remain elusive.

Grafted to narratives of moral nature and moral heritage is the obligatory burden of present generations to provide a legacy for future generations. Here too there are logics worth unpacking. First, despite future-geared promises being central, the precise form that obligation takes remains vague and disputable. Second, the exact substance of the legacy presupposes that aesthetic or intrinsic value must necessarily override an argument of utility. At a fundamental level there are genuine difficulties of imputing any general obligation to the human species, many of whose members have already been deprived the access to those utilities they are supposedly obliged to bequeath to the future (Soper 2000: 259–60). Ironically, those who consume the greatest resources through excessive life-styles are very often guilty of chastising the world's poorest for simply attempting to survive. Called to mind are the impoverished villages on the edge of Kruger that are reprimanded by park ecologists for using firewood or utilizing "alien" species as food sources. Put simply, why should the needs of living people's be trumped by those of coming generations? Bryan Norton (2005: 332), the guru of sustainability predicts that if "our generation and successive generations act on these beliefs, it is reasonable to hope that humans of the future *will* share a community with us and that the special places that are preserved may remain for them shrines to cultural, intellectual, and moral ideals that unify and give meaning to our culture." But this teleology assumes a stasis and, since green politics really only began during the 1960s and 1970s (Deese 2009), this presumption is optimistic. Environmentalists today lament their failures in reaching the global public or impacting politics, as the 2009 Copenhagen Climate Conference laid bare. The post-environmental lobby regrets that "in the name of indisputable facts portraying a bleak future for the human race, Green politics has succeeded in depoliticizing political passions to the point of leaving citizens nothing but gloomy asceticism, a terror for trespassing over Nature and a diffidence toward industry, innovation, technology, and science" (Latour 2007).

Future Thinking

In the foregoing I have argued that commonalities have emerged between nature conservation and cultural heritage formulations. Greatest value is accorded to sites considered unique and of scientific or aesthetic merit. Value is assumed to be intrinsic to sites and is not tantamount to either use value or exchange value (see also Lafrenz Samuels 2008). Such qualities are typically embodied in pristine spaces unmarked by human modifications since "man" is considered a destructive agent of change. Land use legacies and human histories are erased in these romanticized productions of place. Indigenous communities of the past, however, have been considered more attuned to the balance of conservation than modern indigenous groups. Either they are deemed worthy natural objects and part of the fauna or rapacious consumers with an undifferentiated drive to destroy everything around them (Tsing 2005: 255). Given the centrality of European thought to these constructs, it is ironic that European national parks are today often landscapes of traditional agriculture and small-scale settlement. The ecology and aesthetics of these places has developed through human interaction rather than absence with the goals of preserving the traditional local culture and a vibrant sustainable economy (Hamin 2002: 340). These lived-in, working land-scapes present a very different balance of nature and culture than that presented for much of Africa, evidenced by this chapter's opening quotation from Latour.

I have suggested here that global crises surrounding natural resources have become entangled with cultural resources, landscapes, and values. This "fossil fuels" template of the world attempts to restrict utilization and save our stocks for future generations. Concerns over dwindling resources, risk, and sustainability now regulate cultural heritage discourse about site usage, occupation, and lived traditions, often undervaluing them when it comes to indigenous owners and stakeholders. The past is thus transformed into a raw material and finite resource that must be cordoned off or enclosed. Heritage agencies the world over typically struggle with the realities of human occupation, encroachment (Latour 2007), ongoing traditional practices, visitation, and appropriation in and around signifi-cant sites. There are exceptions at the local level, though these struggles have often been hard won in places such as Australia (Lilley 2000b; Lilley and Williams 2005), or remain ongoing sites of contestation between local and international bodies, evinced in debates over preservation and management of sites across Southeast Asia (Byrne 1991; 1995). Just as animals, plants, and landscapes have been deemed part of the national estate for moral and scientific uplift from the Victorian era onwards (Garland 2008; Ritvo 1987), archaeological and historic sites are often wrested from their immediate inheritors for the global good of others.

While the above propositions first developed in the sphere of natural heritage protection, I suggest that they have been overlain upon the material remains of the past and, since a great many such sites survive in seemingly "natural" settings, it is not surprising that such congruent treatment has emerged. However, the stakes are considerably different for archaeological contexts, steeped as they often are in living traditions, continuities of visitation and use, and archaeology's cen-trality for identity formation and maintenance. A different suite of relations can be established with the materiality of the past and its continued possibilities for successive cultural reworking, though this is not to say that connections to nature and place making are not deeply complex and socialized. In fact, archaeologists have slowly recognized that any simplistic demarcation between cultural and natural sites can be problematic to disentangle in the past, as now. Irrespective of position, whether one claims that "nature" and "culture" are clearly differentiated realms or that no distinction can be made between them, all our thinking remains premised upon the humanity–nature antithesis (Soper 2000: 15). Tracing the consequences of that antithesis in South Africa – for people, heritage, and conservation – is at the heart of the chapters that follow.

With legacies of pristine wilderness, exotic tribes, and colonial attitudes that positioned Africans as closer to nature, archaeology must exert considerable effort to overturn the stereotypes of good nature, bad natives. When ecotourism, safaris, and natural assets are seen to bring much needed foreign currency injection, cultural heritage must struggle to present itself as valuable, complimentary, and constitutive of the nation. In high-profile destinations like Kruger National Park, efforts to trade off natural against cultural heritage – and against the histories, occupations, and anthropogenic modifications of the park – reveal complexities that ultimately challenge a strictly green model of value. Multiple histories of the park from our human origins, to Iron Age settlers, colonial administrators, and resistance fighters all add to the rich and deeply stratified picture of the park. This should not be a zero-sum game. Struggles to comprehend what is "natural" in order to maintain some designated ecological balance and preserve an aesthetic "wilderness" in counterbalance to human intervention proves neither scientifically credible nor socially progressive. Indigenous knowledge and intangible heritage may instead offer inroads to traditional practices and understandings around natural and cultural patrimony (Deacon and Foster 2005; Deacon, Mngqolo, and Prosalendis 2003; Deacon *et al.* 2004; Masuku Van Damme and Neluvhalani 2004). While these models have been proposed and successfully implemented at some rock art sites in Southern Africa, their broad implementation in mainstream archaeology and across national parks has been negligible. Australian management of cultural and natural heritage is often held up as a model for South Africa. Yet because of their respective histories their heritage context also differs: Aboriginal people have a very different relationship to history, their intangible heritage is often linked to the deep past that present co-occupiers of the land do not share. South Africa has carved out its own unique path toward past mastering. However, a new democratic nation cannot remain crippled by being deprived of its deeper history. By choosing to gloss over the complexities of the past, recuperation will always be attenuated leaving apartheid's legacy to prevail.

Notes

1   http://whc.unesco.org/en/activities (accessed November 20, 2009).
2   http://whc.unesco.org/en/donation (accessed January 15, 2010).
3   http://globalheritagefund.org/index.php/our_approach/our_vanishing_heritage_principal_threats (accessed January 17, 2010).

4   http://www.globalheritagefund.org/news/publications/annual_reports.html (accessed November 20, 2009).

5   http://www.conservation.org/learn/culture/pages/overview.aspx   (accessed November 23, 2009).

6   http://www.international.icomos.org/risk/index.html (accessed December 7, 2009).

7   http://whc.unesco.org/en/107 (accessed November 20, 2009).

8   http://www.worldwildlife.org/who/History (accessed November 20, 2009).

9   http://www.wmf.org/content/annual-report (accessed November 20, 2009).

10 http://www.un.org/popin/icpd/conference/ngo/940909224555.html,   (accessed November 23, 2009).

11 www.sustainablepreservation.org (accessed November 23, 2009).

Chapter 2

Making Heritage Pay in the Rainbow Nation

Heritage is not an acquisition, a possession that grows and solidifies; rather it is an unstable assemblage of faults, fissures and heterogeneous layers that threaten the fragile inheritor from within and from underneath. (Michel Foucault, *Nietzsche, Genealogy, History,* 1977)

Always end your book with Nelson Mandela saying something about rainbows or renaissances. Because you care. (Binyavanga Wainaina, *How to Write About Africa,* 2005)

Part of the fascination surrounding heritage in South Africa is the panoply of practices, places, and things that actually constitute it: wild animals, meteor craters, archaeological sites, archives and museums, local crafts, contemporary art, sport, and so on. Everything is someone's heritage in South Africa. Some of that heritage is the stuff of empowerment and capacity building, and some must be considered inherently negative heritage, the type typically jettisoned from the crafting of new nations. Certainly not all new heritage is configured around Africanity or the recovery of black pasts. Some heritage claims have spawned new racisms rather than engendered reconciliation. *Unity in diversity* may have provided a rousing anthem for the birth of a nation, and was leveraged internationally for investment, aid, and tourism, yet it has been tested at home by ethnic prejudice and stark economic realities. With the end of apartheid the ANC inherited an economy that had suffered two decades of stagflation, sanctions, divestment, and public debt of R230 billion (Terreblanche 2008). While economic opportunities have benefitted a new black middle class, between 45 and 50 percent of the population now live in poverty, and the plight of the black poor has notably worsened under the ANC's neoliberal policies (Ferguson 2007). The government's promise of a people-centered society has receded in the face of political denial and unwarranted optimism. Against this backdrop I examine the role of post-apartheid heritage making, comparing the expedient political rhetoric of the 1990s with the subsequent problems of implementation and transformation. Heritage was relentlessly promoted as a socio-economic driver in South Africa, especially for its vulnerable citizens and particularly in the face of dwindling government services and failed delivery. This continues despite all evidence that such measures offer unrealistic fallbacks (Meskell and Scheermeyer 2008). The challenges of healing the nation while simultaneously providing capital injection to the nation's poorest areas, then, brings us squarely to Kruger National Park, beginning with Mandela's centenary speech setting out his dream for the park's future. The complex issues outlined in this chapter, I argue, were to find full expression in Kruger at the inauguration of the new nation.

South African heritage is called upon to labor, not only in the service of the state but also as a palliative for the nation's poor and historically oppressed and their reintegration into new civic and economic spheres. A person's historical persecution, their traditional knowledge, tribal identity, association with a land-scape, use of natural materials, craft production, or their ancestor's graves are potentially all valuable assets that can be harnessed to "capacitate" and develop themselves and their communities. The troubling inheritance of tribalism and its reinvigoration under the promotion of the Rainbow Nation is further entwined with many liberal heritage ventures. Tangible and intangible heritage can all be brought into play (Scheermeyer 2005), ever widening the centrifugal promises of the past to provide for the future. The economic dimension of South Africa's cultural and natural heritages is vital, indeed the point underlies a key argument of this book. Yet I argue that heritage operates as a more complex form of self-compensation or therapy. Capitalizing culture under neoliberal restructuring is too convenient a catchall for these unfolding processes; this mistakenly undercuts the particular historical context of South Africa. Making heritage pay is also more complicatedly about fulfilling the social, spiritual, and therapeutic needs of the majority of South Africans in an era of uncertainty.

Elements of South Africa's liberalized program to "make heritage pay" may be symptomatic of many modern states. Parallels exist in North Africa, where exter-nal directives from the World Bank have targeted historic sites and districts for economic growth and social cohesion (Lafrenz Samuels 2009; 2010). While we might identify this as a global trend, I maintain that South Africa represents an extreme example for numerous historical reasons. This is a state-sponsored program, rather than the result of international intervention; South Africa's democracy is little over a decade old; the disempowered constitute the majority not the minority; and the state comprises both first-world and third-world econo-mies. The new nation has also compelled new subjectivities in the shape of active, responsible, entrepreneurial citizens who do not seek to rely on direct state intervention but would heal themselves (Ferguson 2010). Private–public partnerships and NGOs have increasingly replaced state functions that we also see reflected in heritage and conservation management. In terms of expertise there are glaring deficits in the educational system pertaining to heritage and the pre-colonial past. Heritage as a commodity was thus called upon to mitigate state shortfalls in impossible ways. It is for these and other reasons that South Africa provides such a compelling context to investigate the category of heritage and the particular types of work it now performs globally.

The past, observes Wendy Brown (2001: 5), is "less easily reduced to a single set of meanings and effects, as the present is forced to orient itself amid *so much* history and *so many* histories, history itself emerges as both weightier and less deterministic than ever before." Heritage then has come to resemble *muti*, the traditional medicine favored by black South Africans, because both call upon the ancestors in their efforts to heal and transform individuals and society. Invoking the past, performing new rituals, and celebrating diversity are the authentic guarantors of economic and spiritual security. In the burgeoning post-apartheid heritage sphere there are trauma tours conducted by ex-Umkhonto we Sizwe members (Grunebaum and Henri 2003; Grunebaum-Ralph 2001; Meskell 2007b), township tours (Nieves 2008; Witz 2007), cultural villages such as Lesedi and Shakaland (Rassool 2000; Witz, Rassool, and Minkley 2001), living San exhibits (Geldenhuys 2004; Meskell and Weiss 2006), and a multitude of ethnic craft initiatives. Some of these ventures rely implicitly on familiar Bantustan (apartheid-rule ring-fenced ethnic homelands) identities that many of us imagined would have vanished with the new nation. Indeed, the detailed inventorying of cultural practices, accompanied by public performances, was keenly embraced under apartheid as a necessary constituent of separate development (e.g., Malan and Hattingh 1976) and has long been part of identitarian politics, one way or the other, throughout the nation's history. Inventorying heritage is not simply motivated by private enterprise, but is avidly fostered by the state (Meskell 2005c; Sack 2003), chiefly through programs administered by the Department of Arts and Culture (DAC). Some of these strategies fold back upon themselves, reinforcing apartheid-era stereotypes. Others may indeed create new ethno-futures that supersede reified ethnicities by transforming tribes into corporations (Comaroff and Comaroff 2009: 8). For the Comaroffs (2009: 150), the commodification of ethnicity is an inherently modern practice, imbued with neoliberal expectations and capitalist desires for choice and consumption of cultural identities. One might well cast these South African developments as inherently entrepreneurial, modern – or indeed post-modern – and liberating, especially after repressive decades of apartheid rule. Yet this turn to culture and heritage is not a mere consequence of market forces. It is marked by South Africa's particular colonial history, in which racial and cultural differences were marshaled as the basis for unequal rights and privileges (Garuba and Radithalo 2008: 36), and more lately those same differences fueled the democratic revolution. Since 1994 those diverse cultural heritages, coupled with natural heritages, are being leveraged in order to cultivate new opportunities.

Struggles around culture and difference in South Africa have historically constituted a powerful domain of political resistance, whereby culture or ethnicity was a shorthand for political, social, and economic claims. These claims are increasingly being enacted in the sphere of heritage and are themselves underpinned by state failures over equity, access to resources, and recognition (Garuba and Radithalo 2008: 37). Globally too, recognition politics have been premised on distinctiveness, by appeals to cultural difference in regard to historical injustice and restitution, specific attachments to place and practice, particular lifeways, and so on. The recognition and accommodation of identity-related differences typically provide a route to the realization of human interests and are not simply ends in themselves. Yet South African identity categories resist any simple bifurcation of First Peoples and colonizers as understood in other post-colonial nations. In defiance of all other colonial settler societies, South Africans often reject the appellation "indigenous" to heritage and other forms of tradition and culture. Internal national politics have seen colored, Indian, and other minority heritage sidelined or subsumed by dominant black ANC official memorialization and preservation projects (McGregor and Schumaker 2006; Meskell and Scheermeyer 2008). This has sparked violence in multi-ethnic townships like Kliptown and undermined national solidarity. One notable exception to this trend is the long-standing heritage and memory work around the District Six museum (Hall 2006; McEachern 2002; Rassool 2007; Rassool and Prosalendis 2001). In nations such as Australia or the United States where the majority population is white, liberal attempts at recognizing indigenous alterity have resulted in other ways of constraining and controlling difference (Ivison 2002: 44; Povinelli 2002). In South Africa, issues of identity and "indigeneity" are, unsurprisingly, more multi-dimensional.

This inevitably gives rise to the complex question of who constitutes the nation's indigenous. If "indigenous" is taken to broadly encompass the non-white population, then the term covers the majority of South Africans. San, Khoekhoe, colored and the majority black population were historically victimized under white, colonial occupation and apartheid rule. In that way their subject status under colonialism and apartheid is similar to the experience of native peoples in settler societies of Australia, Canada, New Zealand, and the United States. But if indigenous refers only to "First Peoples" then it excludes everyone save San and Khoekhoe descendents. Even if we take the category "African" to equate to indigenous status, many white South Africans have hijacked the term asserting that they too are African by birthright. Liberal philosophers argue that "indigenous" can refer to "peoples who lived in that territory before settlers arrived and the process of colonization began. This relativizes the definition to prior occupation rather than first occupation" (Ivison 2007: 614). This is generally how the term is used throughout this book. Finally, self-description as indigenous has recently been cast as a connection to land (Hodgson 2002a: 1038; Sylvain 2002: 1076). However, this definition has been critiqued for the implicitly European belief that true citizenship is a matter of ties of blood and soil (Kuper 2003: 395). Certainly, most of my interviewees who describe themselves as black argue for restitution on the basis of owned and managed lands and settlements that were appropriated by whites, many of which episodes have occurred in living memory. Yet the issue of land and connection can also entrap rural communities in a legacy of primitivism, anti-development and anti-modernization (Sylvain 2002) and pays no heed to urban populations. It is also fraught with historical readings in South Africa since the removal and relocation of peoples were state strategies during colonial and apartheid times. These politicized geographies, premised on scripted tribal identities, had disastrous consequences felt to this day.

The Tribal Trap

In the desire to make heritage pay, post-apartheid South Africa has unwittingly embraced, if not reinvigorated, much of the same racial and ethnic categorizing that was instrumental in the very logics of minority rule and majority subjugation. *Plus ça change, plus c'est la même chose.* Tribalism, then and now, was both a form of power and a form of revolt against it (Mamdani 1996: 218). Understanding apartheid racialism and its consequences is vital for tracking the progress of the past and the relationship between cultural and natural heritage since 1994.

During apartheid tribes were positioned as nations with their own Bantustans or homelands situated on inferior lands. However, sizable portions of some homelands like Gazankulu, Bophuthatswana and KwaZulu had already been absorbed into protected areas. Independent homelands meant that blacks would be citizens of their own states, rather than the nation, ostensibly denying them South African citizenship. By preserving the trappings of tribalism, the apartheid state essentially prolonged the machinations of colonial indirect rule long after it had been abandoned elsewhere on the continent. South Africa was, after all, the last country to gain independence in Africa. Tribes were embraced as a political technology that fused cultural custom, ethnic identity, and administrative territory (Moore 2005: 14). The Bantu Authorities Act of 1951 was the crucial legislation that established the ethnic reserves and shored up the role of chiefs, who were then responsible for the allocation of land, the welfare and pension system, and development. Apartheid administrators recognized that the greatest threat to racial supremacy came from new class forces engendered by the modern economy that effectively cut across tribal lines, forces that would have been fueled by a racial mode of representation and control (Mamdani 1996: 95). By supplanting "racialism" with "culturalism" the apartheid state could effectively institutionalize separate development, albeit predicated on the tenets of white supremacy. Like other African states before them, South Africans called upon the concept of "culture" to perform the work of "race" in describing difference (Chanock 2000: 18). Rather than talking in outright terms of inferiority, tribes were merely different and, as such, entreated different trajectories. Different cultural groups had separate parliaments with limited self-governance in the tribal homelands, there were traditional authorities and customary law, and some homelands even had their own defense forces. Independent homelands like Venda and Ciskei had something of their own legal system, whereas non-independent territories such as Gazankulu were strictly subject to apartheid laws (Omond 1985) and were constantly in a state of emergency.

Rediscovered traditions surfaced under apartheid, cultural pasts and military histories were invoked, folklore flourished, and cultural symbols were fabricated and rationalized through the tenets of culturalism. Ethnic branding is by no means new, nor was the idea of unity in diversity. Black communities were encouraged to revive origin myths and ancestral practices, along with traditional ethnic dress, games, cooking, music, and dance (Harries 1991: 108; Ranger 2010). Bantu education promoted craft-based education such as weaving, not mathematics, as Verwoerd famously preached that such subjects would never be of practical use for blacks (Leibhammer 2005: 123). Anthropologists were central to those processes (Dubow 1995; 2006), and later, during the 1980s, the South African Defence Force (SADF) was their largest employer (Gordon 1987). Different languages and customs were stressed in National Party efforts to foster tribal solidarity and cultivate rivalries between groups. Racial mapping further escalated tensions between the Shangaan and Venda around Kruger National Park in the 1960s coupled with forced removals and arbitrary divisions of territory. Some archaeologists also succumbed to the ideology of tribalism and the unchanging Bantu (Hall 1984). Pretoria University's excavation of Mapungubwe during apartheid and their desperate efforts to secure radiocarbon dates that fitted the "late arrival of Bantu" model was politically motivated. Enforcing ethnic identities lay behind the passage of the 1970 Bantu Homeland Citizenship Act that claimed to "develop the spiritual and cultural assets of that national milieu and to help develop a healthy self-respect and pride" (Harries 1991: 106). This has the eerie ring of post-apartheid heritage uplift as well.

Under the new dispensation, the ANC sought to eliminate tribal rivalries, but not tribes themselves. Tribes would remain the centers of culture and community but not the locus of political solidarities (MacDonald 2006: 100). Resurgent nativism can be seen in the establishment of the Native Club by high-profile ANC members (Hamilton 2009; Ndlovu-Gatsheni 2008), illuminating the public scripting of elite ethno-culture. Customary courts and Houses of Traditional Leaders, both holdovers from homelands legislation, have also been welcomed in the new democracy (Oomen 2005: 84). In 2008 the controversial Communal Land Rights Act (No. 11 of 2004) handed control of communally owned land back to traditional leaders for administration. Communities bordering Kruger, including the

Dixie and Makuleke, were involved in the protest that claimed that this was taking them back to "apartheid-era tribal units" (Claassens and Cousins 2008; Groenewald 2008). Where the National Party decoupled race and culture as a means of separation and white supremacy, the ANC has held to the same distinction of non-racialism for reasons of national unity and democracy. Advocating non-racialism under the ANC has enabled black and white elites to prosper while the poor have remained marginalized (MacDonald 2006: 127). The old fault lines of inequality and discrimination have simply been papered over by other forms of social injustice and hierarchy, namely those of rich and poor (Daniel, Southall, and Lutchman 2005). One particular remedy that poor black South Africans have been offered is to again "develop" their own "culture." Before and after 1994, the strategy for the disenfranchised requires that they look to the past to forge their future.

The narrative of "progress" from a racist past to a nonracial present and future marks the critical modality in the post-apartheid era. South Africans are effectively living in a "double temporality," with the apartheid past as the constant referent in current understandings and future projections. The public sphere is infused with a "consciousness of the history that preceded and informs the current conjuncture, an awareness of living with the past in the post-apartheid present – and into the foreseeable future, for that matter" (Farred 2004: 593). Like other purported post-colonial settings, the appellation of *post* is seemingly premature. The new nomos is haunted by the old nomos according to Farred; the old nomos is inescapably part of the new one and that duplicity is laced with concern, regret, anger, or inevitability. Living in double time lays bare the impossibility of remaking the nation without recourse to its multiple pasts, not simply the apartheid years but the long dureé of colonization and repression of indigenous peoples across southern Africa. This particular positioning, some might say impasse, is key for those of us investigating post-apartheid shifts in the cultural productions of history and heritage, museums and tourist locales, as well as constructions of nation, identity, and politics. We are poised at the very moment, this dual orientation, in which South Africans find themselves acknowledging, reconciling, and even re-crafting specific pasts.

Developing Heritage

The decade following South Africa's liberation offers a unique window into the discursive creation of a new nation's heritage landscape. Government officials rewrote the dominant, racially motivated historical narratives that the apartheid government's decades of indoctrination imprinted on its citizens. In tandem they launched a campaign of socio-economic initiatives targeting the past as a corrective for redressing the ills of the past regime and simultaneously shoring up African identities in the present. This new suite of public discourses centered on the concepts of the Rainbow Nation and the African Renaissance. Reflected in the wording of the new national heritage legislation, the ANC leadership claimed that heritage "helps us to define our cultural identity and therefore lies at the heart of our spiritual well-being and has the power to build our nation." And further that "our heritage celebrates our achievements and contributes to redressing past inequities. It educates, it deepens our understanding of society and encourages us to empathise with the experience of others. It facilitates healing and material and symbolic restitution and it promotes new and previously neglected research into our rich oral traditions and customs" (Republic of South Africa 1999). As a new apparatus in the ANC arsenal, the past was summoned to serve the democratic state, to have economic, social and therapeutic benefits.

To the government's credit, early efforts were made to incorporate the hurtful histories of white rule. This assimilative strategy often appears under the rubric of the Rainbow Nation and saw full expression in the African Renaissance speeches of former president Thabo Mbeki. The term "Rainbow Nation," coined by Archbishop Desmond Tutu to reflect a new post-apartheid, democratic, multicultural society in South Africa, was quickly taken up by Nelson Mandela in his inaugural address. "Each of us is intimately attached to the soil of this beautiful country as are the famous jacaranda trees of Pretoria and the mimosa trees of the bushveld – a rainbow nation at peace with itself and the world" (Mandela 1994). Rainbow-ness could encompass nature and culture while successfully avoiding all reference to race in any specific terms of color. It was merely symbolic of the diversity of the nation's unspecified racial, ethnic, or cultural groups. Like culturalism before it, the rainbow narrative could be deployed politically and materially, whether for public performances or in the regalia of the state flag. The ANC deployed the rainbow mythos at the famed van Riebeeck celebrations commemorating European arrival in South Africa, previously associated with apartheid rule. Jan van Riebeeck and his wife, Maria de la Quellerie, were imputed as beginning "a 350-year struggle for national unity" in which purportedly everyone fought, and which ultimately led to a multicultural, rainbow-hued South Africa (Witz 2003). The supreme whiteness of van Riebeeck and de la Quellerie shifted to a rainbow color, dressed up in the language of multiculturalism and diversity. In a remarkable display of spin, Nelson Mandela declared that Jan van Riebeeck was one of the founders of the South African nation. The crafting of such originary myths makes the security of a new South Africa dependent on quasi-fictive narrations of nationhood to which it may not be capable of standing up; its future is perched on a dangerous precipice of fabrication. This is similar to other racist fantasies, like Manifest Destiny, or the fundamental right to appropriate another's country, constituting the very rationale for colonization thereby forcing indigenous constituencies to celebrate their own oppression.

The Rainbow Nation represents a failed decolonization project. Though conceived as a lack it was produced through excess: an excess of history, an overburden of pastness, and inscription of history always onto the present. As Farred (2004:

594) would have it, "the past is too constitutive of the present." Tired of the hollow rhetoric and governmental desires to homogenize South African society, one Indian academic explained the dilemma, "in this post-rainbow nation euphoria, we've all become the same color. I don't think it's got to do with color, I think it's got to do with culture, and the culture of mass consumerism." The Rainbow Nation story, like the wider pan-African embrace of the African Renaissance, might have bolstered nation-building fervor during political transition but, more than a decade later, its promise is tired and unfulfilled. Both narratives rested on novel understandings of heritage and past culture, not only black African, as the van Riebeeck celebrations attest. Rainbow Nation-ness is the epitome of an imagined community à la Anderson (Lazarus 2004: 620). Yet it is this very lack of attention to history that fuels repeated ethnic and racial tensions and misunderstandings in post-democratic society. Instead of unraveling and making public the complexities of the deep past, the state would rather revel in the glories of re-enchanted history, on one hand, while simultaneously projecting them forward as exemplary models for progress on the other. South Africans are being educated through various cultural productions about what is best remembered and what it is best to forget. The very recent past of liberation can be underscored, yet the longer, more complex colonial history of the country, and the reasons why apartheid was successfully entrenched in the first instance has been subsequently downplayed.

Building upon the domestic vision of the Rainbow Nation, the African Renaissance demanded a cultural re-engagement with the rest of the continent with South Africa at the helm. At the philosophy's heart is a reliance on a suite of cultural (read archaeological) achievements from Southern Africa and beyond: San art, Great Zimbabwe, and so on link to the monumental efforts of ancient Egypt, Carthage, and Axum (see Mbeki 1996; 1998). Spearheaded by Mandela and promoted vigorously by Mbeki, the theme of an African Renaissance enjoyed regular public and media fanfare. With rousing pan-African zeal Mbeki famously addressed the Constitutional Assembly in 1996:

> I am an African . . . I owe my being to the Khoi and the San whose desolate souls haunt the great expanses of the beautiful Cape . . . I am formed of the migrants who left Europe to find a new home on our native land . . . I am the grandchild of the warrior men and women that Hintsa and Skehukhune led . . . My mind and my knowledge of myself is formed by the victories that are the jewels in our African crown, the victories we earned from Isandhlwana to Khartoum, as Ethiopians and as the Ashanti of Ghana, as the Berbers of the desert . . . I am the grandchild who lays fresh flowers on the Boer graves at St. Helena. (Mbeki 1996)

This speech also reflects the cultural mythos of rainbow identity, a Rainbow Nation where black can expropriate Khoekhoe, San, and white histories (and presumably visa versa) with the ultimate aim of cultural therapy, thereby healing historic wounds and promoting interracial understanding. Such easy isomorphisms may have emotive appeal yet fail to take seriously histories of cultural difference, not to mention colonial genocide and apartheid repression, for the sake of a willing amnesia.

President Mbeki's rhetoric around the African Renaissance was a clear example of this strategy to revive, regenerate, and reconstruct the past for the present, showcasing South Africa's achievements for national and international audiences. Like other aspects of early ANC rule, the nation's cultural heritage was primarily connected within Africa, rather than to the West or globally. Yet at the same time it was firmly rooted in a Western capitalist value system with a strong neoliberal agenda. He re-engineered continental institutions like the Organization of African Unity (OAU) and formed new ones, including the Southern African Development Community (SADC) and the New Partnership for Africa's Development (NEPAD) (Kagwanja 2008: xx). Heritage, then, had a dual mandate, to operate within the purview of the African Renaissance but also to be highly consumerist, which was one of the hallmarks of Mbeki's particular style of government. While heritage was easily touted as a wellspring for national pride and for economic growth, the enabling infrastructure and linkages made between resources and outcomes remained tenuous. After the 1994 elections, revitalizing a program of specifically African heritage was a necessity, albeit secondary to the agendas of restitution and civil infrastructure development. This might explain why the desire for making heritage pay continues to be so strong, yet heritage legislation, particularly at the provincial level, has been slow in implementation. Apartheid governments placed greater emphasis and directed far greater capital toward the promotion of natural heritage in the form of national parks and reserves. Mbeki's government was ultimately no different in terms of funding. There remains a general unwillingness to balance support for natural and cultural heritage since environmental tourism proves so lucrative and ensures injections of foreign currency. However, as some of the chapters in the book demonstrate, the naturalizing of culture and past communities, specifically in an African context, has negative and racist implications for certain communities today.

While politically expedient at the fragile moment of transition, critics have subsequently attacked the candy-coated myth of peace for temporary stability that has prevented real transformation in South Africa (Erasmus 2008). People I interviewed from various backgrounds expressed themselves as "tired" of Rainbow and Renaissance narratives; they felt that changes in social perceptions were being forced rather than developed. Their sentiments were summed up incisively by a young conservator: "I think they can be very empty terms if people don't have water to drink or a place to sleep or get the practical aid and help that they've been promised." Rainbow and Renaissance culture was undoubtedly inflected by the ethos of the Truth and Reconciliation Commission that permeated post-apartheid society. Remembering but also forgetting was deemed a vital therapeutic strategy for forgiveness and recovery during the 1990s (De Kok 1998; Mamdani 1996; Ndebele 1998). Some, like Brink (1998), argued that healing and social transformation can only be achieved after requisite forgetting, that ignorance can be politically expedient when precipitated by the state. Prescriptive state-sanctioned forgetting might ward off the dangers intrinsic to remembering past wrongs and quell fears over the endless chains of vendetta that revenge can unleash (Connerton 2008: 61). Forgetting can also be constitutive in the formation of new identities, which were needed after 1994. But newly crafted memories are frequently accompanied by a set of tacitly shared silences. Cultural critics also see dangers in the conflation and fabrication of historical narratives, arguing that the historicity of the past will be elided and that with forgetting comes the potential for future reprisals. It is perhaps no wonder, then, that the historical details of the South African past, its colonial oppressions and inequities, proved to be challenging for an emergent nation to publicly present, much less celebrate.

Instead of focusing much needed attention on the nation's own deep history, the new government gave substantial funds to Mali to conserve and make available historic, early manuscripts in Timbuktu in an effort to help cement South Africa's precolonial linkages across Africa (Jeppie and Diagne 2008).[1] When I visited Timbuktu in 2008 the archives were impossible to access and there was no visible acknowledgement of South Africa's financial support. Such gestures sadly have not changed South African's perception of their own history as embedded within this larger frame, nor curbed violent xenophobia toward other Africans (Boonzaier and Spiegel 2008: 202). More seriously, at the time of writing, the government's continued support of Zimbabwean president Robert Mugabe, its recent blocking of UN resolutions against ethnic cleansing and human rights abuses, and its unwillingness to condemn rape and civilian attack in Darfur have led South Africa to be branded a "rogue democracy" (Kagwanja 2008). Emancipatory rhetorics rather than facticity may have been instrumental in forging an ultra-democratic, postcolonial state, yet today the African Renaissance fails to resonate with many South Africans in either spiritual or economic domains.

Neoliberal Heritage

The heritage sector is booming in South Africa; there are new heritage agencies, NGOs, UNESCO World Heritage sites, and cultural patrimony is now interwoven with various government ministries and parastatals. Yet the state is attempting to contribute less in way of infrastructure with the expectation that private enterprise, the provincial sector, and international agencies will make up the deficit. Many new national initiatives are expected to be self-sustaining through private partnerships with business, and are based largely on the competitive tender system. As a result, new heritage venues are peculiarly promoted as centers for weddings, receptions, corporate events, and the *indabas* (or workshops) of which South Africans are so fond. New sites of heritage production, including the Origins

Center, Maropeng, Didima, and the Cradle of Humankind, advertise widely as corporate or civic venues that are incidentally located in heritage landscapes. This trend is also visible in the parastatal organizations such as SANParks where much of the nation's cultural heritage resides. In 2005 SANParks boasted impressive increases in numbers of black visitors, up from 4 percent to 19.7 percent because of successful transformation. In 2007 it was discovered that the 62.2 percent of black visitors to Mapungubwe National Park (South African National Parks 2006) were attending conferences and workshops.

At the beginning of new dispensation, tourism was targeted as a priority for South Africa's economic development. Developing tourism was premised upon three principles: it would be government led, driven by the private sector, and should be community-based (Republic of South Africa 1996). The precise relationship between the state and private sectors was never specified, nor exactly what would constitute "community-based tourism" (Binns 2002; Hughes 2007: 273). Speaking during Heritage Month in 2009, the ANC's Chief Whip stressed the yet unfulfilled need to leverage South Africa's cultural and natural heritage for poverty eradication and socio-economic development (Motshekga 2009). Part of the difficulty results from a split portfolio with cultural heritage falling between two ministries, the DAC and the Department of Environment and Tourism (DEAT). More than any other sphere, tourism provides the linchpin. The number of international tourists has risen dramatically since the release of Nelson Mandela and lifting of international sanctions and stands at around seven million annually (Hughes 2007: 270). While domestic tourism is also growing, much of the cultural heritage discussed here remains the purview of the international market for a whole host of social and political factors.

NEPAD and the African Union (AU) effectively treat culture and heritage as integral to sustainable development programs across Africa (Jordan 2006a). NEPAD considers that escalating poverty levels, underdevelopment, and the continued marginalization of Africa require countries like South Africa (but also countries like Morocco, see Lafrenz Samuels 2009) to harness every economic asset they possess. Influenced by the tenets of the African Renaissance, former minister for Arts and Culture Dr Z. Pallo Jordan expressed great pride in "the fact that Africa is the Cradle of Mankind" and in the "ancient kingdoms of Africa we find the earliest examples of abstract human thought." On the question of sustainable development he warns that "we can no longer rely on traditional methods of conservation and protection. The pressures rooted in under-development and poverty have created serious new threats to heritage sites. One of the challenges of the African Renaissance is empowering Africans to know, and to take pride in their world heritage sites, which are equal to those of other peoples of the world" (Jordan 2006a). While this might be true, it participates in the unwieldy logic that impoverished people are the problem for, and the main beneficiaries of, heritage. Pallo Jordan's personal dedication to the African past ensured the establishment of key initiatives at the Kamberg Rock Art Center, the Origins Center, and

Thulamela, as well as in Mapungubwe National Park. Indeed, many fear that the status of archaeology and heritage in South Africa will be further weakened by his loss from the Arts and Culture portfolio in Zuma's new cabinet. Disastrous resignations from the Robben Island World Heritage Site and accusations of homophobia over an exhibit at Constitution Hill immediately plagued the next minister, Lulu Xingwana, herself soon to be replaced (Van Wyk 2010).

Heritage in South Africa has been called upon to fulfill numerous state level agendas: on the domestic front it is to provide social and economic regeneration as well as identitarian politics of nation making. On the international front, national heritage has to connect to the rest of the continent, to constitute a precise Africanity, to contribute to the narrative of origins and achievements that underpins the African Renaissance, and to fulfill globalist fantasies of self-sustainability. This was evidenced during the 2002 World Summit on Sustainable Development when then President Mbeki and Kofi Annan famously visited Sterkfontein Caves. Their imprinted footprints are now on display accompanied by a plaque with Annan's words of caution: "The lives our distant ancestors led here millions of years ago hold a clear lesson for us today: while their footprints on nature were small, ours have become dangerously large. The World Summit on Sustainable Development of 2002 must set humankind on a new path that will ensure the security and survival of the planet for succeeding generations." As Shepherd cleverly notes, Annan's words convey a biblical injunction in regard to salvation of the earth's resources. Salient for the project of this book, it summons the language of "sustainable development" to describe the nation's cultural heritage as well as the historicizing of the African Renaissance. Africa remains central, then, to world affairs, both because of its "originary status" but also the context of its plight today, which implicates the rest of the globe historically (Shepherd 2003: 826).

Taking a closer look at the Cradle of Humankind, a UNESCO World Heritage Site inscribed on the "Cultural Property" list, and specifically its flagship museum, Maropeng (Setswana for *the place where we once lived*), underlines the preoccupations with the rise of public–private enterprises, consultancy culture, and new urgencies around environmental risk, extinction, and resource depletion. Opened in 2005 by Thabo Mbeki and costing some R347 million, the Maropeng Visitor Center at the Cradle of Humankind World Heritage site was developed through a public–private partnership between the Guateng Provincial Government, the University of the Witwatersrand and Maropeng a'Afrika Leisure (Pty) Ltd. Typical of many new government-driven heritage ventures, there is a heavy and overt reliance upon the private sector, market principles, and corporate solutions (Comaroff and Comaroff 2009: 128). The international consultants were a British firm that specializes in theme parks, as can be seen in the proliferation of interactive zones, noisy media displays, and the underground boat ride that is similar to a Disneyland attraction. A plaque at the entrance celebrates a 2005 award by the British Guild of Travel Writers, and etched in the background is the predictable string of free-floating signifiers: local economy, local community, responsible,

Figure 2.1   Maropeng, part of the Cradle of Humankind UNESCO World Heritage Site. Courtesy of the author.

sustainable, tourist potential, and education. Other awards include "best market-ing campaign" and "best business unusual product or service." The Maropeng complex boasts not only a Visitor Centre with several restaurants and cocktail bar but also a 24-bedroom 4-star hotel and conference facilities for up to 500 delegates. Commercial advertising in brochures and magazines also directs clients to the Cradle Nature Reserve (and Game Reserve), specializing in weddings and confer-ences and home to the acclaimed Cradle Restaurant.

Maropeng was designed to celebrate South Africa's rich fossil record, which effectively charts our human evolution. Yet rather than promote cultural heritage or human history, the focus remains squarely with a "Commitment to the Environment," as their vision statement demonstrates. The Sustainability Wall explores themes like tool manufacture or fire usage and relates them to contem-porary global crises. Instead of exploring the historic or contemporary practices of South Africans, their achievements such as gold smelting and iron working, early international trade or production of art, it jumps ahead to the contemporary focus on environmental catastrophe and degradation. Burning houses, polluted landscapes, shanty towns, unsustainable foods are all showcased with alarmist graffiti asking "will we destroy ourselves" and papered over with posters featuring Mandela, Che Guevara, anti-globalization, anti-animal testing, anti-apartheid, anti-war, AIDS, clean air, and women's rights campaigns. Pressing social issues like education, poverty, migration, unemployment, and hunger, so rife in South Africa, are collapsed in the singular call for environmental sustainability. The social has been replaced by the environmental, the cultural with the natural, and certainly the techniques of archaeology to uncover the fossil record with those of conservation. It is noteworthy that Maropeng is hardly a paragon of sustainability: it uses copious amounts of water internally for a fountain and outside to keep the grass on its tumulus green; it is constructed as a vast concrete and metal bunker; its displays use significant amounts of electricity as well as plastics, metals, glass, and paper. Maropeng's profligate cost has not been matched by visitor numbers, which are largely constituted by school groups, making the center itself unsustainable. Maropeng dramatically evinces the porosity of cultural and natural heritage designations and the tenacity with which environmental discourses permeate all sectors of public life.

Politicians have used Maropeng and other prehistoric sites like Mapungubwe and Thulamela to develop the idea of African civilization in the present, and contrast this with Western empires that are cited as responsible for violence, oppression, and degradation. The majority of speeches begin with the acknowledgement that "humanity first emerged in Africa. Africa is the Mother of humankind . . . Africa was, indeed, the first civilization, held in the highest esteem in antiquity" (Mancotywa 2007). African qualities like *ubuntu* need to be recouped in order to save the nation morally first, whence other benefits will follow.

> Heritage – not only is it a strategic resource for our country but it is a DNA of our society. The apartheid government created a wrong impression about our heritage, that it was only about buildings, bricks and mortars, hence monumentalising of [*sic*] heritage. In dealing with challenges facing the heritage sector it is important for us to ask ourselves, what is the role of heritage in nation building and national identity? (Mancotywa 2007)

Since 1994, the answers have congealed into a mantra: national cohesion, reconciliation, and regeneration. Resuscitating African civilization, therefore, will ultimately guarantee economic benefits and transformation and halt the moral decay. As Maropeng highlights, the state now endorses a recombinant neoliberal heritage constituted from national emancipatory rhetoric and commercial production, and in doing so has missed the opportunity to educate its citizens about the complex history of South Africa's past.

By the mid-2000s South Africa's romance with cultural heritage had waned, as was reflected in the shift from impassioned political speeches to those demanding asset delivery. The onus was placed on the past to be self-sustaining. The shift from heritage as an inalienable asset to heritage as an economic driver was outlined in a speech by Pallo Jordan at the Donor's Conference for the African World Heritage Fund, an African-inspired initiative supported by UNESCO.[2]

> The concerns raised by the management of Africa's natural and cultural sites calls for a holistic approach that will make them less of a burden on the fiscus. To attain this we will have to change our attitude to our heritage sites. The manner in which we manage Africa's World Heritage Sites can transform them from fiscal burdens into economic assets. This site, where we are [Maropeng], for example, every

weekend receives in excess of 300 guests. On long weekends, that figure escalates to more than 800. During holiday season it rises even higher, and many of those visitors are tourists from abroad who will spend their money here and in the surrounding towns and villages. Innovative management means the sites having a direct impact on the communities that surround them. (Jordan 2006b)

In less than two decades South African heritage was cast as a burden under apartheid and as an asset for the new nation's revivalism, then recast again as a burden on a strained fiscus and before once again being cast as a potential asset. Heritage has been made and unmade since 1994.

We might recall here that South Africa started the European phase of its history not as a colony of some far-flung nation or empire, but as an outpost for an international company. Capitalism was there from the beginning. It was about stockholders not citizens. So there is something oddly circular about the government's restructuring of the nation within a system of global capitalism (Terreblanche 2008: 122). The ANC's version of non-racialism has simply privatized and culturalized race (MacDonald 2006). It has also transformed South African culture, and de facto race, into an international brand (Chanock 2000: 24), in essence capitalizing culture. This assumes that "culture" is permanent and deeply historic, premised upon stable communities with shared structures of behavior and belief. Culture is then conservative rather than dynamic, it can thus be reified, mobilized, and put to work. Like the separation of church and state in a liberal democracy, race is relegated to the private, unofficial sphere (except for Black Economic Empowerment or BEE). This also gives "race" some traction. It can be celebrated under the banner of tradition, but it can also create enclaves and exclusions. The government's financial and commemorative investment in Freedom Park (Baines 2009), Walter Sisulu Square, and Constitution Hill celebrating a largely black, ANC vision of South Africa and its democracy is indicative. As a private, embodied, and cultural asset, "race" can be hived off to create a livelihood as well as remaining an inalienable property. The substitution of race for power/culture has played out since the 1994 elections: Mbeki employed racial nationalism to underpin democratic government during his presidency; he used democratic government to endorse capitalism, and finally turned to capitalism to materialize the importance of racial nationalism (MacDonald 2006: 127). In a country that claims to be nonracial, by which they mean race is not society's organizing principle, race continues to be absolutely inescapable. That race continues to assume the mantle of culture is a reminder of the tenacity and vitality of colonial categories.

Rainbow Materialities

Many liberal intellectuals have pointed out that "ethnicity" and tribalism are forms of false consciousness promulgated by the apartheid government's grand plan for homelands and separate development policies (Robins 2001: 837). In the post-apartheid era this has impacted negatively upon certain groups that have claimed special status and recognition, particularly the San and Khoekhoe minorities. In this rather unstable landscape of ethnic making and unmaking, it is still the case that indigenous groups, often territorialized in the ways colonialism and apartheid subdivided the nation (Mamdani 1996; Mbembe 2000; 2001), are being encouraged through government initiatives, development schemes, and private enterprise to present themselves as culturally distinctive through the making and selling of their ethnically respective cultural objects and identities. Such artisanal economies are often supported by neoliberal policies (Colloredo-Mansfeld 2002: 113), often operating under the rubric of development and in South Africa, specifically, they are hitched universal tropes of cultural diversity and potential benefits. The performance of craft making, with all the associations of "primitive" otherness and essential difference, coupled with tourist-oriented "tribal" performances are promoted as recuperating African identities while promoting self help and a sustainable local economy. Some years ago the minister for Arts and Culture outlined:

> poor communities are in many instances, owners of assets – natural and material resources, human resources, cultural assets, indigenous knowledge, traditions and customs that can be the key agents for social and economic development. South Africa is blessed with a rich cultural tradition with artistic individuals and communities living in all corners of the country. Any poverty alleviation programme which aims at creating work opportunities must begin with these assets. We need to invest in people and their ability to make objects and artefacts, production and music. (Sack 2003: 4)

Material culture is one critical component here, particularly the fiction of a specific, ethnically bounded materiality that sediments identity in a pre-modern era and stands as an unchanging hallmark of "black" and "colored" peoples. These contemporary "primitivisms" reflect the earlier, and much critiqued, colonial reifications of a simple way of life. Rewriting the past and being attendant to strategic essentialism in the present, we also need consider "both the fixity and fluidity of racial categories" and how people "reworked and contested the boundaries of taxonomic colonial states" (Stoler 1995: 199). Failure to do so simply compounds historical ignorance and allows dangerous prejudices to flare as they did around the 2006 opening of the Origins Center at the University of the Witwatersrand. Radio callers in Johannesburg were angered by the use of the term "First Peoples," and the inference they took from it that San and Khoekhoe arrived prior to black settlement. It was this notion of "Firstness" and primacy that black South Africans found offensive in its reinforcement of old apartheid narratives of their own late arrival. Yet instead of new alliances between San, Khoekhoe, and black constituencies, the flattening of historical processes spawns new discriminations that Rainbow Nation narratives have done little to ameliorate and that appear renewed and multiplied, like the proverbial hydra.

It could be said that South Africa has been a "state looking for a nation" (Appiah 1992: 262). One of the most performative arenas in which that process can unfold is in the heritage sector, replete with material symbolism that can be drawn upon for celebration and legitimation. Attention to archaeology, I would suggest, has been rather overshadowed by the predominance of human origins within the global fraternity of "cradle of humankind" sites on the one hand and celebration of the liberation movement, what is commonly known as "the struggle," on the other. The latter is reflected in the nine Legacy projects endorsed by Cabinet: the Women's Monument, the Anglo-Boer South/African War, Constitution Hill, the Chief Albert Luthuli Project, the Nelson Mandela and Samora Machel projects, the Ncome/Blood River Projects, the Khoisan Project and Freedom Park (Jordan 2004). McGregor and Schumaker observe that

> state-led commemorations of nationalist achievements and struggle histories have been highly selective, liable to elevate ruling party histories and heroes over others, often ignoring unions, youth or women, and dealing with violence selectively or not at all. It is interesting that the heroes and sites of early colonial revolts have been remarkably absent in public monuments, testimony perhaps to the growing marginalization of rural populations, the lack of local meaning . . . or the difficulty of harnessing important living mediums and sacred sites to state projects. Rather than promoting national unity as intended, state heritage projects have often provoked controversy and resistance, particularly when combined with mounting popular disaffection, shifts towards authoritarianism and closure of the public sphere, the pressures of economic decline and gaping inequalities enhanced by neo-liberal adjustment. (2006: 8)

The real problem, I would argue, is the inattention heritage has paid to history. Heritage provides a hollow spectacle that is rarely educational or deeply historical: Freedom Park or Walter Sisulu Square provide pertinent examples (Marschall 2006b; Meskell and Scheermeyer 2008). This fails to address educational deficits perpetrated on South African citizens by decades of apartheid government. School texts and curricula encouraged racial and historical fictions and erased African achievement (see Esterhuysen 2000; Shepherd 2003; 2005). ANC ministers like Kadar Asmal have worked tirelessly with a small group of historians and archaeologists to change the textbooks, but the results are slow and certainly archaeology is yet to attract a new generation of black professionals.

Heritage might indeed be everywhere, but it is often nebulous, celebratory, and frequently without historical substance. Historians, working in conjunction with a younger generation of archaeologists, have begun to produce more detailed accounts of the deep and recent past that are both socially and politically relevant (see Bonner, Esterhuysen, and Jenkins 2007; Bonner, Esterhuysen, and Swanepoel 2009; Delius and Hay 2009). The 500 Year Initiative[3] is one such project that is actively working between history, geography, social anthropology, and archaeology with documentary, material, and oral evidence. Rather than adhering to the hard and fast categories of colonial tribalism, this project more than most has tried to track the emergence of modern South African identities. As we have seen, the attachment to tribalism has remained resilient through apartheid and post-apartheid eras.

Post-apartheid fetishizations of tribal culture are still haunted by the specter of homelands and separate development, taxonomies of primitivism, and often by the de-privileging "First Peoples" like the San and Khoekhoe. Whites, too, have been engaging in forms of cultural promotion and ethnic separatism, as the case of Orania makes clear. The town is a whites-only Afrikaner Volkstaat in the Northern Cape with its own flag and currency, premised upon the cultural pres-ervation of the Afrikaner culture. Afrikaners feel that their special kind of histori-cal persecution under the British, and now their marginalization under black majority rule, justifies their use of language and culture as instruments of identity politics and resistance (Garuba and Radithalo 2008; Kuper 2003; Nasson 2000; Stanley 2005). Yet as many interviewees have asked me directly, why are there no Afrikaner cultural villages or craft stalls? Afrikaners claim to be African too, some even desire to be considered "indigenous" (see Kuper 2003: 389). Perhaps this inequity resides in the judgment that "Boer" culture is not suitably exotic for tourist spectacle, much less aesthetically appealing, and lacks the necessary histori-cal substrate of continuity and tradition (but see Schutte 2003: 282). Afrikaner culture has visibly changed since the Great Trek; are we to be seduced into believ-ing that Zulu culture has not? Some heritage development in South Africa has clearly been empowering, much of it is targeted towards tourism and reflects global trends, while other dimensions serve to reinforce boundaries and ossify identities. I have witnessed a range of schemes that defy easy determination or judgment, from pragmatic small-scale projects aimed at passing knowledge onto the next generation to desperate development-oriented projects instigated by well-intentioned NGOs that are "built to fail."

Arts funders, craft routes, and glossy art books all neatly divide South Africa into nine provinces with "culture at a glance," a rainbow of "traditional lifestyles" where distinct "tribal" material goods are sold: Tswana pottery, Pedi woodwork, Venda musical instruments, San beadwork, Tsonga weaving, Shangaan textiles, Ndebele murals, Swazi beadwork, Zulu baskets, Basotho blankets, Xhosa pipes, and Pondo woodwork. Communities are thus being branded, commodified, and recuperated though tribe-specific productions (Comaroff and Comaroff 2009: 37; Meskell 2005b). Promoters of these craft routes, like *Due South* (Eskom 2006), argue that regional tourism, particularly in rural areas, will not only benefit com-munities economically but change the anonymous face of craft production. Funded by Eskom, South Africa's power and electricity giant, and endorsed by the environment and tourism minister, sustainable development and cultural diversity remain the touchstones of this "crafting legacy."

Despite the promises made by governments, NGOs, and corporations alike that heritage promotion has obvious socio-economic benefits, the depressing images

Figure 2.2   Artists working at the !Kun and Kwe Development Project, Platfontein. Courtesy of the author.

of failure and futility are the ones that persist: !Kun and Kwe women sitting on cold floors in tin sheds at Platfontein painting versions of ancient rock art in an assembly line of development (Weiss 2005), women beading jewelry in a deserted movie set that is now Shakaland, men in their eighties from impoverished villages bordering Kruger National Park who want to lead community tours showing how "the blacks live today" and telling stories about their ancestral sites. Franz Fanon (1963: 224–5) is invoked endlessly on this issue, to the point of cliché, yet his observations were undeniably astute: "the artist who has decided to illustrate the truths of the nation turns paradoxically towards the past and away from actual events. What he ultimately intends to embrace are in fact the castoffs of thought, its shells and corpses, a knowledge which has been stabilized once and for all." The material expression of those solidarities implicates archaeologists and anthropologists alike and also calls for critical historical analyses (see Herzfeld 1991; Leibhammer 2005) rather than romantic presumptions. Perhaps the most poignant example of this notion of material culture as uplift and national pride comes from Mbeki's speech on national heritage day:

> We are fortunate that there are still some ordinary men and women of our country who are daily weaving a memory, beading a legacy, cutting a spoor, telling a story and loading into these into bowls of history, a future for all our people . . . the weavers of iHulzo and Isilulu, the baskets from Hlabisa woven with care by Reuben Ndwandwe and Beauty Ngxongo, the makers of Ntwana dolls, the Litema of the Basotho women, the iNcwala, the reed dance – these are only some of the traditions that have survived the passage of time. (2004)

Five years later and the celebration of heritage is downplayed while the harsh realities of implementation are laid bare:

> The greatest challenge for the ANC government is to transform the heritage sector as it is primarily exclusive of the majority of black people in terms of ownership and management of heritage sites. Unless there is collective ownership of the herit-age sector in South Africa, the existence and survival of heritage sites will remain threatened as the majority of the black people will perceive these sites as fiefdoms to enrich those unscrupulous individuals who exploit the poor as cheap labor. (Motshekga 2009)

The question remains, would indigenous people choose to perform these pasts if they had other alternatives? The rate of unemployment casts a bleak pall over this issue, especially in rural areas. A landscape littered with endless empty craft stalls and swamped by failed development schemes suggests that there are few options for many South Africans. Easy as the critique may be, few of us have been suc-cessful in providing viable alternatives. As decades of research have demonstrated, we would do better to abandon the top-down implementation of participation and development projects for a bottom-up program of capacity building and indigenous management (Cooke and Kothari 2001a; Lafrenz Samuels 2009; van der Waal 2008).

Perhaps this re-enchanted enthnicized landscape is the expected outcome of liberal heritage in countries like South Africa, as it has been in other parts of Africa and elsewhere (Bruner 2005; Bruner and Kirshenblatt-Gimblett 1994; Fontein 2005, Hodgson 2002b; Kirshenblatt-Gimblett 1998; Thomas 1994). Perhaps the Bantustan model has enjoyed such a long history that it too has become "tradi-tional culture" despite black empowerment and mobility being high on the national agenda. Across Southern Africa foreign tourism has encouraged the expansion of "traditional villages" and commodified re-inventions of authentic local life. An entire spectrum of cultural villages now operate in South Africa (more than 40 nationally) from those of single ethnic groups such as the San (Meskell and Weiss 2006; Robins 2001), the Shangaan on the edge of Kruger National Park, or the Zulu at Shakaland, which pays homage to the Hollywood film set rather than a proud history, to the multi-ethnic enclaves like Lesedi Cultural Village. Cultural villages or ethnic villages, while having widespread popularity with tourists, retain a number of troubling aspects over cultural fixity, primitivism, and the reinforcement of ethnic stereotypes and cultural hierarchies, not to mention the repetitive futility of labor for those employed in such enter-prises (Adams 2006; Bruner and Kirshenblatt-Gimblett 1994; Edensor 2001, Kirshenblatt-Gimblett 1998; Meskell 2005e; Notar 2006). Naturalizing uneven development in this way has relegated certain groups to a particular stage in the human past, thus extending old ideas about civilization and barbarism (Huggan and Tiffin 2007: 2). Many scholars have pointed to the specter of apartheid ethnic categorizations and segregations in the South African examples that simply resurrect a pre-democratic semblance of the past (Hughes 2007: 266; Rassool 2007). Despite copious deconstructions the desire for ethnic tourism and its more deeply rooted substrate, "the tribe," has been reinvigorated since 1994 with great alacrity.

Lesedi Cultural Village on the outskirts of Johannesburg is a prime example of the congealed ethnicities being performed daily to the delight of many. Visitors to Lesedi begin their tour by being funneled through four segregated villages representing South African culture: Xhosa, Sotho, Zulu, and Pedi. Ironically, there has been so much intermarriage between performers from different "tribes" that Protea Hotel management struggle to keep individuals in their correct tribal locations. When tourists arrive various performers scurry back to their spatially and socially discrete cultural groups: such separations are impossible to maintain, even at the level of artifice. Brokering tightly bounded and scripted identities clearly has its limits. Lesedi relies upon a heavy materialist focus to inform visitors about cultural types: the Xhosa smoke particular pipes, the Zulu wear certain animal skins, the Sotho make one type of mat, and so on. As with most cultural villages, such didactic renditions are trapped in time, so there can be no modern Zulus or Pedi. Moreover, sexual stereotypes are reinforced and transacted between semi-clad young Zulus and foreign visitors as part of an authentic African experience. The imaginative worlds created by northern tourists in the global south have distinctive material and symbolic features. According to Ebron (2002: 165), they are underpinned by geopolitical fantasies: the smug sense of northern privilege, and the southern dream of opportunity and wealth in the north; the northern search for "something missing" that might be found in the south, and the southern pride in heritage. Such encounters are redolent with nineteenth-century images of pulsating tribes and the performance of ethnographic spectacle that seduces some tourists into imagining that they are partaking in the "real Africa" (Witz, Rassool, and Minkley 2001). This is not to say that cultural and historical traditions cannot be embraced or publicly celebrated, but by performing as "cultural others" many South Africans are inevitably re-living the past in public arenas rather than being presented as members of a new national modernity.

Travelling far south of Johannesburg, Ulundi is an impoverished and increasingly crime-stricken tract of KwaZulu Natal abutting apartheid's industrial wastelands, where Shakaland (like Lesedi) is managed by Protea Hotels. It epitomizes the fascination with tribal exoticism, hyper-masculinity, and Zulu warrior culture, set amidst clashes with colonial forces. Shakaland is its own kind of cultural desert: a depressing wasteland originally built for the Shaka Zulu television series and now branded as a high-end cultural village charging R600 per person per night (Schutte 2003: 481). We are welcomed to the "great Kraal as dedicated in the international TV series Shaka Zulu – now a living museum to the old Zulu order, please tread with respect." Visitors sleep in beehive huts, vividly painted and tackily decorated, amidst an assortment of aloes and cacti as well as goats, cats, and chickens in the sham simulacrum of a Zulu settlement. Trapped by the iso-

Figure 2.3   Waiting for the tour buses at Shakaland, KwaZulu Natal. Courtesy of the author.

lated location and regimented by the daily schedule, my colleague Thembi and I found the experience almost as dispiriting as the live-in workers at Shakaland. The sense of repetitive futility is palpable and workers seemed ground down by the tedium of life under the looking glass. At the tour's end a group of women assembled their beadwork on mats as if preparing for hundreds of tourists instead of two. As we passed through the official Shakaland shop a clichéd repertoire of "African" objects bore the tag "Made in China."

   From the vantage of natural and cultural heritage, I suggest that the re-enchantment of South Africa's tribal heritage capitalizes upon various historical and contemporary projects described in this chapter. Many craft initiatives, heritage projects, and cultural villages are reminiscent of ethnic homelands as well as foreign tourist desires for African primitivism. In the new South Africa such productions are sanctioned forms of making heritage, creating jobs, boosting tourism, and celebrating culture and ethnic pride in the Rainbow Nation. They entreat the universal virtues of cultural diversity following on from biological diversity, as set out in Chapter 1. What is left unquestioned is whether cultural diversity is "naturally" a good thing, why promoting people's difference and maintaining distinctiveness is beneficial or morally worthy. It is another example where overlaying an ecological model onto cultural heritage may be misplaced and have untoward consequences for the people it presumes to protect. Are we more concerned about saving cultural and material differences rather than allowing people to choose from a number of future-oriented lifeways? We may want to preserve a wide range of human conditions because it allows free people the best chance to constitute their own lives, yet this does not entail enforcing diversity by trapping people within differences they long to escape (Appiah 2006). A more cosmopolitan approach to heritage would not always endorse a preservationist stance (Meskell 2009b: 4), nor attempt to congeal people within some preserved ancient authenticity.

Making Heritage Pay in Kruger

South African scholars have cogently critiqued cultural villages for years (Rassool 2000; Rassool and Witz 1996; Schutte 2003; Witz, Rassool, and Minkley 2001), and I was convinced that researching those forms of heritage making would likely duplicate their findings. Archaeologists are often drawn to representational issues, to the spectacular contortions of our data in the public arena. One of the many reasons Kruger National Park was a captivating field site was the dearth of research into the more mundane parastatal organizations that would promote the African past in their efforts to forge bold new futures. More importantly, there was the complexity of issues around heritage, economics, empowerment, and race that were being juggled by the state, donor agencies, corporations, and park officials. New techniques of government (Ferguson 2010), embedded in an economy of debt and payment, had reconfigured conservation and heritage by welcoming the private sector and community partnerships and engaging in didactic strategies to create new heritage citizens. Kruger was also generally indicative of the South African situation. It occupied the space of double time (Farred 2004), ever-cognizant of its formidable and repressive past, always looking back over its shoulder, and at the same time desperately trying to re-imagine itself, always future perfect. Nelson Mandela captured that particular double temporality during the park's centenary celebrations in 1998. The challenge was neither to "forget those who had to surrender their land to make it possible, often through forcible removal, nor those who for generations were denied access to their heritage except as poorly rewarded labour." His vision for the park's future was rehabilitation via a new liberalization program that would benefit the previously disenfranchised, and indeed all South Africans, who could now enjoy a reconfigured Kruger National Park. He argued that "tourism occupies a strategic place in our overall strategy for reconstruction and development, embracing the spirit of partnership that underlies all our achievements as a newly liberated nation." Specifically, he acknowledged the major role the private sector would play, "whether it be through the promotion of conservation; direct assistance in the upliftment of communities neighbouring on parks; or as business with an interest in the sustainable growth of the industry." Mandela's dream for Kruger importantly included an acknowledgement of the past and pointed to a liberal, developmental future. And as it transpired in the decade following his centenary speech, some economic elements of that dream have largely been realized.

SANParks was effectively realigned with the ANC's policies for corporate liberalization and transformation. This commercialization strategy followed the dominant paradigm of neoliberal economic thinking in South Africa, specifically the policy framework of Growth, Employment and Redistribution (GEAR). That also meant conservation science, for the first time, had to be traded off against the goals of privatization, tourism, black economic empowerment, and the awareness of countless communities and their development. SANParks opened its gates to consultancy culture with McKinseys, private luxury lodges, international foundations, development agencies, and foreign researchers. Apartheid-era branding gave way to an inclusive Africanity captured in the *Xa Mina i Xa Wena* motto ("It's Mine, It's Yours" in Tsonga) coupled with aggressive marketing and commodification. SANParks' mission today is to "develop and manage a system of national parks that represents the biodiversity, landscapes, and associated heritage assets of South Africa for the sustainable use and benefit of all.[4] After much reworking, SANParks' operations are today founded on three pillars: (i) biodiversity conservation; (ii) nature-based tourism; and (iii) constituency building towards a people-centered conservation and tourism. A thoroughly modern park would come in tandem with modern science in the form of biodiversity conservation and new expertise from social ecology, but it was not seen fit to employ trained archaeologists or heritage experts. However, Kruger drew international attention at the moment of democratic transition by claiming the first collaborative archaeological project between blacks and whites of the new nation with the site of Thulamela. And they had struck gold.

In the 1990s the past looked as if it were going to have a real place in crafting a new future for Kruger National Park and its descendant communities. It was already promoted as a font of African pride, but it was promised to leverage economic partnerships, to offer grounds for reconciliation, and to find its niche alongside natural heritage. Liberal heritage was not simply a technique of governmentality but a spiritual resource serving up socio-economic benefits, reconciliation, and African revivalism. For many reasons, historic and contemporary, clusters of things that we call cultural and natural heritage, material culture, archaeology and rock art, indigenous knowledge, and tradition were all harnessed within the project of recovery and restitution. However, the central challenges of education, capacity, racism, and poverty remained. Past legacies and materials were called upon despite the public ambivalence to history, particularly the pre-colonial and colonial past that was largely ignored in the national arena in favor of very recent events (Meskell and Scheermeyer 2008). History offered up a negative reminder of apartheid's shadow and the complicity of Kruger Park: it was political, factional, and racial. It was a wound that might impede transition or breed further conflict, and addressing the past had the potential to tear the park asunder through successful land claims. Cultural heritage, moreover, was in danger of being hijacked by ecological urgencies around diversity, resilience, and risk that overshadowed people and their histories. The placing of the past and its relationship to natural heritage in Kruger was still unresolved. There was so much history and so many histories, as Brown would say, that history itself seemed more vital and yet ever more fleeting.

Notes

1   http://www.loc.gov/exhibits/mali (accessed April 13, 2011).
2   www.awhf.net (accessed December 31, 2009).
3   http://web.wits.ac.za/Academic/Science/Geography/Research/500YearInitiative (accessed February 22, 2010).
4   http://www.sanparks.org/about/vision.php (accessed February 21, 2010).

Chapter 3

It's Mine, It's Yours
Excavating Park Histories

M: *What does Skukuza mean?*
J: *I'm not sure. These people who were robbing us and robbing animals.*
M: *Was he a black man or white?*
J: *I haven't met the man. I don't know. He worked with animals.*

Skukuza Stories

There are many Skukuza stories, starting with the name itself. It was a derogatory title given to the park's first warden by the local Shangaan people, meaning to "strip bare" or "sweep clean." There are the much lauded tales of Col. James Stevenson-Hamilton and his "making" of the park and "saving" of an African "wilderness," the indigenous histories that have been silenced for so long, and the newly created narratives of reconciliation and inclusion through heritage under ANC leadership. The latter is captured in the slogan *Xa Mina i Xa Wena*, brandished liberally on park signage. In this chapter I focus in on some particular historical moments but also on some long interconnections that have remained largely untold. Certainly some stories have more currency than others. White histories have left a tangible material imprint on the park and remain difficult to dislodge, despite the efforts of the new custodians. Part of the power of material heritage is its tenacity to endure and survive successive regimes: the park is littered with memorials to white times and white heroes that continue to overshadow unmemorialized black history, genealogy, and achievement. Two images

The Nature of Heritage: The New South Africa, First Editon. Lynn Meskell.
© 2012 John Wiley & Sons, Inc. Published 2012 by Blackwell Publishing Ltd.

of colonial materiality remain fixed in my mind, although I could choose innumerable others.

The first is the dog cemetery at Skukuza, adjacent to the Stevenson-Hamilton Museum and Library, itself a musty relic of the colonial era. Engraved tombstones in *Little Heroes Acre* commemorate the dogs of successive officials dutifully buried and remembered over the decades. They attest to the "close bond that existed between the animal and its master" according to cemetery signage. The ways in which dogs were defined, used, and treated, provide important insights into the nature of colonialism (Gordon 2003) and later apartheid (Coetzee 2000). While domestic animals, throughout the park's history, were supposedly excluded from the park – especially since they were associated negatively with African hunting practices (see also Tropp 2002), animals belonging to white rangers and wardens were the exception and were greatly revered. While hunting was officially forbidden, white senior rangers were allowed a monthly game quota to provide meat for their dogs. The entrails were subsequently given to black field rangers until David Mabunda, the first black CEO of Kruger, banned the practice in the 1990s. While easily overlooked by many park visitors and workers who daily walk by the site, it was several black employees concerned with African heritage who first drew my attention to the dog cemetery. One woman once actively involved in struggle politics explained to me that the continued presence of the burial ground was an affront to the memory of all those who once lived in what is now Kruger, who died or were killed in processes of appropriation and eviction when their livelihoods were seen to threaten conservation, and even during apartheid times when their heroism led them to cross the park's military patrolled borders. She explained that there are likely thousands of people buried within the park, but these remain unmarked sites.

Why is the dog cemetery noteworthy? It is a material mnemonic that privileges animals over people (*read* Africans) and celebrates the comradeship of white man and dog while symbolizing the very negation of human dignity between "men" that characterized the colonial and apartheid eras. But like all uncomfortable material remnants of repression, or negative heritage, the new black management has chosen not to erase or replace the vestiges of repressive regimes. As with the very public discussions of the dismantling of Paul Kruger's statue, a decision has been taken not to disrupt the status quo (Ramutsindela 2004: 67). Such strategic conciliatory understanding reflects the nation's historic imperative for a negotiated settlement rather than radical change. But it may also signify that the ghosts have not been laid to rest (Ramphele 2008). Or this might simply be inertia, reinforcing the secondary position of cultural heritage and history in the new agendas for Kruger Park.

My second example is closely related to my first. In the southern section of the park there are a series of heritage markers widely dispersed along the arterial roads. Round bronze medallions about 30 centimeters in diameter exhibiting the image of a striding terrier have been set into brick pedestals about 1 meter high. Some are damaged and many show signs of corrosion, some pedestals have lost their medallions altogether. These heritage markers are represented on all maps and guides to Kruger, and they are considered historical not because they relate to real events or individuals but rather to the celebrated canine hero of Sir Percy Fitzpatrick's popular book, *Jock of the Bushveld* (1907). The story of Jock echoes colonial travel writing but also national parks' narratives: the region is devoid of an indigenous population, all the heavy work is done by local men emasculated by being called "boys," and most of the stories involve white hunting (Woodward 2008: 103). Fitzpatrick's novels are stories of white, male heroism set in the discourse of nineteenth-century colonialism: man and dog against the elements, in harsh uncivilized terrain (Carruthers 2005; Ritvo 1987; Woodward 2008: 93). Yet it is the dog, not the white master that is celebrated and materially commemorated. Jock is still extremely popular in South Africa, possibly because of the centrality of the nation's natural heritage in general and Kruger National Park in particular. His name was also bestowed upon Jock Safari Lodge, a resort in the south of the park that caters primarily to Afrikaners. But as David Bunn observes (2006: 361), Jock's pervasive presence proved problematic during Afrikaner nationalism when it was regarded as an offensive ideogram of English presence. The heyday for Jock was the 1930s and 1940s, dark days indeed for black inhabitants of the park and those systematically being expelled from their traditional lands. Older white South Africans see them as charming tales of yesteryear, younger readers are discovering Jock anew through a massive centenary campaign. In 2009 the Skukuza bookstore was filled with more books and merchandise devoted to Jock than ever before. It is puzzling why these "historic" markers should remain as heritage today, to be memorialized at the expense of many real and heroic individuals, and in this age of recognition that must surely include black rangers and park workers (Bunn 2003; Carruthers 1995: 96) who literally made and manned Kruger National Park and continue to do so.

There is, then, a certain irony that Kruger's heritage officer and I are tasked with recording these heritage markers, spending days on the road documenting their preservation alongside other archaeological and historic sites. Stemming from the initiatives of the South African Heritage Resources Agency (SAHRA) to inventory cultural heritage in South Africa, monuments to Jock stand commensurate with the San rock art sites and Iron Age archaeology, and in fact have greater visibility and marketing for tourists. Recently a new Kruger guidebook (see Frandsen 2009) has finally included a map detailing historical sites, although only a total of 54 for the entire park. Five refer to Jock, and only three sites document the prehistory of the park, the remaining illustrate white history. Jock's markers are indeed popular stopping destinations. Our survey found over and over again that the brick markers offered the perfect cover for tourists trapped between rest camps responding to the call of nature. Behind many of the markers we found clumps of rotting toilet paper, the obvious intrusion of tourists into Kruger's landscape.

Canine hagiographies like *Jock of the Bushveld* evince a kinder, more blameless theme in what was essentially a human history of dispossession. Within the colonial apparatus, enlisting these animals to defend their masters from wild nature, and thus ultimately preserve wild nature, is portrayed as an intimate and noble defense. These two episodes in Kruger's past and present seem especially telling for my purposes, moreover, because they reflect the wider malaise surrounding cultural heritage generally, and black history specifically. But they are far from isolated examples. The emphasis on white histories of conquest and commerce remain unchallenged, and we know more about European rangers, wardens, traders, and military leaders than any African in the history of the park (Cock 2007: 149). The bookshelves at Skukuza's library and bookstore are lined with their accounts (e.g., Bryden 2005; Krüger 1994; 2002). One need only think of the celebrated adventures of Harry Wolhuter (1948), the preserved archaeological site of João Albasini's trading post (Bunn 2006), or the more recent interest in the wartime exploits of the Steinaekers Horse regiment (van Vollenhoven, Pelser, and van den Bos 1998). This white focus was not simply confined to the apartheid years; as research applications in the Skukuza files suggest, there has been continued archaeological interest in revisiting and re-excavating white sites or those that are imagined to yield "treasure."

Essentially, this is a story of deep disregard, as Ann Stoler (2008) would say. Pre-colonial history in the park does not occupy pride of place, nor is it central or critical enough to trouble addressing, redressing, erasing, or much of anything else. However, the history of the environment is a concern, whether animal migration patterns, disease landscapes, or the effects of fencing (Bengis, Grant, and de Vos 2003; Whyte, van Aarde, and Pimm 2003), and Africans obviously play a role in those stories. Yet the place of the cultural past resists any easy formulation, especially in the years since apartheid's end. There have been no dramatic erasures, no dismantling of statues that accompanied the fall of other fascist regimes or the erection of new monuments, rather there is a tacit ambivalence that has produced sites of charmless heritage across the park. This ignorance and disregard is reinforced when talking to park officials. They do not decry San or black heritage, but they are largely unaware of it and not particularly interested in developing their knowledge. There is a carapace of carelessness, a learned ignorance on the part of white and black managers and researchers that reaches right back to the beginnings of the park and is increasingly intractable. Ignorance and ambivalence was key to the sustained processes of colonialism, and found its form in institutional arrangements. The National Parks Board (NPB), and its successor SANParks, inherited that legacy. As students of colonialism we accept that cultivation of ignorance and the vitality of empire go together, the latter being "in the business of limiting, distorting, and obscuring knowledge" (Stoler 2008: 248). Ignorance, then, is an ongoing operation, a cumulative, *achieved*, and labored effect. But in the case of South Africa these are not processes relegated to colonial history, they have been implicitly instantiated in present post-apartheid practices and structures (Bunn and Auslander 1998; Cock 2007: 164). Therein lies the sobering aspect of my own project, that given the new dispensation and rhetorics of change, so little has changed.

There are endless examples of neglected archaeological heritage across the park: the falling walls at Thulamela (Meskell 2007a), ancient ceramics broken and discarded in a Skukuza storeroom, a colonial museum display untouched since the 1970s. I recall an image of moldering artifacts in aged glass cases at the historic site of Albasini: pieces of chipped porcelain, rusted metal, a model of the trading post, coupled with the obligatory photos of white men like Louis Trichardt and João Albasini himself all fester amongst dust and dead insects. A sound recording was once supposed to accompany the artifacts, but it has long fallen silent and stubbornly refuses to work no matter how many buttons are pressed. This situation is made more frustrating because some small excavations have been conducted there since the late 1990s by contract archaeologists, yet this work has not been effectively presented to the public. Visitor's logs suggest that people really do visit the site, only to witness the years of sedimented disinterest and decay. Adjacent to the thatched hut housing the display cases and the brick foundation of the trading post is the burial place of a prominent black man named Nkayikayi Samuel Mavundla. He was one of the only people allowed to reside in the park after the era of removals, and he died in late 2000 (see also Bunn 2006). Weeds and long grass obscured his grave and we struggled in vain to locate it, ever mindful of the fact that we were walking further into the veld unarmed.

How do we position the role of ignorance, the seemingly harmless, "not incompetent" role of the administrators, managers, researchers, and workers, the people throughout colonial and apartheid history that Stoler (2008: 245, 249) refers to as a few calm, good men. This willfully learned ignorance went hand-in-hand with the vitality of empire where it enabled hierarchical relationships and facilitated mutual co-existence. Working in South Africa, and especially around Kruger, I have interviewed numerous people with troubling worldviews, racist beliefs, and bitterness toward other South Africans and black Africans. It is not unlike my experiences growing up in Australia, as many of my interlocutors perceptively pointed out. Some South Africans are proud to wear their racial prejudices on their sleeves, rather than resort to the hypocrisy they see as manifest in places like the United States (Crapanzano 1986: 189). They are happy to project the narrative of "economic apartheid" onto Europe and the United States as a way of excusing or justifying past social policies. How exactly does one adequately portray such individuals, to humanize them in ways that make their interior selves legible, as J.M Coetzee has ably managed (see Attridge 2005; Coetzee 1980; 1988; Durrant 2004; Meskell and Weiss 2006)? Coetzee's strategy is one that implicates us all in the project and aftermath of colonization. It is not something "out there," nor can such relationships easily be brushed away to reveal past glories (Meskell 2005e). Neither is anything "gained by flattening colonial history into a neat story of colonizers pitted against the colonized," and as Stoler (1995: 199) reminds us, "the reification of a colonial moment of binary oppositions may speak more to contemporary political agendas than to ambiguous colonial realities." As I argue throughout this book, eliding history can impinge upon post-apartheid reconstruction by simply papering over historic and long-lived inequalities and injustices. Some repressions are difficult to deconstruct, erase, or rewrite in the scripting of a new Rainbow Nation, and their residues can still be felt in realizing the effective operation of nation and national park alike.

The Past of the Park

There has been very little work in Kruger that meets the standard of modern archaeology, certainly much remains unpublished and languishes in brief reports to SANParks. Each decade seems to have had a particular episode and profile of research. In the 1970s, the Iron Age site of Masorini was excavated; the 1980s saw surveys by archaeologists from Pretoria University that located around 1000 archaeological sites as well as a program of faunal analysis; Iron Age Thulamela was excavated in the 1990s, and in the late years of the 2000 decade research started on palaeoclimate. The park has never been intensively surveyed, and most of the identified sites tend to fall near rivers or established areas: a pattern that underscores the dearth of research carried out for the majority of the two million hectares. Section rangers and field rangers have long picked up notable finds without properly recording them or their findspots (Miller 1997: 31), only for them to end their days deteriorating in the Skukuza storeroom or discarded altogether. I remember seeing six Stone Age axes adorning the desk of a senior manager as he bemoaned the state of archaeology, saying "we need more ladies like you, more professors." Publications by National Parks own staff (Verhoef 1986) that document hundreds of sites spanning 100 000 years of human occupation in Kruger, have been conveniently forgotten. While archaeological science garners some interest, support for rigorous survey or excavation of sites has remained a low priority. Archaeological research agendas that contribute to environmental knowledge are deemed useful, those that focus on prehistoric peoples, less so. What follows is an attempt to piece together an archaeological account of human presence in the park from published materials, since this still remains a contentious narrative and one that national parks like Kruger and others elsewhere across the globe still refuse to fully acknowledge or promote.

The area that today comprises Kruger and its immediate environs has a considerable cultural history. It stretches back more than 1.5 million years, from

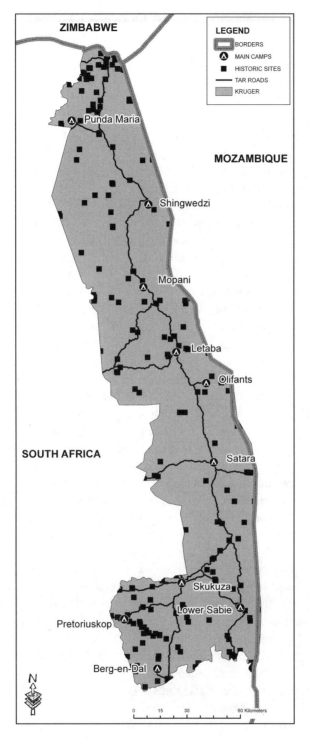

Figure 3.1 Map of Kruger National Park showing camps and known historical sites. Courtesy of South African National Parks, Geographic Information Science and Remote Sensing.

the evidence of hominid remains and Early Stone Age tools at sites in Pafuri, Stolsnek, and Makhadzi near Letaba (Verhoef 1986: 151). Middle Stone Age finds (250 000–40 000 BP) were recorded at Stolsnek and Malelane (Mason 1962). The Later Stone Age (from 20,000 BP) occupation of the park is evidenced by lithics and ostrich-eggshell beads and by hundreds of rock art sites (English 1990). Sites extend from the southern edge of the park around Berg-en Dal and the Mthethomusha game reserve (Hampson *et al.* 2002) to the far north in Pafuri in the Limpopo Province (Eastwood and Blundell 1999; Hall and Smith 2000), and to the east near Olifants Gorge and the lower Crocodile River. During this period the bow and arrow was developed and the ancestors of the San exploited animals such as zebra, warthog, and various antelopes. Larger animals were driven into pits and speared, fish were caught, and digging sticks were used to procure tubers and roots, and a wide variety of fruits and vegetables were collected (Delius and Hay 2009: 30).

Scenes of hunting, spirit trances, humans, and animals were all captured, whether by paint or engraving, on rock surfaces that can still be seen today. Since there are no historical records of San living in the area, this has led scholars like David Lewis-Williams to suggest that these sites are probably thousands of years old. From linguistic analysis, it is likely that people who created the images would have spoken a Southern San language akin to !Kwi languages such as //Xegwi, ≠Khomani and /'Auni (Barnard 1992). New research into geometric rock art associated with later Khoekhoe herders has revealed sites in the north of Kruger in rich grazing environments. Employing both linguistic and rock art data, Eastwood and Smith (2005: 72) argue that interaction between the proto-Khoekhoe and the autochthonous San was established in the Limpopo basin at the beginning of the first millennium AD. Khoekhoe also influenced the first Bantu-speaking farmers of the region. Ehret (1998) has convincingly shown that Bantu-speaking communities in the southeast borrowed a range of Khoekhoe herding vocabulary, such as the generic terms for sheep, cattle, and milk, replacing older Bantu root words.

Perhaps it not surprising that a national park would focus its investigations around human and animal interactions. Archaeologist Ina Plug worked extensively during the 1980s analyzing faunal remains from 22 sites across the park, the oldest from Skukuza dating to 7000 BP. Some 170 000 bones from ash pits, shelters, and stratified deposits date to the Stone Age, 11 Early Iron Age, and 8 Late Iron Age sites (Plug 1989b). Sites were predominantly located along the Luvuvhu, Letaba, Olifants, Sabie, and Crocodile rivers, and population numbers were thought to reach about 15 000 during this period (Mabunda, Pienaar, and Verhoef 2003: 5). A wide range of wild animals was present, some with much greater distribution patterns in the past than today, such as black rhino and roan antelope. Her evidence also shows that sheep were introduced into the area by Early Iron Age pastoralists, as were cattle. She compares the relative abundances of species, in prehistory and in the present, finding that the species most often hunted in the past are also the most numerous today: impala in the Later Stone Age, zebra in the Iron Age, followed by wildebeest and buffalo (Plug 1989b: 114–15). She argues that today Kruger's animal distributions are artificial, because fencing has impacted on changing migration patterns and dams and boreholes have provided water. When compared to modern animal census figures, however, Plug demonstrates that impala, kudu, buffalo, and elephant were under utilized in the past, whereas zebra, wildebeest, roan antelope, warthog, giraffe, and tsesebe were over utilized compared to other species, yet these animals were never in short supply. It was only with the introduction of firearms in the nineteenth century that near extermination of game occurred.

Contrary to popular opinion, and to some of Kruger's own scientific researchers, we know that pastoralists entered what is now South Africa at least two millennia ago. Sheep bones from Blombos Cave in the southeastern Western Cape Province and at Spoegrivier in Namaqualand, have been directly dated to the first century AD, which implies a northern presence some centuries beforehand (Mitchell and Whitelaw 2005: 214; Sadr 2003: 205). Depictions of sheep in rock art are well documented from the Limpopo Valley in association with herder-associated ceramics (Eastwood and Fish 1996; Hall and Smith 2000). Almost two millennia ago Bantu-speaking farmers arrived with a mixed economy that included sheep, goats, and cattle, but also the cultivation of cereals and legumes. They brought new ceramics styles and technologies such as metalworking; iron tools enabled land clearance and cultivation that in return supported population growth and dispersal (Gronenborn 2004; Mitchell 2002a 259). From the northern Limpopo they quickly reached the limit of the summer rainfall zone around 33.5° S and much later expanded beyond the savannah into the interior grasslands in the fourteenth century AD (Mitchell 2004: 3). This contradicts the thesis of parallel arrival of blacks and whites that was politically expedient during the apartheid years and still has ramifications for land claims, restitution, and recognition politics, as we will see later.

Early Iron Age settlements in Kruger tend to be situated on high riverbanks above the estimated 10-year flood line (Plug 1989a). Sandy banks were preferred to gravel banks, presumably for their agricultural potential. Settlements at Tshokwane and Letaba cover up to six or seven hectares and show no signs that game supplies dwindled during occupation. Later sites like Thulamela are estimated at nine hectares (Mitchell 2002a: 324). The presence of cattle at several sites indicates that the region was free of *nagana* (Animal African Trypanosomiasis) between AD 300 and 900 (Plug 1988). This was also the case around 1725 when Dr W.H.J Punt (1975) recorded his travels through the region, noting flourishing communities. It is worth remembering, too, that occupation of the landscape can also encompass shifting settlement patterns (McCann 1999), influenced by social factors as well as disease vectors or rainfall, and does not always have to comply with our presentist notions of established, continuous settlement. The modernist equation that only continuous occupation equals possession has disadvantaged native peoples across Africa, Australasia, and the Americas.

Perhaps the most well known archaeological site is the Iron Age settlement of Thulamela (c. 1440–1640) that was part of the broader Zimbabwe Culture. The main hilltop settlement has several stone-walled enclosures, beyond which lie the non-walled residential areas. The first phase of occupation has been dated between AD 1410–30, then a decade later impressive stone walls were constructed and ceramics appear resembling those from Great Zimbabwe. International trade contacts are reflected by metal gongs from West Africa, glass beads, Chinese porcelain, and seashells, and there is evidence of industry, including gold and ivory working (Grigorova 1998; Küsel 1992; Steyn et al. 1998). Metal harpoons, spears, hoes, ingots, and blades were recovered, along with scores of spindle whorls, ceramics, groundstone implements, and the famous gold beads and wire (Miller 1997). Occupation continued until the site was abandoned around 1640 (Mitchell and Whitelaw 2005: 241). Some time later new immigrants established themselves in the area (Vogel 2000: 54). Radiocarbon dates taken from the regional capital, Dzata, suggest that this was not before 1690. What followed was the construction of new stone-walled settlements associated with the Venda. More recently, people from the Makuleke, Mhinga, and Makahane communities farmed the area until 1946 (Esterhuysen n.d.) and still continue to live in Pafuri.

A number of Iron Age sites in Kruger were probably linked to Thulamela, including the unexcavated site of Makahane (c. 990–1300) now in an off-limits "wilderness" zone. Makahane is a stone-walled hilltop settlement with commanding views (Eloff 1966; Eloff and De Vaal 1965) and a long oral tradition depicting the cruel exploits of King Makahane. Many of these oral histories were recounted to me in various visits to the community in Musunda. Matjigwili (c. 1400) is a large terraced site with stone walls and a large monolith that is related to Makahane (Küsel 1992); it is also connected to the rock art sites of Xantangelangi and Mashakiri Poort. The settlements of Dzundzwini and Thula Mila and a third unnamed site near the Punda Maria gate (Miller 1997: 35) are also only visible now as terraced stone walls, and they too have not been properly recorded, much less excavated. Further east, in the Lebombo Mountains, the site of Shilowa (1200–1600) has only middens and hut floors preserved. Unfortunately, the Bowkers Hill complex at the Mooiplas Ranger Station has had both graves and stone walls destroyed through construction of the ranger's house (Miller 1997: 35). Human occupation has a very long history in this region, and despite the pervasive notions that malaria made habitation unfeasible, indigenous communities must have had some management strategies as many of my informants outside the park attest. Many more known sites are listed in an Afrikaans-only publication describing the history of the park (Pienaar 1990), making it all the more remarkable that the official story of minimal black habitation has changed so little.

The Iron Age sites of Masorini, Shikumbu, Sekgopo, Khotwani, and Vedogwe on Kruger's western boundary fall within the area of Phalaborwa and have long constituted a mining landscape. Despite claims that Masorini was a very recent site, archaeological evidence points to occupation around Phalaborwa dating back to the eighth century AD (Gordon and van der Merwe 1984; Van der Merwe and Skully 2003: 179). Archaeologists suggest that there were probably hundreds of smelting sites (copper and iron) in the area and about a dozen furnaces have been recorded. In the 1970s some 15 terraced settlements with circular hut floors were excavated, producing ceramics, groundstone mortars, beads, metal tools, and faunal remains. Settlement sites like Vedogwe reveal large enclosures 12 meters across that were used as stock pens. It is likely that there were two major phases of industry and habitation. During the tenth–thirteenth centuries open villages were built on flat land, while between the seventeenth and nineteenth centuries terraced settlements exploited their defensive advantage (Miller, Killick, and Merwe 2001: 407). As noted by others (Plug and Pistorius 1999: 159), there has never been a full publication of the excavation at Masorini by the University of Pretoria. A complete picture has been hampered by the practice of rangers indiscriminately picking up numerous copper artifacts around Masorini and Shikumbu, their provenience and any other information, now lost. Some are now on display at Masorini, other finds were simply boxed and shipped off to Skukuza when staff at Letaba Camp threatened to dispose of them.

I would argue that archaeological work carried out over the decades, however scant, can still be marshaled to demonstrate a long and complex sequence of human habitation. Recent work on climate change is also informative for human modification of the landscape and more likely to be given attention by park ecologists and managers. Results show that the last 700 years in Kruger were marked by climatic variations with warmer and wetter periods, transitioning from a warm period ending in the fourteenth century, to the cooler, drier conditions between 1400 and 1800 (Gillson and Ekblom 2009). After 1800 there is evidence of significant human intervention, when maize was grown and localized fire increased. As Gillison and Ekblom's research demonstrates there is an extensive history of environmental management within Kruger, not simply the last hundred years of white science. The scarcity of archaeological investigations has led to the untenable notion that there was little farming or other anthropogenic influence. In fact, African communities had a mixed economy growing cereals such as millet, sorghum, pulses, and cucurbits, and they kept sheep, goats, and cattle (Mitchell 2002a). Iron Age cattle were able to tolerate hot, dry conditions and could grow relatively large on this type of grazing (Plug 1989a). Employing data from pollen cores, charcoal analysis, diatoms, and isotopes, Gillison and Ekblom's work suggests that farming was small scale and did not impact the environment adversely. Increasing charcoal levels may be linked to occupation of sites like Thulamela, intensified clearing, and slash and burn agriculture. Data from Thulamela may also support the idea that settlements were regularly occupied throughout in the

Limpopo valley, despite dry periods or later episodes of tsetse vectored trypano-somiasis, because of the documented reliance on wild game (contra Huffman 1996). In the century between 1750 and 1850 there was an increase in maize pollen and larger charcoal particles that signify the firing of vegetation for cultivation. Despite political upheaval at the time, maize production was increasingly popular, it was produced above requirements and was traded with others, as recorded by early travelers in Pafuri (Elton 1873; Gillson, and Ekblom 2009: 182). By the end of the 1800s cultivation had declined, although cattle herding continued. Rinderpest, also known as cattle plague (Spinage 2003), would have affected both wild and domestic species between 1895 and 1897. Moving into the twentieth century, stringent controls on black communities changed hunting, herding, agri-cultural, and firing practices.

Trade boomed between 1500 and 1800, spurred on by the desire for ivory but also for commodities like salt, copper, tin, fur, ochre, cattle, and grain. Masorini was one of the major copper working sites at this time, and traders moved across the Sabie–Lydenburg area, through the Lebombo Mountains on Kruger's eastern border to Delagoa Bay (Mozambique), where the Portuguese had their trading post (Delius and Hay 2009: 41). The flourishing ivory trade had a vast impact on wildlife, and in 1768 alone some 26 000 kilograms of ivory went through the port of Inhambane in Mozambique (Mabunda, Pienaar, and Verhoef 2003: 6). From the seventeenth century, European incursions into what was to become Kruger were geared toward securing natural resources and subduing local people. Colonial history in the park begins well after 1652 when the Dutch East India Company began sending expeditions into the interior with the aim of tapping into the indig-enous gold trade. Their corporate motivations were the conquest of trade rather than people or territory. On August 9, 1723 Jan van de Capelle, a Dutchman in charge of Delagoa Bay, dispatched 19 men to the Blue Mountains, only to be forced back by native inhabitants. De Cuiper led Capelle's second expedition to the goldfields of the Northern Transvaal and, on July 10, 1725, he crossed the Crocodile River, and in doing so recorded numerous black settlements in the region. He was the first European to see the Transvaal and to document valuable details about local geography, customs, place names, linguistics, and the trade in gold, iron, and copper. But de Cuiper was attacked by Chief Dawano's men and retreated to the Lebombo Mountains, where he was forced to abandon the journey. His expedition has been immortalized on a bronze plaque on the Crocodile River Road in Kruger National Park (Couzens 2004: 12–15).

At the close of the eighteenth century powerful chiefdoms like the Pedi, Swazi, Ndebele, and Ndwandwe were active around this southern portion of the park, what is today part of Mpumalanga Province. Evidence remains today of many extensive stone-walled settlements across the region, and in the eighteenth century alone archaeologists estimate some 40 000 people lived on the escarpment between modern-day Machadodorp and Lydenburg. These communities were not divided into fixed or isolated tribes but instead were comprised of diverse individuals

(Delius and Hay 2009: 36). The new century began with great political upheaval south of the Limpopo River during what has been called the *Mfecane* (Zulu for "the scattering"), when Shaka conquered and dispersed various tribes (Harries 1991: 83). Archaeological and historic evidence then speaks to the past dynamism of human endeavor in what is now Kruger, rather than a sterile account of empty lands and pristine wilderness.

Colonial Incursions

The portrayal of colonial history in Kruger often assumes a rather romantic and wistful aura; the oft-used 1930s sepia photo of an elegant woman leaning out of her car to photograph a lion comes to mind (Bunn 2003). But the history of white incursion into the Lowveld was more menacing and exploitative, as only recent histories in South Africa have been able to portray (Carruthers 1993; 1995; 2001; Delius and Hay 2009). The Boer occupation of the Transvaal, the eviction of black communities, and enforced labor schemes, followed by decades of apartheid victimization are some of the worst periods in park history. Understandably, I was told during my very first days in Skukuza that no-one wanted to know about the "bad old days" anymore. The past is being forgotten in different ways. For example, several young black scientific researchers who lived in the research camp with me had never heard of members of the armed wing of the ANC, the MK, being shot in Kruger during their lifetimes, much less the history of the *trekpas*. Men like Aaron Makwa, Watson Majova, Peter Zitha, and Patric Baloyi were just some of the men killed in Kruger during the late 1980s who are named in the *Lives of Courage* list.[1] These histories never registered with my colleagues, and this learned ignorance has many surrogates; apathy, censorship, disinformation, and secrecy. Certain topics are discouraged, some knowledge runs roughshod over people and things, and particular research is lost and never to be recovered (Proctor 2009). Historical ignorance has a complex political geography: in Kruger it is exacerbated by an inaccessible archive, deficits in funding and capacity, past and current political imperatives and compromises, changing public and political discourses, as well as institutional pressures. In the Rainbow Nation some forgetting has been deemed necessary for therapeutic purposes, allowing a once divided citizenry to move forward. Rather different motives were at play during the last days of apartheid, when documents held at Skukuza were destroyed, a poignant object lesson in the making of ignorance in Kruger National Park.

This effacement of African history was not always the case. Stevenson-Hamilton's *The Low-Veld: Its Wild Life and Its People* (1929) devoted considerable attention to the region's indigenous inhabitants and their recent history without denying their long relationship with Kruger's landscapes. He wrote about existing communities of Shangaan and Swazi along the Komati and Crocodile Rivers, the

Swazi and Sotho among the foothills, the Shangaan toward the Letaba, and large numbers of Venda across Pafuri (Stevenson-Hamilton 1929: 180–1). This complicates the emerging picture of African history within the park: it may be the case that black history and presence was more consequential in colonial times than in post-colonial ones. Since the colonial era more white histories of the park have been produced; these narratives also have a diminished profile in post-apartheid Kruger, although they could hold great political purchase depending on their presentation. Perhaps it would be fair to say that history itself has come to play a lesser role today and, like archaeology, it has been eclipsed by ecology.

In the early 1800s, whites explored the Vaal River region, and in 1836 Louis Trichardt was the first Voortrekker to cross through what is now Kruger. Nagana destroyed his cattle en route. In 1852 the Boers established the Zuid Afrikaansiche Republiek (ZAR) from the Vaal River to south of the Limpopo and west to the Portuguese colony in Mozambique. Securing land from the Pedi and Swazi kings was fraught, and consequently the Boers took control of lands belonging to many smaller and less powerful chiefdoms and communities (Delius and Hay 2009: 51). Africans were never considered citizens nor was provision made for them in this land grab. Whites were given title deeds, even to lands not under Boer control, but this did not mean that they had the necessary labor to work their farms. Some sold their land when farming became unprofitable. Unwilling to do menial labor, whites demanded African labor as a form of tribute. They raided black communities for children to labor on their farms (called "inboekelinge" or *booked in people*), or they traded with the Swazis for children from neighboring African groups in the Eastern Transvaal (Delius and Hay 2009: 57–60). About 1000 children were taken each year until the 1860s when greater resistance from communities and pressure from the British and others to halt child slavery forced its decline.

A popular trope in park-sponsored documents, influenced by long-standing English–Boer hostilities dating back to the Boer War (see Carruthers 2008), is that the English were primarily responsible for the decimation of game through sport hunting (e.g., Mabunda, Pienaar, and Verhoef 2003: 6). Before the Boers arrived the region teemed with wildlife. Between the 1830s and 1902 there was wholesale slaughter for meat, skins, and ivory, largely because many Boers were too poor to farm and turned to hunting (Delius and Hay 2009: 55). The elephant population was decimated through the ivory trade, and it was only with competition over these resources that racialized recriminations firmly took hold (Carruthers 1989: 190). Colonial explorers and hunters like de Santa Rita Montanha, Das Neves, Mauch, Erskine, and Napier have left traces of this hunting history in the documents as well as etching it on baobab trees (Dladla 2000: 90). Wildlife was gradually being transformed from an economic resource available to everyone to a commodity reserved for the benefit of the ruling whites. Game was considered *res nullius* (or no-one's property) under Dutch Roman law and was thus subject to state protection and control (Carruthers 1989: 190), creating in return new zones of trespass and "poaching." In a new environment of impending scarcity, racialized competition over resources, and a looming battle between Boer and English interests in the colony, officials began debating the merits of establishing a protected reserve in the Transvaal.

Historian Jane Carruthers has soundly demolished the myth that Boer President Paul Kruger was instrumental in either protectionist policies or in establishing the Sabie Game Reserve, laying the foundation for Kruger National Park. It was more likely that Volksraad members Richard Loveday and J.L. van Wijk forced the government's hand in establishing the game reserve by introducing the motion in 1895 (Carruthers 1994: 269). The president's own memoires make clear his belief that game should be cleared from the land. Stevenson-Hamilton famously quipped that Kruger "never in his life thought of wild animals except as biltong" (cited in Carruthers 1994: 274).[2] Though he may have signed the document, there is little to suggest Paul Kruger was ever an ardent conservationist.

NPB officials like Deputy Director R.J. Labuschagne, perpetuated apartheid nationalist mythology, stating that on March 26, 1898 Kruger proclaimed the park after a 14-year battle to establish a wildlife sanctuary:

> the President himself fought tirelessly for an idea that often involved him in bitter controversy. In 1884, a year after his election as Head of the State, no one could foresee that the threat of extinction would soon confront wildlife in the game-rich Transvaal. But President Kruger's remarkable courage, conviction and foresight enabled him to over-come every difficulty. His victory over opposition was all the more noteworthy because it was achieved when gold was being mined in the vicinity of the area and when there was alarming unrest and disorder, deputations of gold miners demanding more rights, an uncontrollable influx of all kinds of adventurers and undesirable elements, the Jameson Raid, clashes with Native tribes; events which led, barely eighteen months after the establishment of the game sanctuary, to the Anglo-Boer War. (cited in Carruthers 1994: 265)

What the president would be more useful for was the use of his name in the 1920s in an era of heightened nationalist fervor and Voortrekker nostalgia. Kruger was marshaled to unite and solidify a specifically Afrikaner attachment to the land and its game, rather than the region's people and their history. Afrikaner nationalism was deployed until surprisingly recently when park authorities used "unity among Afrikaans-speaking white South Africans" as an apology for their own ethnic and racial politics during apartheid. Moreover, Afrikaner victimhood and ethnic rallying is portrayed in post-apartheid times as "an active uplift program" after the ravages of the Great Depression and Boer War (Mabunda, Pienaar, and Verhoef 2003: 13).

With the cessation of the Boer War, a British cavalry officer named James Stevenson-Hamilton was appointed warden. He enlarged the Sabi Reserve and began an immediate program of forced evictions of some 2500 Africans (Pollard, Shackelton, and Carruthers 2003: 430). Conversely, he allowed others to stay in

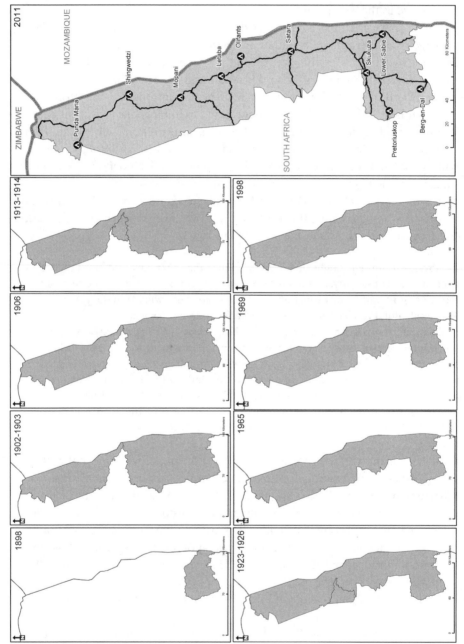

Figure 3.2 Map of Kruger National Park acquisitions through time. Courtesy of South African National Parks, Geographic Information Science and Remote Sensing.

the northern Singwitzi portion when he realized native labor was needed. Today official park historiography mentions only "isolated black families" (Mabunda, Pienaar, and Verhoef 2003: 8), tending to reinforce the dual fiction of *empty lands* and *worthless lands*. But there were some 3000 residents at this time in the Singwitzi Reserve alone, and they were permitted to continue agriculture and herding. A report on the Sabie Farms Reserve dated September 4, 1902 by the Native Affairs Department records numerous settlements, including 20 kraals and 200 people under a Swazi chief called Mambatine. Numerous families had moved from the Crocodile and Sabie Rivers and the Lebombo hills, and there was a considerable population noted north towards Oliphants River where there were no white men save a few traders. We might recall, too, that in the Transvaal, the Shangaan tribe alone numbered over 82 000 (Junod 1926). And while Kruger comprises only part of the province, Junod recorded numerous groups that once occupied this territory including the Nondwane, Shiburi, Masilane, and Maluleke.

In May 1905 it was decided that the considerable number of Africans in the game reserves should, like other squatters on crown lands, be subject to the payment of squatters' rents. From this date onward Africans who resided in game reserves became a source of considerable revenue (Carruthers 1995: 43). As the warden wrote, "Our native residents had to pay their taxes to the native commissioners of the different magisterial districts in which the reserve was situated . . . After the first year or two I was able to save them the trouble of making tax collecting expeditions to the reserve, either by collecting on their behalf, or by sending the natives to their stations to pay there" (Stevenson-Hamilton 1993: 113–14). In a brutal twist of fate, those Africans living in the reserve were considered bad for nature, but also a necessary labor force to "construct wilderness" in a landscape already of their own making. As indigenous inhabitants of that landscape they were either forced from their homes or allowed to remain as designated "squatters," but immediately fined for their trespass. Paying that penalty entailed their unpaid labor as indentured servants transforming the landscape for whites. The unrelenting coercion of settler control through enclosure and exclusion re-ordered and re-assigned both humans and animals to serve an emerging commercial economy (Van Sittert 2002: 117). Farmers were transformed into "squatters" and hunters turned into "poachers" overnight (see also Igoe 2004; Steinhart 2006). It is for these reasons that Stevenson-Hamilton was given the name Skukuza ("he who sweeps away") that is still used today by descendant communities around Kruger.

Trekpas and Trespass

The archives at Skukuza are kept in a vault near the director's office, literally a bank vault that one can easily become trapped in, as I did on one occasion. In those archives I discovered a single box labeled *Argeologie File B/3 (1912–1983)* that held papers on mining, treasure hunting, and squatters. Perhaps everything extractive and historic could be glossed by my own discipline. Squatters, I soon discovered, referred to Africans who were living within park borders and underwent that taxonomic reversal from being inhabitants to interlopers. Importantly, these "squatters" were testament to the continued black settlement throughout the park at camps like Pretoriuskop and Satara that were home to several hundred people and their livestock. Their "invisibility" may be due to the fact that Africans were not permitted to walk on the public roads, so that visitors could reasonably claim to be unaware of their presence (Carruthers 1994: 275). But they were certainly visible to park authorities. Apart from the census lists, the box-file contained dozens of copies of the *trekpas* ("papers to move on" in Afrikaans), the documents giving Africans 90 days notice to leave the reserve. I held copies of the trekpases that were issued to men from Lower Sabie, Tshokwane, and the Saliji area. In reality, throughout the length of the park the trekpas was issued, people were caught and punished, pressed into labor, and uprooted from their homes. The Vagrancy Act of 1879 stated that anyone "loitering" or "wandering" near any enclosed place, such as a farm or kraal, could be convicted and then would be incarcerated or indentured for up to three months (Van Sittert 2002: 114). As late as the 1950s there were "squatters" recorded around the camps at Shingwedzi, Punda Maria, Satara, Pretoriuskop, each listing hundreds of people and their animals.

During my fieldwork in Kruger I was interested in meeting individuals who had once dwelt within the park boundaries and were forcibly evicted during either colonial or apartheid administrations, or who were descendants of such people. The Mkhabela were one such group, and I met them over several years to track the changes that were directly affecting them. Historically, the Mkhabela family, today some 100 people, lived at a place called Esitakweni, near Pretoriuskop. Between 1950 and 1960 they were finally evicted from the park. Joseph Mkhabela, grandson of Chief Nyongane, explained that in the early days many groups were forced to bring their cattle to one place, and they were all killed together in a mass operation. Park officials, in a now familiar story, claimed that such measures were necessary because of disease, but no satisfactory explanations were given and, to this day, the Mkhabela and many other communities I have interviewed assert a more conspiratorial agenda. Trickery and the tsetse fly were usefully allied for provincial conservation authorities arguing for the removal of Africans and their animals (Brooks 2005: 236). By stripping African communities of their cattle, with all their social and economic significance (Beinart 2003: 338; Shutt 2002; Tropp 2002), the park was effectively sealing their fate. Cattle killing represented a complete annihilation: no compensation was ever offered. Joseph says that his grandfather died two years after the incident from a broken heart.

None of the park authorities I encountered, with the exception of one black heritage officer, were interested in hearing such stories, largely because "compensation" has become such an acrimonious issue in South Africa. Land claims in Kruger have been viciously debated in the press and on SANParks' own web forum in vitriolic language that underlines how racism continues unabated in South Africa. Many intelligent people, inside and outside Kruger's fence, still choose to believe that Africans were recent arrivals, never lived or toiled inside the park boundary, and therefore have no rights to any sort of compensation, let alone land restitution. Significantly, Stevenson-Hamilton attested to the wholesale destruction of native livestock in his own 1937 memoires: "On my return I found the elimination of all native stock, cattle, sheep, goats and pigs nearly complete. I visited the place where the park's herd had stood. In one day a 'green and pleasant valley' covered with sleek healthy animals had been converted into a stinking repulsive Golgotha" (Stevenson-Hamilton 1993: 290). Poignantly, he actually recorded the destruction of cattle belonging to Joseph Mkhabela's grandfather.

> Some three thousand native cattle in the park were destroyed, none reported to be infected. For the natives the loss was serious. Besides being used for plowing among them, cattle to a large extent represent currency. When six hundred head were shot at Nyongane's on the western border, the native owners stood by in absolute silence, though I was told that it was only the chief's influence that prevented a demonstration. (Stevenson-Hamilton 1993: 291)

Few could dispute the veracity of this account or the piteous tone that underlies it. He went on to describe the killing of all small stock that ostensibly deprived people of their meat supply and forced many to move out. When Stevenson-Hamilton mentions monetary compensation, which he had the unfortunate duty of distributing, he concedes that it was not generous and was often paid much later. "As one headman remarked when I handed over to him £70 in notes, 'What is the use of all this paper money? Probably it will get burnt or eaten by white ants, and even if not, it will quickly be spent at the stores and soon be finished, while the cattle would have been increasing every year'" (Stevenson-Hamilton 1993: 291).

The testimony of Stevenson-Hamilton further complicates the position of colonial conservationists who were obliged to stand by while government veterinarians eradicated stock (Beinart, Brown, and Gilfoyle 2009; Spinage 2003), themselves believing this was the scientific course of action. Stevenson-Hamilton realized it was not simply destruction of these herds that crushed the economic and social backbone of the tribal tradition and power; it was the colonial control and intervention into their day-to-day lives.

> Having thus been cleared of domestic stock, the park was declared an "infected area" and no animals, such as equines or dogs, might be moved from it without permission from the veterinary department, and then only after disinfection of their feet under official supervision. The natives asked how it was that while they might not

send a donkey to the store a mile outside the park to get a bag of meal, the zebras and wildebeest could travel backwards and forwards at will! "Can they not then also carry infection on their feet?" Henceforth there was no fresh milk in the park, which came rather hard on young children, and it was not always easy for the natives to buy artificial substitutes. (Stevenson-Hamilton 1993: 291)

It has been estimated that in the 1939 campaign some 14 000 animals were killed in the Crocodile River area alone (Bunn 2006: 368).

The Mkhabela remember the burial places of their chief and other members of the family in Kruger, as well as the hundreds of slaughtered cattle. Usually families visit the park during December to ensure that the graves are tidy and to perform the rituals: December, like Easter, is a good time for reuniting everyone. As on the occasion of our visit, the family, young and old, male and female, arrives in cars and old vans. My colleague enables them to come into the park without paying the levy and arranges for us to visit the graves on foot, something that a regular visitor would be forbidden to do for the sake of safety. Though we are a big group, there is no ranger with a gun, and nobody wants to walk at the end of the line. Hidden amidst the long grass, chief Nyongane's grave is marked by a roughly hewn headstone and is covered with the material things from his life, an old kettle, his walking stick, and so on. What may look like a haphazard array of items is actually a suite of intimately biographical objects steeped in memories for his descendents. Members of the family carefully cut back the grass and remove weeds from the grave.

After this visit Mkhabela elders returned to Skukuza to arrange for a commemorative plaque to be inscribed and installed near Chief Nyongane's grave. The Mkhabela family had to petition Kruger officials to visit the site on September 24 (National Heritage Day) as part of the memorial ceremony. Given the wealth of the park and the simplicity of the gesture, it struck me as sad that the community then had to pay for their own plaque, yet they seem cautiously optimistic, saying that this is just the beginning. That such interventions are now possible is a mark of the trust that has been established, especially through members of the People and Conservation unit. Yet all such encounters scarcely seem to inch forward toward some kind of resolution. Our meetings were always somber and professional, reflecting the enormous power differentials created by the fence and all that history.

On occasion we met to talk about other historical events. During work in the archives I found a letter dated June 20, 1946 entitled *Boundaries of Kruger National Park – Pretorious Kop Area*. From this document it appeared that park authorities had constructed Numbi Gate on land that cut three-quarters of a mile into Native Trust Land. When faced with the dilemma, it was clear that the park intended to keep the land with the idea of developing it, deeming it of "utmost value to the park . . . also of national importance that it should be retained within the park." Colonel J.A.B Sandenbergh, the park warden wrote, "knowing the Native mind I am certain they are already resenting our possession of this ground, and their resentment will probably take the practical form of poaching, well knowing that in law we cannot proceed against them for trespassing." Sandenbergh was later fired for alleged financial malpractice unrelated to this incident (Carruthers 2008: 222). Although it was an illegal encroachment, this over-extension served national park goals and a deal was finally struck with the Native Affairs Department. With the sweep of a pen, 3500 people were told to move, although some 2000 were permitted to remain on the land if they agreed to labor for the park building roads and infrastructure: overnight they too would inhabit the category of squatters.

Holding a sheaf of fragile, yellowing paper, we look over copies of the trekpas with the Mkhabela representatives, Simon, Phineas, Nelly, Boi, and Joseph. No one present remembers that the trekpas was basically an eviction notice, since their generation has lived largely outside the fence. Several cannot read the English, so I tentatively recite those named in the documents from the 1950s. Gradually some of the names are recognized and there is muted discussion about their relatives. A man they recall, Monte Mkhabela, was given 90 days notice to "remove himself, his family and his possessions from the confines of Kruger National Park and seek residence elsewhere." These moments are poignant connections with a past that consists of these familiar yet brutal decisions and retells a history for which they are still suffering. For the Mkhabela one remaining problem is information and access. One man told me "our fathers, our grandfathers were ignorant . . . because people didn't have enough knowledge to argue" against what was happening to them. "It wasn't the park that came first, this was our place."

More recent incidents also trouble the community. While working in the park in 1998 Nellie Mkhabela's sister was killed by a buffalo. Kruger officials denied any responsibility, claiming that she was not a park employee but, rather, was working for their employees. Indignantly the family told me that white people don't explain anything to black people. Understandably, the relationship between the park and the Mkhabela soured during the 1950s when apartheid policies were brutally enforced, but their interactions had improved since the new dispensation. They believe for that relationship to be equitable they need their land in the park and have a land claim pending. The Mkhabela cannot move back into their ancestral area but are interested in seeing how such places could be managed. The Mdluli Tribal Authority has already had some success in pursuing its land claim and is now engaged in conservation and tourism ventures inside and outside Kruger (Ramutsindela 2004: 114; Spenceley 2003: 23–5). In the interim, it would like to see the name of Numbi Gate, taken from the name of the mountain outside the park, changed to Nyongane Gate after the chief now buried in the park. Kruger has not complied with the 1998 South African Geographical Names Council Act (Mphahlele 2009) to restore the dignity of indigenous place names after their erasure during former administrations. The Authority also seeks proper compensation for the destruction of its people's cattle. During our conversations, the

heritage officer apologetically explains that he has no power to implement reparations, but promises to raise it with those higher up and explains in detail how they
might craft an official document. Since late 2008 the government has amended its
land claim process, stating that financial settlements will replace all potential land
restitution in protected areas. The controversy rages over returning successfully
claimed land in Kruger (Groenewald 2009a; Ramutsindela 2003), with angry
whites arguing that black litigants will now have exclusive control and use of their
wilderness.

Joseph Mkhabela phoned me after one of these meetings to see whether two
of his daughters could assist me with my research. We discussed an internship
based in Kruger, focusing on Mkhabela family history and documentation. Gaining
permission from the park, however, proved to be another issue. I approached one
of the senior black staff tasked with community liaison, whom I imagined to be
sympathetic, but she was dismissive and annoyed at the very idea. "Those people
out there," she argued, "are just after money and not interested in learning about
their own history." She scolded me for my naïveté and assiduously ignored the
matter. The new developments toward access, transparency, and transformation
that SANParks proudly broadcast were being tested in practice, but not simply on
the basis of race or racism – the convenient foil of a white manager impeding
research on black history. Instead its failure turned on new modalities of class and
power, irrespective of color. It was about the widening gap between those that
had "made it" socio-economically and those on the margins who were still poor
and powerless. South African inequality is now intra-racial and fuelled by two
income gaps: first between a multiracial middle class and the rest, and then
between the African urban industrial working class and the African marginalized
poor (Seekings and Nattrass 2002: 222). Recall, too, that South Africa has a Gini
coefficient of around 0.6, making it one of the most unequal societies in the world,
a recipe for destabilization, ethnic tension, and violence (Kagwanja 2008: xxxvi).
Discussing the official response to the Mkhabela request with my black and colored
colleagues, they readily accepted that this was commonplace in the park and
outside and had stock taxonomies, like *wabenzi* (referring to the current penchant
for owning a Mercedes Benz), for the new black elite who has forgotten too
quickly their comrades in the struggle.

Military and Juridical Histories

From the outset, conservation enforcement and law enforcement in South Africa
have had blurred boundaries. This same nexus can be traced internationally across
the United States, Indonesia, Nepal, Thailand, Congo, Colombia, Kenya, and so
on (Bannon and Collier 2003; Price 2003). In the 1880s the United States army was
called to protect the Yellowstone National Park, they established its headquarters

called Fort Yellowstone and later a permanent military presence was decreed. The Yellowstone model provided an acceptable template for conservation management worldwide. When Stevenson-Hamilton was appointed warden of Kruger in 1902 he took on 10 native police and paid them in rations. The "respective duties of the game reserve and customs police were interchangeable; that is, while the latter acted in all ways as native rangers, the former became responsible, when stationed at border posts, for carrying out such customs work" (Stevenson-Hamilton 1993: 113). Today there is a police barracks adjacent to Scientific Services in Skukuza. From time to time the police launch raids on the Staff Village and arrest anyone, usually wives or family members, who is not in possession of the correct permit. On occasion these arrests involve scores of women and children, who are forced to wait dejectedly outside the police station before being dumped outside the park gate.

Historically, Kruger has relied on forced native labor whether from local inhabitants who were designated as "squatters" or from prison labor. Illegal immigrants from Mozambique were seized crossing the park and arrested by reserve officials for trespassing. This offense came with a sentence of two weeks imprisonment and about 1000 men were caught annually. After their time was served they were given a "pass" that enabled them to work as cheap labor on Transvaal's farms or in the mines. Many exchanged their penalty for two weeks labor for the park, typically in building the vast network of roads. The government eventually found this type of "laboring" incarceration unsatisfactory and insisted on a program of formal detention at the main camp. The issue was solved in 1924 with the use of mobile lock-ups that could be moved throughout the park wherever labor was needed (Carruthers 1993: 15). Other native labor was channeled "legally" through the park. From 1920 onwards, the Witwatersrand Native Labour Association conveyed native recruits from Portuguese Territory through the Shingwedzi Reserve from the Limpopo–Pafuri river junction to Punda Maria (Stevenson-Hamilton 1993: 186). Their headquarters stands today in the northernmost section of the park, a white-washed colonial outpost that is considered by many to be a significant heritage site and, as such, is marked on park maps (Hansen 2008).

The desire to find work in South Africa remains desperate, and today increasing numbers of illegal immigrants from Mozambique and Zimbabwe have fled their homes and braved the park in an effort to escape war and poverty. After the crisis in Zimbabwe, armed soldiers heavily patrolled the borders of Kruger and Mapungubwe National Parks. Immigrants pay guides from Mozambique to take them through the treacherous northern sector of the park. Everyone who officially visits, works, or lives in the park must stay in a vehicle when traveling outside the camps. But those who are willing to risk everything for a better life in South Africa cross the border on foot with few possessions, save what they are wearing and carrying. Novelist Nadine Gordimer has written emotively about the ordeal of one desperate family making the perilous journey from Mozambique through Kruger: "a kind of whole country of animals . . . some of our men used to leave home to work there in the places where white people come to stay and look at animals" (Gordimer 2003: 36). During my fieldwork I witnessed several refugees running through the long grass, afraid that we might be there to apprehend them. Like most of those fleeing, they were following the vast electric cable lines that run through the park that are a constant reminder of the human power that shapes Kruger. Because of this established pattern of migration, Kruger's lions have learnt that their defenseless prey have a specific route through the park, with dire consequences for their human quarry. Some of my colleagues have helped refugees who were close to collapse, putting themselves in potential danger, whereas others have turned a blind eye. Bodily dispossession and vulnerability persist in a post-apartheid Kruger: whether in the veld or the worker's compound in Skukuza (Meskell 2006a), the story of bare life is not relegated to history. One can scarcely imagine the desperation that causes people to navigate such landscapes. Few refugees return to their homelands to recount their ordeals and many relatives wait years, even decades, for any word concerning these border crossings (de Jongh 1994; Rodgers 2009). It is a grim situation that South Africa, and more specifically Kruger, consistently acknowledges yet does little to ameliorate. With unemployment, AIDS, poverty, and instability these *deurlopers* (through walkers), as they are called in Afrikaans, are described by both black and white park rangers as a type of parasite.

Globally, many national parks have a shared history beyond conservation that participates in the politics of national borders and conflicts, military operations, policing, and punishment (Brockington 2004; Cock and Fig 2002; Igoe 2004; Keller and Turek 1998; Reid *et al.* 2004; Spence 1999; West, Igoe, and Brockington 2006). A chilling example is Sperrgebiet National Park, recently proclaimed in Namibia, which forms part of a Peace Parks initiative with South Africa.[3] Meaning the Forbidden Territory, Sperrgebiet is infamous for the genocide of the Herero by Lieutenant General Lothar Von Trotha and German colonial forces and for the world's first extermination camp on Shark Island.[4] National Parks often serve as strategic staging grounds and buffer zones: South African parks like Kruger and Mapungubwe offer dramatic examples. Mapungubwe is notorious as a place for rehabilitating soldiers recovering from shock therapy and surgery because of their homosexuality during apartheid (Fleminger 2008: 105; Kaplan 2004: 1415; Van Zyl *et al.* 1999). During fieldwork there in 2008 I stumbled across a Special Forces training camp in old apartheid-era bunkers at Poacher's Corner bordering Botswana. Testosterone-laden men in military fatigues proudly sported their unit's motto, *Born to Fight, Trained to Kill, Ready to Die, We fear naught but God*. The chief officer explained that his men were being sent out alone at night to camp in the bush and learn survival skills. He denied any suggestion that this was linked to patrolling the Botswanan border or preventing a new influx of immigrants entering South Africa through the park.

My interest has been both archaeological and ethnographic in tracing the Limpopo, in northernmost Kruger where the borders of South Africa, Zimbabwe and Mozambique intersect. This meeting ground was ominously dubbed Crooks Corner as testament to the histories of exploitation, both human and animal, that Southern Africa has suffered through colonial regimes, in the brutal regimes of apartheid South Africa and the former Rhodesia, through war-torn Mozambique, and the forced relocations and displacements of people more recently (Connor 2003). This point of triangulation, a no man's land of sorts, has witnessed some of the most aggressive poaching and illegal trading of animals, gun running, movements of military and insurgents as well as untold numbers of refugees. For over a century this has been a stain on the map – a lawless area that has defied containment. This region was where apartheid forces launched chemical weapons assaults into Mozambique against the anti-apartheid resistance forces Frelimo (Frente de Libertação de Moçambique) (Cock and Fig 2002), using perhaps the nation's most positive emblem of heritage as a staging ground for crushing the resistance across national borders. Park managers in the early 1990s may not have had full control of the area, since the park was patrolled by a military unit trained by the SADF 111th Battalion (Ellis 1994: 67). Yet as we shall see below, SANParks archives reveal a good deal of military documentation that suggests some degree of participation.

The politics of destabilization, poaching, and the illegal ivory trade were long played out in Kruger. In 1992 a report commissioned by the Environmental Investigation Agency in London uncovered evidence that from the 1970s to the 1990s the South African government funded their war on Mozambique and Angola with elephant ivory, rhino horn, and gems in vast quantities (Austin, Currey, and Galster 1992; Duffy 1997; Ellis 1994). In the 1990s, despite moves toward a new black government, members of the security forces, and police established the "Third Force," which was responsible for violence and atrocities aimed at halting negotiations with the ANC (Ellis 1998). During de Klerk's presidency the illegal trade continued and Kruger was the linchpin, with SADF and possibly Third Force members operating across the park. Kruger runs the length of Mozambique and supported 95 percent of the country's elephant population, so it was vital not only for operations against the resistance in Mozambique but also for preparedness at home in the event of a black majority government. Col. Gert Otto (SADF Special Forces) was head of military operations in Kruger and regularly crossed into Mozambique to meet with RENAMO fighters (Resistência Nacional Moçambicana, formed by Rhodesian secret service officers in the 1970s). Trained and armed by the SADF, they had covert bases in the north of the park and their headquarters for staging attacks was in Phalaborwa (Austin, Currey, and Galster 1992: 31). The rest of the elephant-ivory smuggling story reads more like tropical gothic farce involving SADF trafficking, apartheid cover-ups, a Portuguese ex-encyclopedia salesman turned millionaire, a Greek hotelier, plus some Taiwanese carvers and their carving factories in Pietersburg and Durban. And while this might seem like a dramatic chapter in the park's history, we might recall the long colonial history involving natural resources and conflict. The case of Kruger was not an isolated

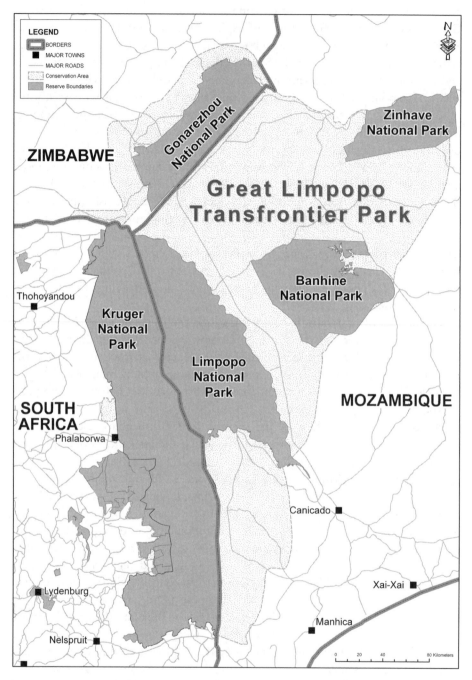

Figure 3.3 Map of the Great Limpopo Transfrontier Park linking South Africa, Zimbabwe, and Mozambique. Courtesy of South African National Parks, Geographic Information Science and Remote Sensing.

one. In 1989 anthropologist David Webster was murdered by a SADF death-squad when his fieldwork in Kosi Bay brought to light evidence of ivory and weapons smuggling into Mozambique (Ellis 1994: 66).

In the 1990s controversial plans for a Transfrontier park linking South Africa and Mozambique, funded by Afrikaner millionaire Anton Rupert, were indicted as yet another strategic deployment of conservation for South African intervention and control. Rupert was closely associated with the Broederbond ("band of brothers"), the Afrikaner nationalist secret society established in 1918 (see also Brockington 2009: 105; Ellis 1994). He was a close friend of WWF International's first President, Prince Bernhard, who was publicly sympathetic to the apartheid government. During the 1990s the SADF endorsed the Transfrontier proposal, hoping to use the scheme to stabilize the area next to the Kruger National Park and to gather intelligence information. Ramutsindela (2004: 124) shows that initially the Transfrontier Peace Park had very little to do with nature conservation or peace promotion and was primarily intended to reinforce white domination in the region. Toward the end of apartheid the SADF, the largest single landowner in South Africa, "turned its attention increasingly to matters of conservation, lending land under its control to conservation and musing on its possible peacetime conservation role" (Ellis 1994: 68). Given the continuing strategic importance of the Mozambique–South Africa border, the political imperative was central. Moreover, ex-military personnel were thought to make good wardens and rangers, accustomed to the outdoor life and trained in the use of weapons, deemed vital in the war on poaching. You can clearly see the connection between the military and conservation every day in Kruger, ex-soldiers serving as pilots, authorities who still wear the old epaulette uniform from the apartheid years (Maguranyanga 2009: 88), and many have a military bearing and military moustache.

Rupert and the World Bank did go on to fund the GLTP, and the new South Africa has still been roundly criticized for its de facto domination and economic self-interest in the region (Büscher and Dressler 2007; Draper, Spierenburg, and Wels 2004; Rodgers 2009; Wolmer 2003). South Africa's new territorializations represent the capitalist turn in environmental governance aimed at boosting privatization and commercialism, while communities on the Mozambican side have been forced out and deprived of their livelihoods (Büscher and Dressler 2007: 604). Critics argue that the new park hardly stimulates, and possibly even undermines, the realization of the African Renaissance ideals of regional cooperation, emancipation, cultural reaffirmation, sustainable economic development and democratization (van Amerom and Büscher 2005: 159). The entire notion of an international park in such a context, that traverses three countries experiencing dire poverty, the HIV/AIDS pandemic, unemployment, violence around immigration, and displacement, seems to test the limits of possibility.

Today we are left with only scattered documents, letters, and maps in the file marked NK/13/4 SADF in the Skukuza vault as compared with many decades of ranger's diaries, meeting minutes, and Mozambican labor reports. Secret documents outline the apartheid security structure devised for the park in the 1980s, with zoning for specific military units, control points, and the numbers of commandos and black soldiers allocated to each section. In the southern third of Kruger there were 123 white commandos and 29 black, with 77 "others" being listed. It is hard to imagine park authorities failing to spot these men, and it is tempting to consider that the other 77 may have been drawn from park employees. In total, 347 men were stationed throughout Kruger, with Skukuza forming the military nerve center. In a secret document sent to park warden Dr Salomon Joubert, dated September 20, 1988, Col. J Van Heerden requested that the activities of both the parks board and SADF be coordinated in the north of Kruger, ensuring an economic use of manpower and exchange of intelligence to halt ANC infiltration. Patrols were deployed along a grid and on all park borders at intervals of 2 kilometers. Van Heerden promised military air support if needed.

An operations handbook was compiled for Kruger's military officers in their efforts to apprehend suspected resistance fighters traversing the Lowveld, instructing them on how to recognize members of the ANC, how to disarm them, and even how to identify potential informants among black park workers and train them, specifically how to extract information and betray their fellow comrades in Kruger. Van Heerden insisted all illegal immigrants be searched for dental fillings, toiletries, new clothing, and foreign labels that could indicate overseas training. Other indicators were possession of tinned food, passport irregularities, an inability to speak the local Shangaan language, and even a discoloration on the right shoulder from ANC rifle training. A Top Secret communication from Van Heerden to the Kruger Park Commando Unit on the July 19, 1988 states that all teams "must capture or kill if arrest is not possible." One operation conducted in Pafuri was called "Deception and Destroy" and was designed to trick ANC operatives into investigating the appearance of SADF stockpiling in the north and then ambushing them. We have no idea whether the operation, rather simplistic in its strategy, proved successful or not. However, we do know that if insurgents were captured, the site of Maritenga on Kruger's western boundary was where they would be interrogated.

The symbol of the Kruger Park Commando Unit was the lion's paw print – a fitting symbol for the power and predatory skill of a dominant aggressor. *Snuffels*, their bi-monthly report featured the lion paw print coupled with a cartooned commando rat following animal and human spoor in the bush. Two confidential reports remain today in the Skukuza files for June/July and August/September 1986. In the first, compiled by Intelligence Officer Major T.L. Marais, instructions are given to infiltrate communities bordering the park by training informants. He suggests that (white) section rangers in the park extract information from their black field-rangers. What follows are lengthy instructions on how to identify potential black informers: someone young and socially accepted, ill-treated by radicals, with a defective belief in "witchdoctors" who was thus amenable to a new ideology (Marais 1986: 2). Rangers were key to this structure of infiltration and informing and, while some park authorities may have avoided such encounters, the records state that other rangers complied. In June 1986 field rangers arrested 120 trespassers and SADF arrested 117. In July the rangers caught 343 people and the soldiers 127: they claim 2411 border crossings in July alone. Marais begged rangers to give the detention of insurgents and the training of infiltrators their highest priority, not in terms of quashing resistance but for "voortbestaan van die Park as erfenis vir ons kinders" (the survival of the park as a legacy for our children) (Marais 1986: 7).

Military documents from the 1980s and 1990s provide additional charts calculating numbers of refugees per month, the numbers of people who were apprehended, those who escaped, or were turned back, wounded, or even killed. Recent testimonies from Mozambicans who regularly traversed the park during the 1980s reveal that some park personnel were very sympathetic to their plight, and archival records further indicate that senior officials were troubled by their "duty" to turn people back after they had crossed into the park (Rodgers 2009). Other records detail more minor infractions such as general unrest around Pretoriuskop Camp and Numbi Gate, including black workers singing in the compounds "Mandela must be released otherwise our boys will fight." While marked "Secret," these papers belong to the SANParks archive and should be viewed both as official documents of the apartheid government and similarly of park authorities and their operating procedures.

There are more mundane correspondences concerning the SADF that escaped the vigorous shredding in the last days of apartheid. The army set up temporary bases throughout the park that seriously impinged upon Kruger's dual mission of conservation and tourism. Soldiers were variously charged with killing and disturbing game, lighting fires, leaving rubbish, obstructing tourists, and generally being a negative presence, but ultimately the military had jurisdiction. This led to bitter conflicts with park personnel, and at least one white ranger was arrested when he confronted a group of soldiers about an incident at their camp. While the apartheid years seem especially turbulent, warfare and conservation have a shared history and they often find themselves working in unison. White military occupation has a long, if uneven history in Kruger, as the historical site of Steinaecker's Horse shows. During the mid-1990s archaeologists from the National Cultural History Museum excavated the outpost of Colonel Ludwig von Steinaecker and his British military unit referred to as Steinaecker's Horse. Dating to the Anglo-Boer war, the site is 15 kilometers northeast of Letaba Camp. The soldiers complemented their tinned military rations with wild game and domestic animals. And like their successors, they segregated the Native Police troops from the white soldiers (van Vollenhoven, Pelser, and van den Bos 1998). Archaeological finds from the 1920–40s suggests that people continued to occupy the site long after the cessation of fighting, for which there is no official record. Much older finds from the Middle Stone Age and Iron Age attest to a much longer prehistoric sequence.

Both the published accounts and fragmentary archives sketched here reinforce the fact that Kruger National Park has served as both a military zone and a wilderness corridor that shielded the state from political resistance and insurgency. It has operated as a buffer to safeguard the nation from illegal immigration, while at various junctures exploiting those same refugees as a labor force. In 2009 SANParks CEO David Mabunda welcomed the military back to patrol the eastern border as part of a R2 million operation to stop rhino poaching. Mozambicans were cited as the main culprits. Bizarrely, Mabunda claimed that SANParks was also selling off rhinos as "state assets" that would then directly fund anti-poaching (Groenewald 2009b). With the demise of apartheid, the military presence in the park has continued unabated: today the xenophobia surrounding refugees has created a landscape of prejudice that undermines any sort of acknowledgement of the histories of linked ancestry, not to mention oppression and freedom struggles that black communities from across Southern Africa share.

Strongly intercalated with its military role, Kruger National Park has operated like a state and has always exercised various degrees of juridical and disciplinary power (Carruthers 1995). In a letter to a Mr Duvenage dated April 27, 1944 we read that with "Proclamation 731 of 1933 the Warden of the Park was created an ex officio Assistant Native Commissioner over the area in question, on the understanding that his responsibilities should be confined to criminal jurisdiction in respect of game and forest laws, and the protection of national relics such as Bushman paintings which are found through the area." From this and later letters the warden could impose fines and sentence people to jail for a month, but it is also significant that he was charged with the protection of San paintings in much the same vein as the natural patrimony of "game" and "forest." Archival records outline how such responsibilities were enacted: in one case native children, two years of age, were prosecuted for starting a fire. Adults were charged with an array of offenses including being drunk, not paying their taxes, being "deranged," trespassing, poaching, and even for their own disappearance. Vague offenses are noted in the correspondence, such as "natives causing trouble." Exactly what "trouble" they caused is later clarified: they were observed "walking through the park" (see also Van Sittert 2002: 118), and black labor was preferably invisible. Nowhere in the correspondence is concern voiced about workers being attacked by wild animals. And yet there were always a few notable "honest and loyal native" types who "never had a conviction" to set against the masses who were criminal, lazy, or just a nuisance (Bunn 2003; Carruthers 1993).

Of course these "illegalities" were not one-sided. Land transfers and shifting boundary lines, for example, obviously benefited the park on numerous occasions, as we saw with the example of Numbi Gate. Motivation for these acquisitions was the exchange of good land suitable for conservation for poor grazing land suitable for natives. The Pafuri land exchange with the Makuleke tribe was a glaring

example of discrimination and collusion (de Villiers 1999). Letters from the Park
Warden in 1953 document his surprise that the Pafuri natives were still flourishing,
along with his hope that their numbers would soon be insignificant. Acting very
much like a state in terms of land transfers and acquisitions, the Department of
Native Affairs challenged the park's actions arguing that Pafuri was incredibly rich
agriculturally and Kruger was duping both the natives and the government if they
continued to pretend that the land they offered in return was comparable. Suffice
to say that the episodes I have sketched here were typical of their time; they reveal
the blindness and racial prejudices of a circumscribed community who mandated
their own limits of care extending to Europeans and to nature. Ethics were not
entirely absent; rather their own ethics provided moral exemptions for the park
and its authorities so that the plight of indigenous groups living in the park or
that of native laborers was largely peripheral. These histories reveal the ingrained
habits of sanctioned ignorance and self-deception (Stoler 2008: 256), and they have
much in common with the learned ignorance surrounding the deep history of
African presence in the landscape, and the social and ecological shaping of that
landscape.

A Post-Apartheid Park: Your Heritage,
Your Park, Your World

A decade after the first democratic elections I moved into my rondavel at
Nwatshisaka camp with its thatched roof and all the accompanying animals;
elephants at the fence and monkeys at the ready to raid my kitchen. The camp
was both exotic and familiar. Bathroom tiles, sheets, crockery, and soap were all
emblazoned with the old insignia of the park, the kudu, with the words *Custos
Naturae*. The institutional stamp reminded me of my years spent in Cambridge
and Oxford Colleges, unsurprising given the British colonial history of the park
and its first warden, James Stevenson-Hamilton. Intense branding reflects the civilizing mission of the park, a curated gentility in the midst of a proclaimed as
"wilderness." It was also horribly dated and reflects an Anglo rather than an
African history and context. The colonial genre of architecture is maintained
across the park with a loving sense of nostalgia: there are no plans to re-inscribe
these older spaces with a new post-apartheid aesthetic. New private safari lodges
in Kruger, however, have moved to an African contemporary aesthetic with luxurious ease. The overall effect is a kind of double-time (Farred 2004), trapped between
the tropical gothic of colonial times and the hyper-consumerism of post-apartheid
Kruger with its new lion logo brandished upon hundreds of predictable products,
be they wine glasses, beer-can holders, clothing, jewelry, candles, or lotions.
Such commodification blurs into ancillary advertising campaigns promoting a
new inclusivity for post-apartheid parks: *Your Heritage, Your Park, Your World.*

Heritage here should not be confused with cultural heritage, it refers to Kruger as legacy from the last days of the Transvaal Republic that has been recast under various regimes. Following the recommendations of McKinsey & Co consultants, such terms provide an economically geared catch-all that targets greater public (read black) buy-in, reinforced by "your park" and more universally, "your world."

Kruger has become its own brand in the new millenium, inspired by the recommendations of McKinsey's consultancy report. Post-apartheid transformation was not only racial or organizational; it would be fiscal, developmental, and neo-liberal. A twenty-year commercialization strategy was instigated in which private concessions (Cock 2007: 88), consultancy culture, outsourcing, audit, and performance measurement would become part of Kruger's core business. SANParks now claims to operate in two industries – conservation and tourism – that provide public goods (conservation) and private goods (eco-tourism) in a public–private management system (Soundy 2004). There are internal tensions between the two missions (Zhou 2009) and one senior figure in Scientific Services repeatedly likened SANParks' push for tourism to prostitution. No corporate unit existed during apartheid management, since the NPB received direct funding from the state. Many of the old guard dislike the new corporate mission and are vehemently against the drive for greater tourism. Economic liberalization provided opportunities for SANParks to pursue market-driven strategies of revenue generation, and this effectively enabled the organization to fund conservation and made it acceptable to inject an entrepreneurial spirit into park management (Maguranyanga 2009: 43). In the face of South Africa's structural adjustment matters of national development still prevail over green rhetoric (Baviskar 2003: 315). Another priority old-style constituencies still resist is the expected increase in participation of historically disenfranchised sectors of society and the call to be institutionally and socially responsive to policy imperatives and adjacent communities respectively (Nyambe 2005). Kruger's decision making often takes shelter under the banner of technical efficiency and moral conservation goals, thus insulating it from political contestation, public accountability, and participation. Conservation efforts thus have to be balanced with fiscal imperatives, which in turn have to be traded off against community development, and this has led to palpable hostility within Kruger. While the desire for beauty and wilderness fenced people out during the twentieth century, the new technocracies of biodiversity, resilience, and complex systems perform many of the same exclusions today.

Nelson Mandela encapsulated the pivotal challenge confronting SANParks over a decade ago, entreating South Africans to "recall these threads in our history not to decry the foresight of those who established the park, nor to diminish our enjoyment of it . . . rather to reaffirm our commitment that the rural communities in and around our parks should also benefit from our natural heritage, and find in it an opportunity for their development" (Mandela 1998). Similar to the rhetorics of "archaeology as therapy," CEO David Mabunda would go on to present SANParks as a "healing" institution that would ameliorate the depredations of apartheid. The organization would join forces with the ANC and impoverished black communities alike to create socio-economic opportunities and develop people (Maguranyanga 2009: 7, 15). Democratization and economic liberalization would be realized in post-apartheid parks and Social Ecology, then later People and Conservation, would be the designated conduit. But the reality of transformation has been met with considerable institutional resistance and the concerns of neighboring communities, whose empowerment, participation, and development have been sidelined. In tandem with this response, the cultural heritage of these descendent communities, a past that for many of them lies inside Kruger, has similarly been ignored. The most recent Management Plan for SANParks (2008b) is illustrative: archaeology fails to appear in almost 60 pages, the word "heritage" has been co-opted into the term "biodiversity heritage," and the seven uses of "cultural heritage" appended to the end of long lists is followed by "etc." Cultural heritage, supposedly one of the pillars of the new black organization, has been absorbed under the category, Ecosystem Management. Archaeology and heritage are literally off the map.

So how does culture figure within Kruger's new dispensation? Culture is seen very much as contemporary practice rather than ancient heritage, though there are attempts to link the two through the concept of indigenous knowledge (Masuku Van Damme and Neluvhalani 2004). Despite this recognition internationally, indigenous knowledge is seldom incorporated into project designs that would ensure significant transformation and a radical questioning of modern assumptions about nature and culture (Escobar 2008: 14). Strikingly absent is any celebration of "indigenous stewardship" within Kruger that has become a popular trope in representations of Australian Aborigines (Jacobs 1996), the archetypal Massai (Homewood, Kristjanson, and Trench 2009; Igoe 2004), or even the San across Southern Africa (Gordon and Sholto-Douglas 2000; Robins 2002; Sylvain 2002). Rather than being co-opted to the cause of nature conservation as "indigenous conservationists," as has been the pattern in countries like India, Brazil, and Australia, the past inhabitants of Kruger have once again been left off the map, absence being preferable to agency.

Heritage today is largely trapped in the negative association of public works and poverty relief and has been relegated to the production of arts and crafts and performing primitivism, in that familiar beaded and feathered way: young men in impala skins dance for money outside Skukuza's rest camp; local crafts sold at stalls by tourist gates attempt to "develop" communities. One social ecologist purported that craft initiatives were the most successful development projects of the new democratic era. The grounded reality is rather more complex, as various staff members reiterated, the quality of local craft is not up to international tourist standards and has thus failed. Craft stalls are depressing, and deserted outposts and local goods have been excised from the main commercial center at Skukuza.

Yet support for developing craft industries is often touted within Kruger as a vehicle for socio-economic uplift, while in reality it operates more successfully as a public relations exercise.

 Neoliberal heritage exists because Kruger is unwilling to support heritage ventures and People and Conservation has a limited budget in comparison with its biophysical counterparts (Edgar Neluvhalani, pers. comm.). Biodiversity as the core mission of the park is not under comparable pressure. When heritage development is entertained, consultants are called in to produce reports, brochures, and management plans that are inevitably filed away and forgotten. In 2009 a consultancy report pointed to dramatic failures, particularly in Kruger's disregard of history, and concluded that the solution lay in appointing an Interpretation Manager and another manager for Interpretation Design and Publishing. Retired rangers are paid for knowledge of rock art sites gleaned while employed by SANParks and academics, for years of research in Kruger previously published or never to appear. The same individuals with historic ties to the park are invited back again and again, regardless of their previously poor record of delivery. Consultancy culture is de rigueur, yet none of those individuals I encountered were trained as archaeologists or were necessarily interested in bridging natural and cultural heritages. Kruger's heritage offers the perfect retirement strategy, poised between the culture of amateurism and opportunism; archaeology is thus relegated to the unprofessional and unscientific sphere. Conversely, the biophysical sciences do not engage amateurs, and park scientists and managers conduct game capture, wild dog research, or invasive species management, though there is very limited scope for volunteers though the Honorary Rangers program.

 Let me be clear, I am not advocating a major program of new archaeological fieldwork in the park, there are many archaeological sites and projects that already exist and that could be developed and promoted for shared socio-economic benefits. However, the appointment of trained archaeologists in SANParks seems an obvious requirement, as does an organizational commitment to rethink Kruger's landscape as a socio-natural one. This chapter has sought to highlight some ignored historical moments of Kruger, including the deep prehistory of the park so often glossed over. There could be other attendant histories written, those of black rangers, white scientists, immigrants, and laborers; or histories of biodiversity, burning, poaching, or disease – all would be welcome and fascinating. Jane Carruthers' prolific historical work on Kruger still remains exceptional. More specifically, I am suggesting that to ignore the anthropogenic and peopled aspect of protected areas fosters a dangerous fiction. The loss of history remains detrimental to both cultural and natural heritage profiles. If transformation is a goal for conservation, with communities being fully integrated into parks programs, then the peopled history of these landscapes must be incorporated and supported. Historic and archaeological studies can be as scientific and rigorous as biophysical research and potentially as beneficial, as luminaries like Nelson Mandela recognized.

Notes

1   www.sahistory.org.za (accessed November 20, 2009).
2   Biltong is the dried meat South Africans prepare.
3   http://ppf.org.za/News_1090000000_0_0_0_0_791_Sperrgebiet+proclaimed+a+nati onal+park.htm (accessed April 13, 2011)
4   http://www.dailymail.co.uk/news/article-1138299/The-Holocaust-Horrifying-secrets-Germanys-earliest-genocide-inside-Africas-Forbidden-Zone.html   (accessed January 3, 2010).

Chapter 4

Why Biodiversity Trumps Culture

Who are these people, I wondered, who love animals so much that they are willing to kill us for them? (Amitav Ghosh, *The Hungry Tide*, 2004)

Wide empty spaces and game are critical – Africa is the Land of Wide Empty Spaces. When writing about the plight of flora and fauna, make sure you mention that Africa is overpopulated. (Binyavanga Wainaina, *How to Write About Africa*, 2005)

The United Nations declared 2010 International Year of Biodiversity. It is also the Year for the Rapprochement of Cultures. Such a conjuncture might signify that we are now recognizing the intercalation of natural and cultural domains. However, 2009 was simultaneously the International Year of Reconciliation, International Year of Natural Fibers, and the Year of the Shark. Sitting in the Paris headquarters of UNESCO's World Heritage Center, everyone around the table agrees that biodiversity is the current mantra. It currently overshadows the cultural past and its scientific experts wield greater leverage than their cultural counterparts. Discussing these issues in the context of South Africa, I discovered that Kruger National Park had once prepared a UNESCO nomination on the basis of outstanding universal value. That "value" was calculated on the basis of science, conservation, and natural beauty. No mention was made of cultural history. This episode is salutary for those of us curious about why so little has changed after the end of apartheid. Why is black history still peripheral, and how might the new nation rebalance the discursive projects of nature and culture? These questions are, in part, what began to direct my research.

The Nature of Heritage: The New South Africa, First Editon. Lynn Meskell.
© 2012 John Wiley & Sons, Inc. Published 2012 by Blackwell Publishing Ltd.

Spaces like Kruger reveal that there are ever more entanglements between science, morality, religion, law, technology, finance, and politics, but never less (Latour 2007). Instead of our classifications becoming more closely defined, so that we can say with certainty what constitutes heritage, biodiversity, or even a "national" park, today we are confronted with new and increasing complexities, connections, and attachments. An example of this is the very idea of studying the present past in Kruger. It is not possible to neatly parse out archaeology and heritage from the role of governments, development programs, international agencies, or corporations. In any such attempt we find interpolated among these broad concepts particular histories, agendas, ecosystems, and the agency of humans and non-humans. From this vantage Kruger can no longer be revered as a wilderness, a people-free landscape, or a pre-colonial reservoir of biodiversity. Historical–geographical processes continue to fashion the park, including material practices, ideological structures, social relations, cultural traditions, language, and bio-chemical physical actions that taken together comprise socio-nature (Hannigan 2006: 35). Geographer Neil Roberts (2003) argues that over much of the earth "First Nature has probably never existed; certainly not, for example, in Africa where plants, animals and humans have co-evolved over millions of years. And even where it has, it is far from clear whether it is reasonable to consider it as an original and truly typical baseline against which the effects of later human actions can be judged." While my own research in Kruger cannot hope to offer the expansive new synthesis of social and natural histories that is needed, it does explore some increasingly forgotten social histories of the park and suggest why cultural heritage is still precariously placed.

Today, Kruger National Park is the largest game reserve in South Africa, frequently touted as "the size of Israel," extending 350 kilometers north to south and averaging 60 kilometers east to west. There are six ecosystems across the park, Baobab sandveld, Mopane scrub, Lebombo knobthorn-marula bushveld, mixed acacia thicket, Combretum-silver clusterleaf woodland, and riverine forest. Kruger's biodiversity scorecard includes 148 types of mammals, 118 different reptiles, 505 bird species, and 1990 plant taxa. There are also over 1000 archaeological sites dating from the earliest human history, to San rock art, Iron Age settlements and recent colonial period sites. Our penchant for this type of inventorying, however, does little to convey the dynamism of the landscape or acknowledge long-term anthropogenic factors. During the millennia of human presence, Kruger has witnessed hunting, grazing, agriculture, terracing, mining, settlement, burning, and other forms of landscape modification. Nature and society are entwined and our understandings of both people and the physical landscape call for explanations of mutual constitution and inseparability (De Jonge 2004; Swyngedouw 1999). Producing "nature" then becomes a more transparent enterprise that dynamically configures spaces including national parks. Presciently it recognizes that contemporary intrusions, whether scientific, managerial, or research driven, though often occluded, are in fact accepted practices which themselves have long histories.

Kruger National Park exhibits varying but significant degrees of intervention into its "wilderness." Management policies including suppression of fire plus a controlled burning regime, extermination of predators, animal relocation, culling, drilling boreholes to provide water, fencing, exclosures, and test plots are but a few. There exists a dense network of roads, camps, resorts, research facilities, and monitoring points. Parks, and other forms of sacrosanct nature whose laws should remain untouched by human values, actually need our constant care, our undivided attention, our costly instruments, our hundreds of thousands of scientists, our huge institutions, not to mention exorbitant funding (Latour 2007). At one major meeting, Kruger's Head of Scientific Services speculated, "it's more like an art than a science what we do." Our shared difficulty in relinquishing *wilderness* or *wildness* is bound up with romanticism, modernism, and our attachment to the bifurcated taxonomies I set out in previous chapters. National parks are particularly susceptible to these attachments in their fulfillment of our desires for untouched nature, their propensity for masking colonial dislocations and obliterating the history of those dislocations, along with the history of the spaces that existed previously (Neumann 1998: 31). Nature and its legacies are essentially presented as raw, timeless, unchanging, finite, endlessly beneficial, and governed by universal laws. Conversely, culture is historical, divisive, destructive, ever changing and hence fleeting. Nature assumes the background against which culture elaborates itself, the contrast that distinguishes difference from the given and the inevitable. Culture is then deemed an active, largely negative force, reworking and enlivening nature in the process of making it function for our historically and geographically variable uses (Grosz 2005: 45).

Kruger National Park, South Africa's self-proclaimed flagship of conservation, biodiversity, and wilderness heritage, is an appropriate setting to study the current tensions surrounding the privileging of nature over culture and the continuing sacrifice of historic recognition for the "greater good" of conservation. Irrespective of leadership or regime change, the mobilization of state power devalues the archaeological past and its human histories. What subsequently emerges as a dominant concern in the new South Africa is a distinctive articulation of nature as biodiversity. SANParks (South African National Parks 2005a) define biodiversity as encompassing compositional, structural, and functional elements of ecosystems, each being manifest at multiple levels of interconnected organization ranging from genes to landscapes. However, the park was long declared a reserve on the basis of aesthetics and the prevalence of game for hunting (Igoe 2004: 57) rather than its ecological diversity. Since 1994 ecologists and managers have expediently re-imagined the park to be both rich in biodiversity and aesthetic wilderness. Nature as scenery is giving way to nature as a scientific object. Biodiverse environments do not necessarily meet aesthetic goals (Eaton 2008: 349; Graber

1994), nor does a wildlife habitat always mesh with a managed wilderness. I should point out that Kruger itself is *not* a biodiversity hotspot (Magome and Murombedzi 2003: 117). Embarrassingly, scientists and researchers agree that there is more actual biodiversity in the poverty stricken rural sprawl that constitutes Bushbuck Ridge on Kruger's western boundary. When this fact was made public at a Conservation Services meeting in Skukuza one shocked section ranger shouted "then we need to change the indices, change our definition of biodiversity!" It is important to note that within Kruger itself the region of Pafuri in the far north contains 75 percent of the park's biodiversity. Pafuri was home to some 2000 Makuleke people until they were evicted in 1969, thus highlighting the positive impacts of indigenous management that the park has chosen to overlook (Cock 2007: 152; Fabricius and de Wet 2002: 144).

States and Parastatals

South Africa has been lauded by the United Nations as a "Champion of the Earth" because of its efforts to protect the natural environment. Some 7 percent of the nation's land surface is either a protected area or a private reserve. Its ecological richness is unparalleled and, despite its relatively small area (1 219 912 km^2), it is the third most biodiverse country on earth, a *world in one country* as the tourist slogan proclaims (Carruthers 2006: 806). While synonymous with nature in the form of dramatic wilderness and exotic game, South Africa also has an appalling environmental record and is under considerable pressure to reduce its greenhouse emissions (Cock 2007; McDonald 2002a). Natural degradation, pollution, and toxic landscapes have been linked to environmental racism that was spawned during the apartheid era. The ambivalent place of nature for South Africans today was surely fashioned during apartheid, and spaces like Kruger have become emblematic as racist stains on the map. During the 1990s culture and nature were sometimes deployed interchangeably in the political rhetoric of South African transformation. Environmental mottos like *apartheid divides, ecology unites* and the *greening of our country is basic to its healing* (Carruthers 2006: 805) parallel the claims I have underscored for culture and heritage. Moral environmentalism connects to moral citizenship with its concerns for healing and the well-being of future generations. More recently, some victims of South African apartheid have begun to seek solace and healing by ecotherapy in the wilderness of the Drakensberg mountains (Cock 2007: 24–8). The National Peace Accord Trust has taken some 2000 people on trips to aid trauma recovery. Many of these men were ex-combatants who, like their comrades leading heritage-based trauma tours (Colvin 2003; Meskell 2007b; Witz, Rassool, and Minkley 2001), describe the connection with nature and ancestors as transforming and rehabilitating people through a spiritual experience. As the following chapters demonstrate, natural and cultural heritages

in Kruger National Park have been invoked intermittently to ameliorate past depredations, with short-lived success.

Recuperation would also be sought from a more economic perspective. From
the 1980s onward, international development and conservation discourses
reframed economic development and "modernization" in terms of environmental
sustainability (Hayden 2003: 48–9). Noting that "poverty and environmental
degradation have been closely linked" in South Africa, the ANC made it clear
that social, economic, and political relations were also part of the environmental
equation (Gibson *et al.* 2008). Environmental inequalities and injustices would
be addressed as an integral part of the party's post-apartheid reconstruction
and development mandate. Indeed, the new South African Constitution, finalized
in 1996, includes a Bill of Rights that grants all South Africans the right to an
"environment that is not harmful to their health and well-being" and the right
to "ecological sustainable development" (McDonald 2002b: 2–3). Like many
of the new constitutional rights, the majority of South Africans may never
see them operationalized. When the Rural Development Plan was disbanded
in 1996, the Environmental Affairs and Tourism portfolio was assigned to the
ANC's high profile minister Mohammed Valli Moosa, who later became president
of the IUCN. In the 1990s, when the ANC transformed SANParks, the socio-
political dimensions of conservation policy were similarly responding to international agendas for poverty elimination, reflected in the Millennium Development
Goals. National parks and protected areas were considered weapons in the
ANC's arsenal to combat the problem of economic development and to positively
provide local, regional, and national services (Carruthers 2006: 814). Valli Moosa's
successor, Marthinus van Schalkwyk, was former leader of the apartheid-aligned
National Party. This signaled to some commentators the low political profile
and impact of the environment in the current government (Carruthers 2006: 805;
Patel 2009). Fragmentation is a salient issue for the ANC and as of 2011 there
are four national and ten provincial agencies managing protected areas in South
Africa (Zhou 2009: 18). Archaeology and heritage have been in a worse predicament, being split between the two departments respectively responsible for
the arts and culture and tourism and the environment, DAC and DEAT, and
managed by various national agencies and councils as well as provincial authorities
(Deacon, Mngqolo, and Prosalendis 2003; Meskell and Scheermeyer 2008;
Scheermeyer 2005).

The South African media is flooded with platitudes of sustainability, biodiversity, conservation, empowerment, and chemical safety, while innumerable workshops and *indabas* (meetings) are held to discuss endlessly their monitoring and
projected futures. Typical of the mood, a special section of the *Mail & Guardian*
newspaper called "Greening the Future" (2005a) reported that conservationists,
racing against time to prevent massive extinction, had developed a new weapon
– the concept of mainstreaming biodiversity. According to Saliem Fakir, director
of the IUCN South Africa, mainstreaming ambitiously targets major segments of

the economy such as agriculture, forestry, tourism, mining, and so on. The same newspaper runs an annual competition, the *Investing in the Environment Awards*, to acknowledge and reward best practice in environmental management. More coercively, 2006 saw the launch of the "Green Scorpions," a task force of over 600 Environmental Management Inspectors with state powers to question and arrest individuals, inspect premises, establish roadblocks, and generally enforce environmental law. The vast majority of these new enforcement officers are none other than SANParks employees. Such spectacles have become commonplace as new styles and ambitions of government inculcate better behavior towards the environment on the part of citizens and those who are themselves conservation subjects. Despite these moves, South Africa lags behind other nations on the environmental index. It was ranked 115 out of 163 countries in the 2010 Environmental Sustainability Index (ESI) that monitors water quality, maximization of biodiversity, and international co-operation. The ESI covers 21 elements of environmental sustainability, including protection of the global commons and the nation's ability to improve future performance. In turn, these variables are translated to reflect back upon the nation's commitment to good governance, including robust political debate, free press, lack of corruption, and rule of law, that supposedly correlate with environmental success (*Mail & Guardian* 2005a: 7). Surprisingly, one of Kruger's senior managers claimed that mining companies were actually "greener" or more "eco-friendly" than the park, and that the organization was lagging behind in practice. Yet the concerns of environmental science have become theoretically paramount, and are similarly reflected in the organizational and research priorities of SANParks. At present the natural sciences dominate all aspects of Kruger's programmatics and research, whereas the social sciences are a negligible, but growing area of the park's remit, considered by some interviewees to be the "soft," politically correct, "little sister" of biodiversity conservation.

Kruger is a parastatal organization; it operates as an arm of government, is answerable to the minister responsible for the Environment and Tourism (DEAT), and is now expected to be financially self-sustaining. But more than its programmatics, Kruger operates like a state and has always exercised a significant degree of disciplinary power. Its central administrative node and main tourist hub is Skukuza. The Tsonga name with its connotation of scouring reform, was conferred upon the first warden of the park, Stevenson-Hamilton, in the early 1900s by the local Shangaan people (Carruthers 1995; 2001), and it is telling. His measures to rid the park of its indigenous inhabitants became synonymous with the structure and identity of the park: particularly with systematic histories of erasure. Elders whom I interviewed from the northernmost park border at Pafuri south to regions around Lilydale and Numbi on the western border, who once lived inside the confines of the park and were evicted between the 1920s and 1960s, still refer bitterly to the entire Kruger National Park as *Skukuza*. The name Skukuza, the action of stripping away all that existed before, has come to represent the politics of the park to this day. Skukuza, as both noun and verb, continues to have a strong resonance.

Africans were forcibly removed from their ancestral lands to make way for game parks like Kruger. Billions were spent preserving wild flowers while bare life for poor colored and black people in the townships meant inadequate food, shelter, and clean water (McDonald 2002b: 1). During apartheid the issue of the environment was considered a white, suburban issue of little relevance to the liberation movement, while environmental policy was seen as a tool of racially based oppression. In scores of interviews around the park borders, dislocated residents see Kruger as the state, irrespective of its former apartheid-era white National Party or current black ANC management. But the most painful period in their history, and one that still awaits recognition and apology, is that of their expulsion. "We were born there; our fathers were born there," explained an elderly man now living outside Kruger at Lilydale. "We cannot trust Skukuza that is what we know." Mr Khoza was born near the Sand River in the 1920s and recalls a thriving agricultural community in Kruger before they were forcibly moved. Others agree and recount the settlements at Lower Sabie, Komatipoort, Satara, Tshokwane, and Crocodile Bridge. With visible disgust an old woman named Mandisa told me how park authorities chipped away at their existence bit by bit. First they killed their cattle and then her people were given 24 hours to move on. "There was no malaria, the animals weren't infected; they just wanted to rob the black people." Outpourings of denial and anger accompanied my every mention of Kruger's official history of disease-ridden and inhospitable landscapes. "The whites are writing lies" people would insist. The residents of Lilydale and nearby villages desperately want to record their own histories while those who can remember are still able to do so.

New histories would act as a corrective to the official scripts while also creating bridges with the younger generation. One of the stories Mandisa wants to tell is about the days when a bus would come from Mozambique to Shingwedzi in the north, picking up people along the way and testing whether they were fit for mine labor or not. If you were deemed fit you were sent to Johannesburg to the mines, if unfit you were sent back. As compared to their stories of Skukuza, the tale of dubious mine recruitment dons a rosy hue (see Mavhunga and Spierenburg 2009; Rodgers 2009). Mandisa does not care to see the park again but her neighbors want to return to visit graves and sites, to collect their old grinding stones and harvest thatch or plants for medicinal purposes. Several women explain that they know the locations of ancient sites and would like to share this information with park authorities. But tensions typically flare at the mention of access and natural resources. "This is our own place, no one can tell us we can't go in there and cut trees," one old woman said defiantly; "there is no way for the communities to interact with the park, the relationship is so sour now, the park is not interested." Despite these grievances, relations between the park and its forcibly relocated neighbors have improved since the democratic elections of 1994. An entire unit,

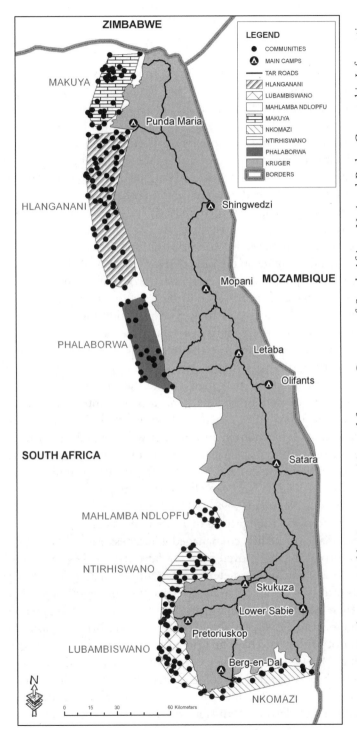

Figure 4.1 Map showing neighboring communities and forums. Courtesy of South African National Parks, Geographic Information Science and Remote Sensing.

People and Conservation, was established to facilitate community relations and employment. Importantly, this is the unit that also manages cultural heritage, although SANParks have no qualified archaeologists on their staff in either their administrative offices or across their 22 national parks (see Chapter 5).

Many black South Africans, long excluded from the park on racial grounds (other than as service workers or guides), have understandably seen Kruger as an exclusive enclave catering to the cultural and recreational tastes of the white and the wealthy (Beinart and Coates 1995; Brockington 2004). SANParks' post-1994 discourse of stakeholding and community involvement is aimed at creating the appropriate disciplined environmental citizens. And coincident with the "rhetoric of stakeholding comes a certain provisional language of representation and participation, expressed through the intertwined idioms of compensation, investment, and incentive-building" (Hayden 2003: 8). In South Africa, as elsewhere, rural people, researchers, and governments are "all encouraged to buy in to the globalizing project of biodiversity conservation and protected areas with the promise of dividends dangling in the future" (Hayden 2003: 8). Throughout many interviews, I have enquired whether people are proud of the park as a national treasure, an international icon, a beacon of biodiversity, and the pinnacle of conservation. Most reply that they still await an explanation for their eviction; they wait for compensation, for the right to freely enter the park, see the animals, visit the graves and sites of their ancestors and have their children and grandchildren given employment by the park. Many more are angry that dangerous animals escaping the park's confines destroy their crops, attack their cattle, and threaten personal safety and that nothing is done to protect or compensate them. If they retaliate and kill the animal, they face possible prosecution. Yet the park bears no responsibility for the destruction (in 2006 Kruger was deemed legally responsible rather than state or provincial agencies). So common is their plight that researchers refer to their rogue escapees as DCAs (Damage-Causing Animals). Much of the "human cost" of wildlife has been elided from the preservationist discussion (Fortmann 2005: 202; Neumann 1998: 190–1).

In attempting to correct the picture of Kruger and its parastatal relationships, much has been made of the first co-managed wilderness area with the Makuleke, an indigenous group forcibly moved from the far north in 1969 that then legally reclaimed some 250 square kilometers in 1995 under ANC rule. However, the preconditions of return ensured that biodiversity and conservation would remain paramount; there would be no mining, prospecting, or agriculture; no residential use other than tourism; SANParks would continue to perform its role as the management authority and would have first right of refusal on any sale (Magome and Murombedzi 2003: 115–16). Framing a contractual national park in this manner, however, has itself been decried as ecological apartheid where the familiar tropes of communal tenure and tribal authority are still in play. To win their claim the Makuleke endorsed biodiversity's mission and promoted ecotourism – a strategy that has not been entirely financially successful. The coercive nature of conservation continues irrespective of regime change in South Africa and demonstrates that the decolonization of nature remains a thorny issue for postcolonial states.

While indigenous peoples and conservation organizations may share overlapping interests, their respective perceptions about what is at stake are very different. Conservation biologists view nature as being significant apart from human involvement, whereas many indigenous groups do not, and the former want to protect wilderness areas from human predation and exploitation (Langford 2003: 91–2). Evidence from around the globe today suggests that the exclusion of people from wilderness is actually damaging to the conservation mission (Brockington 2009: 132). At an international scientific networking meeting in Skukuza this resistance was illustrated when several Australian ecologists, including an Aboriginal researcher, suggested incorporating indigenous firing practices and were rejected out of hand. Education and development efforts are, hence, unidirectional. Anthropologists occupying various roles have long advocated the participation of local communities in both planning and management of protected areas like Kruger. Many have highlighted issues of social justice, arguing that the typically poor and marginal inhabitants of protected areas should not bear the costs of conservation. Others invoke human rights, by which local populations have entitlements as citizens of the states that administer the protected areas, or as native or indigenous peoples with specific claims to sovereignty over their territories (Orlove and Brush 1996: 333–4). To date, these strategies have found little purchase in the overall management of SANParks.

The Nature of Biodiversity and Bad Citizens

The global Convention on Biological Diversity (CBD) defines biodiversity as "the variability among living organisms from all sources including, *inter alia*, terrestrial, marine and other aquatic ecosystems and the ecological complexities of which they are part; this includes diversity within species, between species and of ecosystems" (Orlove and Brush 1996: 329–30). "Biodiversity" as a construct entered the stage of science and development in the late 1980s, while its textual origins can be traced to the CBD in 1992, the Global Diversity Strategy (fostered by the World Conservation Union, United Nations Environment Program, World Resources Institute) in 1992 and the 1992 Earth Summit in Rio (Escobar 1998: 54). For South Africa, the end of apartheid and the shift to a democratic neoliberal state came at the very moment that the mandate of biodiversity achieved global recognition, and this synchronicity is particularly salient. One senior scientist explained it as "an intersection between a political opportunity, or a window of policy change, that we've seen right through the legislation in South Africa and these changes in ecological thinking." Biodiversity is conceived as cosmopolitan and neutral, belonging to no single person, group, nation state, or corporation

(Litzinger 2006: 69) but instead to a common humanity, coercing us all to participate in its mandate. While biodiversity has "concrete biophysical referents, it must
be seen as a discursive invention of recent origin. This discourse fosters a complex
network of actors, from international organizations and northern NGOs to scientists, prospectors, and local communities and social movements" (Escobar 1998:
54). And this ties neatly into developments in South Africa from the mid-1990s
onwards when the new democratic nation first became involved in this series of
international networks.

The new black leadership avidly supports the international biodiversity mandate,
trading it "off against social needs such as health care and other welfare services,"
stressing that "to achieve the 10 per cent IUCN ideal, some 50 000km^2 of additional
land (2.5 times the size of Scotland) must be acquired" (Magome and Murombedzi
2003: 109) for protected, conservation areas. This is especially controversial in
South Africa since land reform under the ANC has been slow and heavily criticized
for its reticence to disrupt nationally profitable white farms. In 2005 more than
17 000 land claims had yet to be processed and most successful claims now entail
financial compensation rather than land settlement. The potential losses to
Kruger's biodiversity through land restitution have been dramatized in terms of
local black communities turning "wilderness" into theme parks and casinos
according to SANParks representatives (Groenewald and Macleod 2005: 6) – a
caricature that also featured heavily in the *2005 State of the Nation Report* (Walker
2006: 68). The global security of nature has gained currency as the driving force
behind protected areas (Ramutsindela 2004: 108), and those anxieties effectively
trump the recognition of communities, past and present. Conservationist capital
assumes a triple resignification for Escobar (2008: 105): nature is recast as a biodiversity reserve, local communities are enticed to be stewards of nature, and local
knowledge is retrofitted to save nature. In reality biodiversity's immediate beneficiaries are often few and occluded.

The Paris Declaration on Biodiversity (2005) describes it is a "source of aesthetic, spiritual, cultural, and recreational values; it provides goods that have direct
use values, such as food, wood, textiles and pharmaceuticals; it supports and
enhances ecosystem services on which human societies depend and provides
opportunities for human societies to adapt to changing needs and circumstances,
and discover new products and technologies." These are far-reaching and, importantly, integrated aims between nature and culture. For SANParks the significant
social benefits of biodiversity are greatly stressed across interviews and public
forums in which park managers and scientists participate, yet individually many
feel that these assets cannot and should not provide benefits for communities
bordering the park who were the original custodians of the land. The socially
responsible dimensions of the Paris Declaration are useful in garnering public
support for Kruger's core mandate but are ultimately elided in the practice and
management philosophy of the park. In one chilling interview a senior official
argued that raising the living standards of impoverished communities on the

park's edge would only result in greater needs, whether food, wood, or electricity. Her strategy was one of deception and disregard: communities should be kept ignorant of what Kruger possesses so that there will be no such requests. For such powerful decision makers in Kruger's future environmental responsibility, ecological apartheid can still be operationalized through the lofty goals of biodiversity and conservation.

Biological diversity promises enormous benefits and, increasingly, poverty reduction. It is globally promoted as crucial for human well-being by organizations like the UNEP listing deliverables such as pharmaceuticals, tourism, employment, carbon emissions offset, food, and fuel (Secretariat of the Convention on Biological Diversity 2009: 7). South African experts purport that savannahs provide wood, medicines, and food; freshwater contributes fish; and nature-based tourism comprises 5 percent of the nation's GDP (Gibson *et al.* 2008: 191). These are exactly the same resources that are requested by communities bordering the park and that are regularly denied on the circular logic of diminishing biodiversity. So communities are being coerced on the basis of projected benefits that they will rarely, if ever, receive. Some in Kruger sidestep the issue benefits by arguing that conservation and poverty are quite different problems and that parks cannot be held responsible for tackling the global challenge of poverty. Without concrete evidence that protected areas contribute to the livelihoods of the poor, this sets up biodiversity conservation as a constraint on poverty alleviation, not a means to achieve it (Adams and Hutton 2007: 164). Instead, the ethical mandate to protect this biodiversity for the good of humanity is held up as a moral imperative that can legitimately transcend local rights (West 2006: 179–80). Biodiversity comes to work in other ways for South Africa, not long ago a pariah state on the world stage, by offering a new suite of benefits for ecologists and the conservation lobby. It bestows modernity and international connections, ensures support and funding, is profit oriented, both scientific and moral, and seemingly bypasses racial divisions while attempting to address with poverty and inequality. In South Africa biodiversity is forward looking, it does not dwell on the nation's past, makes little reference to historical processes, and attempts to nullify restitution, including land claims, for a presumed planetary good. These are just some of the reasons why parks authorities, whether black or white, find these more pressing concerns than that of alternative histories, cultural heritage, natural resource sharing, or community issues. I would argue that unless some balance with history is achieved alongside real benefit sharing, the ideals of conservation and diversity remain imperiled.

Conservation is not simply about sustainable nature or moral worth; it has come to signify global goods and services whether the setting is Africa, Latin America, or Europe. Escobar (2008: 143) opines that biodiversity discourse is an elegant gimmick for the continued exploitation of nature by capital. This trend is observable in countries like Costa Rica where "green consumerism" opportunities and corporate standards, not government action, have spearheaded environmental protection. Here forest protection is closely aligned to biodiversity conservation, watershed protection, and carbon trading, thereby constituting a neoliberal arena that promotes payments for environmental services (Liverman and Vilas 2006: 344). In the 1970s Mario Boza, the first director of Costa Rica's national parks system, helped establish a private, nonprofit foundation to attract and manage international resources with the intent of sidestepping "bureaucratic red tape involved when the central government receives and uses donated funds" (Pearson 2009: 721). The most well-known parastatal environmental organization in Costa Rica is INBio. Combining state and private bodies, INBio operates by market principles but has access to public biodiversity resources. International attention may have focused on bioprospecting contracts yet, like South Africa, Costa Rica's vision of neoliberal nature is also entrenched in inventorying biodiversity and promoting environmental education (Pearson 2009: 722)

National Parks, Peace Parks, and protected areas are firmly rooted in a capitalist system that benefits nation states and corporations alike. Nature is increasingly neoliberalized and can be routinely re-regulated for commodification (Igoe and Brockington 2007). Marketing campaigns by SANParks and the GLTP for the 2010 Soccer World Cup hope to capitalize upon this very potential through new foreign injection (Büscher and Dressler 2007). During my visit in 2009 countless items of clothing and camping equipment brandished the World Cup logo, but the exact linkage between biodiversity and soccer remained puzzling. Neoliberal conservation aims for more than just an economic win–win equation, it hopes to benefit corporate investors, national economies, biodiversity, local people, Western consumers, development agencies, and conservation organizations (Igoe and Brockington 2007: 435). More cynically, we could point to key members in prominent conservation agencies from the GLTP and WWF to the Nature Conservancy, who are either engaged in or close to industries like mining, logging, and dam building and are thus working towards corporate interests rather than communities (Brockington 2009: 114–16). Big conservation is increasingly embedded in transnational spaces, enclaved environmental resources, declining state authorities, and increased militarization and coercion (Ferguson 2006: 46). From a more positive perspective, paralleling the notion of cultural heritage uplift, nature is increasingly administered as a healing force. Here again nature is lauded for its spiritual benefits, not simply its economic promise. Such heritage is not reducible to the goods of individuals nor is it a *means* to the good, rather it *constitutes* the good (Ivison 2002: 59).

SANParks has an explicit management plan following the National Protected Areas Act (57 of 2003), which places biodiversity at the top of their core mandate. This is framed by SANParks in terms of "Biodiversity Values." The use of the term "values" implies that biodiversity extends beyond scientific enquiry to arenas of a more social or moral human nature. From a governmental perspective, the understanding and operationalization of biodiversity has essentially been hitched to other modes of transitional development in South Africa: "Biodiversity understanding and management must reflect the social imperatives (e.g., transformation, equity, efficiency, empowerment, growth) of an emerging African democracy" (South African National Parks 2005a). Thus, the implementation of environmental programs and the creation of environmental citizens have been explicitly positioned as a national good. Specters of crisis and urgency underwrite the language of "building co-operation" and reveal a didactic plan for subjects outside the park, whereas "compliance auditing" may well refer to those within the park's working boundaries. "We strive for continuous, and co-operative, improvement of public perception of our rationale for conservation practice and beneficiation of biodiversity / ecosystem services" (South African National Parks 2005a). "Public perception" is key, not necessarily public delivery. In the meetings I attended at Skukuza between scientists and section rangers, language laced with biological or environmental overtones also functioned to create a sense of the overarching scientific and moral mandate that superseded the needs of individuals or communities. Scientists acknowledged the thorny, if not weedy, debate over what is deemed *natural* or *unnatural* about Kruger, and yet they chose to retain the word *natural*. There was a reflexive concern, some might say masking, in avoiding terms like "designer vegetation communities" to describe the processes that have led to Kruger's current landscape. Some members of Scientific Services also prefer the word "wildness," instead of "wilderness," arguing that the latter is an aesthetic judgment.

Wilderness is a richly laden concept that emerges after the forces of industrialization and urbanization require a wild nature in both economic and intellectual terms. Impelled by specifically American visions of the frontier, the loss of the wild was considered detrimental to North American identity, particularly masculinity. Such imaginings were easily transposed onto Africa since the continent could still boast large mammals (not hunted to extinction as elsewhere); it was considered more natural, wild, and remote, and traditional lifeways were still practiced by indigenous people who were themselves considered "natural" against the backdrop of the metropole (Adams 2003a: 34–5; Neumann 1997; Wolmer 2005). What shifted during the mid-twentieth century was the idea that indigenous Africans who were once acceptable as part of the landscape were now considered a threat to nature and to colonial rule: hunting became poaching, collecting or harvesting became law-breaking, and farming threatened conservation (Neumann 1997; 1998). This tension between acknowledging the human social past, and even more recently celebrating traditional methods (Masuku Van Damme and Neluvhalani 2004), while still securing protectionism and bolstering biodiversity goals, remains unresolved in the organization of SANParks. This impasse was astutely observed by one resident of Welverdiend who protested, "they will never make us love these natural resources by arresting us."

Kruger's management "implies a 'minimum interference' philosophy except where anthropogenic influences warrant direct, even severe, interference to achieve a biodiversity custodianship mandate" (South African National Parks 2005b). This might include controlled firing practices by rangers to provide bushfire buffers or more dramatic programs such as the species culling. Kruger's managers might sell animals or kill them and stockpile ivory (some 48 tons), employing various justifications, whereas indigenous communities may not. National Parks, such as Kruger, are

> a storage house of ecosystem goods and services, and cultural resources. These may be sustainably utilised as long as this use does not compromise the biodiversity mandate for that national park. A policy and strategy for this use must be developed. It would consider *inter alia* issues of game capture, translocation and sales, culling, alien biota control (not in itself a sustainable practice but an important cog in sustaining biodiversity), and management of cultural resources associated with the biodiversity estate. (South African National Parks 2005b)

Talking about the *need* for a policy has supplanted the development and implementation of a policy and in effect produced the desired outcome for park policy makers.

Recently the mantle of scientific truth has come under fire, most notably with the planned elephant "cull" of several thousand animals and the public outrage (van Noort 2005a; 2005b) over the purported necessity of "killing" for the sake of biodiversity. Elephants, as the archetypal charismatic mammals, are powerful symbols that have come to stand for Africa itself (Fortmann 2005; Garland 2008), and their protection and management has become highly charged in the public arena. Trapped between two discourses of salvage for the global commons, saving "endangered" fauna or saving biodiversity, SANParks has struggled to stay credible, particularly in light of the admission that elephant numbers cannot be scientifically marshaled to determine the degree of diversity loss, only to hypothesize the possibility of loss. The mere suggestion that something called "biodiversity" might indeed be a cultural construct remains one of the sure-fire ways I can induce my colleagues in Scientific Services into a heated debate.

Permitting communities to enter Kruger to access resources has not been considered feasible, whereas the converse has been more readily adopted. Representatives from Kruger have gone into buffer communities and told people to cut down their mango trees because they are an invasive species. They might indeed compromise Kruger's biodiversity mission but such callous demands ignore that mangoes offer one source of nutrition in these impoverished villages and can also be sold to generate a meager income. Entreating communities to conserve nature and combat diversity loss, global warming, or alien biota should not become the new *sjambok* to whip Africa into line (Mavhunga 2007: 441). Ever-narrowing subsets of acceptable nature repeatedly push humans further out, except as subjects for management science to regulate, effecting a radical purification of nature (Cruikshank 2005: 258). This is marked by the current fixation upon invasive species, now a vast, somewhat paranoid issue in South Africa and globally (Beinart and Middleton 2004; Clark 2002). This is matched by concerns over ecosystem domination by aggressive super-species, no less. The bio-invasion of especially "thirsty" foreign species such as Black Wattle, Hakea, Lantana, and Jacaranda poses a significant threat to the native flora and they have been attacked using biological agents and even targeted burning from aircraft. Couched in the language of alien invasion, foreign plants and fish were a consistent concern in the fraught meetings between scientists and rangers because they impinged on South African biodiversity. One scientist said the unsayable – these migrating and threatening organisms were like Mozambicans illegally crossing into South Africa through the park. Extensive programs for the eradication of alien biota utilize dramatic and violent techniques, and the insinuation of any parallelism was chilling in light of the park's covert activities during the apartheid years (Meskell 2006a). Translocated biological life whether human, animal or plant (Clark 2002), is unwelcome. In the current climate of xenophobia, migrants from bordering countries are viewed as pariahs (*kwerekwere*) in the emergent nation, taking jobs, bringing AIDS, and so on (Comaroff and Comaroff 2001). To invoke the Afrikaans word *deurloper* (through walkers) as one ranger did, reminds us of the racist history that Kruger National Park has yet to slough off. But more generally these sentiments reflect the view that any socio-historical human presence, outside the prescribed enclaves of research and tourism, is undesirable and must be eradicated – and even the latter is scarcely tolerated out of fiscal necessity.

Building on Foucault's notion of governmentality, the notion of "environmentality" offers a provocative terrain for investigation into SANParks recasting under the ANC, particularly in terms of the kinds of subjects and subjectivity implied therein. Following Agrawal (2005: 166), I use the term "environmentality" here to denote a framework of understanding in which technologies of self and power are involved in the fashioning of new environmental subjects. However, it is in the interstices, between the efforts of subjects and the consolidation of institutional power, which proves most telling. Hayden (2003: 83) rightly asks what kind of participation and subjectivity is being recognized, impelled, forged, and articulated through the promise of biodiversity. SANParks has preferred didactic programs of environmental education whether "Kids in Kruger" or "Keep Kruger Clean," which are all aimed at training black South African youth to be good environmental citizens. During a 2006 campaign, Kruger's Director Bundile Mkhize sermonized that "cleanliness was next to godliness" to hundreds of black people with garbage bags at the ready to do their part to clean the park (Figure 4.2). Instead they were assembled on the road immediately adjacent to the entrance rather than actually in the bush. More bizarrely, "fake" garbage had been poured out in front of them moments before, making the entire exercise staged and futile. Later I was told by local elders that building "contractors take rubbish from the park and dump it outside in our communities, this happens regularly and those working at the gates have told them, the trucks have come from inside. And then they have cleaning campaigns but *inside* the park. It's a problem with the management."

Figure 4.2   Photograph of Keep Kruger Clean Campaign. Courtesy of the author.

   Salvage politics are typically united by incentives of common goods and depend upon webs of participation, compensation, discipline, and sacrifice that discursively shape desirable heritage citizens. In an Orwellian tone, interventionist policies that control the past also serve to predict future outcomes, promising sustainable development, betterment, and socio-economic uplift. What must be sublated in the present will be recouped in the future by coming generations, while international elites and the adequately resourced will be able to enjoy the spoils of conservation and heritage in the present in the form of cultural and ecological tourism and research. Such promissory strategies tend to de-privilege indigenous and minority communities, the disempowered constituencies whose land, livelihood, and legacies have been appropriated. While good environmental subjects are strongly desired, with an emphasis on the indigenous populations surrounding Kruger Park, their own knowledges and practices cannot be interpolated into park management strategies. Gradually, some within the organization are recognizing their programmatic deficits, recognizing that "biodiversity means nothing to rural people if it does not mean something on a day-to-day basis. If their demands are not addressed, biodiversity conservation will never become their priority" (Hendricks 2005: 4).
   At a major meeting to discuss new national policy concerning benefit sharing, one senior scientist attempted to

> dispel the myth that black people are smashing up their own lands – never mind that they were crowded in there in a bloody iniquitous system for over twenty years, and all the insults that happened on all the landscape because of all the people being put there and all that bloody history – the point is that it is unbelievably resilient.

Naturally I am drawn to the invocation of "bloody history," yet the real issue in this excerpt is the *resilience* of bordering communities. Another ecologist insists that if buffer communities had "been on a bed of shales then it would have been totally trashed. But because it's on granite, the system functions in a way that will actually creep back up in 10 to 15 years." Framed in this way, geopolitical reasoning both explains their victimhood and abrogates responsibility for the plight of communities because their now depleted environments are adaptive and can potentially regenerate. Given the lengthy timescales involved, the effects of "bloody history" can be seen as transitory and epiphenomenal.

Ecosystem resilience is the capacity of an ecosystem to tolerate disturbance without collapsing into a qualitatively different state.[1] A resilient ecosystem is one that can withstand shocks and rebuild itself when necessary. Resilience in social systems has the added capacity of humans to anticipate and plan for the future. This thinking has led to the creation of the Resilience Alliance and its spin-off, Panarchy. Panarchy, which was first developed to describe global governance, encapsulates the precept that changes within the system – whether they are economic, ecological, or social – are evolutionary, transformative, and adaptive. It has since been adopted by some ecologists to rationalize the interplay between change and persistence, between the predictable and unpredictable,[2] all of which is rather obvious and descriptive rather than explanatory. Ecological science has been used to generate technocratic recipes for managing nature and has coined terms and concepts drawn from thermodynamics and engineering, such as system, energetics, equilibrium, and feedback, to describe nature. Conservationists, schooled in ecology, see themselves in some senses as "engineers of nature" (Adams 2003b: 224–5). A small number of archaeologists have been influenced by the Resilience Alliance and Panarchy (Redman 2005; Redman and Kinzig 2003), mainly olderstyled processual archaeologists who once sought environmental determinants to explain social change and have transformed their concerns into those of sustainability, adaptation, and degradation.

Irrespective of our own scholarly debates, many of the poorest people I interviewed do not understand what biodiversity entails, and yet most representatives of SANParks believe that they do and are largely supportive of this united venture (Meskell 2006a). While targeting schoolchildren has been the park's priority, one boy explained that Kruger was for foreign tourists who had killed all the animals in their own countries and so needed to come to Africa to see theirs. In a recent survey of 100 respondents in nearby Makoko, 81 percent of people were found to believe that Kruger exists for tourists, 73 percent, that the land is used by park employees for grazing their own livestock (Rademan 2004: 139). Most see little or no social or economic benefits from having one of the world's great conservation enclaves on their doorstep (Saayman and Saayman 2006), rather, they applaud the more tangible benefits provided by private reserves such as those run by AndBeyond. Moreover, people living on the edge of the park clearly understand that hunting in nearby private game farms by rich tourists is differently configured to traditional hunting practices. The taxonomies of "hunting" for sport or survival might seem porous to an outsider, but have serious legal ramifications to those who once lived inside the park and are now very much on the outside. One man, jailed numerous times for poaching in Kruger put it well. "It's all about money, who can afford to hunt and who cannot." He connected this immediately to the indices of race and power; being black means that killing an animal has different significations and ramifications. How might such "disaffected" individuals, the bad subjects of conservation, and their descendents be brought into line, so to speak, with preservationist efforts?

In 2005 four black Kruger employees were fired for killing several impala in a laundry compound at Skukuza, and talk of the scandal spread like wildfire across the park. They were then handed over to the police on charges of poaching, illegal hunting, and possession of a wild animal's carcass (*Mail & Guardian* 2005b). One employee explained it in terms of hunger. He recounted angrily that SANParks does not pay people properly, particularly the most lowly ranked general workers such as these men. The irony that tourists can buy impala hide products or impala pâté at the Skukuza store and then eat the meat at the park restaurant was lost on most of my colleagues. Kruger's own *Annual Reports* demonstrate that over the years more impala have been shot to feed black workers like these men than was ever killed by poachers. Food rations have long been given to black (not white) workers as wages. When elephant culls are underway the animals are butchered in mobile abattoirs and distributed as rations to black workers and sold cheaply to poor communities bordering Kruger. White rangers continue to kill impala and either consume them or feed them to their dogs. Some rangers flaunt the rules further by keeping hunting dogs and training them in the park. One ranger gave an impassioned speech about a warthog killed by locals then in the next breath went on to describe how he hunts warthog on a farm nearby. This leads one to ask what is the difference between poaching and culling around Kruger, if not the fine line represented by a fence? Bad subjects start at home.

Dreams of *Terra Nullius*

Biodiversity is viewed today as an ecological workhorse, an essential raw material for evolution, a sustainable economic resource, a font of aesthetic and ecological value, a global heritage, genetic capital, and the key to the survival of life itself (Hayden 2003: 52). Given this enormous potential and the future-geared, promise-based rhetorics of rescue, is it surprising that archaeological pasts seem weary and moribund ruins that are not living up to their earning potential? Perhaps as a result of this lack of interest, and given the recent volatile struggles over land claims in Kruger and elsewhere, narratives of *terra nullius* or "empty lands" have resurfaced in dangerous and familiar ways. The now discredited discourse is coupled with celebratory discourses of conservation and biodiversity in interesting ways, as both pertain to global desires for pristine wilderness, minimal human intensification, the erasure of anthropogenic landscapes, the primacy of non-human species and future generations. Without recognition of the complex and continued human history in Kruger's landscapes there is little chance of historical justice and restitution for black South Africans.

John Locke is largely blameworthy for the trope of *res nullius*, the idea of the globe as a common possession that effectively disregards historically existing property rights. In his philosophy, *private property* follows from *private appropriation*, namely from the work of one's hands, the labor of one's body, and so on. European expansion deployed Locke's treatise to justify colonial appropriation of lands. In the first instance, indigenous lands were considered given to all "in common." Secondly, they were worked by the industrious and thrifty (read "European") for the benefit of all and so were doubly possessed (Benhabib 2004: 31). Just as native fauna in South African have been proclaimed *res nullius*, or belonging to no one, Kruger has been branded as *terra nullius*, a land empty before the onset of white exploration and settlement. An attendant moral absolutism attaches to *terra nullius*, as it does to the constructs of nature and wilderness, with humanity being oppositional and negatively juxtaposed. Nature, in this binary equation, is intrinsically valued, whereas people and their material histories are intrusive, destructive, artificial, and devalued (Soper 2000: 19). Deep ecology and green politics have further bolstered these hierarchies, divisions, and narratives of blame (Cock 2007: 49). Despite the Green Movement's nods to indigenous knowledge and participation, the remnants of colonial conservation ideologies remain. Neutral nature is seen to trump the greed, waste, and devastation of people and societies, past and present.

Narratives of *terra nullius* hitch to the imaginings of powerful international bodies and regulations including the WWF, UN, IUCN, and the Convention on International Trade in Endangered Species of Wild Flora and Fauna (CITES), who want to privilege and preserve flora and fauna over and above people (or even the evidence of people) in the name of the global commons. They are distinct yet related discourses and both are enshrined in a "protected areas" strategy developed largely from a US model of national parks and wilderness reserves that historically separated humans and nature, nature and culture (Adams and Mulligan 2003b: 10). Separation has meant that nature is destroyed in productive spaces and culture is erased from the leisured spaces of parks (Shetler 2007: 236). More and more nature is designated a special precinct to be protected from livelihood-linked activities, and although nature's territory is expanding, our theorizing remains conceptually thin (Zerner 2003: 56). Human occupation and intensification is negatively inflected from the outset, whether in pre-colonial, colonial, or postcolonial contexts, and classified alongside hunting, mining, deforestation, resource depletion, and so on.

Biodiversity and conservation may today be global constructs, but they are imagined in South Africa in very specific, historically charged ways. Myths of emptiness have been vigorously dismantled in Australia and North America yet they have significant resilience in South Africa whether through lack of education or the association of archaeology with the apartheid state. Whatever the causes, Kruger's indigenous history remains a deep wound in the landscape and one that is painfully ever present for the indigenous communities that live on Kruger's borders (see also Mavhunga 2002). Equally, Ranger's Zimbabwean fieldwork has illustrated that the Matopos landscape has a rich human history and that only in the light of this can the scenery itself be understood (Ranger 1999: 289). Whites emphasized the natural heritage of the Matopos, while those struggling for freedom emphasized black cultural rights. Like South Africa, the settler version of history supported the myth of wilderness conquest. Indigenous groups have the most to lose, or win, in the recognition and restitution that might logically follow acknowledgment of history. Without an admission of the human past, recognition premised upon historical and genealogical grounds cannot move forward in the present. In cosmopolitan terms we need to counter South Africa's continued residual racism that implies that certain people do not matter (Appiah 2006: 153).

To underline the continued diminished position of the archaeological past I draw upon its recent rendering in Kruger National Park's public documents. It is puzzling that in 2010 they still claim that,

> Bantu people entered about 800 years ago, gradually displacing the San. The available evidence suggests that humans occurred at low density and were mostly confined to the more permanent river-courses. It is reasonable to assume from the continuous presence at some sites that humans and wildlife existed in harmony, with no major impact of humans on wildlife or the reverse. The arid nature of the environment, together with an abundance of predators and diseases would have played a role in preventing large-scale human population growth and settlement. Nevertheless, sophisticated cultures already existed by the 16th century.[3]

The first myth is that Bantu-speakers (read "black Africans") arrived at the recent date of 800 years ago, which is challenged by archaeological evidence that suggests their advent at least two millennia ago (Mitchell 2002a, see Chapter 3). The former still participates in the apartheid mythology of concurrent arrival of black and white immigrants in South Africa, specifically when they reached the Western Cape. These deeply flawed constructions of history and culture have had a lasting legacy, felt to this day, but most palpably felt over the apartheid years since they were used to create racial hierarchies and structure unequal living experiences for both black and white South Africans.

Second, the myth of low density is highly speculative as so little systematic park-wide fieldwork was done during the apartheid regime. Moreover, the archaeology within the park – for example, the Iron Age sites of Thulamela, Makhahane, Shilowa, and Masorini – suggests significant industrial activity and occupation. These are material facts that are never engaged with, even by the researchers in Scientific Services or the foreign scientists who come to conduct research on the flora and fauna of the park. For the scientific community in Kruger, population density is determined teleologically: not by archaeological investigation but by current observations about impacts and modifications on the landscape. As Hayashida points out,

> because of the time lag in ecosystem response to disturbance and environmental change, current ecosystem structure, function, and composition cannot be fully understood or explained without a historical perspective. The lasting effects of past human actions (termed "land-use legacies") include changes in species composition, successional dynamics, soils, water, topography, and nutrient cycling. Many seemingly natural areas have a cultural past that is part of their ecological history; their conservation today requires knowledge of that past and assessment of the value of continuing or replicating past cultural practices. (2005: 45)

Given the forced relocations of people who lived in the park over the last century, the determined efforts to re-instate something imagined as a pristine wilderness, and the absence of any serious systematic archaeological survey, the lack of substantive human trace is undoubtedly in the eye of the beholder. Yet we can say there are over a thousand sites across Kruger's vast expanse: early hominid, Paleolithic, San rock art, Iron Age, historic, and recent. Even under National Party rule several publications recorded early and continued black history in the park, documentation of early European explorers passing through their territories (Punt 1975). More than 170 historic place names have survived to reflect indigenous settlement, industrial sites or sacred places (Kloppers and Bornman 2005; van Warmelo 1961), undoubtedly a mere fraction of the original. Even when the first warden, Stevenson-Hamilton, published *The Low-Veld and its People* (1929) a significant proportion of his book was devoted to African inhabitants across the park and their recent history. These histories too have been gradually sidelined or forgotten.

The third myth is the apartheid fable of aridity and predator activity that is the specious basis for the purported low population and lack of landscape modification. Archaeological evidence and new palaeo-environmental research challenge this picture (see Chapter 3). SANParks must dismantle the devastating myths of empty lands and late arrivals that de-privilege indigenous South Africans and erase their historic achievements in the materiality of the past and present. There is a growing movement that recognizes that even at colonial contact many landscapes were as fully anthropogenic as those found in Europe (Clark 2002; Lane 2009; Shetler 2007). Recognition of this point would, however, be troubling for the mandate and ambition of SANParks, which needs to preserve the more barren notion of Kruger as predominantly pristine. While culture is all about fluidity and movement, nature is ideally meant to stand still.

I find myself asking why the peopled past is so problematic in Kruger's landscape, even after the apartheid years. During 2005 I was asked to participate briefly in a collaborative interdisciplinary project about disease landscapes in Kruger, this time assuming my role as an archaeologist. When I presented the established evidence for early and continued human occupation in the region it was greeted as both unheard of and unwelcome. Eagerly I pointed to their own apartheid-era Parks Board publication from the 1970s that assembled historical accounts of the first Europeans in the area and their encounters with significant black populations (see Punt 1975). My first invitation to the project meeting was also, significantly, my last. Others note that archaeological and historical evidence is deemed peripheral or speculative at best in the face of biophysical science. Carruthers (2006: 817) believes that conservation managers use simple stories about the past to bolster policy, but remain reticent about conducting historical analysis, are ignorant of historical context, wary of professional historians, and unsure of how best to combine the humanities and conservation science. And there are other foundational reasons why the past remains problematic: years of sedimented disinterest within the nation; the lack of any archaeologists employed in SANParks or within Kruger; the prioritization of the biophysical sciences; researchers, rangers, and trackers who have other tasks and no interest in cultural resources; and the residual inertia of racism and lack of education. There is a long way to go in terms of site management, tourism development, the upgrading of museums and displays, curation, the creation of inventories, and even the securing of the return of archaeological objects from other institutions. Positive steps are gradually being taken, but the disparity between management of nature and culture remains salient. The work of heritage in South Africa is always in process, it is future perfect.

When interviewed, the then Director of Kruger National Park revealed that he had never visited the nationally celebrated site of Thulamela and, when pressed on the scale of Kruger's cultural heritage, resorted to stock answers from the park's Public Relations materials. With its impressive stone walls and dramatic discoveries of smelted gold, the site has been used in speeches by cabinet ministers and presidents (Jordan 1996), and yet it has quickly fallen from public and park interest. There exists a general feeling that safari tourism featuring charismatic mammals (faced with the threat and danger and extinction), offers a more reliable fiscal return. The success of the UNESCO uKhahlamba-Drakensberg Park, under the management of Ezemvelo KZN Wildlife not SANParks, with its rich rock art and heritage ecotourism suggests that culture can be successfully capitalized upon in South Africa. One can easily imagine apartheid park wardens and administrators privileging nature and wilderness at the expense of the historical cultural achievements of the black South Africans they victimized. Less easily envisaged is that the recent black ANC management has similarly chosen to sideline archaeological heritage and marginalize human history within the park, which is palpably felt by communities along the park's edge. Willingness to address the past, or better still, to ethically recount its specificities, is a necessary condition for justice and reconciliation in the present. But as indicated here, people of various political commitments and affiliations in South Africa today disagree profoundly over the details and consequences of historic injustices for thinking about future reparation. It impinges upon our respective notions of justice, and those of responsibility, freedom, and identity (Ivison 2002: 93–4). More than half of Kruger's land is now "threatened" by indigenous claimants in South African courts, and since Kruger is the jewel in the crown of African parks, and the most financially viable national park across the nation, black management is in a predicament. Public debate is volatile regarding conservation areas, justice, identity politics, and common goods (see Chapter 7).

Historical injustice goes hand in hand with reparations, of which Ivison (2006) outlines three modes: restitution, compensation, and recognition or acknowledgement. These can take the practical forms of financial payment, apologies, affirmative action, constitutional provisions, and so on. Most importantly, recognition acknowledges the victims and the harm enacted against them and involves the act of restoring or compensating those who have suffered. Recognition can also take the form of public apologies and forms of collective remembrance, as has become commonplace in post-apartheid South Africa; these are themselves political acts. Around Kruger numerous communities have petitioned for various kinds of reparation. For example, some, like the Mkhabela clan, have suggested a change in the name of the Numbi park gate to Nyongane, a symbolic change that would cost little in financial terms. They have asked for acknowledgment of the burials of their elders and some 350 cattle situated within the new borders of the park (see Chapter 3). The Malatji have been more vigorous in launching a land claim that will entail land transfer or a financial compensation (see Chapter 5). While not all reparations are costly or financial they do overturn the fiction of *terra nullius*. Legitimate procedure is crucial to these ongoing processes of reconciliation and potential restitution. The challenge for postcolonial liberalism, as Duncan Ivison argues (2002: 22), is to orient ourselves toward the local, while similarly providing an account of the conditions and institutions that distinguish this effort from merely deferring to existing power relations. This seems key in an emergent nation like South Africa where regime change may have ousted segregation but has failed to combat issues of class and race that remain central vectors of inequality.

Skukuza: Nation without History

Many authors have pointed to the continued colonial, national, and governmental overtones of conservation and biodiversity management (e.g., Adams and McShane

1996; Adams and Mulligan 2003a; Brockington 2004; Duffy 2002; Greenenough and Tsing 2003; Honey 1999; Keller and Turek 1998; Moore 1998; 2005; Moore, Kosek, and Pandian 2003; Neumann 1998; West 2006). Some impute that, discursively, biodiversity does not exist, rather it conveniently "anchors a discourse that articulates a new relation between nature and society in global contexts of science, cultures, and economies" (Escobar 1998: 55). Yet much of its networks of models, actors, theories, strategies, and objects, remain hegemonic. Kruger is reliant on international funding agencies, philanthropy and donor aid, and NGO assistance: it operates on American and European support. The organization is also cumbersomely bureaucratic and juridical, with its own policing and border enforcement powers. Big conservation has had to embrace big business, and this is reflected in SANParks post-1994 corporate structure and mission. Kruger sometimes flirts with the notion of development, embarks on education programs for HIV/AIDS, and minimally entertains notions of sustainable resource use. Is it any wonder that various researchers from very different disciplines describe Kruger's workings as "schizophrenic"? During my own fieldwork I have continually struggled to find coherence in the philosophies and management strategies for natural and cultural heritage within the park. Kruger is a lumbering beast that refuses to be brought into line with the nation's other parks and the wider organization of SANParks. Its history of triumphal nationalist conservation coupled with long-term successful policies of human removal and erasure has made it near impervious to development and, ironically, adaptation.

Over the years I have come to view Kruger National Park as a state within a nation. One park official explained her idea for a passport system with entry stamps for Kruger and, despite the obvious marketing ploy, she had succinctly captured the nationalist spirit of the place. Kruger is psychically over-determined in the white South African imaginary. According to the influential left-leaning *Mail & Guardian* newspaper, "it is an irreplaceable repository of the pre-colonial environment, the nearest thing we have to South Africa before the arrival of the Dutch and British. As such, it is as deserving of preservation as Mapungubwe or the remains of Tswana Iron Age settlements. Conservation in South Africa is a nationalist issue" (2005c: 24). This perplexing position indirectly foregrounds the importance of black heritage and at the same time attacks human activity. Segregating nature and culture in this conundrum of modernity tells the story both ways: tradition saves nature, tradition destroys nature (Tsing 2005: 254). The fact that white colonists destroyed a landscape shaped by Africans is then turned against their descendents, who now claim that same land back as their right. There is no mention of the archaeological sites in Kruger like Thulamela, but instead those far afield like Mapungubwe. Furthermore, "Kruger must be seen as a precious custodian of biodiversity on a continent where indigenous wildlife is under acute threat . . . Like the Amazon rain forest, it is a heritage held in trust for all humanity" (*Mail & Guardian* 2005c: 24). The nature we are most likely to hear about today, writes Cruikshank (2005), is increasingly presented as endangered, pristine, or biodiverse, excluding other ways of seeing and making it more difficult to appreciate unfamiliar points of view. We cannot dislodge the view that certain landscapes are natural because we have been trained to expect a particular vision through centuries of painting, poetry, literature, and landscape design (Neumann 1998: 10). Environmental politics like those expressed in the *Mail & Guardian* buttress the idea that wilderness can be re-imagined as uncontaminated by humans.

In asking why diverse nature might offer a more compelling suite of possibilities for South Africans than cultural diversity and preservation, a number of differences are laid bare. Nature is considered neutral, supra-racial, existing and entreating protection beyond race: it can be embraced by the new, multicultural concept of South Africa as the Rainbow Nation (Meskell 2005b; 2006b). Nature is immediately legible with real-time collective consequences for the planet if we fail to meet our protective agendas. Thus, a truly cosmopolitan engagement is required, whereas the archaeological and historical past requires decipherment, translation, and education, and is packaged in South Africa as peculiarly local. Cultural heritage is identity-specific, factional, and, while seemingly important for crafting a new national identity, archaeological remains are currently configured to particular communities in partial, exclusionary, and politically divisive ways. Multiple-stakeholder sharing of the past can be understandably difficult given the repressive histories of colonial and apartheid rule. Species diversity is universally recognized and consumed, irrespective of race, nation, religion, gender, ethnicity, and so on. It is also globally supported by an organizational and fiscal infrastructure that further operates an index of modernity, civilization, and alignments to First World priorities. The language and scope of biodiversity is inherently modern, neoliberal in ethos, and positively configured as scientific, sustainable, developmental, and experimental. Nature has increasingly been treated by development agencies, national governments in the north and south, organizations regulating global trade, and some conservationists, as a public good in the name of one worldism. Private and state-sponsored environmental education programs, especially those targeting schoolchildren, throughout and beyond the borders of Kruger, exemplify these hallowed concerns for creating environmentally right-minded subjects whose primary goal is conservation for the future. The underlying trope is that African adults are beyond repair and are not concerned with conservation (Cock 2007: 56).

Let me finish by reiterating that I understand the grandeur of Kruger National Park and appreciate its many histories and values. This was brought home to me when another Australian, a visiting ecologist, asked me whether I considered Col. James Stevenson-Hamilton a genius for founding Kruger and "leaving us *this*" he exclaimed, looking around wide-eyed. "That is one perspective," I ventured, "another could be offered by the countless residents along the park's edge who saw Skukuza stripping them of their land, their livelihoods and their history." His bemused look suggested he had not entertained these "other" histories of the park. Yet we are beginning to see moves toward a greater balance between natural and cultural values beyond the fence. Bryan Norton suggests that we concentrate more on the natura–cultural dialectic since this might shift focus toward the processes that have created and sustained the species or elements that currently exist, rather than on the species themselves (2005: 188). He believes that this would add to an existing heritage of co-evolution that has shaped both humans and nature. Such a heritage provides a sense of place for communities and nations. The commitment to sustain certain features of one's cultural and natural history is a commitment to an ongoing community and to the place it occupies. Furthermore, he believes that the social sciences, including economics, anthropology, sociology, and political science, must have important research and practical roles to play (Norton 2005: 302). Capturing that social dimension of biodiversity is long awaited in Kruger while natural heritage remains privileged and paramount in the hearts and minds of those who research, manage, and represent the park "for the benefit of all South Africans."

Notes

1   http://www.resalliance.org/ (accessed January 11, 2010).
2   http://www.resalliance.org/593.php (accessed January 11, 2010).
3   http://www.sanparks.org/conservation/transfrontier/great_limpopo.php (accessed January 10, 2010). This same text also appears in the newly commissioned brochures for the GLTP.

Chapter 5

Archaeologies of Failure

We have no right whatever to touch them. They are not ours. They belong partly to those who built them, and partly to all the generations of mankind who are to follow us. The dead have still their right in them. (John Ruskin, *The Lamp of Memory*, 1849)

Perhaps it was my feeling of defeat, or more likely guilt that much of my research was producing a decidedly negative account of transformation and past mastering in Kruger – and an even more starkly depressing view of the place of archaeology since 1994. Toward the end of my field season in Kruger, in 2006, I kept recalling the kindness, generosity, and general interest in my work that so many people had expressed during my years in the park. Park managers, administrators, and scientists in Kruger were always ready to be interviewed; they included me in their meetings and workshops, and made me feel a valued researcher. These were smart, savvy professionals who had always indicated that social science research was part of the core mandate for SANParks – some expressed the opinion that heritage was integral to the overall conservation effort in the new South Africa. Like all ethnographic work, a tension unfolded between what people told me during interviews and what I witnessed in practice. Park authorities spoke eloquently about the importance of heritage, but the on the ground archaeological pasts were held in a general disregard and nature trumped culture at every turn. Charmless heritage sites were an embarrassment not lost on visitors or researchers: neglected sites, derelict displays, and a colonial presentation style. One could dismiss this as ignorance, but hardly malice.

While this story of disregard was crystallizing I was also being pressured to deliver a positive, uplifting narrative of the new democratic state by some of my

The Nature of Heritage: The New South Africa, First Editon. Lynn Meskell.
© 2012 John Wiley & Sons, Inc. Published 2012 by Blackwell Publishing Ltd.

South African colleagues. Then a social event took place that proved formative. It was a farewell party for one of the scientists held in the Staff Village to which scientific services personnel were invited, by which I mean it was a predominantly white event. It was themed as The Kalahari Picnic. This was a fancy dress party where people were requested to come dressed as a ranger, a tourist, an animal, or a "Bushman." A number of senior people decided on the latter. Men and women changed out of their khaki uniforms and into blankets and cheap garments, some wore rattles around their ankles, and the women padded themselves with pillows. Their faces were blackened with cocoa powder, their bodies hunched over walking sticks, and some brandished bottles of cheap South African brandy called Klipdrift. These scientists and conservationists performed their own prejudices about indigenous bodies and movements, mimicking their dancing, and the perceived alcoholism of San communities. Decorating the walls of the neat little village hall were painted panels depicting silhouetted Bushmen against a backdrop of a flaming Kalahari sunset; other panels were decorated with copies of San rock art. I was not invited to attend this stark tableau, rather I heard about it the following day from a colleague who confessed mixed feelings about the event. His own ancestry combined Khoekhoe and colored peoples, and he always occupied an uneasy position in Kruger – not white enough for the apartheid authorities and not black enough for the ANC empowerment schemes.

The institutionalized racism and segregation of apartheid was publicly overturned in the mid-1990s in front of a global audience, whereas the banality of everyday racism and disaffection has proven more difficult to combat. Quotidian racism lies directly under a surface of civility and can be excused as frivolity and good humor; such racisms are often applauded for their honesty in contrast to their counterparts in the United States or Australia where they are often masked or publicly denied. In terms of indigenous history, the Kalahari picnic provided one of the only spaces where archaeological heritage, in the form of rock art, was given any visibility at all, albeit without much recognition that Kruger itself boasts hundreds of rock art sites. The African past thus serves as a gloss or backdrop, metaphorically and literally, for which the real work of nature conservation and biodiversity necessarily takes place.

The ordinariness of racist acts presupposes that individuals possess a complex interiority and make daily choices about their actions (Stoler 2008). When I asked about transformation in the park since apartheid's end, Kruger's senior staff said things like "my role in life is to help black people" or "I socialize with black people." Another claimed to be a "visionary" who "came back to South Africa to help through the transition." Contradictions would gradually emerge through the deeply ingrained perceptions of black people in and around Kruger. One woman told me that she did not care for the way black people lived. Others complained that their neighbors were "not really poor or starving and so we don't think they should have resources, and so we won't make them accessible." Another man feared a "swarm" of black tourists would come to the park even though he was

employed in the tourism sector. What remains in Kruger is the underlying architecture of apartheid that is so difficult to encapsulate, let alone excise. From my
first days in the park I was often warned not to dwell on apartheid history, and
was told repeatedly "we all know this, it's our history, it's not interesting." Another
example of this refusal to confront apartheid's legacy is the continuing failure to
relieve the appalling housing conditions for the poorly paid black workers in
Skukuza and other camps (Meskell 2006a). Hidden behind fences, concealed from
tourist roads and camps, and hardly ever encountered by policy makers, being off
the map fuels the fiction of transformation. Maintaining an "ethical shelter" in
this case also enables park elites to live amidst the starkly drawn socio-economic
inequities of the park – a shelter that does not necessarily extend to others. Many
white South Africans necessarily have to live the "vital lie" (Simmel 1908). They
have to participate in the indispensable untruths and concealments that sustain
orderly social life. I continue to struggle with how best to describe and discuss
these good men and women, many of whom avidly profess not to "see race" or
claim that African heritage is important to the park's mandates. The lie is a social
relationship – a communicative act that requires the compliance of the Kruger
community – and the lie is founded upon a deep history of structured inequalities
that many want to bury.

Unresolved racism and the deep disinterest in Kruger's African past are fundamentally connected. They are never stated and may even appear disconnected in
the minds of park policy makers, scientists, or rangers. However, the few young
SANParks heritage officers I encountered during my research were quick to make
the connection and express their disillusionment in the organization. Race is ever
present, from Lockean fictions of *terra nullius* to the racial profiling of poaching
to differential living conditions, political promotions within the organization, and
the creation of entire directorates like People and Conservation that must deal
largely with black rural poverty. It was these young People and Conservation
representatives who first brought my attention to dog cemeteries being maintained while storerooms of artifacts decayed, skulls were kept in cupboards, and
black histories were progressively lost. They also alerted me to the sub-standard
housing for black workers in Kruger.

As outlined in the previous chapters, cultural heritage is seen as racialized in
ways that natural heritage is not: it looks backwards rather than forwards and
provides fewer obvious tangible benefits. In this chapter I examine two projects
that were initiated within SANParks to highlight diverse heritage and possibly
provide benefits, both of which ultimately faltered: one focused upon Iron Age
archaeology and the other on San rock art. In part they failed because of a lack
of expertise and monitoring, but more significantly because of the uneasy position
that archaeology occupies within the umbrella mission of conservation. Straddling
the secondary aims of community participation, restitution, education, and development, heritage has not yet proved itself to be truly valuable, physically or economically. No matter that politicians have endorsed its potentials, an archaeological

past has fallen short on providing a better future. Of course biodiversity has yet to deliver too, but the promise and the lure are inherently First World, modern, and entrepreneurial. As I go on to argue, attention to the past is compromised not only by the very aspects that have given it such political valence, its African and aspirational associations, but by its positioning as a disciplinary field within SANParks. As we will see, positioning cultural heritage under the People and Conservation directorate and linking it with development and benefits beyond boundaries potentially aligns heritage with community empowerment, land claims, and valuable resource sharing – all of which has become increasingly fraught for the powerful biophysical sciences and conservation lobby. So, paradoxically, the political resonances and uses of heritage in the new South Africa have become their undoing within Kruger.

How exactly is Kruger's rich archaeological heritage placed in a post-1994 landscape, managed as it is by an organization charged with the mandate of biodiversity? Issues that are social or historic, those that involve claims to access, co-management, and reparation, have become flashpoints and unwanted burdens for Kruger. Universalisms like conservation, on the other hand, are seen as constantly opening the way for improving truths and livelihoods (Tsing 2005: 9), despite the fact that they rest upon the same asymmetries that characterize South Africa. Mandating certain forms of environmental progress and coercive participation is a form of neocolonialism, but has gained such global momentum because it embraces various private and public agencies and promises so much that it resists simple critique. Cultural heritage institutions cannot hope to match the private or non-governmental funds of the Nature Conservancy, WWF, IUCN, Peace Parks, Gates Foundation, Packard Foundation, Pew Charitable Trust, Hewlett Foundation, Ford Foundation, and Rockefeller, to name a few that have a specific focus on the global environment. Environmental agendas can be hitched to education or poverty relief, as the McKinsey Report (2002) elucidates, thus allowing SANParks to tap into millions of rands for support. In such a climate, conservation brings major economic injections, political capital, international recognition, ethical participation, and the stamp of First World modernity.

Misadventures at Masorini

Both my archaeological and ethnographic work was administered and facilitated by colleagues in the People and Conservation division, particularly the heritage officer attached to Skukuza. Social ecologists from Letaba or Pafuri regularly assisted and accompanied me during interviews with community members. Over my years in Kruger we often visited the Iron Age site of Masorini (Meskell 2005a) since it was one of only three archaeological sites open for visitors in Kruger.

There was also a vibrant Pedi community bordering Kruger in Makushane, the Malatji, who have declared the site as their own and recently won a land claim on the basis of their forced eviction from 1914 to 1953. The community visits the site every few months and conducts religious rituals annually between September and October. Masorini had been excavated in the 1970s, the reconstruction of the site was typical of its era and the presentation of the site was in desperate need of updating. The site was a terraced hill (*koppie*) with a series of thatched furnaces at ground level and rondavels clustered upon the levels above. From archaeological and visitor perspectives, site presentation was outdated and uninviting. The huts at Masorini were small, cramped structures, and the furnaces were bereft of thatch. Broken pots were strewn around courtyards along with scatters of flints, slag, and other artifacts. The recently constructed site display consisted of an open rondavel exhibiting iron tools and ceramics strewn on tables without proper protection or supervision. A young attendant explained that during his tours when the display was unattended various objects have been stolen; yet no security provisions were made. Tourists would often stop at the adjacent picnic spot to barbeque (*braai*) but many never ventured past the visitor facilities.

Masorini is a set piece in Kruger's charmless heritage. There had been complaints from the Malatji about factual inaccuracies in the dates and locations of activities displayed and, since the thatched huts were in poor condition and incorrectly constructed, park officials agreed the site should be remade in the traditional manner. Archaeology would be the vehicle to employ the Malatji, it would bring new stakeholders into the park and address their concerns, the site would receive its "authentic" facelift and presumably the park would be rewarded with tourist revenues. There was an excitement about these developments, particularly amongst social ecologists and key members of the tribal authority like Bishop and Evans Malatji at Makushane. Masorini's promise reminds me of what one inspired young biophysical researcher opined: "the cultural landscape does not stop at the fence. It's only the artifacts and the sites that are here. But the cultures that include them, they go much further and this is something that we can use as a strong, strong sort of bonding chain between us and the communities."

In June 2004 I visited Masorini with Skukuza's heritage officer in order to check on the progress of community negotiations. To our horror we found great swathes of the site burnt. Black field rangers were still carrying out "controlled" burning when we arrived and the areas around the furnaces were still smoldering. Burning an archaeological site is not the same as when rangers burn fire-breaks or do controlled test burns, nor is it an appropriate "clearance" strategy, although that was the explanation we were given. Stripping and clearing the archaeology and the site reconstructions was exactly the thinking that lay behind these moves. Burning was deemed the most expedient way to rid Masorini of the old wooden superstructures and thatch before new reconstruction could begin. Despite the

Figure 5.1   The remains of burning at Masorini. Courtesy of the author.

concerns we raised, we were assured that only the modern huts were burned. However, I documented patches of burning on the higher terraces where other archaeological materials had been recorded. Expedient erasure did in fact damage the archaeological remains and artifacts that had extensively covered Masorini hill and its vicinity. There are many ways to view this act of instrumental ignorance, as tragedy, as crime, as provocation, as strategy, as stimulus, as obstruction, or as opportunity (Proctor 2009: 24). Disregard for the past, I would suggest, cannot be de-coupled from disregard in the present.

Besides this archaeological clearance, Kruger's section ranger has decided to halt the participation and construction work designated to the Malatji and instead to continue using field rangers to complete the work. The proposed project of employment and stakeholder involvement had foundered. Rangers from Kruger, already paid for their daily duties, were taken off their regular patrols and were put to lashing the poles together for the new huts. It was unclear whether they had the requisite skills to construct the huts traditionally and how the Malatji would respond. The incident left a number of uncomfortable questions, including why the Malatji missed out on the building and thus the remuneration? Whose traditional views were being instantiated here and whose were sidelined? Indeed, how seriously was the park taking its commitments to indigenous collaboration, outreach, and responsible heritage presentation? What began as a promising set of negotiations between Kruger's administration and Makushane had faltered. Skukuza's head office and regional section rangers had different, plausible understandings of procedure, yet good intentions about community development backfired, with dwindling finances cited as the cause. In the discussions that followed, Evans Malatji complained that they had too few people and too little time and, when Kruger did not provide the materials on time, they could not adequately complete the job. What transpired was ostensibly a disagreement between the Malatji in the role of workers and Kruger in the position of boss. While transformation has been central to the upper level of management (Maguranyanga 2009), according to one biophysical scientist, it has been slow to filter down to rangers and guides. On the ground, evidence of transformation can be difficult to detect.

From the park's perspective the decision not to employ community members was purely economic. Social ecologists explained that the Malatji had asked for R27 000 to rebuild each hut and since there were 22 huts this became too expensive. When park officials refused it was then agreed that community members would be paid R10 an hour like the regular park workers. Evans felt that the money was not their prime consideration. The Makushane community was taking control of the project and felt good about the collaboration and would have done the work for an hourly rate of R5 if it meant they could be involved in their own heritage. Later it emerged that certain individuals preferred a monthly wage, some claimed improbable hours, and there was no supervision. Contracts were made with individuals not the community, so follow-up negotiations were hampered. On a more positive note, Evans Malatji conceded that the failure of the project was an organizational matter rather than a racial one and the community members had not experienced discrimination. Generally, I had seen good working relations between social ecologists and the Malatji, but rebuilding Masorini was primarily contracted with the local section ranger and his field staff. At the end of the project we were to see further carelessness as field rangers burnt the remaining construction materials on the site, just as they had burned down the original standing huts to expedite the job. The field rangers were unsupervised, uninterested, and certainly uninformed about Masorini as a heritage site, about the fragility of its landscape and that Kruger's mission of conservation might also extend to cultural remains.

Coupled with the aforementioned events, there were other related episodes of archaeological clearance. At Letaba Camp social ecologists presented us the results of recent field ranger collections: boxes of unprovenanced objects picked up on various walking surveys of the region. It is likely that these Iron Age examples were connected to smelting activities at Masorini, yet all the contextual and spatial information had been irretrievably lost. We were summarily handed these boxes to take back to Skukuza, there was overt lack of interest and casual jokes that they would soon be dumped if we did not retrieve them now. My colleague was visibly upset and attempted to counsel her fellow employees, begging them to record the find spots of archaeological materials with their new Cybertrackers – a handheld device that field rangers carry to notate biophysical conditions. Archaeological finds and landscapes are not, to date, part of this park-wide systematic monitoring. Social ecologists and heritage officers have campaigned unsuccessfully to convince their biophysical colleagues to integrate "culture" into their successful program of natural heritage monitoring, as has been done elsewhere (see Dyson, Hendriks, and Grant 2006; Lepczyk *et al.* 2009). "There are many loose ends within Kruger in terms of cultural management and cultural mapping," a senior policy manager explained, and he complains that social ecologists are now responsible for every-thing from community development to cultural resource management. Moreover, social ecologists typically have only studied to first-degree level, and have done so in nature conservation rather than cultural heritage. There are other reasons why archaeology has fallen short more generally: the history of apartheid archaeology (Hall 1988), inadequate transformation of the discipline (Smith 2009), deficits in education (Shepherd 2003; 2005), the lure of the private sector, lack of adequate staffing and funding, and so on.

Putting Archaeology in its Place

The complex tensions that surround the management of natural and cultural heritage can also be traced through the negotiations around developing San rock art for the purposes of tourism and indigenous development. Historically, the archaeology of African agro-pastoralists proved challenging for South African heritage makers, whereas rock art was perceived as a more appealing option. This was because the San have been romanticized, naturalized, and, more worryingly, they were conveniently considered extinct (see Blundell 2004; Garland and Gordon 1999; Gordon 1992; Prins 2009; Robins 2001; Skotnes 1996; Sylvain 2002; Weiss 2005). In recent years several attempts have been made to publicly showcase the significant paintings within the park, attempts that I have both participated in and observed. Hundreds of rock art sites have been located and mapped, with hun-dreds more awaiting discovery within the two million hectares that comprise the park. There has always been great public interest in San rock art, even during apartheid times, when the San were accorded a "special" status, particularly in national parks. During the 1930s Piet Grobler, the South African Minister of Lands, allowed the San to remain in the Kalahari Gemsbok National Park, but only because they were classified as part of the animal landscape. In 1941 Denys Reitz, the Minister of Native Affairs, claimed that the San were part of South Africa's fauna, they killed fewer antelopes than lions and it was "a crime to let them die out" (cited in Ramutsindela 2003: 43). Such metropolitan romance, according to Tsing (2005: 160), produces the categories by which we know "indigenous people" and "wild nature" and quickly spiral into fantasies around tribal survival, spirituality, and harmonious stability. They have little utility in helping us understand the particular histories of socio-natural landscapes, yet groups holding diverse political affiliations are loath to relinquish them.

Resurgent post-apartheid interest in San heritage and the empowerment of San descendents is exemplified by the collaborative interventions of the Rock Art Research Institute (RARI) at the University of the Witwatersrand (Blundell 1996; 2002; 2004; Smith *et al.* 2000). In the early 2000s RARI funded a rock art field school and training program based at Berg en Dal camp in Kruger's southern sector. The plan was to train rangers and other staff alongside university students in rock art site management and heritage planning. For the fieldwork component of the course they required an armed ranger provided by the park and, since rangers were planned participants, this should have been a straightforward request. But there were problems over ranger participation and even availability. As the days of waiting dragged on it became impossible to begin fieldwork and the project collapsed. More embarrassingly, San descendants were also invited to come to Berg en Dal to discuss new interpretive displays, but no SANParks representatives arrived at the meeting and they too left in disgust.

A second attempt at collaboration was made when RARI was invited to draft a management plan for Kruger. They began by designing an intensive stakeholder survey to maximize collaboration, inclusion, development, and tourism. Just as the previous training initiative foundered so too did attempts by the three young black researchers from RARI to glean information concerning relevant stakeholders, their concerns, ideas, and needs surrounding rock art. These African researchers, from Zimbabwe, Uganda, and Kenya respectively, complained to me of racism and xenophobia during their interactions in and around the park (see Erasmus 2008: 176). They encountered everything from disinterest to resistance from the very people who they were reporting to in SANParks. Some park workers felt threatened that the researchers were there to replace them; others complained that they were indifferent to cultural resources and development projects across Kruger. Arrangements within Kruger were fraught, they told me, meetings with various SANParks representatives were cancelled, they were dissuaded from meeting the director, questionnaires were not distributed at gates and lodges, interviews were sometimes hostile, and access to neighboring communities stalled.

During that period another rock art mapping and development project was granted a SANParks permit, this time led by an elderly retired ranger who had spearheaded the recording of the art some decades ago but lacked any formal training. With support from the People and Conservation unit, and in dialogue with rock art specialists, several walking trails for rock art were proposed. Trails would be led by qualified guides and rangers to ensure the protection of visitors and fragile rock art. With their SANParks research permit in hand the team began recording rock art in areas like Afsaal. But they were quickly admonished for leaving a vehicle on a dirt road in plain sight of tourists who were paying hundreds, if not thousands, of dollars daily. The southern sector of the park is home to the majority of Kruger's rock art and is also promoted as a prime "wilderness" zone. Traffic of any sort was considered unwelcome because of the close proximity of Kruger's luxury game lodges – private fee-paying concessions that operate quasi-independently within Kruger but pay the organization handsomely for long-term leases. Visitors to these luxury lodges were afforded walking tours that included visiting rock art with the aid of an armed escort, but such experiences were not open to ordinary visitors to the park. The team also incurred strong disapproval from section rangers who, for the most part, did not want to be responsible for anyone's safety, despite the long tradition of walking trails in Kruger. During mapping we frequently encountered elephants that had no difficulty traversing the steep rocky slopes and outcrops where many of the paintings were located. Under the banner of safety, rangers dismissed the rock art trails: they were short staffed, had to patrol great swathes of territory alone, monitor their black field rangers, and were constantly on call for fires, animals, tourists, accidents, and other incidents. It was simply not going to be possible. A solution came in the form of a rock art specialist and tour guide who was a trained ranger himself and had worked extensively both inside and outside Kruger at various private game lodges. Conrad was eminently qualified to handle the rifle and the narrative about San history and cosmology, having received training at RARI. This option too was rejected, on the basis of insufficient funding.

To date, no concrete steps have been taken to consolidate the work done to develop a public program of rock art. The retired ranger refused to publicly present his materials to his colleagues at Skukuza because he feared reprisals for his focus on cultural heritage. He reminded me that he still had a son working in Kruger and was worried it would adversely impact his future in the organization. He harbored deeply contradictory views about the significance and visibility of archaeology in the park. In the next breath he snapped that Kruger was *not* a cultural park, but a natural one, and should not be developed with its archaeological resources in mind. At the time he was working in Kruger as a consultant, sharing his knowledge of rock art gleaned during his years of employment and was preparing to commercialize this in a coffee table book. He was adamant that archaeology should not be mobilized in land claims and vehemently opposed people returning to live in the park. This same man took me to numerous archaeological sites, spanning Paleolithic to recent historical times, lamenting the state of their preservation, their lack of recording or research, and their ultimate loss to memory. While he had no archaeological training as such, he was one of the few people I met who demonstrated any real commitment to the archaeological past and its public presentation.

These events were simply the last in a long series of attempts to showcase Kruger's rock art heritage. A decade before the National Geographic Society had

Figure 5.2 Conrad recording rock art in Kruger National Park. Courtesy of the author.

approached the park with a project, but social ecologists in People and Conservation were unhappy about the lack of community involvement or potential benefits and subsequently blocked it. National Geographic would have propelled Kruger's San heritage into the public spotlight, but at the same time rock paintings held no interest for Skukuza's People and Conservation unit, whose primary responsibility is liaising with neighboring black communities. Hector Magome (2004: 130), Executive Director of Scientific Services for SANParks, explains that the unit "was created ostensibly to involve local communities adjacent to all national parks so that they could, in turn, support its national conservation." As an act of enlightened self-interest SANParks began focusing on community-oriented support programs at a time when the organization needed a new public persona as a "community-oriented" agency (Maguranyanga 2009: 82). Conflicting objectives, multiple mandates, and the massive burden of need together put archaeology in a difficult place.

The placing of archaeology under the People and Conservation directorate is, then, critical. The consequences are that cultural heritage must vie with the more pressing goals of education, empowerment, and employment across SANParks. Archaeology is not put on an equal footing with the biophysical sciences, nor is it considered a science at all, and thus de-privileged and mis-understood throughout the organization. The tension witnessed over National Geographic's participation underlines another fallout from this arrangement. Social ecologists understandably consider development and education that targets previously disadvantaged stakeholders to be their core function, not the promo-tion of an archaeological landscape from which unknown or limited benefits accrue. Explaining an archaeological project to one social ecologist in Skukuza, he urged me to be brief: "my chairs have nails on them, so people don't spend too long." At the institutional and national scale a more serious disjuncture emerges. The very reason why heritage is promoted by the ANC turns on the self same reason why archaeology fails and is de-privileged in Kruger: the archaeological past is positioned within social and developmental discourse. Archaeology is not represented as a science or even its own discipline, neither is it considered "modern" or profitable like biodiversity conservation. Archaeology is perceived as a vehicle to elucidate the African past, connecting to particular stakeholders rather than representing the entire nation. Operating under the umbrella of People and Conservation thus renders archaeology across the rest of the organization as merely a conduit for development, education, and public relations, primarily for poor, rural, black South Africans. And that, as I was told innumerable times, is not the business of Kruger. So what elevates heritage in the new South Africa has subsequently buried archaeology within the park.

Ecologies of Heritage

Archaeologists and other social scientists conduct research through collaborations with social ecologists in People and Conservation, whereas natural scientists are managed through Scientific Services. People and Conservation, once known as Social Ecology (1995–2003), was perhaps the most important development in the transformation of national parks. Social ecology has gone through various per-mutations: first being a unit, then being elevated to a directorate, and finally, demoted to a division in 2009 (Masuku Van Damme and Meskell 2009). Today their mandate is to "create the crucial connection between the daily work of rangers and the South African people. Talking to people is a core business for SANParks – nowadays just as important as tourism and conservation."[1] Their mission includes community-based education, environmental education, and cul-tural heritage. In fact, all "black" issues, whether the problematic apartheid legacy, addressing impoverishment on park borders or heritage management, are out-sourced to People and Conservation so that the work of nature conservation can continue unhampered. However, just because national parks are managed by black South Africans, according to Maguranyanga (2009: 102), it "does not necessarily mean that they will automatically deliver meaningful benefits as well as respond favorably to the needs and interests of neighboring black communities." As institutional ethnographies have revealed, elite-pacting emerged between new black managers and older style white managers. This had the unintended consequence of sustaining operations and practices aligned with former apartheid rule and ensured opposition to radical changes in park management (Maguranyanga 2009: 106–7). This resistance to change is nothing new (Cock and Fig 2002: 152); it has been a sustained problem since the new dispensation in the 1990s.

Social ecology is a philosophy that views ecological problems as entwined with deeply rooted social issues that are themselves the product of structural inequalities (Bookchin 1996). For the National Parks Board of the 1990s, social ecology was conceived as a strategy to foster a new philosophy and approach toward interacting with neighboring communities as well as creating mutually beneficial partnerships. Admirable at a level of rhetoric, but more difficult to implement, they struggled with how best to harness the transformative capacity of social ecology in overhauling park management practices. Maguranyanga has demonstrated that there was strong resistance within the organization to embracing social ecology, and park managers generally did not consider it integral to their core activities. In the 1990s, as now, it is often relegated to outreach and problem solving. Starkly, the place of social ecology represented the clash between two racial worlds and competing visions of transformation and conservation (Maguranyanga 2009: 86). What remains today in SANParks is still a white technical core of managers and scientists that contributes toward both the perceptions and experiences of racism and the lack of transformation among black employees. Failure to transform at the managerial and scientific levels is a constant reminder that the architecture of apartheid persists.

Dr Yvonne Dladla was appointed to manage Social Ecology in 1995. She was the first black woman director in the history of the National Parks Board, and she proposed significant measures to transform the organization (Moore and Masuku Van Damme 2002). Her appointment was perceived as a threat to the core philosophy of park management coupled with "suspicions of hidden political agendas, general uncertainty, and also anxiety about the future" (Magome 2004: 129). For the purposes of my study, Dladla was significant since she produced comprehensive cultural heritage handbooks that rival anything produced subsequently, yet sadly this too has fallen from memory (Dladla 1999; Masuku Van Damme and Meskell 2009). In the current literature People and Conservation always presents its cultural heritage mandate and has elevated it as a corporate strategic objective, but the accompanying projects outlined are often couched in service of environmental education (see, for example, Maguranyanga 2009: 167; South African National Parks 2008a; 2009). This situation is possibly because of the dearth of successful archaeological projects SANParks might publicize, or it may alternatively reflect the more pressing needs of development and education.

Archaeological excavation and survey has never been extensive across the 22 national parks' currently in SANParks' portfolio, but it has been further reduced in recent years, probably because a new generation of social ecologists have, quite rightly, expected archaeology to shed its old apartheid image of disinterested science. Tense relations developed with an older generation of archaeologists who struggled with modifying their field practices in accord with post-apartheid transformation. Long-standing research permits, I learned from my colleagues, were not automatically renewed when it became clear that research objectives and community participation were not aligned. Important exceptions to this include new Stone Age and Iron Age research in Mapungubwe National Park, survey work in Brontebok National Park, Paleolithic research in West Coast National Park, and small-scale excavation of Boer War sites in Kruger.

Environmentality provides a salient lens through which to view these developments, involving as it does the entanglement and co-evolution of governance, environment, and identity (Agrawal 2005). Environmental regulation and management has come to serve as a new form of international governance, one that has profound and concrete effects on the lives and practices not only of communities but also of scientists (Hayden 2003: 83). It is a particularly pertinent optic through which to view the transition from apartheid to post-apartheid park governance and politics regarding social issues. During transition, major figures like the National Parks Board former director Dr Hall-Martin vigorously opposed Social Ecology, suggesting that the organization was abandoning its core business and becoming a development agency (Masuku Van Damme and Meskell 2009: 78). Like many, he believed single-mindedly that their legislative mandate was to defend nature conservation rather than promote socio-economic development and broader transformation objectives. Early on this view was challenged from within the organization by progressive white managers (Fourie 1991). Maguranyanga has also argued that black managers like Dr Msmiang shirked their responsibilities to empower social ecology. Taken together, park managers viewed the social ecology unit as a pacification effort to mitigate criticism that the organization had not meaningfully engaged local communities. And because their function was a detached structure, then and now, issues surrounding social ecology could neither command power nor organizational muscle (Maguranyanga 2009: 177). I witnessed these tensions daily during my fieldwork in Skukuza during meetings, conferences, and daily negotiations between colleagues. There was little overlap between the operations of People and Conservation and Scientific Services: project meetings were attended by scientists, community visits were conducted by social ecologists, fieldwork was carried out separately, and the two groups might come together around intense public issues such as elephant culling that involved scientific data and public backlash. The annual Savannah Networking Meeting run by Scientific Services was intended to bridge the two; however, the vast majority of presentations involved biophysical research with only one session devoted to social approaches. In 2004 the Social Science Research Unit was established under People and Conservation to address the historical disparities in the conservation landscape (Masuku Van Damme and Meskell 2009: 80). However, with the loss of its director, Sibongile Masuku Van Damme, in 2008 the unit faces further challenges. According to those in the unit, an exciting and potentially transformative new generation of research is being conducted, although it has yet to impact the bastions of biophysical management.

Social ecologists describe their encounters with natural scientists in the language of "struggle." Senior managers like Patricia argue that "all along, it has been about conserving and conservation has been detached from people." Fences have become symbolic of the rift between conservation and people. She was one of the most disaffected people I encountered at Skukuza; she was constantly worn down, considered moving on or doing another degree, yet was ultimately bound to the institution in deeply personal and conflicted ways. After 20 years of ingrained practice, she had watched biophysical scientists being forced to finally consider communities. Patricia describes this as culture shock, "half the time, other than me battling with them, I feel pity." Despite these fraught encounters, she believes that there has been substantial progress. Others assert that not enough has been done since 1994. They purport that the mission of social ecology has been ill defined, insufficiently funded, and then politically paraded to illustrate corporate social responsibility. Tangible benefits are more difficult to identify and, according to another manager, "the people we're dealing with don't have the intellectual capital to thoroughly interrogate what we're doing." In some instances, speaking about capacity building, or "capacitating" in popular parlance, seems to have substituted for actually putting it into practice.

All of these problems bring us back to the configuration of SANParks' research and mission, where nature conservation is isolated not simply from social research but also from the peopled dimension of parks. Scientists and policy makers are thus insulated from the external impacts of the park, both historically and presently. In this bifurcation, social issues, whether black heritage or black poverty, need not impinge on the core objectives of the organization. Nelson Mandela warned against this very situation in 1998 at Kruger's centenary celebrations. He asked that South Africans "remember the great sacrifices made by rural black people who had to surrender their land to make way for the establishment of the park. For the best part of the life of this conservation area, successive generations of black people were denied access to their natural heritage – only being suffered to come in to provide poorly rewarded labor" (Mandela 1998). Conservationists cannot divorce themselves from those who have sacrificed their land and livelihoods, nor can they discount the exigencies of natural resource use, co-management, and benefits beyond boundaries. The very people who have paid the price must now negotiate the future of the conservation mission beyond the fence. Moreover, by shunting the entire burden of social injustice toward the social sciences those disciplines are conflated with, and unfairly weighed down by, conservation's negative legacy. This is another example of Kruger's refusal to take responsibility for its recent past. Within SANParks Corporate Structure the Core Functions are currently divided between Conservation Services and Tourism and Marketing: People and Conservation have been left off the map. As social ecologists struggle for recognition, parity, and support within the organization, they must somehow service the desperate needs of transformation and fulfill their mission for education, participation, and, where possible, development. Therein lies the dilemma for placing archaeology. Many People and Conservation employees I interviewed do not regard cultural heritage as one of their core functions, although they do recognize the importance of black heritage in the broader sense through indigenous knowledge and tribal traditions. Archaeology is thus considered outdated, antiquated, and disengaged from living communities. It is an addendum to development, as it is to nature conservation.

The core business of People and Conservation is represented by a five-pointed star in the service of Constituency Building for Biodiversity Conservation: Social Science, Youth Outreach, Community Relationships, CRM and Indigenous Knowledge, and Environmental Education (see Figure 5.3). That all these vectors should be directed to constituency building for biodiversity is in keeping with the neoliberal imperatives put forward by the McKinsey report (2002). SANParks is right to support multiple values, but it should not expect that individual values like Cultural Heritage should exist simply to build support for Biodiversity Conservation. Moreover, a "value" like Cultural Heritage cannot be considered equivalent to an "activity" or program such as Youth Outreach or Environmental Education (see Lockwood 2006; Verschuuren 2007). This is not to say such programs are not vital, simply that they are different to values and assets. Emphasis on education and outreach could of course be beneficial for archaeology too, not simply biodiversity, and would be in keeping with therapeutic rainbow narratives of the 1990s. However, given the lack of heritage professionals or archaeologists employed, the more pressing urgencies of land claims and restitution, and the desire for employment and benefits from Kruger, liaisons with communities are transacted around these imperatives instead of historical ones.

Grafting education to development further severs the connection between disenfranchised black communities on the borders and Kruger's scientists and managers, who openly claim that theirs is not a development agency. Environmental education is a core function of People and Conservation and substitutes as the public, gentler face of Kruger. Didactic programs can be positively participatory but also coercive (Peluso 1993; Scott 1999), as we saw with the *Clean up Kruger* campaigns and those combating invasive biota in the buffer zone. Nature protectionists, according to Norton (2005: 331), see the protectionist effort as a process of community building: conservationists are not just saving special places, they are also accepting responsibility for projecting the value they feel toward protected areas into the future. This added commitment includes both the development of institutions and the development of narratives and traditions. Cultural resource management and indigenous knowledge systems could complement conservation

Core business of People and Conservation

A focal area of the Core Business of SANParks includes to build constituencies for biodiversity conservation through the People and Conservation programme, at International, National and local levels

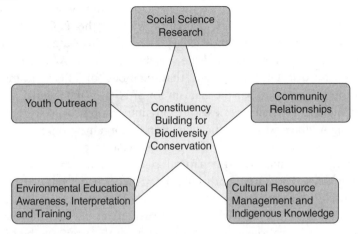

Figure 5.3 SANParks diagram setting out the Core Business of People and Conservation. Courtesy of South African National Parks.

in South Africa (Deacon *et al.* 2004; Scheermeyer 2005) as they do currently in Botswana (Segadika 2006; Segobye 2005; 2006). Bundling these concerns could prove progressive and mutually advantageous. Yet there is also the possibility of a dangerous muddying of the waters where material and immaterial heritage is channeled instead into biodiversity efforts at the expense of indigenous constituencies.

Unless some equilibrium between concerns internal and external to the park is attained, Kruger faces what it calls a Threshold of Potential Concern (TPC). The concept of the TPC is much favored by scientists in the park to describe the upper and the lower levels of accepted variation within the set of operational goals that together define the conditions by which Kruger is managed (Foxcroft 2004; 2009; Gillson and Duffin 2007). To date researchers have documented landscape function, degradation, threatened biota, fire in the landscape, and plant and animal dynamics. While the concept has been developed as a model for managing eco-systems and specific environmental vectors, this model might also be brought to bear on issues such as resource sharing or the current state of heritage in the park. The state of sites like Albasini, Masorini or Thulamela could all be reaching the upper limits of their TPCs. Thresholds are derived directly from Kruger's manage-ment and research objectives: cultural heritage is purportedly a consideration within ecosystem management (South African National Parks 2008b: fig. 2.3). Thresholds are essentially upper and lower limits along a continuum of change and a suite of TPC's together represents the envelope within which ecosystem changes are considered desirable. When the upper or lower TPC levels are reached, or when modeling predicts that they will soon be reached, this prompts an assessment of the cause of the extent of change. As part of Kruger's adaptive management model this assessment provides the basis for deciding whether management action is needed to moderate the change or whether the TPC itself should be recalibrated in the light of new knowledge.[2] Given the flux state of archaeological sites, their need for monitoring, and the various factors involved in site presentation and benefits distribution, I suggest that the model of TPC assessment might be an appropriate and familiar mechanism for SANParks managers.

In sum, significant challenges exist in fully integrating social science research generally and heritage work specifically within the organization. Kruger National Park remains the most resilient to change in SANParks' portfolio because of the long-standing dominance of the natural sciences and acrimonious relations with its neighbors. I was frequently told that other, smaller national parks were more amenable to integrating cultural heritage and communities into their core responsibilities. During a high-level research meeting at the Pretoria head office I heard it said that "social science research was the little sister" of the biophysical research program in SANParks. This positioning was all the more patronizing as it came from a senior, white, male scientist who was addressing a younger, black female colleague leading the new initiative. Social science research, encompassing archaeology, history, and ethnography, is not recognized or integrated within conservation. Unless one understands the differences between archaeology, site management, biophysical sciences, and community development before these elements are integrated, then mistakes like the burning of Masorini are inevitable. Archaeology will retain its second-class standing and continue to be palmed off as a failed community employment scheme.

An Alternative Vision of Cultural and Natural Heritage

In South African conservation and heritage management two frames of reference are often invoked, the United States and Australia. All three countries confront the issue of national parks, indigenous heritage, and potential co-management. The United States is generally considered a historic leader in conservation and park management, whereas Australia is thought to be most progressive regarding Aboriginal rights and claims, integration of culture within parks, intangible heritage, and ideas of cultural landscapes. The Australia ICOMOS Burra Charter (1999) is most frequently invoked as a model for South African heritage agencies (Deacon *et al.* 2004). Yet South Africa's history and contemporary challenges make easy comparison or simple duplication fraught with problems. A senior rock art specialist described the fault lines. "One of them has to do with a perception in South

Africa that heritage is not very complex, that it is not very important, and that the skills it takes to manage wildlife can be easily transposed onto heritage management." Antecedents for this thinking can be traced to colonial perceptions of indigenous people being closer to nature. He asserts that "animals in South Africa have always been something sacred, even for a white middle class," and during apartheid it was possible to still celebrate the country's beauty and its animals, marketing them through tourism. Natural diversity, not cultural diversity, might then excuse or cleanse apartheid's stain. His final point is that indigenous heritage was never marketed, but since 1994 there has been a huge pressure to change that. But "rather than bringing new people and new ideas, heritage has become tacked onto the conservation side of things, because it's what they know." These views neatly summarize many of the perspectives I observed in Kruger.

The foregoing provokes the question, Is there some other model for embracing cultural and natural heritages within the framework of national parks? Might there be another way of considering both objectives in Kruger? As a useful comparison I offer a brief examination of the Australian context, specifically in the state of New South Wales (NSW), which faces many similar challenges around indigenous heritage management yet has produced a broader vision of heritage in parks (see also de Villiers 1999; Parr, Woinarski, and Pienaar 2009). Unlike South Africa, almost all park management in Australia is managed at the state level, with the exception of a few federally managed parks including Kakadu and Uluru-Kata Tjuta, both of which are co-managed by Aboriginal custodians. Currently the NSW parks service employs some 14 archaeologists and around 80 cultural heritage staff, primarily Aboriginal heritage officers who focus on prehistoric and historic Aboriginal heritage and natural resource management. These hard-won developments reflect the Australian government's particular history of relationships with Aboriginal people as a continuing site of legal, economic, and social negotiation.[3]

Since 1788 Aboriginal people have fought for their land rights, and in every state they have long been engaged in a struggle to be recognized as citizens. Courts and state governments alike typically refused their rights and amendments to rights of citizenship, including addition to the national census, and it was only in the national referendum of 1967 that indigenous affairs shifted to the Commonwealth and thus enabled census rules to be modified. Yet even this acknowledgment did not produce a radical shift in the life experiences of Aboriginal people. The NSW Aboriginal Land Rights Act of 1983 provided a means for compensating Aboriginal people for the loss of their land. However, it was only in 1992, with the Mabo court decision, that the doctrine of *terra nullius* was finally overturned and the government seriously began to address the issue of native title (Lilley 2000a; Smith 1999: 109). Today, Aboriginal groups are still battling the politics of self-determination and attempting to secure restitution from the exploits of governments, pastoralists, and mining companies. As in South Africa, many Aboriginal people have questioned the privileging of archaeological knowledge and its management (Langford 2003) since the discipline has been perceived as a technology of government (Lilley 2006; Lilley and Williams 2005; C. Smith 2004; L. Smith 2000: 109; Smith and Campbell 1998).

The Department of Environment, Climate Change, and Water (DECCW) manages natural heritage and Aboriginal cultural heritage in NSW. Built heritage (the immoveable component of non-indigenous heritage) is administered through the Department of Planning (Alpin 2002: 211). DECCW's broad remit includes more than 793 national parks, nature reserves, Aboriginal areas, historic sites, state conservation areas, and regional parks covering 6 725 069 hectares,[4] more than 8.39 percent of all land in NSW. DECCW is responsible for managing Aboriginal heritage across the state, both in parks and outside their borders. The DECCW integrates "natural, cultural and community values," making sure that cultural heritage and community values are instrumental within the planning process (Byrne, Brayshaw, and Ireland 2001: 22). In addition to Aboriginal heritage, cultural heritage practitioners employed by DECCW have also investigated the migrant experience in Australia (Byrne *et al.* 2006) with heritage projects for Vietnamese and Macedonian stakeholders (Thomas 2001) as well as Arabic speakers. At the start of 2010 there were more than 35 cultural heritage research projects completed or ongoing, 28 books published, and numerous articles.

Like their South African counterparts, Australian park authorities naturalized cultural heritage during the 1980s and 1990s. Places and objects were perceived statically "because they occur in a physical landscape, are part of the natural world" (Byrne, Brayshaw, and Ireland 2001: 21). This was aggravated by white society's propensity to classify and collect Aboriginal heritage objects and places as if they were natural. There is an increasing effort to enlist rangers with cultural training, since historically they have entered the program holding biological science degrees, like their counterparts in South Africa. Apart from targeted recruiting, rangers already in the service are given heritage training by heritage staff, including Aboriginal cultural awareness training, thus reinforcing the importance of a strong cultural heritage presence within the service. Aboriginal culture is foregrounded within Australian parks and framed specifically around archaeological landscapes. Cultural heritage enjoys wide connectivity within the landscape. Not only are people linked to landscapes, but to plants and animals, adding a dense stratigraphy of meaning to place. However, managing cultural heritage entails more than just conserving the physical remains of the past, it is also about understanding and protecting the places, things, traditions, and stories that remain significant to people over generations.

How did national parks achieve this position in regard to Aboriginal heritage management? This is an important question for its comparative application in countries such as South Africa. Byrne, Brayshaw, and Ireland (2001: 23–5) examined the historical process across all land categories in NSW and describe the process in three stages. The early phase (1969 to 1980) was marked by the first protection of Aboriginal "relics" in 1969, although formal lobbying began in the

1930s and concern for places and objects can be traced back as early as 1788. Significantly, archaeology was deemed to be providing the "primary expertise," signifying the centrality of the discipline within the organization of parks. For the first time, Aboriginal people were brought into the field of heritage management. The next phase (1980 to 2000) marks the era of Environmental Impact Assessment archaeology, which was first developed in the state of NSW. Aboriginal consultation on heritage management issues became standard practice, and the number of consultant archaeologists also rapidly increased. Yet it was only in 1997 that national parks initiated a research unit in cultural heritage, some 20 years after the establishment of a research program in nature conservation. Relevant to the South African context, this late move has been deemed "symptomatic of a perception that cultural heritage management was comparatively straightforward and 'obvious' whereas the work of nature conservation required continual innovation based on solid scientific research" (Byrne, Brayshaw, and Ireland 2001: 25). In the third phase, from 2000 onwards, the DECCW has adopted a more holistic approach and Aboriginal community heritage values have attracted even greater attention and additional resources.

Instructive for SANParks, the NSW parks authority has a formal Statement of Reconciliation[5] mandating the greater involvement of indigenous communities in heritage and conservation initiatives and partnerships. In the case of NSW, an obvious way to implement these new directives is through Aboriginal co-management of national parks and reserves. Under an Aboriginal co-management arrangement, the government and local Aboriginal people share responsibility for park planning and decision-making. This ensures the continuing practice of traditional and contemporary culture in the management of land, yet still allows access to larger publics (see also Commonwealth of Australia 2000; Hill and Press 1994; Igoe 2004). The success of co-management depends very much on the existence of park management skills within indigenous communities and on there being skill-transfer programs in place. It is not enough simply to employ Aboriginal people: appropriate skills and university training must be encouraged and matching resources designated. While there are obviously contextual differences between Australia and South Africa regarding indigenous populations, land redistribution, institutional capacity, and archaeological management to name a few examples, the case of NSW offers insights for the integration of natural and cultural heritages and for re-instating indigenous pasts and presents.

Despite the myriad complexities of the South African context, the Australia ICOMOS Burra Charter (1999) provides the closest approximation to indigenous understandings of living heritage, stakeholding, and multiple claims. The principles that underpin the charter were set out in 1979 (updated in 1999) and identify the desire to encompass aesthetic, historical, scientific, and social significances. They have received wide acceptance among Australian heritage practitioners (Byrne, Brayshaw, and Ireland 2001: 4; Smith and Burke 2007), and the Charter has been formally adopted by nations like China and Indonesia. Importantly, the charter recenters the place of culture in a living context termed "places of cultural significance," rather than as a static object of outstanding artistic or scientific merit. Moving beyond the reductive notion of sites and objects, national parks recognizes that Aboriginal culture is a living set of practices interleaved with the environment. While Aboriginal archaeological sites form a vital constituent of Australia's national heritage, and many are on the Aboriginal Heritage Information Management System (there are over 60 000 documented Aboriginal sites in NSW and 10 000 in grey reports), they have even greater salience for Aboriginal communities. These sites provide a direct link with their traditional culture: "Land and waterways are associated with dreaming stories and cultural learning that is still passed on today. It is this cultural learning that links Aboriginal people with who they are and where they belong."[6] Because this is a living cultural heritage, Aboriginal people require access to these sites and landscapes so as to renew their cultural learning. Legislation ensures that living Aboriginal heritage must be considered as part of land management through management planning and physical protection.

Past Mastering in the Park

Skukuza, the process of stripping bare or sweeping clean that was conferred on Stevenson-Hamilton and later on the park's main camp, remains a forceful technique. Throughout the history of Kruger it has been an effective mechanism to remove people, excise the traces of their past, and even to clear archaeological sites like Masorini. Mimicking the practice of fire breaks or patch burns for regulating biodiversity, rangers can manage heritage sites by the same sanctioned tactics of clearance. Environmental management methods have been literally transposed onto archaeological heritage, whether burning at Masorini or protecting wilderness at the expense of rock art accessibility. Developing rock art for various publics would see heritage challenge, and lose out to, the two major pillars of SANParks post-apartheid mission, biodiversity and tourism. First, the promotion of ancient art directly confronts the ideology of *terra nullius* with deep human history materially attested by the presence of the San. Equally, constructing heritage trails would threaten the maintenance of "wilderness" and, while trails can be tolerated for "nature," they cannot be imagined for "culture." Consuming wilderness, offered by high-end private concessions in the south of the park and a significant fiscal generator for SANParks, must also be protected. Ambivalence toward the archaeological past is materially enacted in such negotiations across Kruger National Park, and its fugitive status has itself become a tactic of past mastering.

The current impossibility of heritage, its no man's land in the People and Conservation unit, is the product of concerted moves to manage the past. More critically, archaeologists might see it as a strategy to enclose and segregate its spaces and effects. Effective past mastering, or the processing of history is hampered because people have been alienated from heritage sites, a lack of heritage expertise abounds, misreadings thrive, and the old ghosts are never laid to rest. Refusing to acknowledge diverse histories and instead condoning ignorance and celebrating the non-human constituents of protected areas may lead to future recriminations and reprisals. The profusion of indigenous land claims filed for land bordering and within Kruger National Park is testament to this interleaved history of exclusion and disempowerment. Enclosing sites and fencing people out represents a failure. I was repeatedly told that the sites of Masorini, Albasini, and Thulamela are falling apart, yet they could be revivified through indigenous participation and co-management, as is often the practice in Australian national parks. This is what communities like the Malatji have repeatedly proposed to the park and to researchers like myself. Charmless heritage could be re-enchanted. While diverse archaeological pasts were supposed to provide for the nation's poorest, socially and economically, archaeology's circumscribed existence coupled with the prevalence of willing amnesia makes Mandela's dream a rainbow-tinted fiction. Archaeology is actively undercut, allowed to collapse or become overwhelmed by the undergrowth, while dog cemeteries are carefully raked and tended and Bushman's Picnics are performed in private spaces. The past is not just ignored; it can be actively overwritten, misread, scorched, or even parodied.

Despite the failures documented here, there persists a strain of valiant optimism within the organization, often voiced by a younger generation of black and colored managers and researchers, typically holding degrees in the natural sciences. One young man enthusiastically expounded his dreams for past mastering in Kruger:

> rock art sites, old village sites, possible trade routes, the way we have picnic spots or stop-off points. We could have information up there that is explicit to a historical site, and people can actually look at the information and put it into multiple scale contexts. So you can find the trade routes, or in Pafuri where the laborers came here to work on the mines, and put it in a national context. People can see that Kruger Park is not this little paradise that has always operated in isolation, much as it does today. That it was part of a broader spectrum of human events, which make up Southern Africa's history.

There is still hope that a younger generation may be able to balance natural and cultural heritages, that archaeology can be considered both a social and scientific discipline, much as ecology might now be understood. That rapprochement was hard won in Australia, so we may have to wait it out in new nations like South Africa, where the past is still very much in process and remains future perfect.

Notes

1   http://www.sanparks.org/people (accessed December 14, 2009).

2   http://www.sanparks.org/parks/kruger/conservation/scientific/mission/tpc.php (accessed December 14, 2009).

3   http://www.alc.org.au/culture-and-heritage.aspx 4 (accessed April 13, 2011).

4   http://www.environment.nsw.gov.au/resources/whoweare/deccar0809appendices_09579.pdf (accessed February 22, 2010).

5   http://www.environment.nsw.gov.au/NPWS/StatementOfReconciliation.htm (accessed December 14, 2009).

6   http://www.environment.nsw.gov.au/nswcultureheritage/Aboriginal PeopleAndCulturalLife.htm (accessed December 14, 2009).

Chapter 6

Thulamela

The Donors, the Archaeologist, his Gold, and the Flood

The three major themes of this book are neatly interwoven at one archaeological site in Kruger called Thulamela. Here we can see how heritage was called on to compensate for past deprivations and bad governments; it would form the basis for reconciliation and uplift, and it would need to enlist public and private partnerships to fulfill its mandate. Fashioned as a fantasy love story about the first archaeological excavation involving blacks and whites in the Rainbow Nation, Thulamela could be sold at home and abroad as a parable for the emergent democratic state. Very quickly, however, the relationship faltered, expectations were dashed and the promise of therapy morphed into platitudes, disappointment, and recriminations. Nature trumped culture in the end and conservation won out over collaboration and communities. Thulamela, as a case study, has one of everything: the lure of gold, tribal conflict, white mischief and new age magic, financial mismanagement, a reburial fiasco, political capital, international media coverage, and a great flood. Rider Haggard could not have crafted a more compelling tale.

Thulamela is a nine-hectare Iron Age settlement (c. 1440–1640) with stone-walled enclosures in the far north of Kruger. It is a picturesque site on the top of a hill with majestic views overlooking Levhuvhu River, near the confluence of the Limpopo. The site was surveyed in 1990 and the first test trench was dug a year later. The park appointed Sidney Miller, a civil engineer, as the lead archaeologist, and a team of local masons were employed to rebuild the walls (Miller 1996). The excavation was conducted over four years (1993–7) and overseen by technical and environmental committees drawn from national parks, universities, and local Shangaan and Venda communities (Nemaheni 2004: 256). The excavation and subsequent analysis was of a standard not out of keeping with much South African archaeology, although the final unpublished report fell short of international

The Nature of Heritage: The New South Africa, First Editon. Lynn Meskell.
© 2012 John Wiley & Sons, Inc. Published 2012 by Blackwell Publishing Ltd.

Figure 6.1   Thulamela from the air. Courtesy of Ian Whyte and South African National Parks.

scientific standards. This undoubtedly reflects the status of archaeology within SANParks, where an archaeologist could direct a project that resulted in his MA degree: a high profile project in conservation or ecology would have garnered a senior scientist. Despite these shortfalls, the project had enormous political mileage and the site was declared a national monument in 1999 (Reid 2001: 140, compare also Fontein 2005 for Zimbabwe). Thulamela was used in rousing government speeches and received significant media attention in South Africa and abroad, featuring on the PBS Nova series in the United States. Economic development was the declared intent and community participation was the medium. Both strategies were trying to change the hearts and minds of disenfranchised and impoverished black people, and both were trying to make them "modern" (Henkel and Stirrat 2001: 183). Indeed, much heritage rhetoric has the ring of global modernity, whereby the new nation needs to be recognized as a First World player on an international stage after years of exclusion, and that recognition is hitched to an established set of sanctioned movements and moral causes. World heritage and biodiversity are just two.

Over a decade on, the shame is that following the enormous media and political attention focused on black heritage, SANParks, and specifically Kruger, failed to support, sustain, and promote Thulamela. Duncan Miller, who worked on the project, captured its initial spirit and promise:

Future archaeologists may look back on the excavation of Thulamela as the critical turning point in the history of the discipline in South Africa. It is not the first time archaeological excavation has been preceded by negotiation with local communities . . . but the multiplicity of interested parties, the extent of negotiation, the ongoing inclusion of local communities in the work itself, the sheer degree of local involvement is novel in South Africa, and will mark a change in how we do archaeology. (Miller 1996)

Looking back over the original proposal prepared for the corporate sponsor, the international mining giant Gold Fields, the project aims seemed exemplary. Gold Fields is, of course, a sister company of De Beers, who have funded rock art, archaeology, and nature conservation alike, creating a densely networked heritage-scape under the mantle of Anglo-American funding. The main priorities were to involve neighboring communities in a more "people-centered participatory approach," stimulate "environmental" education and economic development and validate the history of the Limpopo for the past 2000 years (Verhoef 1995). Significantly, archaeology was the vehicle by which the National Parks Board, under its new black leadership, could establish a credible structure with neighboring communities. Nature conservation had victimized black communities in the past, but the archaeology of their own ancestors promised a more viable connection. The early 1990s were optimistic times and, as I have argued, there was a general ethos that heritage could heal the tensions and ruptures apartheid institutionalized. That philosophy was not bolstered by government funds. Instead it was expected that entrepreneurial efforts to seduce big business or international agencies would carry the day and that culture itself could be somehow self-sustaining. As we will see, this was tried again and again with little historical or fiscal hindsight and was doomed each time.

Like all relationships, this one started with good intentions and progressive ideas. Yet complex entanglements and holdovers prevented the project's full realization under the aegis of Kruger National Park, or perhaps anywhere in South Africa at that moment in time. Duncan Miller put it well when he said, "the archaeological realities risk being drowned in a flood of nationalistic fervor and journalistic hype" (1996). First of all, since no full-time archaeologists are employed by SANParks there was no expertise and no oversight in heritage management or promotion and, given the longstanding indifference across the park, this was not going to come from rangers or ecologists. Thulamela is in the far north of the park, and in the acknowledged north–south divide the north sadly suffers in terms of staffing, funding, and resources. International donors and development agencies did become involved, but their distance and lack of real participation could not save the project in its various incarnations. Perhaps more fundamentally, the project was not instigated at communities' behest and their actual participation was minimal. The exhumation of burials, the reburial ceremony, the lack of access to the park, and their inability to veto either park authorities or archaeologists upset many. The key players could be broken down into the following: the donors, the nature conservationists, the politicians, the media, the archaeologists, the social ecologists, and the communities.

The Money

The Thulamela project and its proposed museum/education center were essentially funded twice over. The gold mining conglomerate Gold Fields was the first donor approached after gold was famously found at the site. Gold Fields donated millions of rand, according to a senior manager: the signed agreement was to fund excavation, reconstruction, investigation of adjacent sites, guide training, and the full institutionalization of Thulamela into Kruger's management. Corporate social responsibility morphed into "casino capitalism," where Thulamela's success became a matter of chance, unrelated to performance, and with no conceivable connection between effort and reward (Sharp 2006: 221; Weiss 2009). The World Wildlife Fund South Africa was approached because of their interest in environmental education. There would be new posts for an environmental education officer and two guides, a permanent display and scale model, but no archaeologist or heritage manager. This omission would prove critical.

From the outset there was a strong directive for marketing Thulamela, for spin-off products and merchandise that would enhance the already neoliberal direction post-apartheid SANParks was taking. Unlike the vast conservation and natural science mission in the park, archaeology would have to raise its own funds by selling itself and capitalizing culture. In 1996 independent consultants were called in to draft yet another proposal to pitch to additional donors. Jewelry manufacture and export was suggested, particularly because of the number of gold items excavated from the site and because the initial sponsor was a gold mining company. An "indigenous jewelry design culture" was proposed with a stamp of authenticity and a Thulamela logo to be applied to all items, ensuring financial returns to the Thulamela Trust. Additionally, the committee pitched crafts, clothing, and bush wear, books, CDs, educational toys, and garden products. To my knowledge none were ever produced.

WWF South Africa employed its own expert to assess the project in 1995, in particular Thulamela's stated environmental education objectives. In a disparaging report the assessor expresses

> a great concern that the project is on the verge of losing the tenuous focus on education it had thus far. On its current trajectory there is very little chance of the Thulamela site becoming the "kingpin of the broader EE program for the northern KNP" or promoting "community involvement and participation" as stated in the terms of reference in 1993. (van Rensburg 1995: 1)

Why did they fail to "produce the goods"? Here was an archaeologist employed short term, a parks official doing environmental education elsewhere, and a community panel that was never integral to the project. Jobs were filled by people who could shoot, not necessarily educate. The audit revealed that Thulamela, along with the other archaeological sites such as Masorini, were inadequately managed. Thulamela was not geared to education nor toward the communities; in fact, joint management was a fiction. The final recommendation to park staff and archaeologists alike was clear, namely "involve yourselves."

The Interpretation Center or Environmental Education Center never really materialized and was a source of embarrassment for the then National Parks Board. Archaeology and a cultural museum were quickly hijacked by conservations for an "eco-site" further diminishing the cultural and historic dimension to people and parks, even though an archaeological site formed its basis. The aim was always to instruct local people, particularly school children, about the importance of conservation and ensure their buy-in. Cloaked in the rhetoric of empowerment, and therefore assumed to have a greater moral value, environmental initiatives within Kruger have significant political value, even if they fail. Nonetheless, it remains a way of talking about rather than doing things (Mosse 2001: 32). The Norwegian Agency for Development Co-operation (NORAD) and the DEAT were then approached and in 2003 began funding the same Thulamela Environmental Education Centre and Museum (South African National Parks 2004: 34). The DEAT claimed that "all South Africans can convert unattended heritage sites into economical and sustainable cultural attractions" but it was unclear what the ministry donated to Kruger, apart from being the intermediary between Norway and Kruger (DEAT 2000). NORAD, however, donated R1 million from their Cultural Heritage Directorate. Kruger's Business Plan for 2000 shows clearly that those funds were allocated specifically to an interpretive center and museum. Apart from a few laminated posters displayed at a nearby picnic site in Pafuri, no center or museum was ever built.

The immanence of failure is palpable around projects like Thulamela, and researchers like myself have to consider the rhetoric, meetings, reports, consultancies, and publicity generated against the material backdrop of languishing sites, incomplete projects, and heavy silences. Some of the evidence of this mismanagement was literally swept away when the most severe floods in living memory swept through Kruger in February 2000. Looking over photographs of the picnic site from 1998 it is possible to discern that some photographs and a few original objects in small glass boxes simply washed away in the deluge. Ceramics and metal tools have now vanished. By the end of March the Pafuri gate was opened again, but there had been serious damage to low-lying park infrastructure valued at more than R70 million.

Another solution to the problem of sustaining Thulamela was sought in 2000 with the Mopani Plan, whereby archaeological sites in the region (Shilowa, Thulamela) could be developed for tourism. At Mopani Camp, some 170 kilometers south of Thulamela, a cultural museum might be built that would present the "cultural history of the people surrounding the park" (rather than admitting that they once lived within its boundaries). This would allow Kruger to retrieve and display the objects that were now closely guarded by Pretoria University – an issue that has never been resolved and remains a point of contention. The idea of a cultural route through the park was floated, an obvious and sound strategy that has never been supported. During this meeting with the Thulamela Board of Trustees (South African National Parks 2000), Mr Magoloi from Mphaphuli Tribal Council raised his concern over the lack of progress at Thulamela, yet no response is on record.

Between 2004 and 2005 there was talk again of an environmental centre being built again at Pafuri that could integrate Thulamela within the broader conservation mission. I had recently completed a scanning project funded by the National Science Foundation that brought together computer scientists, media specialists, and archaeologists. The heritage component featured local elders speaking about the site and interviews in various languages. Our group attempted to resuscitate the archaeological component of the proposed center by offering several computers that could display three-dimensional interactive models of the site and all its objects for educational purposes. We were willing to supply the equipment and the digital expertise, keen to consolidate our collaborations with Kruger staff, and spent a good deal of time outside the fence with community representatives (Meskell 2007a). From the start I worked closely with Laura, who was the heritage officer at the time, and we would spend hours driving from Skukuza to Pafuri in her battered golf Chico. Her degree was in nature conservation, not archaeology, but she was more passionate about heritage than anyone I had encountered in Kruger. As a young white woman arriving in Kruger she had been treated badly by various senior white male staff in nature conservation, she was ignored, patronized, and repeatedly told off. But she persevered, having the temperament of a saint, especially in light of Kruger's deep ambivalence around cultural heritage (Cock 2007: 149). Thulamela and the Punda Maria area were of special interest to her and she went on complete an MA thesis on the old mine recruiting station at Pafuri – but only after leaving SANParks. During construction of the Pafuri Gate Center it became obvious to us both that no archaeological objects could ever be displayed in the rondavels, nor could expensive computers and equipment be housed there. The original design had been completely altered; there were huge glass windows cut into the concrete and thatch huts, which presented a security nightmare. We learned then that the structures had become earmarked for Kruger staff offices. Again, heritage would have to be culled.

Numerous managers and archaeologists have drafted management plans for the future of Thulamela, stretching back to the 1990s. There was Sydney Miller's report-cum-thesis (Miller 1997), Israel Nemaheni's extensive plan (Nemaheni 2003), also an MA thesis, and a management plan submitted by international herit-

age expert Amareswar Galla in 1997. There were other reports and recommendations in the Skukuza files, but none were ever fully implemented. During my last
visit, in September 2009, I discovered that yet another management plan was being
drafted, and I was handed a lavish consultancy document prepared by an ex-
academic who had worked in the region for many years. Thulamela spawned
more reports and management plans than any project I had encountered, and yet
the site only ever deteriorated and languished, out of sight and out of mind.
Having exhausted the donors, NGOs, and international agencies, in 2009 Kruger
petitioned the impoverished local Limpopo municipality to fund the restoration
of settlement walls. So, coming full circle, the very people that Thulamela was
supposed to empower and sustain through its heritage development were now
asked to foot the bill after more than a decade of disappointment. "After all," one
employee explained in justification, "they did change their name to the Thulamela
Municipality."

White Mischief

Infamy and scandal have haunted Thulamela since excavations began in 1994. I
had heard stories since my first trip to South Africa from nature conservationists
like Kobus, who had worked with me for several years. He knew some of the
young students who had excavated at Thulamela but was nervous about getting
them in trouble. At the same time he was angry; he discovered one young man
was wearing a strand of ancient blue glass beads around his wrist. When asked,
the student told him that the beads were from the excavations at Thulamela.
Finding this hard to comprehend, I asked several senior archaeologists who had
experience working in and around places like Kruger, whether this was something
linked to the attitude of national parks or was it an unprincipled strain in South
African archaeology? A senior professor rationalized this particular brand of
"Afrikaner archaeology" that had allowed excavators to take objects from the spoil
heaps. He had witnessed it himself, and partly empathized by admitting that he
might have fallen prey to such thefts when he was younger. This remarkable attitude was reinforced by another academic, who was far from surprised, even
though he had just regaled me about his long-standing reputation of community
collaboration. It "says something about the fatalism of many young white professionals that feel we might as well do whatever we want because we're not going
to get a job anyway. Because if ever there's an archaeology post open it's going
to go to a black person." I was speechless, but he continued without hesitation:
"they say why bother because you know, I have to go and look for a waiter job as
soon as we're done studying. They see a climate where black Zimbabweans are
appointed in South African jobs just because they are black and the institution
needs a black face."

Many park workers I interviewed recounted scandalous incidents, some of which they were directly involved in attempting to put right; others were surely rumors, much like the fabled stories of the Kruger Millions.[1] I was told that gold artifacts were stored under the archaeologist's bed during the excavation season and later had to be removed by force. A gold-plated figure like the Mapungubwe rhino was supposedly found, but then disappeared. Several people told me that city auctioneers had phoned certain excavators within hours of them unearthing the first gold beads. Park authorities were asked to store and protect precious artifacts on their premises before they were moved to personal bank vaults. The gold, I was told in interviews, was then ransomed till national parks paid people properly for their work. Lawyers were called in, people fired, lengthy arbitration ensued, and demands for the final report became belligerent. Whatever the truth in the accounts I was given, and there must be a little despite mischief or malice, relations went badly awry. Writing to the project sponsors in 1997, Kruger's park warden apologized that "the conflicts of personalities, and possibly personal interests, at and surrounding Thulamela have caused considerable embarrassment and damage to what is a magnificent project" (Braak 1997).

Nick was a senior ranger in Kruger during the excavations, an angry no-nonsense man who had kept a huge file on the project even after he had left the park's employ. He was still smarting from what he had witnessed during the 1990s, and in his view they were "all amateurs not archaeologists." They were nothing like the experts he watched on the Discovery Channel, nor were they like the conservationists. He put his hands in the air for quote marks every time he used the word "archaeologist" to make his point. Nick explained that there were tensions from the start over authority and access because national parks personnel were treated like interlopers by the archaeologists. Conflicts surfaced over dominant personalities, possessiveness, and personal gain. In this world-turned-upside-down, some old racial divisions collapsed and white men were "baptized" into the Makahane tribe, whites were being pressured into performing black rituals on site, nature conservation was being challenged by other disciplines, and neighboring communities were being asked for their opinions.

During project meetings, matters of transformation and restitution were paramount. For Nick, the political agenda was clear "in 1994, it was now the new South Africa. We kept getting shoved down our throats that we must empower and we must do this and we must do that. And I remember saying at one of those meetings that whatever the past government did, at least one thing they did do is they protected that area since 1926." It was a strategic move in "1994 with the government changing over and ownership and, and, and. So it probably came at a very good time and one could actually go and promote it that this was probably Shangaan or one could promote it that it's Venda, whichever way you want the thing to actually go."

Stefan, a senior park official in the 1990s with an interest in archaeology and now out of the organization, saw it quite differently. He believed that some of his colleagues were anti-transformation and that staff in Kruger's northern sector were the most resistant to change. Those in the north had not adapted to the new cultural heritage mandate, they were not interested in people, and were narrowly fixated on the "wilderness concept." They refused to appreciate Kruger's cultural landscape, "either people don't want to know about it or there is very, very limited knowledge about it." In Stefan's view, his colleagues saw archaeological sites as isolated and accidental discoveries rather than as constituting a pattern of long-term human habitation and indigenous management. I completely agree. For this he blames the former warden Tol Pienaar and his refusal to translate his historical book *Neem Uit Die Verlede*, literally *Take From the Past* (the title being a version of President Kruger's last message before exile, see Carruthers 1994: 282). Stefan begged Pienaar to do so repeatedly but he "will only let it be translated if it's done exactly as the Afrikaans is." If you look at the environment differently, Stefan explained, and you recognize that it does have socio-cultural, economic, political, and biophysical elements, then SANParks is not only primarily responsible for biodiversity. But it was not simply archaeology that was at issue, it was an entirely new approach that asked nature conservationists to start considering people, past and present. Kruger authorities were already hostile to the new Social Ecology Department that had been foisted on them under the new leadership, and now archaeology was added to that imposition. Thulamela bore the brunt of this reaction. Some archaeologists in South Africa still believe that SANParks wanted Thulamela to fail and possibly even sabotaged the project – harsh accusations indeed.

White Crosses

I cannot tell the whole story of the Thulamela reburials because I was not there to witness it. Excuses are given now, emotions ran high then, and many people I spoke to years later were still incensed and were finding the courage to express it. "A chief must be buried in his place," Freddie Munzhelele told me outside his son's rondavel in Tshikuyu. He was born in 1929 and was considered an authority, so he had been interviewed by other researchers interested in the heritage of Pafuri. When discussing the exhumation which he attended, he said, "none of this was explained to me. Not everybody was involved in the project. It was only whites and a few other people." He was upset that snuff had not been offered to the ancestors when the bones were uncovered, it was a simple respectful gesture, but no one had enquired about the proper rituals. Other elders were vehemently against disturbing the bones, saying it was against Venda tradition (Meskell 2007a), while younger members seem less concerned about research on human remains and were pleased to be involved with the reburial ceremony (Nemaheni 2004). It puts pay to the notion of a homogenous "community" out there and underlines the divergent interests cross-cut by age or gender (Robins and van der Waal 2008). On the other hand, archaeologists a decade later continue to maintain that the atmosphere was supportive towards the uncovering and analysis of human remains and the subsequent reburial in 1997 and that there was community consultation. While participation in the project may have been a form of subjection, the consequences were not predetermined and individuals were never completely controlled (Williams 2004), as the following makes clear.

Listening to the archaeologists, the problems could be traced to a combination of factors at a volatile time. For Lesley, Thulamela

> was huge in the press, especially when the skeletons were discovered. The media presented it as this great mystery that was being unraveled, and my problem was that the archaeologist was presented as a mystic. He played into it. I don't think it did archaeology any good one way or another. And they really played out the whole notion of mystery and just being able to *feel* things.

Another archaeologist asserted that the excavator was "trying to protect what he knew about the site" with the prospect before him of numerous TV documentaries and potential books deals. "That's why the [final archaeological] report is something of a eighteenth century kind of adventure document." But this was very much a white adventure story, and as Lesley explains "it became this very European landscape that was being discovered. So it was on a par with kings and queens in Europe and those things that maybe have a role to play in white psyche." Sidney Miller did harness the hype and mystical frenzy of the time, with white appropriations of black rituals and history (see also Draper 1998). He talked of Thulamela's "air of benevolence" and "unique sense of lightness" (Allen 1996). Miller's actions were typical of the Rainbow Nation narrative being woven by politicians and intellectuals alike into the fabric of the new South Africa. A new set of racialisms and exclusions emerged and were grafted onto revolutionary promises of transformation. Miller thus found it necessary to rationalize his own white interventionist archaeology and science into the realm of black heritage with its attendant religious difference (Meskell 2007a: 392). Nick Shepherd (2003: 825–6) outlines how, on other public occasions, Miller described archaeologists as scientists in ivory towers and pitted them against Venda spiritual representatives and people like himself who worked with black communities. Media pressure only exacerbated these new public performances around Africanity and heritage. In the documentary *African Mysteries* a black television presenter discovers Miller within the walls at Thulamela. "Look, it could be an ancestor," he says to the camera. At which time his female co-presenter caustically replies, "No, he's the wrong color!"

Sidney Miller and other senior archaeologists viewed Thulamela as a Venda site, which therefore privileged the Makahane group over the Mhinga, who were Shangaans, a tribal tension with a long and acrimonious history. In numerous interviews with Venda elders, all problems in the park could be traced to employing the Shangaans, and I was warned to be careful of their powerful *muti* (traditional medicine). Plans for the reburial of two skeletons reflected these ethnic divisions, and it was local practices rather than white professionals that mediated and ultimately ameliorated the tensions. Academic discussion pivoted around lack of documented continuity and oral history, possible architectural parallels, histories of arrival, and so on. Much less discussion focused upon shared stakeholding or heritage-making in the present. Tshimangadzo Nemaheni was heavily involved in the process as a Venda heritage officer once employed by Kruger. He has written about the process, specifically how the community forum requested German Mabasa, a Shangaan *sangoma* (traditional healer) to "throw the bones" to divine who were the rightful descendents of the site. To everyone's amazement she announced that Thulamela was indeed Venda and that the Makahane must continue their annual rituals on site. The Shangaans were not the only stakeholders to experience exclusion. A senior parks manager expressed a similar sentiment, explaining the deep divisions between the archaeologist, the ranger, himself, and the entire Parks Board. The same old-boy connections that put Miller in place would be those that eventually caused clashes. Others, like Lesley, recognized more broadly the complete "disconnect between the archaeology, parks, education, and the community."

On May 31, 1997 the Makahane clan led the reburial ritual. Shangaan and Venda traditional dances were performed, although people acknowledged that dancing did not accompany an original burial ceremony. Kruger donated game so that meat could be distributed. A black goat supplied by the Venda was slaughtered and the blood spilled on three stones. The first goat, provided by the Shangaan, had been rejected. The ceremony was enacted under a full media spotlight. There were recriminations about the authenticity of the ceremony, especially the handling of the skeletal remains. A physical anthropologist recounted how they had originally planned on manufacturing aluminum containers for both bodies, sealing and reburying them with the greatest degree of preservation for future research. Immediately the community objected, saying that "the bones were not allowed to touch metal. We must bring them up in linen bags, in wooden boxes." One Venda participant captured the difficulties:

> So we start down there on the valley carrying two coffins, then we walk about a kilometer from the bottom and before we reach the burial site there we have a resting place, by so doing, allowing the leader to rest. By our cultural tradition we won't carry a person to the burial place without resting him, resting the soul before you can bury that person. Everybody was around, parks board, university, local people . . . this isn't traditional; it is done during the night with no public, only by senior people, family people.

The process of burial was contentious, oscillating between traditional Venda and Christian practices. There was no agreement. In the end a white plastic cross was erected over the two grave sites: one for the male burial that Miller personally named "King Ingwe" or King Leopard and the other belonging to a female he named "Queen Losha" – who just happened to live some 150 years later (Steyn *et al.* 1998). Bestowing Venda names upon bodies of unknown identity and ancestry caused a media storm and further annoyance between stakeholders on the ground (Nemaheni 2004: 259). The fact that this was done by a white man who had perhaps "gone native" only exacerbated tensions, just as the imposition of Christian crosses did. South African archaeologists declared the process unscientific, tourists demanded explanations, parks employees found it contradictory, and many community members were offended. A senior official in SANParks, herself a Swazi, complained,

> it was a sad mockery to see the ancestors of people being buried in a small, white coffin . . . I think that's a rushed issue. I mean in my culture if somebody dies, you don't bury them tomorrow. If somebody died a long time ago and it's a reburial, for me that means planning for at least two years to make sure everything is right. The cultural rites are followed, and people do not just see it as a burial, but a reburial.

In June 1999 the crosses were removed. Looking back many people agree that none of the parties really knew the appropriate procedures. It was a new era calling for new traditions, new fabrications even. "That's the thing with Thulamela, nobody knew how," one archaeologist explained. "The communities didn't know what was expected of them in terms of how to inform us what was happening on site. The scientists that were involved had never really worked on a public participation basis. There were so many unresolved issues and mistakes, but the important thing about Thulamela is not what *was* done but that *something* was done." And while there were numerous problems from the Kruger side, communities such as the Makahane and the Mhinga were capable of settling their own negotiations amicably without archaeologists and parks officials interfering by advancing their own agendas, ultimately sensationalizing other people's past for their own gain and shoring up their own authority.

The Locals

In this story of donors, rangers, social ecologists, and archaeologists, there evolved a new suite of participants that had previously been absent from the managerial machinery of the park. The "locals" in this case were really a select group of elder black men drawn from the Mhinga or Venda communities who represented some of the poorest villages bordering the park like Bendemutale, Musunda, and Tshikuya. Heritage practitioners, similarly to aid workers, assume that we can speak of "a community," and that heritage landscapes are isomorphic with social and administrative boundaries The "local community" has become a catch-all in archaeological discourse, an umbrella term that signifies a certain kind of ethical participation has taken place on our part, when in actual fact we mostly only ever talk to a small group who are empowered by all or part of their community to speak. My own work with tribal authorities, chiefs, or headmen (indunas) rarely enabled me to talk freely with women. I remember taking heritage booklets to distribute amongst the Makahane, making a point of handing them to a group of older women who were sitting on the ground, talking amongst themselves, and spatially separate from "men's business." My actions to include the women, a self-satisfying Western feminist stance, may have caused undue tensions about their perceived position and power after my departure, or it might have been over-looked, but it has troubled me since then. Village elites are afforded opportunities to remake themselves as interlocutors for international expertise, writes Tsing (2005: 256), through their cosmopolitan connections to powerful outsiders. Yet they may also endorse forms of knowledge that are skewed or unrepresentative when considered in the context of local practice. Not every local vision of "community" extends social justice, environmental protection, or heritage reconcilia-tion. The diverse views of people, reflected by fractures and differences in age, gender, status, wealth, and connection, can never be fully captured in archaeologi-cal ethnographies.

The assumption that the "community" is coherent or conflict-free is a fiction and a romanticization on the part of researchers (Mavhunga and Dressler 2007; van der Waal 2008: 60). I have become increasingly unsettled by the relentless invocation of the "local" and about the mainstreaming of community participa-tion. Every archaeological project suddenly has a local community, everything is collaborative, every project has their pet group that is dragged out on a single outreach day per year, photos taken with necessary natives, and so on. There is a danger of community participation becoming a shelter and safeguard to ensure that our fieldwork continues unchallenged. Rather than being about power sharing or collaboration, sometimes "engagement" simply operates as an endorsement. As was once said of ethnographers, archaeologists have come to rely upon their indigenous/local communities more than the reverse.

Thulamela was touted as the first "collaborative" archaeological project of the Rainbow Nation, and in 1996 Nelson Mandela publicly celebrated "the work of artisans in Thulamela and elsewhere. All these are part of our forgotten heritage left by more than (*sic*) three million years of human civilisation in our country" (Mandela 1996). Community participation and training implied that archaeologi-cal skills and other opportunities would be transferred to the previously disadvan-taged. Yet providing work laboring on stone-wall constructions started to look more like accessing cheap labor than actually building capacity, and it is a pattern seen throughout the history of archaeology (Atalay 2007; Colwell-Chanthaphonh 2010; Meskell 2005e). "They were not really part of the project in a decision-making capability," one archaeologist told me; it was typical of Thulamela "that

Figure 6.2   Stone walls at Thulamela. Courtesy of the author.

although yes it was this community, it was very parks driven." Leonard, a local
Venda man who was trained as a teacher, worked on rebuilding the walls in 1993
and then became one of two guides for Thulamela. He is incredibly proud of his
association with the site. "It was the first time to see this kind of work, unique
for this type of excavation, because we involved the local communities, this hadn't
happened before." Leonard took ownership of the project, developed his archaeological knowledge, and through later projects also conducted a great many interviews with elders in Pafuri. Perhaps because of his personal passion and
involvement, coupled with his own education and teacher training, he could see
potentials that were simply not available to more remote members of the community. He now leads tours at Mapungubwe National Park where he can fully
realize his archaeological knowledge.

    Back in 1995 a dynamic social ecologist, Elizabeth Mhlongo, wrote a damning
report that highlighted problems that we now recognize as endemic to many so-
called collaborative ventures in Community Based Natural Resource Management
(CBNRM) and heritage projects. Reporting on meeting between parks representatives, the archaeologist and six political and traditional leaders, she imputed a

different agenda to it than the interactive one it purported to have, saying that it was more of a "telling session than a participative process" where reports were given by Kruger and "people's agreement was sought.'" She describes the "despondency" that resulted from the meetings being conducted in English but was also because people were not involved from the initial stage and they "viewed themselves in the process more as recipients of a gesture of goodwill from KNP." Like many participatory projects led by functionalism and economism, the incentives delivered by the project were vague and also underpinned by the assumption that there was a rational interest to participate, whether for promissory future benefits or to be socially responsible in the interests of the community (Cleaver 2001: 48). Sidney Miller, on the other hand, claimed a successful "development phase," stating that five to seven men found employment for the duration of the project and a total of R200 000 had been paid in salaries, food, medical attention and clothes that absorbed 20 percent of the project budget (Miller 1997: 536). These returns were short-lived, unsustainable, and only concerned a few laborers. Actual involvement in decision making was minimal, and the communities were not involved in the planning or development of the site. In terms of the oft-quoted "capacity building," Mhlongo found it sadly lacking and instead found that the men were unsure of their role in being there. Black representatives felt impelled to agree and did not understand that they had a right to disagree (Mhlongo 1995: 2). More optimistically, the unintended consequences of projects such as Thulamela might be worth considering in the longer term. Playing a part in the process, however limited or unsatisfactory, may have exposed various individuals to elements of political learning in dealing with organizations like SANParks or even researchers. Leonard is a case in point. Through the Thulamela experience new alliances had been forged. Framing future claims for political representation may also be bolstered by the adoption of a new vocabulary learned during negotiations (Williams 2004: 568). Such developments are difficult to see at Bendemutale or Musunda, but more obvious in the example of the Makuleke, who have had more sustained interactions with park authorities (de Villiers 1999; Reid 2001, Robins and van der Waal 2008), the Malatji or the Mkhabela (Bunn 2006; Meskell 2005a).

A decade on, is the Thulamela project truly significant in the lives of people bordering the park? The short answer is no. During my discussions people would answer questions about archaeology if asked, but the real issues were more recent ones whose salience has never dissipated. Old men wanted to talk about the old days and the injustices meted out to them by Skukuza and the park. Alpheus thought he would be shot when the park told him the army was coming to build a base on his land and that he must vacate immediately. That was in the 1960s and there was no food and no jobs, so he turned to poaching. Freddie was also evicted at that time; his family were taken out in vehicles and dumped in an open area with nothing to survive on. They were totally unprepared; they lost everything, even their donkeys, and could only bring the possessions they could carry. No compensation has been forthcoming. A ceremony on a hill with goats and white crosses was not a palliative: cultural heritage may have been tendered as the remedy for apartheid's ills, but it was also viewed as a cheap trick incapable of assuaging the economic, social, and spiritual deprivations perpetrated.

The Thulamela project demonstrates long-established tendencies in the promotion and packaging of benefits for communities adjacent to natural or cultural sites. Cultural tourism for critical commentators like Ramutsindela has the lure of exotic cultures yet relegates local black people to a common denominator. Recreating black culture as part of the landscape, furthermore, conflates cultural tourism with earlier, outmoded ideas of wilderness and noble savages (McGregor 2005; Ramutsindela 2004: 107). The material benefits promised to communities by researchers, donors, and developers typically includes profit generation and job creation in unthinking and undemonstrated ways. With the pact of participation and compliance, local communities are promised economic benefits from national parks and heritage sites that they could not have derived in their absence. In turn, many communities have subsequently absorbed the hegemonic materialism of protected reserves and heritage enclaves. Employing national survey data, Ramutsindela (2004: 110) demonstrates this, detailing that some 85 percent of South Africans believe that national parks provide benefits for local communities with almost half the respondents listing employment as one real outcome.

Papering over historic injustice and decades of grinding poverty with the cultural cachet of royal houses and indigenous knowledge in park promotional materials and the media privileges a kind of culturalism over material deprivation and should be considered deeply suspicious. Deploying culture over the material inequalities that exist between Kruger and its neighbors as if they were unrelated diverts criticism of capitalism and conservation and provides an alibi for inequity, exploitation, and oppression in their modern guises (Mohan 2001: 159). Thulamela did an enormous amount of work in service of Kruger's new image of inclusivity and benefit sharing, encapsulated in proselytizing slogans like *It's Mine, It's Yours* or *Your Heritage, Your Park, Your World.* Thulamela's success was broadcast globally for UNESCO (Dladla 2000) and in numerous international publications (Chirikure and Pwiti 2008; Galla 1999; Nemaheni 2003; Pwiti and Ndoro 1999), sometimes inaccurately, while the park's commitment to the site scarcely continued to their publication date. The visitor statistics tell their own tale: only 430 people visited from January to June in 2001. By 2005 there were only 911 visitors throughout the year (South African National Parks 2005b: 37). In following reports no figures are supplied. The next step was a political shift in responsibility and blame, from SANParks to the people involved, the participants: the archaeologists, guides, the heritage officer, and the communities. Without long-term commitment, economic and ideological, heritage projects like Thulamela or Masorini (Meskell 2005a) are *bound* to fail and are indeed *built* to fail. The language of "facilitation" and "capacitating," so popular in South Africa, can also be a means of abrogating responsibility so that institutions can distance themselves from such

Figure 6.3   Sign outside Welverdiend primary school. Courtesy of the author.

project failures, disown the process, blame the participants, and engage in willing amnesia.

The park publicly promotes community involvement and shared benefits, but it was near impossible ever to ascertain the projects they sponsored or exact monies they shared. In several of the schools bordering the park like Welverdiend Kruger had erected signs saying that they were partnered in "environmental awareness programs for rare and invasive species." When I asked the headmaster what exactly the park had donated to the school, he answered, with a huge grin, "just the sign." Participation branding is exceptionally well done in Kruger. The trope of local participation has lately been recognized as a tyranny (Cooke and Kothari 2001b: 13–14). Mainstreaming participation by organizations and governments alike has, furthermore, inevitably revealed the yawning chasm between actual outcomes and the representations put forward (Williams 2004: 563). The quasi-religious associations of participatory rhetoric and practice often lead to even greater intervention, inequality, and injustice while retaining considerable political value for institutions like SANParks. In these cases, development attempts to be apolitical; intervention is always premised on the conservation mission, specifically in its guise of biodiversity management and invasive species eradication. Educating "the locals" and environmental activism might seem hard to critique, but there is little evidence of the long-term effectiveness of this kind of participation in materially improving the conditions of the most vulnerable people or as a strategy for social change (Cleaver 2001: 36).

Deep Disregard

During the 2000s I conducted both archaeological and ethnographic research at Thulamela (Meskell 2005a; 2005d; 2007a; 2009c). I had been drawn to the site

Figure 6.4   Falling walls at Thulamela. Courtesy of the author.

after reading accounts in the 1990s of successful community collaborations and reconciliation and the effective suturing of natural and cultural heritage. Speeches by luminaries like Mandela and Mbeki drew attention to South African pride in a newfound black heritage and its public presentation. What I discovered was rather different.

Thulamela's walls were falling, the site was periodically overgrown, and there was no budget allocated for its upkeep. When we went to digitally scan the site we had to clear the undergrowth ourselves with machetes. Few experts in Scientific Services had been to Thulamela and neither had Kruger's black director after several years in his post. When asked about the site he obfuscated, "there's a lot of cultural heritage in the park as well . . . especially those camps in the north where we've got a whole lot of cultural heritage. And, even in the south, we do have a whole lot of cultural heritage . . . because as you might know our mandate has always been biodiversity conservation." Culture steps in when nature is lacking and might be usefully engaged as a filler, as the director made clear,

> the northern part is not that famous for wildlife. So, it's about the birds and the flora that is there. So, we want to put more emphasis in the northern part of the park on cultural heritage as well. As you know, that's why Thulamela has a lot of that art. So, we want to diversify in terms of the conservation that we do in the park. And, we're going to be putting more emphasis on cultural conservation in the northern parts of the park.

But this has not come to pass.

The north of the park remains marginal. Rex, a senior ranger in Pafuri, reiterated the strong north–south divisions in the park. He explained that geographical divisions in park management lead to complete breakdowns in communication and fostered atomization and personal fiefdoms. "Things are done differently here," he said from an office that had no computer but hundreds of post-it notes. "We are on our own. We have less resources, we're understaffed, under-funded, and we don't even have enough vehicles." Despite national attention Thulamela is not a priority. In his view, heritage cannot be supported by the park unless it guarantees its own funding. International consultants McKinsey and Co. arrived at similar conclusions, insisting that social ecology programs must bring economically capable visitors to the park to boost revenue, when their express mission is to work with deprived communities on empowerment projects. Under the early ANC the ascendancy of commercialization within SANParks and other conservation agencies privileged specific projects at the expense of others, particularly community conservation initiatives that were deemed unlikely to generate significant revenues. In this regard Kruger is very similar to its neighboring agency, Mpumalanga Parks Board, where King's (2009: 421) incisive institutional ethnography has shown how internal contestations within the organization highlighted divisions over commercialization as opposed to environmental education and community development initiatives. With Kruger we can add cultural heritage to that mix and note that it has been overshadowed by environmental education and strongly allied with community development, both of which have themselves taken a backseat to biodiversity (Meskell 2009c).

During my work at Thulamela our team was based at the far northern camp of Punda Maria. It was a depressing outpost; staff housing was appalling, people were living in army tents, and the extra cash I paid to some workers was immediately spent on alcohol and prostitutes. There was never adequate advertising for the site or its tours and the booking staff was either disengaged or absent. Staff never displayed the brochures, except on the day when a helicopter full of VIPs were jetted in for an hour; but then the brochures were put away immediately afterwards. There was one photocopied sheet explaining that the Thulamela tour could take around five hours and cost R150, about US$20. Game drives were only R130 and took only three hours. Flyers for game drives were ubiquitous and there were daily logs in reception recording animal and bird sightings. Punda Maria was predominantly populated by elderly, white, bird-watching Afrikaners. The *Rough Guide* describes Punda Maria as the *real* Kruger, a relaxed, tropical outpost with 1930s bungalows. The camp was rustic, amenities were poor, the restaurant atrocious, and the game sightings were minimal save for the Nyala antelope. There has been a strong push for educational programs like *Kids in Kruger* or *Morula Kids* that brought in busloads of black school children funded by the National Lottery. Focused primarily on environmental education again, the teachers I spoke to never visited Thulamela. Reasons proffered were the amount of time and organization it took, the cost, and that it was primarily an environmental education trip not one that incorporated cultural heritage.

Despite being the heritage officer for Kruger, Laura had no control over the condition of Thulamela or its objects – the latter reside in the vaults at Pretoria

University with no immediate plan of return. She told me they had waited 10 years for the beads from the excavation to be cleaned and returned, and my own team saw metal objects poorly conserved and decaying when they were taken out for digital scanning. Other objects had disappeared from the inventory, and of course, some had been swept away in the 2000 floods. The archaeologist, Sidney Miller, who was in arbitration with senior management in SANParks over the handling of the excavation, has continued to take tours in the park on an informal basis as part of personal connections and the Honorary Rangers program. Accountability to members of Scientific Services and People and Conservation Departments can thus be bypassed and the mystical stories of Thulamela and other sites can be told. Antjie has an expressed love of archaeology and organizes annual field trips and courses with Miller as part of ranger training. She is impressed by his knowledge because "he can actually make it alive for them, and when there's questions he can give the big picture. And just like a story, a nice story." Antjie is unaware of the depressed state of heritage in the park and prefers to work with Miller rather than Kruger's resident heritage officer. For her, archaeology becomes a personal experience that is entangled with charismatic personalities and their narratives.

A tale of two settlements, then, can be encapsulated by two images: Thulamela overgrown with vegetation and Masorini burned for clearance. In their shadow, black history in the park is similarly left in ruins; all are victims of the discursive geographical space of nature. Stefan, who was a major player in the Thulamela project, admits the site is now suffering. Who does he blame but the new generation of black social ecologists and heritage managers at Head Office in Pretoria: people who have only recently been employed by SANParks. He neither takes personal responsibility nor admits that white archaeologists, managers, or scientists have any share in the blame for this deep disregard (Cock 2007: 149). Despite protests to the contrary, he was clearly annoyed at being subordinate to the new young black elite, tensions ensued and he eventually left the organization. Heritage is always racialized in Kruger and because heritage work was subsumed under Social Ecology during the 1990s and now under the People and Conservation Department. Archaeology, I have argued, is seen as synonymous with development and BEE, a soft option that is neither scientific nor conducive to conservation. In most issues concerning people and parks (e.g., Child 2004; Cock and Fig 2002; Fabricius 2001; Igoe 2004; Magome and Murombedzi 2003; Moore and Masuku Van Damme 2002; Ramutsindela 2004), the "people" here are always read as black people. As a park spokesman said, "if you lean towards the social ecology side of things you're going to negate and you're going to directly harm your conservation effort." SANParks collapsed environmental education, interpretation, and cultural resource management into one portfolio, and there have been more than 15 years of resistance and stigma towards People and Conservation, as my interviews revealed. Over those years many of the dynamic black social ecologists resigned, particularly the women, over the lack of support and transformation.

While there exists a wealth of studies demonstrating the impacts of protected areas upon local populations, fewer studies reveal the internal debates, events, and politics that produce conservation policies and environmental citizens (King 2009: 419). SANParks and Kruger might easily be cast as homogenous and monolithic, but the danger is the glossing of internal tensions between individuals and departments that produce very different accounts of the good and of the institution's mission.

Revealing Archaeology in a New Nation

Thulamela was a touchstone for liberal heritage in 1990s South Africa and, like other national ventures, was haunted by unfulfilled promises of uplift and development before an international audience. Yet given the history of archaeology in South Africa, perhaps it would have been idealistic to expect such an expedient transformation. Historians and archaeologists were considered with skepticism during and after apartheid for their complicity in promulgating racist agendas and their denial of black history. The public acknowledgement of the San people as the earliest inhabitants of Southern Africa at the Origins Center, University of the Witwatersrand is one episode that underscores the consequences of that public skepticism. The seemingly simple historical "fact" of prior San occupation caused controversy on Johannesburg public radio when black callers accused white scientists of attempting, once again, to displace blacks as the first, the indigenous occupants of South Africa. Liberal visions of the nation have given way to narrow sentiments of ethnonationalism, in which nations are now tightly scripted on the basis of common language, religion, heritage, and ethnic ancestry (Kagwanja 2008: xviii). Such misreadings and elisions of the nation's past, specifically its precolonial past, are one of the palpable dangers in sidelining the specificity of an archaeological past and substituting it for a rainbow-hued narrative. In these slippery moments of recounting or rejecting the past new fault lines can emerge, new ethic tensions become inflamed, and South Africans face the danger of repeating history.

The placing of archaeology, then, requires broader examination. During apartheid archaeology was complicit in the political project of buttressing ethnic identity and the maintenance of Bantustans. The apartheid government was very anxious to legitimize its homeland policy throughout the 1970s and 1980s by demonstrating, through the use of archaeology and anthropology, that the communities which were settled in artificially created areas had, in fact, always lived there (see also Pikirayi 2007). Archaeology in the Afrikaans universities, particularly at Pretoria University, was deeply implicated as it was deployed to establish tribal origins. One scholar active throughout these decades explained that, as a result of this political pact, the University of Pretoria was bestowed "sole rights to excavate anything in Kruger National Park," as well as Mapungubwe, whilst other English institutions were denied access (see also Bonner and Carruthers 2003: 44). Many of these excavations in the 1970s were highly militarized. "It was a playground for the University of Pretoria which was desperately trying to prove all these communities like the Venda and Shona have always lived in these home-lands," which was untenable since the homelands were arbitrarily imposed divi-sions (see also Pwiti and Ndoro 1999). Mapungubwe was another major site for apartheid doctrine, but one that was to ultimately confound a racist program through material evidence of black achievement and identity. As a negative legacy, bitter struggles linger today over the wealth of the site, repatriation and display of artifacts, continued excavation, reburial of human remains, institutional monopoly, and efforts to constitute an ethical stakeholding process continue to plague the University of Pretoria and the new custodians of the site, SANParks (Meskell and Masuku Van Damme 2007).

Although some academics were outspoken in their protests during the apart-heid years (Hall 1984; 1988), it is fair to say that archaeology has suffered as a result of apoliticizing the discipline and now must reconfigure itself to meet the demands of a burgeoning tourist industry, new and complex constituencies, the recognition of multiple pasts and the ever-present specter of a heritage that hurts. Archaeology during the 1980s was "a travesty of method," according to one senior archaeologist, whereby the pretenses of science masked ugly racial politics. When the bans were lifted, many archaeologists were free to enjoy international conferences and recognition, but there was still no imperative for them to engage at home. South African archaeology today allies itself with tourism, he observes, and assumes that offering black employment is enough. Archaeologists remain "fatally confused about heritage" and have failed to unpack its significance. While in Australia working-class archaeologists closely allied themselves with aboriginal struggles for self-determination and labor politics (Lilley 2000b), in South Africa many archaeologists remained immune.

More than a decade after transition, archaeology is yet to be considered a black profession, it remains difficult to attract students to the discipline, and those prominent black scholars who hold university posts tend to be from neighboring countries like Zimbabwe. Unlike in other postcolonial nations there is not a general sense that archaeology can tell people about their past, validate their rights, or offer tangible benefits to the wider populace. Archaeology remains a luxury in the face of much more pressing social and economic concerns. "Archaeologists have isolated themselves from the community," one academic admitted.

> It is so much a white profession, and it hasn't made the efforts to change itself as a discipline. There are so few black archaeologists. And archaeologists haven't made the effort to establish a popular discourse to really communicate that. There is no popular consciousness about archaeology, and it remains a very alienating profession in that sense, and that's the problem.

(see also Shepherd 2005). He cites a lack of visibility in textbooks, classrooms, magazines, and the media and contrasts this with the Middle East "where everybody in some respects is an amateur archaeologist." The discipline's survival depends on partnerships with local communities to establish meaningful connections and stimulate interest in the material past. This is bolstered by the view that

> indifference or negative attitudes of local people to heritage is an issue that can be understood only within a political frame and that such attitudes have been one of the lasting legacies of colonialism within the context of colonial resettlement policies which alienated people from their heritage. This is particularly true of South Africa and Zimbabwe, where there was a large settler colonial population and consequent land alienation. (Pwiti and Ndoro 1999: 144)

Archaeology, as a discipline and set of practices and potential cultural offerings, has also occupied a no man's land since democracy. Significantly, it would be historians and not archaeologists who would take the lead in the crafting of heritage legislation and who would be advisors to agencies like the National Heritage Council (NHC) and others. The NHC is a statutory body comprised of "specialists in history, language, culture and the arts." This notion that heritage has become the preserve of historians and art museum professionals became increasingly clear during the NHC's first anniversary conference in 2005. Held at the luxurious Sandton Convention Center, the celebration featured the government's new black elite, an array of self-proclaimed ethnic royals, and a small coterie of well-intentioned white academics, bolstered in their efforts by gourmet hors d'oeuvres and lavish conference packs. Historians, often political figures during the apartheid years, filled the vacuum left by a certain unwillingness on the part of archaeologists to engage publicly. Archaeologists are generally reluctant to assume the role of public intellectuals, and this is especially the case in South Africa. Heritage in South Africa refers most commonly to the arts and culture in a contemporary or traditional sense, framed in recent historical terms rather than ancient understandings. Thus heritage is often immaterial, including music, dance, performance, indigenous knowledge, artistic skill, and so on. These practices are proximally closest to the vast majority of people's cultural experience and knowledge, are avidly consumed as African exotica by international visitors, and shored up by governmental and non-governmental economic initiatives. By contrast, archaeological materials and accounts seem woefully lacking. Indeed, the inherent richness of periods like the Iron Age are further severely curtailed by the relative lack of salient information beyond a description of the remains, a glance at the writings on Thulamela or Mapungubwe would demonstrate the point, although gradually new archaeological findings and research orientations are being made available (Hall 2010; Hall *et al.* 2008; Hall and Smith 2000; Schoeman 2006a; 2006b).

   As we have seen with the archaeological sites in Kruger National Park, the past is expected to labor in the service of the state to generate income and subsume its fiscal responsibilities. On the one hand, heritage is supposed to enhance the national fiscus, as is repeatedly emphasized, and on the other to draw from it for important projects. Yet at the same time resources are being plowed into the national heritage sector infrastructure, including developing entirely new organizations such as NHC. This has led to increased fragmentation and little integration or organizational capacity. Pallo Jordan (2004), then Minister for Arts and Culture, recognized this predicament arguing that "government departments, non-governmental organisations, community-based organisations and individuals have undertaken pockets of uncoordinated initiatives to preserve and popularise living heritage. Whilst these are recognised and commended, a government-led, synergetic approach as well as community driven strategies are required to develop a comprehensive programme that captures the imagination of all South African citizens." Government intervention was called for repeatedly at the NHC conference because, in the words of one delegate, those same "market failures have brought about a skewed cultural industry structure." But more than blaming the economy's performance, implementing a vast national project requires a new generation of trained heritage practitioners replete with a diverse skill set euphemistically referred to as "capacity." Yet capacity is exactly what is lacking in the new South Africa for the very reasons I have outlined. Reasons why archaeology has failed to attract previously disadvantaged students include entrenched racism, educational deficits, an ingrained disinterest in heritage and archaeology, and the failure of many academics to effectively convey the relevance of the past to the present.

The political devolution we observe in the heritage sector, the liberalization of the tender system, the proliferation of private heritage contractors and enterprises like the Apartheid Museum or the Mapungubwe Interpretive Center, and the atomized provincial heritage agencies all reflect the penchant for outsourcing the critical apparatus of state support, to an "ever more outsourced, dispersed, deinstitutionalized, constitutionally ordained governance" (Comaroff and Comaroff 2006: 3). The dispersal of government, observable in so many aspects of post-apartheid society, results in an attenuated set of bureaucratic institutions and operates more as a licensing and franchising authority. Along with liberalization, misplaced spending and commercial branding accompanies tenders, privatization, and outsourcing as demonstrated within Kruger. The NHC itself evinces these tendencies. Taken aback by the profligate and ostentatious conference expenditure at Sandton, I commented to another delegate that no lavish "workshop culture" exists for heritage in the United States, to which she responded, "this is Africa, darling."

At the time of writing, racialized tension continues to simmer around archaeological practice in South Africa. At a series of national meetings young black researchers have been singled out for criticism by a largely white establishment. The latter have argued publicly that black archaeologists have not received sufficient training and risk damaging the material heritage of the nation. This comes at the same time as the Association of South African Professional Archaeologists (ASAPA) has recently crafted an ethical mandate for all heritage and field projects across the country. ASAPA has experienced great successes in raising memberships, creating CRM accreditation, and enhancing their scholarly publication, *The South African Archaeological Bulletin*. However, in October 2007 three South African archaeologists directly challenged the ASAPA council for not being more active in the transformation process. Ndlovu, Mokokwe, and Motloung formed the Transformation Task Team with other Council members and, after considerable debate, constituted a Transformation Charter for the organization (Smith 2009: 87). In March 2008 the charter was presented at the ASAPA meetings and tensions flared over two terms: "black" and "affirmative action." After much wrangling "black" was changed to "African descent," since almost all South Africans see themselves as "Africans, " which is one reason why indigenous heritage is a particularly thorny issue. "Affirmative action" was perceived as too vague, and a substitute for it was broadly agreed in "interventive action" (Smith 2009: 88), though, of course, this too seems nebulous. Some 97 percent of voting members endorsed the charter. Yet, as Smith eloquently argued,

> collectively we had not done enough . . . this has led to suspicions of entrenched conservativism and resistance to transformation. It is up to us to demonstrate that this is not the case. We have a conservative element amongst us, no sector of society does not (and conservatives come in all genders, ethnicities and colours); but there is also a proud struggle history within archaeology and we do not remember this often enough and we have not built upon it in the way we should. (2009: 89).

Harnessing a language of solidarity, equality, and social engagement a younger generation of archaeologists might finally be ready to transform the discipline.

Treasure in the Veld

Archaeological projects in Kruger and Mapungubwe National Parks still bear the scars of years of poor excavation, curation, and public presentation by generations of white archaeologists, underlining the duplicity of the above assertions made by white archaeologists. Expressing dismay at "the amount of damage that has been done by excavations," a senior SANParks official remarked that "we're just fortunate that many people don't know in our communities what has been happening." Part of his mandate has been to "try and put our house in order and see if we can have other sound processes for development." A particular kind of archaeology is called for, not simply an extractive or traditional archaeological practice; instead it would be inclusive, collaborative, and focus on living settlements rather than exhumations. Given this vision for the discipline, it is not surprising that few new excavation permits have been issued in recent years. Archaeology should be contributing public goods in South Africa, offering a source of pride and that is, in one colleague's view, what the ANC "thinks people are doing." Sadly, from his perspective archaeology is more akin to treasure hunting. This recalls the many yellowing papers in the Skukuza vaults pertaining to treasure hunting in the park over the past century, prospecting for gold and cinnabar, and permits to dig for the Kruger Millions fabled to lie buried somewhere in the veld. Lacking any knowledge of the South African past, prehistoric San rock art panels around Kruger are thought by some to be maps indicating the hiding place of Paul Kruger's treasure, buried in the dying moments of the Boer War. To that end treasure hunters have used explosives to dynamite rock shelters, destroying one ancient treasure in the fruitless search for another.

The only documented gold in Kruger National Park was found at Thulamela. The broader value and significance of the site was adroitly recognized at the key moment in the nation's transition. It was believed then that a cultural heritage program in SANParks could effectively contribute towards "nation building and the creation of a common society in South Africa based on cultural sensitivity and awareness. This would involve reversing the ethnic particularism and notions of conservationism enshrined under apartheid" (Cock and Fig 2002: 148). As noted then and now, the significance of national parks is not limited simply to their capacity to preserve biodiversity and promote ecotourism. But as the aforementioned events around Thulamela make clear, the successes of the project, however meager, have not been capitalized upon, literally or metaphorically, and archaeological sites since the 1990s have languished in Kruger. The walls of Thulamela have fallen into disrepair; tumbles of stones that were laid in the 1990s make traversing the site hazardous, while trees and grasses engulf the stone circles, together creating a picture of decaying heritage (Meskell 2007a). This decline is not the product of centuries of abandonment with luxuriant undergrowth threatening to engulf a lost city. It is the material evidence of disregard for a decade-old project of rehabilitation and reconciliation: that too seems strangled by weeds. But before archaeologists lament the loss of site integrity, we should reflect upon the incisive expertise of a senior black archaeologist who had worked at Great Zimbabwe and was present during the 1990s rebuilding program. The walled superstructures at Thulamela, their extent, stone cutting and wall design are all a fiction in his view, not based on archaeological evidence, on existing foundational structures, but on dreams and wishes largely materialized by whites. Their lack of training and expertise, the pressure to provide a vision of Thulamela for the new nation, undercut not only the material traces of black civilization, but destabilized the integrity of archaeology and its ability to forge a viable vehicle for new knowledge, collaboration, and transformation. Whether for the best intentions or for strategic gains, white archaeologists, black communities, foreign researchers, park officials, international media, and black laborers have all been trapped in that fiction. I include myself in that entanglement, working as I did with scientists to scan Thulamela's standing walls, creating 3D models of the site, and interviewing project participants and community elders about the 1990s project and its aftermath (Meskell 2007a). Like others I was drawn to the promise of Thulamela as an uplifting, conciliatory venture between parks and people, black and white, archaeologists and conservationists, that should have constituted the real promise, not simply the romance, of treasure.

Note

1 http://www.umjindi.org/pages/history/history_kruger_millions.htm (accessed March 14, 2010).

Chapter 7

Kruger is a Gold Rock

Parastatal and Private Visions of the Good

I personally am not very interested in animals. I do not want to spend my holidays watching crocodiles. Nevertheless, I am entirely in favor of their survival. I believe that after diamonds and sisal, wild animals will provide Tanganyika with its greatest source of income. Thousands of Americans and Europeans have the strange urge to see these animals. (Julius Nyerere, First President of Tanzania, 1961)

Well Deserved

Welverdiend means "well deserved" in Afrikaans and is characteristic of many of the fanciful names once given to the parcels of land that radiate out from Kruger's borders. Places named Lisbon and Lilydale sounded so genteel and cosmopolitan, but in reality were often poor and desperate places where people attempt to eke out a living by selling fruit and firewood on roadside stalls. Welverdiend seems a rather cruel name in retrospect, suggesting that the poor black families living without proper housing, roads, or resources somehow deserve their lot. Though only a stone's throw from Kruger's fence, tourists would not normally stumble upon such a settlement. Welverdiend was different to the vast rural sprawls of Bushbuckridge or Acornhoek that you had to drive through, with millions of people and soaring HIV deaths, where you could always see funerals being conducted from the roadside. Those towns bordered the park and were situated on the most expedient routes traversing its length rather than along those inside Kruger along which drivers were constrained by the speed limit of 50 kph. A colleague and I had made the trip to Welverdiend to conduct interviews with two

The Nature of Heritage: The New South Africa, First Editon. Lynn Meskell.
© 2012 John Wiley & Sons, Inc. Published 2012 by Blackwell Publishing Ltd.

prominent men we had heard speak at a stakeholder forum meeting instigated by SANParks. Outspoken and articulate, they were not afraid to speak honestly about Kruger and its failings, particularly in providing any tangible benefits for its immediate neighbors (see also Brockington 2004; Igoe 2004). Kruger "forcefully removed our forefathers," Philleos said publicly at the meeting, "but they say they don't owe us anything. They owe us. They still owe us for every generation since they removed us. We need to feel that the park is accountable to us so that the engagement is not rubberstamped for something you've already approved." This statement directly targeted the motives of the forum, itself a process forced upon SANParks by the national government. The parastatal was directed to hold external public meetings with various stakeholders to discuss natural resource utilization, benefits to communities, and issues of access and accountability. This is what led me to Philleos and Andreis.

Philleos was a member of the Hoxani forum and a local school principal. His own family once lived in the park near Satara camp and was forced out some time after 1926. Like so many other people interviewed, he speaks of eviction as a painful history when white officials claimed their livestock were diseased and subsequently destroyed their animals. Not long after, those same officials forcibly removed the communities around Satara. In contemporary scholarly literature park authorities justify their history by asserting that there were only "isolated black families" in the park or that such removals occurred internationally (Mabunda, Pienaar, and Verhoef 2003: 8). Philleos and Andreis believe that there was no disease, rather that this was a calculated strategy to weaken black communities since cattle were the tangible sign of their wealth; they were shot in order to render Africans poor. The strategy was twofold. Robbed of their wealth, Africans were also compelled to work for white farmers in a form of forced labor. Again, park literature renders the action legitimate but ultimately "incomprehensible to the local people and unforgivable" (Mabunda, Pienaar, and Verhoef 2003: 9). In answer to the park's assertion that endemic disease kept the African population low if not negligible, Andreis believes that there were natural remedies to manage various illnesses. He took a cynical view, "if there is no one to challenge the scientists they will continue, if they've written a book they think it's the correct information." Both men named specific historic and ancestral sites now within the park's boundaries, arguing that the area was once occupied by thousands of people, although they were scattered in numerous settlements. At that time, they recount, there was no boundary with Mozambique and people moved freely. An older generation of people still remembered, as Philleos' mother did, and they argued that researchers from Kruger should visit these elders and record their stories before they too should disappear. Elders are cognizant of Kruger's African history and concerned that so many black people worked to create the park, their knowledge was integral to its success, and yet their names are forgotten and never published. "Once we become part of the management," Philleos added without a hint of irony, "we could start to change that picture." When we visited in 2006 they were busily finalizing a book called *The History of Vanhlanganu* to be the published by an NGO.

The residents of Welverdiend, like those I interviewed around Pafuri, Phalaborwa and Numbi, all live close to Kruger's main gates and are afforded a view of the park's visitor numbers. They share similar views that the park must create a "fair, beneficial relationship [instead of] always coming with things benefiting KNP. They do not have the community in their heart." Elder men I spoke with are tired of the endless attempts at control, the empty promises that constitute only lip-service in their words: "Show me what they have done? They have been here for 100 years, what have they to show for it?" Kruger is more concerned with foreigners than locals, and they are "singing their song, *Americans are watching, see the rhino, the elephant, the giraffe . . .*" He calls for a model of "collaboration management" like they have established with AndBeyond and their partner NGO, Africa Foundation. Instead of expressing animosity towards Kruger in spite of its repressive histories, community members continually wanted to forge positive relationships and partnerships, to learn and prosper, and to "develop black people." Plaintively Philleos tells me, "Kruger is our factory," and even more strikingly, "Kruger is a gold rock on which our community can be built." Philleos and Andreis stressed that there was an overwhelming need to empower people locally, because "tomorrow they will manage the park, there are no jobs here, no factory." Such communities in their view are uniquely positioned in terms of the geography, history, and knowledge to both protect the park and benefit from its success. As the Tsonga saying goes, *nhonga yale kule ayilweli* or "a stick that is far away cannot protect."

This episode demonstrates a number of key issues that are threaded throughout the book. First, that there are colossal and unrealistic pressures on conservation and other forms of heritage to address and ameliorate current socio-economic inequalities in South Africa. Second, it underscores that often it is private and non-state actors that are fulfilling these therapeutic roles and attending to the gaps caused by shortfalls in state organization and implementation. Third, the priorities espoused by the inhabitants of Welverdiend do not privilege the past or cultural heritage, but are highly attuned to more pressing matters of survival, although they do still desire the access and ability to showcase their traditions.

Developing Black People

The ANC together with the South African Communist Party (SACP) and the Congress of South African Trade Unions (COSATU) initiated their own home-grown structural adjustment program, beginning with the Reconstruction and Development Programme in 1994 and followed two years later by GEAR. Focused on macroeconomic policy, GEAR fostered a tough anti-inflation stance, trade liberalization, and international financial deregulation. Economic liberalization in South Africa has fostered foreign investment, devalued the local currency, eliminated trade tariffs, offered foreign tax breaks and kept wages low at home. The implication of this crisis, according to Gelb (2003: 39), has meant that big business has become more powerful, "and the acceptance of its property rights in the context of the negotiated transition meant that any capital reform would require big business's consent and indeed its active participation." Most commentators agree that from the perspective of inequality and poverty reduction, macroeconomic policy has been far from an unqualified success for ordinary South Africans.

Economic liberalization, as demonstrated by the Spatial Development Initiative (SDI), involves private and public sector partnerships and investment that fast-tracks large-scale development in tourism, industry, and agriculture. This includes heritage tourism and inventories of cultural assets (Deacon, Mngqolo, and Prosalendis 2003: 42). SDIs are implemented in areas that are rich in natural resources but also have widespread poverty and weak institutional capacity to manage development. These include the Fish River, Richards Bay, Phalaborwa, and the Wild Coast. Privatization of these initiatives is purported to enhance international competitiveness, regional cooperation, and a more diversified ownership base. It is claimed that investment (including financial, technical, and institutional resources) cannot only be made by the public sector and its parastatal agencies but must also make sense for the private sector. This "crowding-in" effect of the new government endorses the policy that infrastructural development projects once financed by the public sector should now be subsidized by private investment and lending. For instance, the Phalaborwa SDI hopes to profit from nature-based and cultural tourism, and in the process to benefit the rural economies of places like Welverdiend (Büscher and Dressler 2007: 603), in order to achieve these goals the lack of modern infrastructure, which seriously curtails such possibilities needs to be overcome; once a matter solely for the public purse this is now regarded as being of mutual interest and requiring mutual funding.

Market-driven development is widely viewed as the only avenue to improving livelihoods in South Africa. Expressions such as "unbundling assets" and "fast-tracking development" have become the jargon of a new elite (Magome 2004: 153; Magome and Murombedzi 2003). Yet conservationists identify GEAR as the critical mechanism for downplaying nature preservation in light of pressing social needs (King 2009: 413). Conservation agencies argue that nature-based tourism can offer a viable strategy for generating economic benefits to previously excluded communities while still meeting the environmental goals set by national and international agencies. Certainly by 2007 tourism was earning more than gold for the South African economy (Varty 2008: 45). One analysis of the economic contribution of Kruger's visitors (on average R4400 per person) demonstrates that most of their expenditure goes on accommodation and park products, and thus remains inside Kruger (Saayman and Saayman 2006: 78). Significantly, the study reveals that Kruger contributes relatively little (0.37%) to the provincial economy of Mpumalanga. Described brilliantly as the "carcass model," the presence of the park does attract other forms of development, such as private game reserves, that in turn contribute additional revenues. While conservation continues to be positioned as a key driver in stimulating tourism, it has yet to make a cogent demonstration of exactly how such revenues are distributed to impoverished communities (King 2009: 413).

Global networks involving agencies such as the International Monetary Fund, World Bank, WWF, and IUCN are increasingly impacting countries like South Africa, where the implementation of Western-oriented conservation models garner economic support. The ideas attached to donor assisted funds are aligned with those powerful constituencies and often serve to further marginalize indigenous groups (Igoe 2004: 11). This situation – coupled with the global proliferation of NGOs (once called charities) that were seen as preferable to governments in terms of accountability, transparency, service delivery, and the promotion of democracy, means that many state functions have ostensibly been replaced. At the time of writing there were over 2000 NGOs and development agencies operating in South Africa. During 2006 Melinda Gates was visiting many of the same communities I had, examining clinics and schools in an effort to determine whether their millions might target the AIDS pandemic in the area. The Bill and Melinda Gates Foundation now funds programs to combat tuberculosis in South Africa.[1] NGOs have increasingly stepped in to fill the gap left by the failures and shortcomings of states everywhere to advance the position of indigenous populations and to strengthen civil society. These developments are acutely observable in South Africa today. NGOs, INGOs, high-profile donors, and other non-state actors have taken up indigenous causes; provided services once maintained by the state including healthcare, education, and general infrastructure; and established programs that protect both nature and culture.

Public–private partnerships are becoming the norm in all aspects of South African society. National parks provide a classic example, where banks, telecommunications companies, American foundations, and charitable organizations build infrastructure and support key programs. This is also part of a global trend whereby governments continue to reduce funding for the management of national parks, and park authorities are forced to turn to their visitors, commercial tour operators, and transnational agencies as funding sources for infrastructure and management (Buckley 2002). In Kruger National Park this has meant that private operators were given 20-year concession contracts to either take over or upgrade existing lodge facilities or choose new sites for development. Under SANParks restructuring and privatization program, known ominously as Operation Prevail (Masuku Van Damme and Meskell 2009), private companies had invested R122 million by 2001 in six sites. By 2010 there were some 16 private concessions offering luxury accommodation. The plan has been for the private sector to own restaurants and a large number of camps across SANParks in order to improve the quality of food and services. In contrast to the official view that the private sector would be responsible for generating the much-needed finances, park authorities continued to sell off wildlife as a fund-raising strategy. In 2001, SANParks sold 21 white rhinos as part of this strategy so that the proceeds could be channeled into land acquisition (Ramutsindela 2004: 86). In 2009 they sold more rhinos to finance their anti-poaching operations (Mabunda 2009).

Following international trends, southern Africa has experienced a significant growth in private sector investment in protected areas, including national parks. According to the Global Environment Facility, in 2002 protected areas across the globe were 36.8 percent financed by the private sector, with governments spending only 13 percent, NGOs 0.39 percent, and foundations 0.03 percent (Ramutsindela 2004: 151). South Africa's state financial contribution to national parks has dwindled over the past years because they have been under pressure to meet the basic needs of the poor black majority. The economic logic of contemporary ecotourism is largely a continuation of commercial interests that have long been entangled with the conservation and privatization of nature. Private investment in conservation has taken a variety of forms, as witnessed in and around Kruger: management under contract of state-owned national parks by private individuals or companies; the inclusion of private land into state-owned parks; the founding of private wildlife sanctuaries or hunting reserves; the formation of conservation trusts through land purchase by entrepreneurs or NGOs; and the management by corporations under contract of community land like that of AndBeyond (Hutton, Adams, and Murombedzi 2005: 353).

South Africa's history of cross-sectoral partnerships in conservation dates back to the 1980s when new national parks like Pilanesberg were established. However, recently the element of "community involvement" appears largely to have disappeared in those partnerships. There is even some concern that public–private partnership is emerging as a potential new threat to community-based conservation activity (Hutton, Adams, and Murombedzi 2005: 352–3). Taken together, researchers must increasingly examine new cosmopolitan configurations characterized by changing networks and alliances. We cannot simply look at heritage or conservation agencies, but must factor in non-state actors, donors, NGOs, and parastatals in a mosaic of spheres. Burgeoning commodification of both nature and culture, with all the attendant promises, cannot be overlooked, nor can the widening gap between rhetoric and reality (Büscher and Dressler 2007: 588).

This is Not a Development Agency

Across SANParks portfolio, Kruger National Park has the highest incidence of adjacent poverty of any park. In 2002 there were 1.5 million people living around the park and another 3.3 million within 100 kilometers. Their average income was

R6791 per annum, or about US$900 (McKinsey Report 2002: 14–15). Out of this poverty, but also out of historically grounded demands for reparation, arise two critical issues for Kruger and SANParks. The first matter is shared benefits, whether communities derive a percentage of gate takings, for example, or have access to particular natural resources. The other is the volatile problem of land claims. Both issues represent missed opportunities for national healing and transition in formerly race-based institutions like national parks. More strategically, the organization could address both issues as potentials for benefit sharing, co-management, and development within a program of Corporate Social Responsibility (CSR). CSR is a global business trend that is increasingly prevalent in South Africa's private sector (Sharp 2006) and is what underlies SANParks rationale for establishing the People and Conservation unit.

Since the late 1990s there has been a concerted move by international and national agencies to add development to the list of business corporations' social responsibilities. South Africa is typical here precisely because the responsibility for development is being shifted from governments to businesses (Sharp 2006). The democratic dispensation and new forms of power and empowerment has come hand in hand with new forms of decentralization, deregulation, outsourcing, and sadly widespread corruption and an inability on the government's part to provide key services or to keep law and order (Comaroff and Comaroff 2006). National parks and heritage sites alike are now impelled to be economically self-sustaining. The disadvantaged communities who were promised benefits from their cultural and natural legacies are now seen as either constituting new markets to boost conservation or selfish agents ready to deplete or alienate those assets. It should be recalled here that parastatals like SANParks underwent their own "development" phases after apartheid, benefitting from the vast resources of international governments, consulting firms, researchers, and NGOs.

McKinsey and Co. consultants spearheaded SANParks liberalization in the early 2000s. The mission as they saw it was to protect biodiversity by protecting park assets and revenues through "improving demographics," "building constituency," and "building good relationships with local communities" (McKinsey Report 2002: 1). Whites were needed as "paying visitors" and constitute a major parks lobby, patronage for the future, and donor support. Blacks, conversely, were perceived as future patrons required for the long-term survival of parks since they comprise 79 percent of the population and then made up only 4 percent of park visitors. Environmental education was the avenue by which South African citizens might be disciplined toward conservation and biodiversity buy-in, yet their attachments to cultural heritage went unnoticed. SANParks was advised to pursue US foundations and did receive $31 million from US donors in 2002. Other proposed targets included the World Bank, Mellon Foundation, the French and Danish governments, the Humane Society US, and private donors. McKinsey suggested selling carbon credits and using poverty relief and education funding as ways to directly support the conservation mission. As a result of their consultancy they also identi-

fied that most conservation science in Kruger is itself outsourced and, more worryingly, operates without any independent check.

The way CEO David Mabunda (2009) tells it, SANParks has emerged as an
economic success. In 2009 he claimed SANParks was the only successful conservation institution in the world that had been able to generate 80 percent of its annual
operational budget of R1.2 billion from sustainable commercial interventions.
Other conservation institutions have, to a greater extent, depended on government funding and other large corporations. Such is their success that Mabunda
expects to host a delegation of officials from the largest and richest national parks
authority in the world, the US Parks Authority, to learn from SANParks how to
revive the viability and sustainability of the parks system. His view is optimistic
given SANParks' heavy reliance on external organizations not only for financial
backing but also for restructuring, development, and institutional direction. Not
so long ago McKinsey and Co. and the Danish government, through the aegis of
Danish Cooperation for Environment and Tourism (DANCED), conducted audits,
and the latter provided guidance on everything from community initiatives, to
social ecology and biodiversity management, to the development of the internationally funded archaeological site of Thulamela. DANCED's annual scorecard in
the 1990s was so damning that the organization subsequently refused to extend
funding to SANParks (DANCED 2001; Magome 2004: 140). A decade on, and
those lessons have been learned and privatization has proved a more expedient
route than appealing to donor agencies.

At the same time that SANParks was undergoing intensive restructuring and
calling upon development expertise, the organization was similarly being asked to
aid in the development of Kruger's neighboring black communities. Both were
enterprises for which the park had little previous experience. In 1997, minister
Pallo Jordan told the National Parks Board that "local communities should be
given access to some of the resources in national parks and be included in conserving the national assets by drawing them into the work force . . . there should be
a symbiotic relationship between the local communities and national parks"
(quoted in Ramutsindela 2003: 45). The same ministry felt that even some land
claims within national parks could be tempered through the development of
partnerships. The challenge remains for conservation agencies to find a balance
between the preservationists concerned with fostering biodiversity and the welfare
of local communities (Romero and Andrade 2004: 578). Nevertheless, SANParks
has insisted that land claim settlements "should not apply to national parks, which
exist to protect biodiversity and are not a development agency" (Groenewald and
Macleod 2005: 6). One ecologist describes Kruger's predicament as "a certain
schizophrenia, is it just a conservation agency, or about research, culture, preservation, education, a development agency?" He believes these priorities have probably
always existed but have waxed and waned through the history of the organization.
It would be naive to imagine, however, that national parks under apartheid
fostered development or education for black or colored communities, or were

particularly concerned with cultures other than an Afrikaner one. My research suggests that the situation did not sufficiently change in the first decade after the end of apartheid. In 2000 Dr Anthony Hall-Martin, Director of Conservation Development for SANParks, made that position crystal clear when he stated publicly that he was "not particularly concerned about communities and people and all that stuff" (quoted in Magome 2004: 138).

While the mantra, "we are not a development agency" abounds within Kruger, there are still concerted efforts to empower, employ, and build capacity in neighboring communities. One woman at the forefront of this venture explained, "we do facilitation, but for the projects that we are running, we don't have a budget allocated. Suppose there's a need for me to train craft workers. I will not have a budget to pay for the training myself." Funding might come from a government department or increasingly an NGO. Her sanguine view was that "if Kruger is not able to live harmoniously with the communities, then Kruger is not going to exist. Kruger tends to see itself as an organization that is fully responsible for conservation. But development is there and that's where maybe we need to change our focus." During my time in the park I repeatedly asked for documentation outlining the dozen or so projects that employed and supported local people, none was ever forthcoming on paper. Employees described schemes like training contractors and employing people for gardening, thatching, sewing, and craft production. Much was made of several failing craft stalls adjacent to the entrance gates, whereas the lucrative park shops were littered with tacky souvenirs made in China or elsewhere in Africa – it was a "quality" issue I was told.

Another complication is that community employment "can also mean white farms and entrepreneurs, but it is meant to be black empowerment" one social ecologist explained. "Even when the opportunity is there, we lack capacity. We don't have the expertise of the Department of Trade and Industry or Department of Economic Development or NGOs outside." From her perspective, the park must partner with external agencies, first to learn how "to capacitate people," second to sponsor the ventures, then third to "ensure that our communities are ready to take the opportunities that we have as a park." All of these steps require outside facilitation and financing. She then concedes, "our core business will always be conservation, but somehow we are also taking the responsibility of doing a certain area of development – of course in conjunction with other organizations." The task is huge, and no single government agency wants to take responsibility; as upper management made clear from the outset, the core mission is to conserve biodiversity (Robinson 1994).

Writing a post-apartheid social ecology policy for South Africa, Christopher Fabricius optimistically set forth that

> cultural resources and local people's values and belief systems should be included in park management plans. Traditional knowledge must form the basis for the conservation of cultural resources. Traditional ecological knowledge is a cultural

resource worthy of conservation in its own right. Local people's intellectual property rights related to cultural and other resources are respected. Local people are adequately compensated when their cultural assets generate revenues. (2001: 15–16)

This far-sighted program extended beyond simply integrating community perspectives into already existing programs. Rather, Fabricius asserted that traditional knowledge must be given ontological power, shaping the way conservation and heritage management was done. Furthermore, there should be tangible benefits as a necessary step towards social justice and restitution: "Parks should proactively research the history of land occupancy in and around the park. Local people should be assisted with speeding up land claims" (Fabricius 2001: 17). This positive interventionist view, while possibly impacting smaller or newer parks like Mapungubwe, has not found much purchase in Kruger. The issue of land claims is pertinent here and one of the many thorny issues that concerns social ecologists and it is often buttressed upon historical and archaeological materials. While land is increasingly unlikely to offer a pragmatic basis for an economic livelihood in terms of agriculture (Engelbrecht and van der Walt 1993), it continues to symbolize citizenship and the realization of democratic rights (Gunner 2005; James 2009: 232). Memory is also vital for recognition, and the past plays a critical role in the constitution and mobilization of contemporary claims. Heritage, from the deep past to contemporary culture, is one of the tangible ways in which identity claims are forged and interpolated into legal frameworks.

There have been huge delays in South Africa's land reform process. There are some 4500 land claims still outstanding that may take till 2014 to resolve. Even though claimants have to recount how they were historically evicted and stripped of their livelihoods there is no guarantee that the land will be returned. Recent estimates suggest that half the park, or one million hectares, is now under claim (Walker 2008: 273). Around 25 000 households could potentially benefit from those land claims. The Makuleke received 24 000 hectares back in 1998 (de Villiers 1999) and the Lugedlane received 1700 hectares. More recently the Makahane and Ba-Phalaborwa have expressed their frustration with the process in Kruger: "First we want title to the land, then we can talk about collaboration with SANParks" (Hofstätter 2008). Claimants like the Malatji must balance the legal costs of regaining their land against the real benefits of restitution (Magome 2004: 47; Magome and Murombedzi 2003). And the state must also balance the imperatives of land reform with the biodiversity mission of protected areas like Kruger. Currently the cost of settling legal claims in Kruger, involving 400 000 hectares, could exceed R20 billion ($US 2.7 billion) according to the Land Claim commissioner, Blessing Mphela. SANParks CEO David Mabunda believes it is worth considerably less. It was DEAT minister Marthinus van Schalkwyk who then promoted the shift from land restitution to monetary payouts (Groenewald 2009a). In this protracted saga Kruger has dragged its feet according to Mphela, and he believes that the land should be restored. The commission has been advising dissatisfied claimants to

Figure 7.1   Interviewing representatives of the Makahane family at Musunda. Courtesy of the author.

fight the decision in court. The Muyexe community in the north of the park remain dissatisfied because they had already been promised their land back with title deeds so that they could establish lodges (Groenewald and Rawoot 2009) in line with SANParks concessions and privatization in Kruger. Their only recourse now is a legal one.

To assuage angry communities SANParks is finally offering access to ancestral graves, permission to perform ceremonies, and a potential tourist levy for some groups. With the threat of huge payouts they have allowed 10 community-contracted fuel stations in the park (Groenewald 2009a). The community levy has been in effect for many years in KwaZulu Natal in parks like Mkhuze, but has been vigorously resisted by Kruger. Contracting out commercial enterprises to communities is exactly the kind of local small business scheme that the park insists it has been running since the new administration took over in the 1990s, but there is little proof of this on the ground. As the Phalaborwa claim demonstrates, SANParks leans towards options that buttress state-centrist, "command and control" management structure, and centralize power in the hands of the bureaucratic establishment. New forms of park management or even re-conceptualizing existing models have yet to be considered. The old system of pacifying local communities with incentives hinders the devolution of any real power sharing (Maguranyanga 2009: 143).

In Kruger's public web forums[2] and across the media discussion of land claims has been vituperative, racist, and historically inaccurate. There are more than 17 000 SANParks forum users and hundreds of postings debating the issue of land restitution. One web posting from Gauteng province states that "R20 billion seems a lot for a land that used to be worthless malaria and 'sleeping sickness' infested land." Another posting from Cape Town argues that "this land has been in Kruger for 100 years. Who can claim that it is theirs if THEY never had it?" Mirroring assertions of *terra nullius*, many postings contend that "historians have stated that most of the population in question's ancestors in fact slowly migrated from the more northern parts as recently as 200 years ago" or that Kruger's own publications point to "very few settlements . . . due to the problems with malaria, tsetse flies and carnivores"[3] They heatedly debate the success of the Makuleke contractual park, the value of "pristine" wilderness, redistributive justice, and the impacts of privatization. In a bizarre twist, numerous postings express dismay that the return of tribal lands will result in the exclusion of Kruger's regular tourists in favor of the privileged few. Why this should occur is never explained, but it is most likely a fearful specter of reversed exclusion, this time enacted by black landholders against white visitors. Deploying this logic, numerous postings then argue that Kruger should not benefit just the few but *all South Africans* – the very argument that is used by SANParks to overturn its white, racist, and exclusionary profile and the core mission of the People and Conservation unit.

During my fieldwork I encountered many staunch opponents to benefit sharing who impute that there are too many people whose needs will never be satisfied, that black South Africans would destroy Kruger's "wilderness," deplete its animals, build casinos, and the like, especially if they were successful in their land claims (Groenewald and Macleod 2005: 6; Walker 2008: 217). Such speculations rest on the flawed but influential tenets of the Tragedy of the Commons, Hardin's (1968) popular description of self-interest and destructive consumption (Igoe 2004: 56–8). One scientist explained that "it's more symbolic – our willingness to give some of the resources away under certain conditions – so that they feel we're actually sharing them. But actually, when you divide it up, there's very little in terms of material resources." The community forum meetings that I go on to describe indicate that SANParks is often unwilling to embrace either state mandates or stakeholder submissions about potential benefits and developments. Many of the proposals presented do not threaten the park's integrity, are not financially crippling, and have precedents existing elsewhere in South Africa. Such community-based proposals fall into two categories: direct benefits and developmental partnerships.

Masterplanning Kruger

"Kruger cannot live in isolation, cannot live by itself. You must come visit our communities to know." That was the plea of one erudite speaker at the Hazyview Forum, a view that is shared by the vast majority of elders I spoke with on the other side of the fence. In 2006 the state mandated SANParks to conduct public meetings with numerous stakeholders adjacent to Kruger National Park from a wide swathe of backgrounds and diverse interests. A senior social ecologist explained that the first level concerned groups within a 20 kilometer radius of western border of the park: there are some 187 villages between Hazyview and Phalaborwa. The second level comprised the Association of Private Nature Reserves bordering the park, while the third included all the farms, mines, and businesses along the park. These meetings provided a forum to discuss social, economic, and cultural matters and were run by members of Conservation Services and People and Conservation. While the stated aims were transparency and participation, during the presentations some facilitators became patronizing and aggressive and turned the process of information sharing into interrogation. Sharon, one of the senior white managers, dressed from head to toe in khaki, berated the Phalaborwa audience in a harsh tone: "Bushman rock art, graves, spiritual sites . . . we need your input. We want to open them up for access." Understandably, members of the audience felt unable to respond to her demands.

Tactics to extract indigenous knowledge or intellectual property from stakeholders can be used for marketing strategies or to "green" the organization (Mavhunga and Dressler 2007; Tapela, Maluleke, and Mavhunga 2007). "We need information from you," she demanded, which sounded like the familiar mining of information from black communities, rather than soliciting their perspectives to shape future directions for the park. Having cursorily mentioned heritage once, Sharon then moved on to her primary mission, namely the discussion of Kruger's reviews, audits, and management plans. She admitted frankly that "we have to do this because the government tells us we have to have community participation." Overly bureaucratic and managerial language served to further obfuscate the process: capacitating, "consultating," bioregional planning, rehabilitating infrastructure, biodiversity lower-level plans, ecosystem health, policy frameworks, management frameworks, and integrative frameworks abounded. A senior black social ecologist was then called upon to inform the audience that "the park is not a development agency." One respondent refused to accept this: "it's painful where we come from, I tell you, you wouldn't like it, but no compensation. Let us manage our resources together." Not to be dampened, representatives from Belfast and Bushbuckridge persistently asked how Kruger planned to assist its communities on their borders. Community representatives argued that Kruger was less "developed" than Sabi Sands and other private lodges who were doing more for communities. Sharon countered this with a Powerpoint slide: "we employ so many people. We train them. Nine thousand people live in the park. Two hundred and fifty-six people were trained from the community, and we spent R43 million in development. Kruger employs more than 2500 people, 1364 people employed from bordering communities." What was unclear from the presentation was the exact situation of the other 6500 inhabitants. Did this figure include tourists, out-sourced businesses and labor, and those employed by universities, NGOs, and private lodges? Were such arrangements temporary or permanent, and what was the skill level? These numbers might simply translate into cheap labor, devoid of any capacity building. But none of this was forthcoming, nor was it what communities sought; they wanted concrete community projects whether schools, clinics, resources, or monetary benefits.

Participants at the forums came prepared with specific plans for partnerships and benefit sharing. Andreis asked about selling agricultural produce to private lodges and suggested that Kruger share its expertise on how to grow various plants and trees. Traditional healers wanted access to particular plants while others need thatch grass for hut construction. Other ideas include collecting firewood within the park to sell back to its lodges or harvesting marula that would provide employ-ment and income for people. At present the neighboring land is being stripped of its resources to provision Kruger's vast needs for residents and tourists alike. The community requested tenders for fence construction, since poor fencing permits dangerous animals to escape and cause damage to people and property. Compensation for such losses has not been forthcoming despite being the park's responsibility by law. Entrepreneurial community members wanted to run tours like those that private lodges currently offer, taking tourists to "see how the blacks live in South Africa. They are not coming for Western culture, they are tired of that." Having local people employed as field guides was another proposition. Another suggestion was access to game meat from Kruger, especially after culling, just as private game reserves such as Timbavati had provided. Meat was sold to them, especially during winter, and this they felt would also combat the problem of poaching. These were all reasonable submissions, akin to those that emerged while interviewing in communities along Kruger's boundaries, and furthered echoed in my discussions with managers at private game lodges such as Singita Lebombo, Bongani, Ngala, and Phinda.

Ten days earlier Conservation Services had held their own Resource Utilization meeting at Skukuza. This was where Kruger would hash out its official position, develop a unified organizational front, and prepare to present communities with pre-determined positions on the question of resource sharing. Rangers and ecolo-gists assembled, with the odd researcher, social ecologist, and a lawyer, to resolve Kruger's policy toward communities. This was the Masterplanning Kruger meeting, facilitated by a senior ecologist from Scientific Services. His opening salvo was this is an impossible meeting . . . the people who believe that there should be no-take zones in parks are the people who believe that society agreed that parks are no-take zones. So those are the values that those people have. Now, the South African law states that you can't adopt that attitude, that you have to consider resource use in national parks.

the group was polarized between those who believe that Kruger should exist as a "no take zone" and those who could envisage some experimentation with resource sharing. Some scientists and managers sought to bypass the entire process: "I think there is a little (*sic*) unclarity about national parks," one manager queried. "I know the Act says clearly Protected Areas, but I think we must make sure that it includes National Parks in protected areas." Puzzled, the facilitator asked whether he was suggesting an exemption from the law? His interlocutor continued,

> Yes, I think that is correct, but I think that we must just make sure how the act reads. I think it's an issue of interpretation. I would think the law says you have to investigate and come up with a management plan and whether or not the use is allowed. That's my interpretation. I don't think the law says you must.

For many scientists and rangers at the meeting the government directive to develop a management plan and examine resource sharing should be taken on face value: develop a plan, have the discussion, but not implement any measures that enable community access or benefits. They had to address utilization but certainly not agree to it. This "getting out of benefits" was staunchly defended on moral grounds. Sharon felt strongly that "we fundamentally shouldn't be altering the landscape. I would say that humans should not be fundamentally altering the profile of a national park. So that would be digging holes or changing the topography." Strict adherence to this position, of course, would halt all scientific research and lodge and infrastructure building and thus cripple the new-found economic viability of Kruger. Quickly, the facilitator backtracked by qualifying that Sharon was not suggesting "that nothing inside a national park can ever be changed. Because, otherwise what she is talking about is just one big wilderness area."

The senior ecologist facilitating the meeting spoke passionately about the severity of community needs and the hidden hypocrisy of the park, sometimes complicit in the former. He had long experience in both field science and management and was not hostile to social issues or social science. "We make ourselves pure," he said, "but we strip other areas. We buy our wood from outside and sell it to burn in the park." Others who had contact outside the fence agreed: "by not allowing them inside the park to use some of our resources, we are raping the communities outside." Another ranger ventured that

> we have a responsibility where we don't harvest wood from inside the park, but there's a lot of wood sold inside the park that comes from somewhere else, and it's

coming from the Phalaborwa area. I think there's just some sort of responsibility to know where it's coming from and who else's resources we're actually taking. For the tourists and the trails camps and everything.

While no one denied the needs of black communities, Kruger's managers and scientists were divided about upholding the government mandate, the principle of resource use, their responsibilities as conservationists, and even the existence of wilderness. Like all discussions about rights and claims, there was much boundary policing: boundaries rule in as much as they rule out (Ivison 2008). With Hobbesian self-interest, Kruger's own personnel were keen to secure their own livelihoods, practices, and interests inside the fence, and were torn between the morality of the conservation effort and the morality of social justice and equity. The other side of rights is duties, the duty of care here falling to SANParks after more than a decade of ANC leadership. There were growing indications that other needs and perspectives deserved serious attention, yet legitimating these duties in the park management plan would prove more exigent.

Doing Well by Doing Good

Back in Welverdiend, Philleos and Andreis spoke fervently about the value of maintaining a conservation area like Kruger. They were not opposed to Kruger's existence, rather they argued that it was time for equity and the sharing of benefits as they had already witnessed in their dealings with private game lodges such as Ngala Private Game Reserve, an AndBeyond concession. Typical of the new South Africa, Ngala involves a partnership between a government agency, an NGO, and a private corporation. Ngala had provided classrooms, computers, and student bursaries; they had renovated the church hall and built a resource and media center with computers for Welverdiend. The village had received direct benefits from AndBeyond, and if a private company could manage to invest in the community a huge operation like Kruger could do the same. Private operators such as AndBeyond have made substantial contributions, while many companies make small, but heavily publicized contributions that are used principally as marketing tools and CSR (Buckley 2002: 26). Philleos accused Kruger of using black communities as their "pride," exploiting their presence to "green" themselves. Whereas in reality "Kruger National Park is here just to control us so that they can run their business well." Communities have been consistently excluded from the consultative process whether under apartheid or in present times. "You cannot separate community and conservation," in Andreis' view, they are entwined, and if "there is no man, there is no conservation." He goes on to suggest that the responsibility of SANParks is to share their knowledge of conservation and sustainability for the community's benefit not simply their own agendas. If there is "no sharing, there will be no conservation." Over two decades ago the founders of AndBeyond (Buchanan 1999; Varty 2008), then called Conservation Corporation Africa (CCA), had come to the very same conclusion.

No one really wants to celebrate commercial conservation and tourism companies. Surely they are part of the problem in countries like South Africa? They represent big business, greedy international interests, and affluent foreigners, steeped in the exploitation and commodification of nature and culture alike. This was certainly my attitude before embarking upon my fieldwork: I envisaged corporate conservation as directly in opposition to the government's efforts to empower, rebuild, and incorporate the nation's disenfranchised, particularly those who had paid the price for protected areas. Further, such organizations were unlikely to be interested in black heritage or living communities. Set up as a comparative test case, I first undertook research at Bongani Mountain Lodge run by CCA, and then two of their other concessions, Ngala bordering Kruger National Park and Phinda in KwaZulu Natal.

Doing well by doing good is the underlying philosophy that steers AndBeyond and its more than 40 African camps and lodges, eight of which are presently in South Africa. *Care of the Land, Care of the Wildlife, Care of the People* is another oft-espoused directive underlining the inseparable nature of efforts around conservation and social responsibility. The organization prides itself on its deep commitment to the renaissance of Africa based upon sustainable multi-use tourism around wildlife and nature conservation, benefiting travelers alongside Africa's land, animals, and rural communities. It is high end, responsible ecotourism which explicitly acknowledges that economic development is crucial for the maintenance of biodiversity and is framed as "the culture of care" (Carlisle 2003; Conservation Corporation Africa 2007). Local communities are acknowledged as both influencing and owning this natural heritage. There is also a firm commitment to cultural heritage, and I witnessed at first hand an attention to the archaeological past at Bongani (Hampson *et al.* 2002). Bongani is advertised as

> renowned by rock art experts and enthusiasts for sheltering one of the world's richest sources of rock art – the greatest concentration of per square meter on earth. San artists painted hundreds of rock art friezes throughout the area, and today, in addition to game-drives in Big Five wilderness, guests at Bongani Mountain Lodge are able to explore this natural gallery, estimated to be 1500 years old. The terrain surrounding the lodge boasts more than 250 sites, with new art constantly being discovered by the resident experts. (Conservation Corporation Africa 2005)

Bongani also publicly promotes its connections with RARI. According to Bongani's managers and rangers, visiting cultural heritage is welcomed by the guests and does not detract from game viewing. Their publications also showcase the history of pre-colonial and colonial times, address the brutal legacy of the white administration's forced removals and subsequent annihilation of cattle, the depredations

of apartheid, and the corporation's own responsibilities under the new dispensation (see Buchanan 1999). Some visitors have "white guilt," I was told, and avoid
visiting communities, but many tourists appreciate this as an indelible part of the
journey. One lodge manager was proud that their community trips were not
staged affairs: "there are no loincloths here, if it's a Sunday visitors might join the
church service, if it's a Saturday it might be a sports day." But he notes that most
participants are international visitors rather than domestic ones, many of who feel
they know the rural landscape and its people. Conversely Kruger's heritage is not
accessible he tells me because "they're stuck with the map of Kruger" and that
becomes alienating. Whereas at Bongani visitors "actually pass right through
[heritage], it is in the community, there is more knowledge about it. Mthethomusha
means *the new rule* and many think this is set against the likes of Kruger. It is about
bringing more benefits and more access, right from the start." In 1992 AndBeyond
founded Africa Foundation, an independent NGO whose primary focus is upon
community equity, income generation, education, healthcare, and infrastructural
improvements. Trustees and patrons of the NGO include Desmond Tutu, Tara
Getty, William Newsom, and Howard Buffet, while their partners include regional
conservation NGOs including WWF South Africa, the Endangered Wildlife Trust,
and Birdlife South Africa.

The big business of ecotourism and community benefits need not be mutually
exclusive, in fact AndBeyond have turned their own development mission into an
international drawcard. During my visits to schools, clinics, gardens, community
centers, and a digital eco-village, I was repeatedly told about foreign visitors from
countries like Germany or the United States who were brought into the villages,
shown what was needed, and promptly signed a check. Some have argued that
such donations lead to their own forms of appropriation and paternalism (Burns
and Barrie 2005) while others question the level of success achieved (Büscher and
Dressler 2007: 602–3; Spenceley 2003). Visits to rural villages like Welverdiend
were cast as an optional tour, something additional and different to wildlife tours,
for visitors to have some direct experience of the South African context. Anna
Spencely, an informed critic of new private conservation, argues that all such
endeavors simply fulfill corporate social responsibility, insure lodge safety, and
deter poaching as well as offering consumers a "feel good" holiday. This is undoubtedly true, nonetheless she concedes that "perhaps the commitment and proactive
activity towards improving livelihoods of the rural poor is rather more important
than debating the ethics of who should pay for it" (Spenceley 2003: 76). Indeed,
who is willing to pay in South Africa? Certainly not SANParks nor the government
whether municipal, provincial, or state. In addition, she reveals that in the 1990s
the Ngala Management Committee consisted of members from Ngala lodge,
Kruger National Park, the Southern African Wildlife College and the Welverdiend
community. However, representatives from Kruger refused to endorse any plan
that gave community members voting rights on conservation management decisions (Spenceley 2003: 77).

Les Carlisle, a founding staff member of AndBeyond, went to school with some of Kruger's management, played cricket with a few of them in true South African style, and yet maintains that their unwillingness to include and develop people is moribund and could be disastrous. He may be part of a highly successful and profitable company, but he lacks pretension, the trappings of wealth, and the certainty of mission with which one becomes familiar. He readily admits that AndBeyond made initial mistakes like failing to ask communities what they wanted and making flawed assumptions. That changed with their first lodge at Phinda, which Les helped construct. The benefits communities receive include employment, resource utilization, education, and empowerment that in turn directly benefit conservation and the company. "Poaching from Phinda is annually a tiny fraction of that from Provincial parks like Mhuze," he contends, because of the partnerships. He adds that the provincial agency, Ezemvelo KZN Wildlife, is vastly better than SANParks, something he attributes to their British colonial roots, something of a "last outpost" he quips. Carlisle's inclusive stance means that fences should be permeable, local people should be licensed to kill certain animals if they escape, and reserves must share excess game meat in winter times when people have no food. Solving Kruger's elephant population crisis is simple in his view. The park should cull the excess elephants and give the meat to poor communities at cost price, particularly at times of need, so that they can utilize or sell and profit from the resource. Carlisle is adamant, passionate, and forthright. AndBeyond subsequently withdrew from Bongani after becoming dissatisfied with the motives of some stakeholders at Bongani who exploited community resources and the Mpumalanga Parks Board for not sharing certain profits with the community. While AndBeyond built schools, clinics, and gardens, Carlisle and others assert that more could have been done. Their policy now is to build lodges that are owned by the community wherever possible.

Carlisle points out that cattle farming produces $16 per hectare annually, as compared to conservation tourism $160 (Carlisle 2003: 17). Phinda provides 8–10% direct benefits for neighboring communities. Of the R5.5 million spent building Phinda Mountain Lodge in 1991 some R2.5 million was channeled back into community through employment. When Forest Lodge was constructed using local building techniques some R3.2 million was plowed back through jobs and sourcing materials (Carlisle 2003: 22). Hiring 110 unskilled workers effectively provided economic support for more than 1000 people in the Phinda vicinity. Success stories abound, like the rehabilitated poacher who now runs his own brick-making business, a charcoal manufacturing scheme, and local resource utilization such as ilala palm wine harvesting, thatch, wood, and medicinal plant collection all based on sustainable yield. Phinda built roads so that rural villages had access to markets and tourists. They donated 985 hippo rollers (large plastic containers designed for carrying water from communal wells), books and videos for the local libraries; installed gutters and water tanks at schools; built a medical center and computer centers at two schools. Bolstered by a US$70,000 private donation for community development, Africa Foundation and Phinda have built classrooms in the

Mnqobokazi, Nibela, and Mduku communities, the Nibela skills training center, the Mbhedula women's market, and a clinic (Varty 2008: 161). The Mduku clinic serves 42 000 patients annually. AndBeyond has built over 40 classrooms in 20 different schools, providing education for 1200 pupils and creating 60 permanent jobs. Additionally, there is a university bursary system that educates between 15 and 20 students annually, several of whom I interviewed; they were incredibly impressive young leaders who have returned to their communities after graduation to share their skills. "Local champions" like Lotus Khoza are community members who are selected and trained and then go on to implement their own projects. Hundreds of students and teachers are also hosted at Phinda Lodge as part of AndBeyond's educational mission, funded through the sale of Wildchild Bracelets at the lodges (Carlisle 2003: 22–3).

In 2007 the company signed a 9500 hectare land-claim settlement with Mkhasa and Mnqobokazi elders in favor of those communities. CEO Steve Fitzgerald remarked "it has also always been our dream to return Phinda's land to the community but obviously in a way that can also benefit the company. We realised that the best way forward was to support the land-claim and then to lease the land back from the communities to ensure ongoing sustainability" (anon 2007: 59). It was agreed at the signing that Phinda would pay the community R18 million upfront to facilitate joint ventures or community empowerment programs. Controversial Inkatha Freedom Party figure Mangosuthu Buthelezi proclaimed the handover "the goose that lays the golden egg," while others cast Phinda in the guise of Robin Hood, transferring the wealth from rich to poor (Buchanan 1999: 103).

Ngala Private Game Reserve has a different history. The land for Ngala was donated to the SANParks Trust, via the Worldwide Fund for Nature, by a private landowner (Buchanan 1999: 119). That land was incorporated into Kruger while AndBeyond has exclusive tourism operating rights over both the land and the lodge. In return Ngala pays a substantial lease fee and a proportion of profits to the National Parks Trust, which then finances conservation expansion (Buckley 2002: 28). In 1992 Dr Robbie Robinson, then CEO for the National Parks Board persuaded the company to manage the 14 000 hectare reserve. Ngala was the largest ever donation to the WWF and SANParks, but SANParks lacked the expertise to run it (Büscher and Dressler 2007: 600). AndBeyond had been started by individuals like Alan Bernstein and Dave Varty (2008: 92), who, ironically, had been at variance with national parks since 1970 because of their ideas of incorporating communities, tourism, and land management, not to mention their endorsement by Nelson Mandela before the first democratic elections.

Ngala has maintained a positive and beneficial relationship with the people of Welverdiend. In 2001 they provided every household with a hippo roller. They raised monies to build two classrooms with furniture, bought televisions, books, copiers, computers, and projectors. The residents of Welverdiend request the same benefits from Kruger and venture that Kruger could provide much more, considering their gate revenues from almost 1.5 million tourists annually. This is an optimistic and localized view considering the hundreds of villages and towns that border the park and the millions of people who look to Kruger to ameliorate their plight. Moreover, Kruger is a parastatal organization, as previously outlined, that is managed by the state but must be fiscally self-sustaining. Kruger is one of only two parks in the SANParks portfolio that generate profits, and those funds are redistributed amongst less viable parks.

AndBeyond is an award winning, recognized leader in high-end tourism and community involvement, but a similar ethos is beginning to permeate other private lodges such as Singita Lebombo, a 15 000 hectare concession within Kruger National Park. "One of the agreements that we had with the Kruger National Park when they set up the concessions was that one of the primary focuses should be on creating employment for local communities. Four or five of us went into two villages and interviewed over 1000 people for junior positions." They created the Singita Lebombo Business Linkage Committee to show their determination in creating small black businesses and empowering the local communities. As with, AndBeyond, staff training, development, and capacity building are central concerns, with the goal of getting more individuals in managerial positions rather than trapped as unskilled labor. Singita's manager expressed his "commitment to empowering the local communities, even if it's just our two little communities outside the Orpen Gate. That's where the majority of our staff come from, their families live, and so if we can make a difference to that little community, then we're starting off on the right foot." In 2006 Singita was the only private concession to provide living quarters for its 140 main staff, while other employees were driven in from the communities on a daily basis. Kruger has a central staff village and a compound in Skukuza, and workers' housing adjacent to its camps dotted around the park, and, while the scale is very different, so are the solutions. Here the architecture of apartheid has proven very difficult to dismantle.

Kruger eKhayelitsha

Skukuza has its own black village, a township of impoverished people living inside the park fence. It retains its old name, "the compound," a telling indictment that this camp, a kraal of sorts, is confined to the lowest paid black workers in Kruger. It houses a racially segregated community that on first glance appears not to have changed since the end of apartheid. Working in the park for several seasons one realizes that the residents of Skukuza never have to enter the compound; they may need to drive past it but, while their domestic workers may live there, there is no reason for them ever to be exposed to its inequities. André Gorz (1994: 50) aptly described the dualization of society as the "South Africanization of social life," accompanied as it is by mass pauperization, the proliferation of service workers, secure enclaves, and the erosion of secure employment and housing. Put starkly, the compound allows Kruger to function. It veils the inner workings of the machine that produces "wilderness." Unsurprisingly, no white staff live in the compound, they all reside in the staff village or the research camp, although there are vague references to the odd young white student or intern trying it out for a time.

The compound foregrounds the brutal material inequities and bare life of apartheid like the townships Khayelitsha or Langa (Field 2007), once referred to as a "black spot." For many, employment remains fractured along racial lines, A and B band workers live in the compound, C band and up reside in the staff village. Although difficult to ascertain from the Human Resources office, I was told there were 1250 in A and B bands across the park and these were all black workers, while only around 60 black people occupied C rank upwards. Female domestics explain that they receive approximately R1925 per month as an A band worker, while B band begins at R2700. Laughter abounds at the suggestion that there could be white cleaners working in Kruger, or perhaps anywhere in South Africa. Incongruously, some women lament apartheid times for the kinds of services that were offered, including trucks that took workers outside the park to see their families. Understandably, the new management did not want to ferry black workers in open trucks like animals, and so halted the practice, but failed to replace it with a bus service or any other organized transport. "We are suffering," one woman says. They now have to pay between R10 and R20 to use a shared minibus outside the Kruger Gate. There is also the matter of children leaving at 6.15 a.m. to get to school during the winter without proper transport. A member of People and Conservation once explained to me that Mercedes-Benz had donated several buses some years ago, but soon after the park surreptitiously sold them to increase profits.

Women in the compound complain that the shop is more expensive now. Before 1994 it was a small local enterprise run by the Parks Board, but today they have a store that is part of the park-wide franchise. During the 2000s workers at the lowest bands, on what is termed the Patterson scale, were given rations in addition to their salaries: no white workers receive rations. "If we really want to transform," I was told, "you cannot start giving your employees food parcels. That is degrading. You give food parcels to people that are not actually working but are suffering. Now what message are you sending? Instead of giving these people money, we are giving them food." Speaking of the power imbalance that is typi- cally, though not always, calibrated around race, one black scientific officer spoke candidly: "if you can't experience it, you'll never understand. You can fight, but you can't fight everything. You're supposed to be happy and smiling. You're sup- posed to wave, they're used to doing it. You can't tell me they don't know what's happening. The management is black." As Ben makes this statement he raises his hands gesturing in inverted commas, "but they are white." Class divisions have simply complicated the racial geometries of apartheid yet they have not been overturned. He speaks nine languages, has a degree, grew up in a modern home in Soweto, and defies anyone to call him disadvantaged. There is an annual staff meeting to hear grievances, although he maintains that each year the same issues are raised; salaries, housing, transport, but only by the A- and B-band workers. "The whites don't say anything. Management just want to relieve stress, see the park. First the director will talk, then he asks for questions . . . then salaries: you said last year . . . same stuff. Ten questions, then you get some PR guy answering for them, this is not a dialogue." Ben reveals that there are a few white A and B band workers, but they are housed in the staff village and keep very quiet about their rank. In some respects little has changed under democracy, and the ANC has been roundly criticized for not enhancing the socio-economic status of its poorest citizens but focusing rather more narrowly on a newly emerging black elite. Poverty alleviation schemes operate in the park; however, it is conservatively estimated that Kruger needs R50–60 million to ameliorate the housing problem.

In the compound's communal buildings I saw eight single beds to a dorm room. Typically people do as they please in those rooms at all hours, some sleep, others have sex, cook, talk, and play music. The women told me about husbands, wives, and babies sleeping in a single bed in overcrowded rooms. One could observe people walking around in towels coming from communal showers: privacy was the number one grievance, followed by ablutions, cooking facilities, and recreation. One man explained it was best to shower at 2.00 a.m. to be assured warm water. During my time there I remember the palpable outrage when an angry email was sent from Kruger's management claiming that if people in the compound could not use toilet paper properly, they would stop supplying it altogether. Apart from single room dwellings (about 550) and dormitories (about 20) there are prefabricated structures and tents in the compound, like those used for refugees. Since workers earn so little and receive no housing allowance they cannot afford to purchase housing outside the park and may have nothing on retirement when they are forced to leave.

During my interviews in the compound, I talked to two women in a single room that was about two meters square. The salient issues were housing, salaries, transport, living conditions, and the strings of broken promises to alleviate their plight. When they both sat on the single bed I could not fit in the room, so I posed my questions from the steps outside. In 1998 they were promised better housing, more space, and less crowding. Beyond the tiny rooms, clustered in several units, the grounds were a desolate wasteland with rubbish everywhere and overflowing trash bins. There was no adequate servicing here because this represents the lowest priority in the park. Of course, these are the very people who clean the houses and yards of staff and tourists alike, but no one services them. We were surrounded by rusting metal, makeshift washing lines, uncut grass, and people have started to create small gardens and grow vegetables – this is to be expected as goods are so expensive in the park shops and Skukuza is many miles from the nearest town. The entire effect is overcrowded and squalid. After one visit I had supper with several ecologists from Conservation Services, and one woman complained bitterly about these residents. "They don't keep things clean" she protested, "they do a good job cleaning other people's homes, but don't bother with their own. They're better in the rural settlements, but they don't know how to live here, they just throw the rubbish over the wall – tell me why do they do that, you're an anthropologist?" She genuinely had not considered that while the poorest paid workers spend their lives servicing the established family homes with manicured lawns like hers, or tending the lawns of the swimming pool or golf club in the staff village, that there was no one else to remove rubbish, clean up, or provide proper services for them in the compound. It echoes Gilroy's (2005: 11) observation that the "natives, whose bodies are comparatively worthless, already exist in a space of death, for which their characteristic lack of industry makes them responsible."

Refusing to see the connection between exploitation and privilege or the dire conditions that prevail in the park, my hosts wanted to foreclose any unpleasant- ness. Instead they adopted a light-hearted tone as if to re-orient me: "but the compound is so lively!" Many white residents at Skukuza imagine that this is typical African village life, and so racially prejudiced stereotypes easily come to the fore. Otherwise the woman with whom I spoke may have more acutely observed that there is no room inside for people, so they have to conduct their lives outside. How is it possible to live in Skukuza for so long and not see or imagine that things could be different, that the current situation is unacceptable? While the people I spoke to were adamant that they were treated better since 1994 and things were generally improving, they also felt that living conditions had deteriorated over the past decade. I ask Ben, why do people forget their comrades, especially those individuals now in power who have experienced the compound first hand? He harks back to the ascendancy of class and status and the spurious sidelining of race and equality. Black elites rise through the ranks and they will- ingly forget their previous experiences, "there is nothing one can do." Kruger stands as a microcosm for South Africa, a state within a nation, where today one cannot simply parse out "race" from other structural inequalities. Instead we are obliged to trace the continuing nexus of racisms and in doing so acknowledge the lines of tension between our scholarly duty to recover and to remain faithful to the past and our moral and political imperative to underline the injustices of racial hierarchy today (Gilroy 2005: 31).

Some of the new young black elite in Kruger are aware of the problems, but seldom visit the compound and also have an "out of sight, out of mind" approach. "We have to consider the fact that the establishment there was during the apart- heid so obviously it was this place that was meant for blacks" a young, black woman charged with black economic empowerment told me. "It had to be like that. But I'm sure the management is in the process of changing that. It's been 10 years." I frequently asked my colleagues why black people require less in the way of housing than white workers in the park and why no husbands, wives, and families were allowed to accompany employees? Almost everyone I spoke to who had lived in the compound described problems with prostitution, violence toward women, drugs, and underage girls being brought in for sex with older men.

Women interviewed told me that there were girls living there who did not work in the park and the intimation was that they were sleeping with men while their wives were out working. It has always been the case that families were not supposed to accompany black workers: theirs was theoretically supposed to be a single life, much as in colonial centers and apartheid mine operations in previous times. Officially 1200 people reside in the compound, unofficially it may be closer to 2000, since family members come in and, if they can get away with staying there, obviously will. "It's a desperate situation," one man told me.

> People know it's going on; they have security at the compound for those reasons, so they know. They do a raid every now and again to see who's staying there, checking permits. They've even built a wall so you can't see in. They don't want you to see. They want more money pouring in, they don't want to fix the problems in the compound.

This situation is completely the reverse of the staff village, with its huge family bungalows, palms, and gardens, post office and tennis courts, and its legion of black workers tending lawns and keeping house. What has changed here since 1994 is that black managers and administrative personnel are now able to enjoy this lifestyle and that, as many interviewees pointed out, is at least something.

Gold Rocks, Public Goods, and Private Gains at the Rainbow's End

Connecting several themes of this book, this chapter has examined recognition and reparation for the past, the place of natural resources, and the provisioning of benefits in the post-apartheid era of public–private partnerships. Developments in Kruger since 1994 reveal the cosmopolitan frictions among transnational organizations, funding agencies, corporations, NGOs, and indigenous communities in and around the place of culture in a nature reserve. Both natural and cultural heritage are imagined in particular local and national ways, and each is influenced and impacted upon by global organizations and mandates. Funding for the running and research aspects of Kruger is supplied by North American agencies, private foundations, universities, research grants, NGOs, and state and private revenues (McKinsey Report 2002). Private–public partnerships ultimately do much of the work of the South African state. Many assert that they float the nation, the danger being that they become de facto agencies for service delivery and devolved responsibility for government (Cheah 1998: 322). Ideas about the local, state, global, and indigenous are all pieced together from this complex mosaic of sources, resources, inspirations, and agendas. One setting where these ideas were effectively played out immediately after the democratic handover, was with the Makuleke and their successful land claim for the Pafuri triangle (de Villiers 1999; Spierenburg, Steenkamp, and Wels 2008: 91). It was heralded as a new paradigm for SANParks, and momentarily recast the specter of *Skukuza* in the euphoric zeitgeist of liberation. Dispossessed in 1969, legally reinstated in 1998, the Makuleke now operate a 25-year contractual park inside Kruger's borders and directly benefit from managing two high-end eco-lodges. This represents the best-attested episode where the "gold rock" that is Kruger compensated and empowered a previously disenfranchised group and still provides a source of hope for other communities like Welverdiend. SANParks celebrates the 24 000 hectare settlement and its attendant benefits as a significant result for the Makuleke, yet the degree of autonomy, success, and corruption has been the subject of scrutiny and debate (Masuku Van Damme and Meskell 2009; Mavhunga and Dressler 2007; Robins and van der Waal 2008; Tapela and Omara-Ojungu 1999). Yet given the current hostility toward honoring claims in Kruger through land restitution, it is unlikely that comparable reparations will be forthcoming.

Poised at the intersection of the controversial GLTP (Mavhunga and Spierenburg 2009), the Makuleke bear the hallmarks of both the "local indigenous" in the arena of ecotourism and tribal promotion and the "transnational indigenous" in political and conservation spheres. They have achieved iconic status for a host of actors, including German NGOs, conservationists, international academics, big business, and the state (Comaroff and Comaroff 2009; Robins and van der Waal 2008). The Makuleke contract with SANParks is one of conditionality, allowing no mining, prospecting, residence, or agriculture, and it stipulates that the land must be used for conservation. SANParks also contributes to management costs and therefore has a strong hand in determining the future of the land. However, the Makuleke have been permitted certain sustainable resource utilization, limited hunting (Macleod 2003), and control of the commercial rights to the land, which enabled them to invite private companies to construct luxury lodges: The Outpost,[4] managed by Rare Earth Retreats and Pafuri Camp,[5] run by Wilderness Safaris. The latter pays 8 percent of revenue generated by the camp to the community. Employment benefits include eight game guards and nearly 50 staff throughout the camp. My visits to these lodges showed substantially less local employment and the preponderance of white management, and there has been additional criticism over lease terms, oversight, and managerial control (Reid 2001; Spierenburg, Steenkamp, and Wels 2008: 92). Archaeology is also entangled in these disputes in now familiar ways. During interviews The Outpost's manager confronted the section ranger accompanying me about the destruction of marked graves by SANParks employees, accusing them of bulldozing historic sites on Makuleke land. In the best light these developments could be interpreted as conservation alliances with indigenous stakeholders or post-apartheid benefit sharing, nevertheless they are closely aligned with SANParks broader privatization scheme. What could be tolerated, even welcomed in the mid-1990s with rainbow rhetoric, is now no longer possible. "Land claims could kill Kruger" (Groenewald and Macleod

2005) is the more recent park response to future co-management with communities like the Makuleke.

Disproportionate scholarly attention has been paid to the Makuleke case, compared to, say, the plight of poor black workers residing in the compound, so that I will not attempt to rehearse it here. Suffice to say that it signaled a positive turning point for healing community relations, but one that has been re-scripted a decade later by various parties as a partial victory, an empowering commercial venture, a legal tangle, or a threat to conservation. It is tempting to view the Makuleke return as a moment that has passed, an event that captured the optimism of the 1990s that has subsequently given way to the opportunism of the 2000s. Environmental justice, like heritage as therapy, held sway in the early years of the Mandela and Mbeki governments but has since fallen prey to inertia, disinterest, and the moral mission of biodiversity conservation. Kruger exhibits remarkable resilience in the administrative ordering of nature and culture. Directions for change, ideas for development, community projects are explored over and over again with no institutional memory and very little delivery. Not enough has changed since democratic transition (Maguranyanga 2009; Ramutsindela 2004), and transformation, where it has happened has been at too slow a pace. While liberalization and commercialization have advanced swiftly and successfully through Kruger, the corresponding developments with communities and workers, and even acknowledgement of their role in the forging of the park is fractional. "We are *almost* the future generation of a particular past," one young black woman recounted, echoing that spirit of double time, the inescapability of past deprivations couple with the desire for a reworked future. Past mastering extends further than merely the processing of history or archaeology; the need to confront and ameliorate the past conveys its rhizomes into issues of territory, conservation, natural resources, public goods, and private pains. "How we deal with that past," she concluded with proud optimism, "will allow us to move forward in a way that celebrates people's heritage, their ancestry, and where they've come from."

Notes

1   www.sangonet.org.za (accessed January 8, 2010).
2   http://www.sanparks.org/forums (accessed September 28, 2009).
3   http://www.sanparks.org/forums/search.php?st=0&sk=t&sd=d&keywords=land+cl
    aims&start=60 (accessed January 7, 2010).
4   www.theoutpost.co.za (accessed March 17, 2010).
5   http://wilderness-safaris.co.za/south_africa_kruger_national_park/pafuri_camp/
    introduction/ (accessed April 14, 2011).

Conclusions
Future Perfect

Alive with Possibility was the national slogan back in 2003. It was an anthem that captured the twilight exuberance of the Rainbow Nation that beckoned the international community to invest, visit, and celebrate the success and diversity of South Africa's decade-old democracy. It is telling, then, that only a few years later that initial optimism was replaced by the marketing motto *South Africa: It's Possible*. A less sanguine statement on the nation's progress and future, yet one that still clings to the dream harnessed by the release of Nelson Mandela in 1990 right through to the hosting of the football World Cup in 2010. After the thrill of liberation has gone and our cosmopolitan romance with South Africa has waned, the specter of history repeating itself casts a pall as the iniquities of apartheid continue to resurface and linger. My own study intended to document a new nation's exemplary refashioning of its archaeological past and the new heritages that ANC statecraft would mobilize to reconcile and rebuild. It examines a country that took seriously its deep past for the realignment of a possible future in a present that no one could have imagined unfolding so peacefully, even a decade earlier. Yet as this book reveals, the modernist fantasy of emancipation and progress has put an excessive burden of expectation upon institutions, individuals, and objects, each with their own sedimented legacies that are not easily shed. Past mastering is always an ongoing project, always unfinished and future perfect.

Drawing together the three major themes of this book I want to reflect back on the past 15 years of heritage work in the Rainbow Nation. I begin with the historical context for past mastering and the early governmental desires to deploy the past in a network of reparation efforts. Past places and objects, it was argued, just like memories and confessions, would serve as a therapy in social, spiritual, and economic terms. Making heritage pay then neatly segues into my second

The Nature of Heritage: The New South Africa, First Editon. Lynn Meskell.
© 2012 John Wiley & Sons, Inc. Published 2012 by Blackwell Publishing Ltd.

major theme, that of emerging private and public responsibilities relating to cultural and natural patrimony. This tension over delivery and primacy is reflected in the modern imperatives for biodiversity and particular forms of celebrated nature in South Africa. Protected nature prefigures cultural heritage in places like Kruger National Park and across the nation. It provides a powerful global optic to scrutinize the ontologies of heritage more closely, its natured legacies, and current trajectories that align the past with matters of diversity, sustainability, and loss. These developments form the third theme of the book. I argue that the ways in which we have come to imagine the archaeological or cultural past, coupled with our managerial and protective agendas, have been deeply influenced by thinking about ecological salvage politics. This was the real discovery in South Africa, that natural ecologies supplanted peopled histories and contemporary social urgencies despite the widespread calls for historical justice, education, and African pride, and the benefit sharing that Mandela inspired South Africans to forge.

"State in Search of a Nation"

Anthony Appiah's wonderful phrase truly captures the dilemma for a new South Africa today, as it looks back to the achievements and symbols of the past to imagine its future, yet without fully exorcizing the ghosts of history. As my daily interactions made clear, South Africa is ostensibly trapped in double time. Governments, organizations, and individuals seek to suspend time in a post-euphoric moment rather than confront the iniquities of the past or the deficits of the present. But in such circumstances the political desire for heritage pageantry is often reduced to the rhetorical, unmoored, and weightless hegemony of new national spectacle. The irony is, following Brown (2001), that history's overburden is both weightier and less deterministic than ever before. In the post-apartheid political economy of debt and payment, heritage is called upon to do too much, while "heritage" as a thing and a practice has lacked the underlying capacity and governmental support to do much of anything. While the past is called upon to re-orient itself given the uncertainty of post-liberation and liberalization it cannot help but fail to provide an adequate map to the future. This is in large part because the onus of provision has shifted from the state to the individual and thus the burden is folded back upon the nation's citizenry to reconstitute their own lives and livelihoods from the shreds of tradition, material culture, and knowledge that were left to them after the deprivations of colonial and National Party rule. Other traditions that are recent, hybrid, creolized constitutions, that intriguingly may signal earlier forms of multiculturalism, are only now taking shape as topics of interest and research (Arnold and Schmahmann 2005; Nuttall 2009). Taken together, these deficits lay bare the impossibility of heritage work, specifically the 1990s phase of neoliberal heritage-making that sought to shape citizens as responsible, self-sustaining, and self-promoting subjects who could market the seemingly allochronic qualities that had subjugated them under the previous regime: their tribal culture, their Africanity, their traditions, and distinctive material culture.

Unity in diversity, first mobilized in Humboldt's nineteenth-century configuration of ecosystems and later as a rallying cry for twentieth-century multiculturalism (Soudien 2008; 2009), was an apposite national motto for South Africa. Yet as many South African commentators have observed, greater attention must be paid to what happened in history, not just that certain things happened to individuals, but that that those legacies remain inescapable today. A great many people are still suffering as a result of long-term historical decisions and processes such as racial mapping, tribal designations and conflicts, forced removals, land alienation, and the destruction of livestock and livelihoods. The candy coating of the past may have been adopted by the ANC as a positive strategy for peaceful transition, yet such strategies have been repeatedly undercut by escalating xenophobia and ethnic prejudice. The flattening out of difference that has transpired through the ANCization and heroization of national heritage projects has angered and further marginalized colored, San, Muslim, and mixed-race communities or those non-aligned with ANC politics (Bremner 2004; Marschall 2006a; McGregor and Schumaker 2006; Meskell and Scheermeyer 2008; Murray, Hall, and Shepherd 2007). In a sense, the nation's complex histories have been jettisoned in favor of weightless heritage and, from that vantage, past mastering in South Africa becomes ever more illusory.

The processing of history, the unmaking and making of heritage, cannot hope to offer the *muti* – the healing or therapy to ameliorate the past and re-enchant the future – without some attention to the specifics of a deeper history. By this I do not invoke history as simply the triumphalism of liberation or the evolutionary progress of the fossil record shrouded in the mists of prehistory, but the complex intercalations of precolonial, colonial, and recent pasts. Like many I am skeptical that the historical reflections and genuflections we have witnessed since liberation have offered tangible benefits to ordinary citizens, have curbed violence, or provided a model for social change. Instrumentalizing the past, primarily through modalities of neoliberal heritage, aims to produce self-sustaining citizens free of governmental support that largely serves state goals for reduced responsibility rather than forging *ubuntu* or healing the national psyche. These strategies to make heritage pay "conform to the economic machinery of weightless capitalism and work best when the substance of colonial history and the wounds of imperial domination have been mystified or, better still, forgotten" (Gilroy 2005: 3). Exposure to the grim realities of the colonial past, Gilroy contends, should be made useful in shaping multicultural, pluri-ethnic relations and revising imperialist notions of sovereignty. ANC visionaries undoubtedly had this in mind at the time of democratic hand-over, envisioning that celebrating the nation's historical diversity and cultural vibrancy could be transformed into an embodied and material vehicle for social change and inevitably progress. The good intentions of reconciliation and betterment were undeniably there in the early iterations of the Rainbow Nation and African Renaissance; it is simply that they have been overshadowed by the understandably "greater needs" of fiscal recovery and development.

Notably, archaeologists provided the aesthetic inspiration for the national coat of arms and state motto crafted from an extinct San language, but it would be literary theorists and historians who performed the work of unpacking public heritage, promoting it and debating the past (e.g., Bonner 2010; Hamilton *et al.* 2002; Mbembe and Nuttall 2004; McGregor and Schumaker 2006; Nuttall and Coetzee 1998; Witz 2003; Witz, Rassool, and Minkley 2001). Those archaeologists who did take heritage seriously are still viewed by the old guard as producing work tangential to the larger academic projects of human origins, Iron Age complexity, or deciphering rock art iconology (e.g., Hall 1994; 1995; 2001; 2006; Ouzman 2005; Shepherd 2002a; 2008; Shepherd and Ernsten 2007). There have been a handful of exemplary projects that have attempted to balance heritage, development, and educational aims, including the Wildebeest Kuil Rock Art Center, the Kamberg Rock Art Center and the Clanwilliam Living Landscape Project. In these cases diverse long-term histories are revealed, conflict and difference are exposed, and the multiple layering of sites and landscapes explored. Notably these projects are all based on rock art heritage, rather than archaeology, which suggests that South African archaeology might still be attempting to shed its apartheid legacy of disinterested science (Shepherd 2003). External consultants, rather than archaeologists, have consistently designed and implemented museums and interpretive centers while private operations like the Apartheid Museum (Bonner 2004) have proven more successful than the state ventures of pomp and pageantry like Freedom Park, the Hector Pieterson Museum, and Walter Sisulu Square that have rankled trauma survivors and those living in the shadow of these monuments to victory. Rainbows and Renaissances have recently fallen from view and intellectual leaders in the early ANC government such as Mandela, Mbeki, Pallo Jordan, and Valli Moosa have either stepped down or been replaced in Zuma's new government. Perhaps even discussion of national heritage and public history projects will be suspended in this unsettling climate of anti-intellectualism, corruption, and disregard for democracy (Hammett 2010).

For all the talk of modernity and the world's most liberal constitution, South Africa's new national geographies have fallen back upon old tribal designations and re-enchanted ethnic performances to promote South African culture and uplift. Culture would increasingly do the work of race to describe difference, and this remains true in the burgeoning heritage sphere. With a new climate of commercialism and branding, ethno-cultures have flourished and ethnic tribal identities have been celebrated, naturalized, and sold. We must recall here too that the ousted National Party also saw ethnic difference and tribal tradition as a way of cementing a certain unity in diversity through a policy of separate development, albeit under a banner of white supremacy. The reinvigoration of Bantustan identities for sale has continued since 1994, but the difference is that new governmental modes of citizen-making have been operationalized, whether in the selling of trauma and victimhood, the celebration of township poverty, the promotion of ethnic enclaves, or the indoctrination of good environmental citizens. Re-enchanted ethnicized landscapes proliferate through ecotourism ventures, craft tours, museum exhibits, land claims, reburial ceremonies, heritage rights, and identifications of archaeological sites. Hardened identity categories and disputes about "firstness," indigeneity, and authenticity are other consequences. And while South African academics are offering ever more nuanced accounts of racialization and identity to counter such reversions (Nuttall 2009), politicians, including President Zuma, are, conversely, telescoping and hardening the categories of race and tribe in the public sphere.

Supplanting racialism for culturalism, whether under apartheid or in the new identity configurations of post-liberation society, however, continues to further victimize the nation's poorest. The old government of the past legitimated itself by promising to deliver more; the new government now flourishes by promising less (Comaroff and Comaroff 2009: 128). The language of people "capacitating themselves" abounds in new entrepreneurial, parastatal spaces like Kruger National Park, but the infrastructure, funding, expertise, and culture of development are lacking. Elite pacting and new class-based allegiances that crosscut race only serve to marginalize the black poor, but without the stigma of overt racism – the consequences of which are still felt by the residents of the compound or in the fraught negotiations with black communities beyond Kruger's fence. That ethno-culture represents some essence of being that was once a source of discrimination, but now can be employed as a palliative, rests upon a flawed and perverse logic.

Public and Private Goods

I have argued that heritage was intended to operate as a self-styled or self-made compensation in South Africa, and that the very indices of prior victimhood have been turned into a cultural capital since 1994. Capitalizing culture, or burdening culture with the expectation of a more prosperous and elevated future, has meant that the objects of heritage, and particularly people as objects, would have to be commercialized. Imposing unrealistic material obligations on South African heritage transpired at exactly the juncture when the work of managing heritage was being ever more outsourced to the private sector. Consultancies, commodifications, and the tender system have become the order of the day internationally: it is about being modern. South Africa is certainly not an isolated case. Countries like Montenegro have recently employed external consultants to write their national heritage legislation, Mali has approached archaeologists from the United States to develop their heritage tourism plan, and financial consultants in Italy are brought in to draft European Union applications for multi-sited heritage grants stretching across Europe. Archaeological projects are increasingly self-styled as NGOs and charities, and are, in turn, supported by other NGOs. World heritage sites across the globe have a longer history of entanglement with World Banks schemes, USAID (United States Agency for International Development) funding and other transnational adventures (Brand 2001; Lafrenz Samuels 2010; Lilley 2009; Mitchell 2000; 2002b). Governments, donor agencies, and corporations have all come to see heritage and tradition as reified public *goods* that could be mobilized for the greater public *good*. But more than simply its economic instrumentality, South African heritage might also proffer a seemingly novel vehicle for national pride, spiritual recovery, and racial reconciliation.

New tribal villages, African-themed casinos, and safari lodges are burgeoning, while museums, interpretive centers, galleries, and archaeological sites have often struggled for financial survival including Maropeng, Thulamela, The Origins Center, Wildebeest Kuil Rock Art Center, the African Window Museum, Johannesburg Art Gallery, even Robben Island. Many of these ventures have reconfigured themselves as public–private venues that are as likely to host weddings, events, and corporate meetings as heritage events or educational programs. Capitalizing culture, literally the attempt to transform culture's liquid assets into permanent heritage capital, has proven more challenging than promoting and consuming the modern and global imperatives of nature conservation and biodiversity. International consultancies like McKinsey and Co. capitalized upon the economic potentials for the modern re-branding of nature in Kruger, enabling foreign injections from international agencies and donors to support its new mission. What would remain constant from apartheid onwards was the successful parallel marketing of a white, colonial fantasy of African wilderness and safari and the ability to promote certain forms of nature to emerging global markets, now freely able to consume South Africa in a guilt-free, pluri-racial setting. This dual re-packaging of nature simultaneously captures the virtues of romantic wilderness and the progressive science of inventorying diversity, simultaneously appealing to multiple moral positions. While it was hoped that cultural heritage would match these fiscal potentials, much cultural work has merely appended itself to the trappings of nature's adventures, whether tribal homestays or ecotourism, or simply tendered the decorative veneer of tribal authenticity to lodges and camps like those in national parks, tantamount to an Afro-chic makeover. The resurgence of tribalism and the performance of new primitivities in faux-exotic settings continue to be troubling consequences of naturalizing culture and diversity.

Environment and tourism was, at the time of writing, effectively sutured at the state level through the DEAT, a structure that is at variance to countries like Greece, Turkey, Egypt, or Italy where art, archaeology, and culture is very much the business of tourism. Despite the affective calls for heritage revivalism and pan–African culture at the dawn of liberation, heritage might now be seen as ancillary to the work of nation building and fiscal sustainability. We might recall here that heritage was cast as a burden under apartheid; it was repackaged as an asset for the ANC in a mood of Afro-nationalism during the 1990s, then swiftly recalibrated as a fiscal drain in the 2000s, only to be re-enchanted once more at the decade's close. Cultural heritage and the archaeological past, from the nation's inception with the arrival of European entrepreneurs and colonists, was deemed more complex, messy, and problematic than the nature's patrimony. Under apartheid rule the black past needed to be erased and misread so as to substantiate late black arrival and justify continued white supremacy. Since liberation that same past proffers new bones of contention, often perceived as too tightly wed to scripted identities and races that could prove partial and exclusionary for a new nation to embrace. Of course, monuments to struggle heroes and sites of resistance have been high-profile public exceptions to this position, yet have subsequently spawned violence, ethnic tension, and vocal criticism of the ANC government.

It was not only cultural heritage, but natural heritage too, that was called upon after 1994 to pay for its own functioning, in addition to shouldering the burden of developing the nation's poorest and in general compensating for the depredations of colonial and apartheid rule. South African culture required effort to manage and integrate, whether under Verwoerdian separate development or Rainbow Nation multiculturalism, whereas national nature was immediately legible as pre-racial or supra-racial and has been acclaimed since at least the nineteenth century as a successful driver for South African wealth and international profile. The task set for South Africa's environmental managers in the wake of apartheid, however, was monumental. They would have to rebuild financially viable, self-sustaining institutions, while simultaneously transforming the racial structure of those organizations. Management were entreated to take seriously, for the first time, their obligations to a new citizenry through education, employment, development projects, and land claims, while concurrently responding to new calls for biodiversity conservation and accommodating a new scale of international tourism. Addressing these challenges in the first decade post-1994 effectively charted new territory in South Africa, by balancing the new desires for ecological diversity with the fiscal imperatives of privatization and enhanced tourist services, that was perhaps most palpably played out in premier parks like Kruger. Newly articulated discourses and urgencies such as capacity building, corporate social responsibility, and environmental education were all newly mapped onto Kruger's mopane scrub and Baobab sandveld landscapes. Millennial Kruger was full of promise for a new suite of actors and organizations: the previously disadvantaged, bordering communities, consultants and entrepreneurs, private conservation companies, NGOs, researchers, and the international donor community. But such changes also signaled further threats and discord, with controversial restructuring and redundancy programs like Operation Prevail (Masuku Van Damme and Meskell 2009: 78). The challenge for the new millennium was to maximize the former and delimit the fallout from the latter, and to a significant degree SANParks has been successful. Yet somewhere in the midst of those momentous transformations and adaptations, the history and heritage of their flagship, Kruger National Park, was relegated to an ambivalent niche, a no man's land of sorts that was increasingly left off the map.

Today, the new mission for SANParks combines the twin foci of biodiversity conservation and tourism. This presents a twofold challenge given Kruger's notoriously fragmented policy integration and lack of a coordinating body (Zhou 2009) on the one hand, and the opposing objectives and material outcomes of promoting conservation and tourism, on the other. In discussion with experts from UNESCO they described this post-1994 multi-use phase of Kruger as possibly impinging on biodiversity through increased tourist infrastructure. Developing biodiversity and tourism in tandem is undoubtedly a socio-economic necessity, and perhaps we should not lament some loss of an idealized ecological "climax state" (Carruthers 2008; Clements 1916) if there are other accrued benefits for a greater number of South Africans. Added to that, I have argued that Kruger's mission of biodiversity, and to some degree business, has also impinged upon archaeological and heritage projects rather than supported their entrepreneurial or conciliatory flourishing. Cultural heritage can successfully be incorporated or even partnered with ecological conservation, be marketed for international tourism, and benefit indigenous stakeholders by novel collaborations and benefit sharing, as shown in the case of Australia. While comparable developments there in NSW did not occur overnight, SANParks has not acted promptly to emulate current best practice but has instead chosen, at least in Kruger, to follow the time-honored colonial tropes of safari tourism, Big 5 sightings, and wilderness adventure unmoored from African history, any acknowledgement of anthropogenic and political landscapes, and the recent trauma of human expulsions and exploitation.

The case of Kruger offers a suitable microcosm for understanding the changes and challenges in post-apartheid South Africa. What has unfolded in Kruger is akin to many developments witnessed across sub-Saharan Africa, namely the privatization of nature and neoliberal development culture (Homewood, Kristjanson, and Trench 2009; Igoe and Brockington 2007; Nelson 2010) that has gone hand-in-hand with entrenched tribalization and romanticism and, strikingly in some places, the rise of celebrity philanthro-capitalism around natural heritage (Brockington 2009), though not around its cultural counterpart. In this new landscape local people are impelled to recast themselves as "eco-rational subjects" in Goldman's view (2001), the "eco" in this case standing both for *economic* and *eco*logical. Capitalizing nature globally has taken place within neoliberal restructuring, requiring new forms of re-regulation that in turn lead to re-territorialization and commodification (Igoe and Brockington 2007: 432). One need only think of Mapungubwe National Park or the Karoo that are in reality a mosaic of private conservation reserves, agrobusiness, mining, tourism, and/or settlement. The corporatization of conservation can be clearly seen in SANParks infusion of new business models, but also in the proliferation of private game reserves in South Africa and across Africa generally.

Many scholars have exposed the empty promise of ecotourism for indigenous communities across Africa and elsewhere (Duffy 2002; Honey 1999; Stronza 2001). A surfeit of studies have demonstrated that those communities which happen to live near or amidst protected nature are repeatedly victimized though international efforts to fence and preserve, whether in Botswana (Hitchcock 2002; Keitumetse 2009), Mozambique (Lunstrum 2008), Tanzania (Brockington 2004; Shetler 2007), Costa Rica (Pearson 2009), or the US Virgin Islands (Fortwangler 2007). Yet at the same time there is a perceived need to "indigenize" certain institutions, whether for purposes of politics or consumerism, and this can be seen in many parks whether one visits Yosemite, Uluru, or Serengeti. By having a native presence, should that involve nods to previous indigenous occupation or modern performances, native communities are co-opted into seemingly supporting the conservation mission, often against their own group rights to access, land, resources, and reparations. Notably, these international trends have scarcely impacted places like Kruger where its strong Afrikaner-identified history has yet to yield to the public recognition of indigenous knowledge, histories, and presence. And, finally, I return to an earlier point that, ironically, European national parks have aligned conservation and development by successfully incorporating human populations and traditional lifeways; participation of and assistance to local communities; and diverse forms of land use, including farming (Hamin 2002).

Modern Nature and Premodern Cultures

This is also a book about the past and present of Kruger National Park, the jewel and the thorn in the crown of South African conservation. Its history is testimony to the effects of enclosure, expulsion, and the erasure of an indigenous South African presence. At the same time, its game wardens and CEOs have reified the moral efforts of preserving "wilderness" and aesthetic landscapes for national pride, the global good, and for the benefit of future generations. SANParks' remarkable achievements include racial transformation in upper management, financial restructuring, expansion of its portfolio, the inclusion of social ecology and community programs, and the ongoing revision of its core mission. Much of this has gradually filtered down to Kruger, yet some within the organization admit that South Africa's most famous national park is also the most resistant to change. Kruger's economic successes, its successful forays into privatization, have not been matched by its developmental progress, either with the myriad communities outside the gate or its own employees inside the fence. I suggest that the profile of African archaeology and history, cultural heritage and collaboration with communities today remains low and that these are interrelated phenomena, the latter predicated to a significant degree on the former. These are some of the irreducible failures that allow the system to cohere and continue, a system that privileges nature over culture and the promise of the park over the recognition of its past.

Just like the fiction of dispensing with race that characterized the early democracy, the illusion that apartheid is indeed *past* participates in the vital lie that there is only the future and history is best forgotten. The willing amnesia I encountered in the park, evidenced by the vigorous reinstatement of *terra nullius* or the deep disregard for archaeological patrimony, is testimony to the desire to dispense with certain histories, primarily African histories. Nature's history in the shape of romantic wilderness, heroic rangers, and loyal dogs, however, offers goods and rewards that can be widely packaged and consumed to sustain the national coffers. Additionally, nature's present and future promise in the guise of global biodiversity ensures modernity, internationalism, and recognition that accrue another tranche of socio-economic benefits. Suspending the historical space of Kruger has been deemed expedient for economic and political reasons so that local and community gains have had to be sacrificed for the national and global good. The rising fear of land claims and SANParks reticence to honor successful legal claims in Kruger, coupled with the resurgent racisms it has spawned, are diagnostic of the wider malaise surrounding the past and its material role in the new nation.

In the current arrangement of SANParks heritage falls within the purview of social ecology in the People and Conservation unit, positioning archaeology alongside environmental education, outreach, and empowerment strategies, rather than as a discipline with its own unique techniques and contributions. The very reason why heritage was celebrated and promoted by the ANC, namely the lived connection to its citizenry and heritage's concomitant socio-economic potentials, signifies its downfall within the organization. It is perceived as too politically grafted to repressive regimes and past inequities that directly funnel into benefit sharing, land claims, co-management, and other forms of costly reparation. Post 1994, spaces like Kruger may once have been imbued with promise, captured in the legal handover of the Pafuri triangle to the Makuleke, but a new climate of conservativism and commercialism has lately triumphed.

Dog cemeteries and fictional canine heroes would prove more embraceable than indigenous histories of Kruger National Park, while the triumphalism of white hunters and traders supersedes native agency, condemning them to a perpetual fugitive status. Masorini and Thulamela, together with hundreds of rock art sites across the park, have fallen victim through different trajectories of neglect. Deep disregard is materialized in the moldering artifacts at Albasini and in the persistence of the Stevenson-Hamilton Museum, filled with mangy stuffed antelope, fetal hippopotami, images of subservient blacks and venerated whites, all riddled with the legacies of apartheid history and archaeology. Across Kruger archaeological sites would languish, some would be cleared, projects would be short-lived and fall from view, and eventually the weeds would reclaim the tumble of stones that once represented a proud past.

Ecologies of heritage, however, must actively seek to incorporate recent histories of socio-nature, not simply reify our own disciplinary interests for antiquity. As I was made painfully aware during my interviews, researchers cannot presume to know what stands for history or constitutes heritage or even a site for descendent communities and other groups with felt connections to place. The bovicides of the twentieth century that prompted the final dispossession of the last indigenous residents of Kruger were most often retold as the events that called for an active past mastering. The inhabitants of Kuruman in the Northern Cape (Jacobs 2003) have retold a similar story of military-style stock massacre in the 1980s, underlining that Kruger's history was simply part of a larger, ongoing mosaic of strategic disempowerment. Acknowledgment of these histories, respect for burial sites and compensation for interlaced losses of people, land, and animals was the negative heritage recounted in almost every conversation outside the fence. The relationship between indigenous communities and archaeological sites, specifically in decision-making, stewardship, participation, and development, was a clearly significant, albeit secondary, heritage priority. A narrowly archaeological view of the past might easily sideline cattle killing, the instigation of the trekpas, or the quixotic legacies of *Jock of the Bushveld*, and in doing so elide historic formulations of nature that conspire to trump particular people and their practices. Critical histories of natural heritage also underscore the differential values of particular species throughout Kruger's timeline, whether in the eradication of lions as "vermin" a century ago or the fugitive plans to cull thousands of elephants to curate biodiversity, and helpfully de-naturalize our categories of conservation. Regardless of species, the ethics of care conveyed toward certain forms of nature, whether wilderness or ecological diversity, has traditionally prevailed over African communities.

Misreading the past is a generative endeavor that allows other imperatives to flourish, supports alternative missions of salvage, and enables other potential futures. Both natural and cultural heritages, I would submit, are severely curtailed by vying for precedence in a zero-sum equation. Today we are poised at a critical juncture when human and natural histories are converging through the recognition of globalization and global processes. From the influential writings of Alexander von Humboldt to Alfred W. Crosby, humans have for centuries have been regarded as biological agents wreaking changes, invasions, destructions, and extinctions in nature. However, one recent development has been the progressive questioning of "pristine" nature, the acceptance of co-evolution of species, and human and non-human co-production of apparently "natural" landscapes. Socionature recalibrates the "commonsense" distinctions that political ecology has erected between nature, science, society, politics, and practice. It troubles the tenets of deep ecology, the division of labor between human politics and the science of things, between our particular attachment to "facts" and "values"

(Latour 2004a). Since the turn of the millenium there has been a dramatic scaling up of these intercalations. Anthropogenic climate change surely marks the most momentous shift in human intervention from biological to geological scales, materializing the deep entanglement of human and planetary histories (Chakrabarty 2009).

National parks are perhaps one unmapped space for the modernist project (see also Bunn 2001; Latour 2004a), reifying as they do human desires to shape individual and global destinies and the hubris that we can fully capture and control nature and natural forces. I should point out that archaeology was similarly premised on the tenets of modernism and emerged historically from a commitment to order, classification, objective science, salvage, and progress (Thomas 2004). But contemporary heritage study, like modern ecology or geography, has become more interdisciplinary, self-reflexive, and more open to other systems of knowledge or ways of knowing that are at odds with the management styles of Kruger. Similar tensions between the academy and field practitioners in cultural resource management and historic preservation has been hotly debated in Britain, the United States, and Australia (Lozny 2006; Patterson 1999; L.-J. Smith 2004). Many park managers also want to preserve those discrete taxonomies since their entire history and raison *d'être* wrests on modernist foundational structures. Colonially conceived parks such as Kruger reveal, in landscape ecology terms, a mosaic or complex system of connectivity. They stitch together lineaments of human history, anthropogenic landscapes, conservation politics, enclosure and policing, nationalist agendas and state-like functions, adaptive management strategies, dreams of wilderness, ideas of progress and objective science, and yet they still foster categorical distinctions between nature and culture, humans and non-humans.

Nature and Culture

A remarkable degree of global coherence is expressed in the cascading crises of preservation, access, sustainability, diversity loss, and non-renewability. As a result of working on South Africa's premier protected area and being immersed in the celebratory narratives of conservation and biodiversity I began to interrogate the origins and interconnectedness of natural and cultural heritage as classifications and practices. What emerges is a very particular modern Anglo-American lineage of ideas and sentiments that has powered the protection and privileging of nature and natural resources, and this ultimately presages the politics of cultural sites. This is perhaps not so surprising given archaeology's development in the shadow of geology, paleontology, and the natural sciences (Trigger 1989). Yet managing past human creations, by their very constitution, necessarily differs from managing natural heritage. Cultural heritage is entirely premised upon human engagement, from its creation to its numerous life histories, followed by excavation, preservation, presentation, access, and our experience of that heritage at local and global scales. This is in marked contrast with much current thinking about preserving the environment and natural resources. I have argued here that the underlying management philosophies that guide cultural heritage have inherited a largely negative view of human engagement, including non-expert participation, occupation, co-management, access and modification to past places. Protecting nature prefigures our own practices of enclosure, whether in Thailand or Britain, so that restricted access to cultural sites has led to another kind of fortress conservation (Byrne 2009; Johnson 2008). Descendant and connected communities are often excluded from policy making, they are seen as authentic only when attending to ancient spiritual values rather than modern social or economic ones. Moreover, fears over loss, site destruction, our desires for representativeness and diversity, and more recently concerns over risk, sustainability, and climate change have entered the lexicons of both archaeology and heritage with great rapidity.

One could argue that this is simply a reflection of international consternation within the academy and the public sphere. However, I would suggest a more entangled connection that can be traced across distinct genealogies that have gradually coalesced into a more coherent and universal preservationist stance. Some of those tracings might include Humboldt's *Kosmos* and his nostalgia for the past (Pratt 1992; Sachs 2007) through to the nineteenth- and twentieth-century removals of Native Americans in US National Parks (Keller and Turek 1998; Spence 1999); the British practice of enclosure coupled with the romantic tradition of venerating brutish nature and monumental ruins (Lowenthal 1985); colonial fictions of *terra nullius* to Manifest Destiny; and the moral argument for expanding protected areas and disallowing human occupation. On a transnational scale we might point to UNESCO's early establishment of the IUCN followed decades later by ICOMOS and ICCROM and culminating in the 1972 Convention on the Protection of the World Cultural and Natural Heritage. Despite some negative legacies there have also been productive borrowings from nature conservation: Community Based Natural Resource Management (CBNRM), participatory approaches, and the incorporation of indigenous knowledge have percolated into collaborative and community archaeologies that recognize diverse stakeholders. The profusion of heritage NGOs modeling their ethos or their working practices on agencies like the IUCN or WWF; the promotion of sustainable heritage that seeks economic benefits and enhanced capacity (Lafrenz Samuels 2010); and even corporate social responsibility programs and sponsorship are some recent influences that have found global salience.

Today there is also enough of a shared ethos and language between critical conservation and contemporary heritage studies to assess these inheritances and intersections and judge whether they are apposite in particular contexts. Natural and cultural heritages, I suggest, are progressively called upon to fulfill a whole panoply of roles and obligations, as the example of South Africa illustrates, from employment and development, providing the basis for new claims sutured to identity or land, restitution and benefit sharing, capacity building, spiritual uplift, national pride, and new knowledges. Equally, our communal legacies embroil us in debates about global patrimony, universalisms, sovereignty, human rights, poverty reduction, and the nature of our responsibilities to future generations. Salvage crusades to preserve the past or the environment, albeit on different scales, enlist overlapping arguments, entreat similar sponsors (Lowenthal 2006), and often fall victim to the same elitist North–South divides. Our respective fieldwork exposes us not only to injustices, coercions, evictions, and exploitation on the ground, but also sometimes to the potentials and successes of small-scale initiatives and co-operation. The gravity of such matters might propel practitioners from both fields into the public sphere, thus carving out a privileged niche for ourselves on moral, scientific, or romantic grounds. Equally, they entangle us in new webs of cosmopolitan ethics, indigenous rights, diverse attachments, and obligations to others, which continue to make our work only ever future perfect.

References

Abu el-Haj, N. (2001) *Facts on the Ground: Archaeological Practice and Territorial Self-Fashioning in Israeli Society*. Chicago: University of Chicago Press.

Adams, J. and T. McShane (1996) *The Myth of Wild Africa: Conservation Without Illusion*. Berkeley: University of California Press.

Adams, K. M. (2006) *Art as Politics: Recrafting Identities, Tourism, and Power in Tana Toraja, Indonesia*. Honolulu: University of Hawaii Press.

Adams, W. M. (2003a) Nature and the colonial mind, in W. Adams and M. Mulligan (eds), *Decolonizing Nature: Strategies for Conservation in a Post-colonial Era*. London: Earthscan, pp. 16–50.

Adams, W. M. (2003b) When nature won't stay still: Conservation, equilibrium and control, in W. Adams and M. Mulligan (eds), *Decolonizing Nature: Strategies for Conservation in a Post-colonial Era*. London: Earthscan, pp. 220–46.

Adams, W. M. (2005) *Against Extinction*. London: Earthscan.

Adams, W. M. and J. Hutton. (2007) People, parks and poverty: Political ecology and bio-diversity conservation. *Conservation & Society* 5: 147–83.

Adams, W. M. and M. Mulligan (eds) (2003a) *Decolonizing Nature: Strategies for Conservation in a Post-colonial Era*. London: Earthscan.

Adams, W. M. and M. Mulligan (2003b) Introduction, in W. Adams and M. Mulligan (eds), *Decolonizing Nature: Strategies for Conservation in a Post-colonial Era*. London: Earthscan, pp. 1–15.

Addison, A. (2007) *Disappearing World: The Earth's Most Extraordinary and Endangered Places*. London: HarperCollins.

Agrawal, A. (2005) *Environmentality: Technologies of Government and the Making of Subjects*. Durham: Duke University Press.

Allen, A. (1996) Stone-walled ruins with a unique 'sense of lightness'. *Independent Online*. www.iol.co.za/index.php?set_id=1&click_id=68&art_id=arch31623be52ec3c3f19 (accessed August 2, 2005).

Alpin, G. (2002) *Heritage: Identification, Conservation, and Management*. Oxford: Oxford University Press.

anon. (2007) Phinda's name fulfilled: Phinda land returned to ancestral owners. *Wildside* 3: 59–60.

Appadurai, A. (1990) Disjuncture and difference in the global cultural economy, in M. Featherstone (ed.), *Global Culture: Nationalism, Globalization and Modernity*. London: Sage, pp. 295–310.

Appadurai, A. (1991) Global ethnoscapes: notes and queries for a transnational anthropology, in R. G. Fox (ed.), *Recapturing Anthropology: Working in the Present*. Santa Fe: School of American Research, pp. 191–210.

Appadurai, A. (1996) *Modernity at Large: Cultural Dimensions of Globalization*. Minneapolis: University of Minnesota Press.

Appadurai, A. (2002) Diversity and sustainable development, in UNSECO & UNEP (ed.), *Cultural Diversity and Biodiversity for Sustainable Development, World Summit on Sustainable Development*. Nairobi: UNEP, pp. 16–19 and 49–50.

Appiah, K. A. (1992) *In My Father's House*. London: Methuen.

Appiah, K. A. (2006) *Cosmopolitanism*. New York: Norton and Company.

Arantes, A. A. (2007) Diversity, heritage and cultural politics. *Theory, Culture and Society* 24: 290–6.

Arnold, M. and B. Schmahmann (eds) (2005) *Between Union And Liberation: Women Artists In South Africa 1910–1994*. Aldershot: Ashgate.

Atalay, S. (2007) Global application of indigenous archaeology: community based participatory research in Turkey. *Archaeologies* 3: 249–70.

Attridge, D. (2005) *J. M. Coetzee and the Ethics of Reading: Literature in the Event*. Chicago: University of Chicago Press.

Austin, K., D. Currey, and S. Galster (1992) *Under Fire: Elephants in the Frontline*. London: Environmental Investigation Agency.

Australia ICOMOS (1999) The Burra Charter: The Australian ICOMOS Charter for the Conservation of Cultural Places of Cultural Significance, http://www.icomos.org/burra_charter.html (accessed May 4, 2011).

Baines, G. (2009) Site of struggle: the Freedom Park fracas and the divisive legacy of South Africa, Border War/Liberation Struggle. *Social Dynamics: A Journal of African Studies* 35: 330–44.

Bamford, S. (2007) *Biology Unmoored: Melanesian Reflections on Life and Biotechnology*. Berkeley, CA: University of California Press.

Bandarin, F. (2007) *World Heritage: Challenges for the Millennium*. Paris: UNESCO.

Bannon, I. and P. Collier (eds) (2003) *Natural Resources and Violent Conflict: Options and Actions*. Washington, DC: The World Bank.

Barnard, A. (1992) *Hunters and Herders of Southern Africa: A Comparative Ethnography of the Khoisan Peoples*. Cambridge: Cambridge University Press.

Barnard, A. (2003) Khoisan imagery in the reconstruction of South African national identity. Inaugural Lecture as Professor of the Anthropology of Southern Africa in the University of Edinburgh, Edinburgh, April 29, 2003.

Barnard, A. (2007) *Anthropology and Bushmen*. Berg: Oxford.

Bartu, A. (2000) Where is Çatalhöyük? Multiple sites in the construction of an archaeological site, in I. Hodder (ed.), *Towards Reflexive Method in Archaeology: The Example at Çatalhöyük*. Cambridge: McDonald Institute for Archaeological Research, pp. 101–9.

Baviskar, A. (2003) Tribal politics and discourses of Indian environmentalism, in P. Greenenough and A. Tsing (eds), *Nature in the Global South: Environmental Projects in South and Southeast Asia*. Durham: Duke University Press, pp. 289–318.

Beck, U. (1995) *Ecological Politics in an Age of Risk*. Cambridge: Polity.

Beck, U. (2009) *World at Risk*. Cambridge: Polity.

Beinart, W. (2003) *The Rise of Conservation in South Africa: Settlers, Livestock, and the Environment 1770–1950*. Oxford: Oxford University Press.

Beinart, W., K. Brown, and D. Gilfoyle (2009) Experts and expertise in colonial Africa reconsidered: science and the interpenetration of knowledge. *African Affairs* 108: 413–33.

Beinart, W. and P. Coates (1995) *Historical Connections: Environment and History*. London: Routledge.

Beinart, W. and K. Middleton (2004) Plant transfers in historical perspective: A review article. *Environment and History* 10: 3–29.

Benavides, O. H. (2005) *Making Ecuadorian Histories*. Austin: University of Texas Press.

Bengis, R. G., R. Grant, and V. de Vos (2003) Wildlife diseases and veterinary controls: A savanna ecosystem perspective, in J. T. Du Toit, K. H. Rogers, and H. C. Biggs (eds) *The Kruger Experience: Ecology and Management of a Savanna Heterogeneity*. Washington: Island Press, pp. 349–69.

Benhabib, S. (2004) *The Rights of Others*. Cambridge: Cambridge University Press.

Binns, T. and Nel, E. (2002) Tourism as a local development strategy in South Africa. *The Geographical Journal* 168: 235–47.

Blomley, N. (2008) Enclosure, common right and the property of the poor. *Social Legal Studies* 17: 311–31.

Blundell, G. (1996) Presenting South Africa's rock art sites, in J. Deacon (ed.), *Monuments and Sites: South Africa*. Sri Lanka: International Council on Monuments and Sites, pp. 71–80.

Blundell, G. (2002) *The Unseen Landscape: A Journey to Game Pass Shelter*. Guide Booklet. Johannesburg: Rock Art Research Institute.

Blundell, G. (2004) *Nqabayo's Nomansland*. Uppsala: Uppsala University.

Bonner, P. (2004) History teaching and the Apartheid Museum, in S. Jeppie (ed.), *Toward New Histories for South Africa: On the Place of the Past in Our Present*. Cape Town: Juta, pp. 140–7.

Bonner, P. (2010) Keynote address to the 'Life after Thirty' colloquium. *African Studies* 69: 13–27.

Bonner, P. and J. Carruthers (2003) The Recent History of the Mapungubwe Area. Unpublished document: NORAD and DEAT.

Bonner, P., A. Esterhuysen, and T. Jenkins (eds) (2007) *A Search for Origins: Science, History and South Africa's 'Cradle of Humankind'*. Johannesburg: Wits University Press.

Bonner, P., A. Esterhuysen, and N. Swanepoel (eds) (2009) *Five Hundred Years Rediscovered: Southern African Precedents and Prospects*. Johannesburg: Wits University Press.

Bookchin, M. (1996) *The Philosophy of Social Ecology: Essays on Dialectical Naturalism*. Montreal: Black Rose Books.

Boonzaier, E. and A. D. Spiegel (2008) Tradition, in N. Shepherd and S. Robins (eds), *South African Keywords*. Johannesburg: Jacana, pp. 195–208.

Braak, H. H. (1997) Letter to Mr M. J. Tagg Gold Fields Foundation, dated April 21, 1997. On file in the Skukuza Archives, Kruger National Park.

Brand, L. A. (2001) Development in Wadi Rum? State bureaucracy, external funders, and civil society. *International Journal of Middle East Studies* 33: 571–90.

Brattli, T. (2009) Managing the archaeological world cultural heritage: Consensus or rhetoric? *Norweigian Archaeological Review* 42: 24–39.

Breglia, L. C. (2006) *Monumental Ambivalence*. Austin: University of Texas Press.

Bremner, L. (2004) Reframing township space: The Kliptown project. *Public Culture* 16: 521–31.

Brink, A. (1998) Stories of history: Reimagining the past in post-apartheid narrative, in S. Nuttall and C. Coetzee (eds), *Negotiating the Past: The Making of Memory in South Africa*. Cape Town: Oxford University Press, pp. 29–42.

Brockington, D. (2004) *Fortress Conservation: The Preservation of the Mkomazi Game Reserve, Tanzania*. Bloomington: Indiana University Press.

Brockington, D. (2009) *Celebrity and the Environment*. London: Zed Books.

Brockington, D. and J. Igoe (2006) Eviction for conservation: A global overview. *Conservation and Society* 4: 424–70.

Brooks, S. (2005) Images of 'Wild Africa': Nature tourism and the (re)creation of Hluhluwe game reserve, 1930–1945. *Journal of Historical Geography* 31: 220–40.

Brown, W. (2001) *Politics out of History*. Princeton: Princeton University Press.

Bruner, E. M. (2005) *Culture on Tour: Ethnographies of Travel*. Chicago: University of Chicago Press.

Bruner, E. M. and B. Kirshenblatt-Gimblett (1994) Maasai on the lawn: Tourist realism in East Africa. *Cultural Anthropology* 9: 435–70.

Bryden, B. (2005) *A Game Ranger Remembers*. Jeppestown: Jonathan Ball.

Buchanan, M. (1999) *The Return: The Story of Phinda Game Reserve*. Rivonia: Londolozi Publishers.

Buckley, R. (2002) Public and private partnerships between tourism and protected areas: The Australian situation. *The Journal of Tourism Studies* 13: 26–38.

Bunn, D. (2001) Comaroff country. *Interventions* 3: 5–23.

Bunn, D. (2003) An unnatural state: Tourism, water and wildlife photography in the early Kruger National Park, in W. Beinart and J. McGregor (eds), *Social History and African Environments*. Oxford: James Currey, pp. 199–220.

Bunn, D. (2006) The museum outdoors: Heritage, cattle and permeable borders in the Southwestern Kruger National Park, in I. Karp and C. Kratz (eds), *Museum Frictions: Public Cultures/Global Transformations*. Durham: Duke University Press, pp. 357–91.

Bunn, D. and M. Auslander (1998) From Crook's Corner to Thulamela, in Y. Dlada (ed.), *Voices, Values, Identities Symposium*. Pretoria: South African National Parks, pp. 32–40.

Burns, P. M. and S. Barrie (2005) Race, space and "Our own piece of Africa": Doing good in Luphisi village. *Journal of Sustainable Tourism* 13: 468–85.

Büscher, B. and W. Dressler (2007) Linking neoprotectionism and environmental governance: On the rapidly increasing tensions between actors in the environment–development nexus. *Conservation & Society* 5: 586–611.

Buttimer, A. (2006) Bridging the Americas: Humboldtian legacies. *The Geographical Review* 96: vi–x.

Byrne, D. (1991) Western hegemony in archaeological heritage management. *History and Anthropology* 5: 269–76.

Byrne, D. (1995) Buddhist stupa and Thai social practice. *World Archaeology* 27: 266–81.

Byrne, D. (2003) Nervous landscapes: Race and space in Australia. *Journal of Social Archaeology* 3: 169–93.

Byrne, D. (2007) *Surface Collection: Archaeological Travels in Southeast Asia.* Walnut Creek: AltaMira.

Byrne, D. (2009) Archaeology and the fortress of rationality, in L. M. Meskell (ed.), *Cosmopolitan Archaeologies.* Durham: Duke University Press.

Byrne, D., H. Brayshaw, and T. Ireland (2001) *Social Significance: A Discussion Paper.* Sydney: NSW National Parks and Wildlife Serivce.

Byrne, D., H. Goodall, S. Wearing, and A. Cadzow (2006) Enchanted parklands. *Australian Geographer* 37: 103–15.

Caldicott, J. (2008) Leopold's land aesthetic, in A. Carlson and S. Lintott (eds), *Nature, Aesthetics, and Environmentalism.* New York: Columbia University Press, pp. 105–18.

Candelaria, M. A. F. (2005) The Angkor sites of Cambodia: The conflicting values of sustainable tourism and state sovereignty. *Brooklyn Journal of International Law* 31: 253–88.

Carlisle, L. (2003) Private Reserves: The Conservation Corporation African model, in R. Buckley, C. Pickering, and D. B. Weaver (eds), *Nature-based Tourism, Environment and Land Management.* Wallingford: CABI Publishing, pp. 17–23.

Carlson, A. (2008) Nature and positive aesthetics, in A. Carlson and S. Lintott (eds), *Nature, Aesthetics, and Environmentalism.* New York: Columbia University Press, pp. 211–37.

Carlson, A. and S. Lintott (2008) Introduction: Natural aesthetic value and environmentalism, in A. Carlson and S. Lintott (eds), *Nature, Aesthetics, and Environmentalism.* New York: Columbia University Press, pp. 1–21.

Carruthers, J. (1989) Creating a national park. *Journal of Southern African Studies* 15: 188–216.

Carruthers, J. (1993) Police boys and poachers: Africans, wildlife protection and national parks, the Transvaal 1902 to 1950. *Koedoe* 36: 11–22.

Carruthers, J. (1994) Dissecting the myth: Paul Kruger and the Kruger national park. *Journal of Southern African Studies* 20: 263–83.

Carruthers, J. (1995) *The Kruger National Park: A Social and Political History.* Pietermaritzburg: University of Natal Press.

Carruthers, J. (2001) *Wildlife and Warfare: The Life of James Stevenson-Hamilton.* Pietermaritzburg: University of Natal Press.

Carruthers, J. (2005) Changing Perspectives on Wildlife in Southern Africa, c.1840 to c.1914. *Society and Animals* 13: 183–200.

Carruthers, J. (2006) Tracking in game trails: Looking afresh at the politics of environmental history in South Africa. *Environmental History* 11: 804–29.

Carruthers, J. (2008) Conservation and Wildlife Management in South African National Parks 1930s–1960s. *Journal of the History of Biology* 41: 203–36.

Castañeda, Q. (1996) *In the Museum of Maya Culture: Touring Chichén Itzá.* Minneapolis: University of Minnesota Press.

Catsadorakis, G. (2007) The Conservation of natural and cultural heritage in Europe and the Mediterranean: A Gordian knot? *International Journal of Heritage Studies* 13: 308–20.

Cengiz, T. (2007) Tourism, an ecological approach in protected areas: Karagöl-Sahara National Park, Turkey. *International Journal of Sustainable Development & World Ecology* 14: 260–7.

Chakrabarty, D. (2009) The climate of history: Four theses. *Critical Inquiry* 35: 197–222.

Chanock, M. (2000) "Culture" and human rights: Orientalising, occidentalising and authenticity, in M. Mamdani (ed.), *Beyond Rights Talk and Culture Talk: Comparative Essays on the Politics of Rights and Culture*. New York: St Martin's Press, pp. 15–36.

Cheah, P. (1998) Given culture: Rethinking cosmopolitical freedom in transnationalism, in P. Cheah and B. Robbins (eds), *Cosmopolitics: Thinking and Feeling Beyond Nation*. Minneapolis: Minnesota University Press, pp. 290–328.

Child, B. (ed.) (2004) *Parks in Transition: Biodiversity, Rural Development and the Bottom Line*. London and Sterling, VA: Earthscan.

Chirikure, S. and G. Pwiti (2008) Community involvement in archaeology and cultural heritage management: An assessment from case studies in Southern Africa and elsewhere. *Current Anthropology* 49: 467–85.

Claassens, A. and B. Cousins (2008) *Land, Power and Custom: Controversies Generated by South Africa's Communal Land Rights Act*. Cape Town: University of Cape Town Press.

Clark, N. L. (2002) The demon-seed: Bioinvasion as the unsettling of environmental cosmopolitanism. *Theory, Culture and Society* 19: 101–25.

Cleaver, F. (2001) Institutions, agency and the limitations of participatory approaches to development, in B. Cooke and U. Kothari (eds), *Participation: The New Tyranny?* New York: Zed Books, pp. 36–55.

Clements, F. E. (1916) *Plant Succession: An Analysis of the Development of Vegetation*. Washington, DC: Carnegie Institution of Washington.

Cock, J. (2007) *The War Against Ourselves: Nature, Power and Justice*. Johannesburg: Wits University Press.

Cock, J. and D. Fig (2002) From colonial to community-based conservation: Environmental justice and the transformation of National Parks, in D. A. McDonald (ed.) *Environmental Justice in South Africa*. Athens: Ohio University Press, pp. 131–55.

Coetzee, J. M. (1980) *Waiting for the Barbarians*. London: Penguin.

Coetzee, J. M. (1988) *White Writing: On the Culture of Letters in South Africa*. New Haven: Yale University Press.

Coetzee, J. M. (2000) *Disgrace*. London: Penguin.

Colloredo-Mansfeld, R. (2002) An ethnography of Neoliberalism: Understanding competition in artisan economies. *Current Anthropology* 43: 113–37.

Colvin, C. J. (2003) "Brothers and sisters, do not be afraid of me": Trauma, history and the therapeutic imagination in the new South Africa, in K. Hodgkin and S. Radstone (eds), *Contested Pasts: The Politics of Memory*. pp. 153–67.

Colwell-Chanthaphonh, C. (2010) *Living Histories: Native Americans and Southwestern Archaeology*. Lanham: AltaMira Press.

Colwell-Chanthaphonh, C. and T. J. Ferguson (2006) *History is in the Land: Multivocal Tribal Traditions in Arizona's San Pedro Valley*. Tucson: University of Arizona Press.

Comaroff, J. and J. L. Comaroff (2001) Naturing the nation: Aliens, apocalypse and the postcolonial state. *Journal of Southern African Studies* 27: 627–51.

Comaroff, J. L. and J. Comaroff (2006) Law and disorder in the postcolony: An introduction, in J. Comaroff and J. L. Comaroff (eds), *Law and Disorder in the Postcolony*. Chicago: University of Chicago Press, pp. 1–56.

Comaroff, J. L. and J. Comaroff (2009) *Ethnicity, INC*. Chicago: University of Chicago Press.

Commonwealth of Australia (2000) *Uluru–Kata Tjuta National Park – Plan of Management*. Yulara: Parks Australia. Also online http://www.comlaw.gov.au/Details/F2007B00594/Supporting%20Material/Text (accessed May 4, 2011).

Connerton, P. (2008) Seven types of forgetting. *Memory Studies* 1: 59–71.

Connor, T. K. (2003) Crooks, Commuters, and Chiefs: Home and Belonging in a Border Zone in Pafuri, Gaza Province, Mozambique. *Journal of Contemporary African Studies* 21: 93–120.

Conservation Corporation Africa (2005) *Bongani Mountain Lodge, South Africa*. Travel Brochure: CCA.

Conservation Corporation Africa (2007) *Simply Safari*. Travel Brochure: CCA.

Cooke, B. and U. Kothari (eds) (2001a) *Participation: The New Tyranny?* New York: Zed Books.

Cooke, B. and U. Kothari (2001b) The case for participation as tyranny, in B. Cooke and U. Kothari (eds), *Participation: The New Tyranny?* New York: Zed Books, pp. 1–15.

Coombe, R. (2003) Works in progress: Traditional knowledge, biological diversity, and intellectual property in a neoliberal era, in R. W. Perry and B. Maurer (eds), *Globalization under Construction: Governmentality, Law, and Identity*. Minneapolis: University of Minnesota Press, pp. 273–313.

Coombe, R. (2005) Legal claims to culture in and against the market: Neoliberalism and the global proliferation of meaningful difference. *Law, Culture and the Humanities* 1: 35–52.

Coombes, A. E. (2003) *History After Apartheid: Visual Culture and Public Memory in a Democratic South Africa*. Durham and London: Duke University Press.

Couzens, T. (2004) *Battles of South Africa*. Cape Town: David Philip.

Crapanzano, V. (1986) *Waiting: The Whites of South Africa*. New York: Vintage.

Crosby, A. W. (1986) *Ecological Imperialism: The Biological Expansion of Europe, 900–1900*. Cambridge: Cambridge University Press.

Cruikshank, J. (2005) *Do Glaciers Listen? Local Knowledge, Colonial Encounters, and Social Imagination*. Seattle: University of Washington Press.

Cuno, J. (2008) *Who Owns Antiquity? Museums and the Battle Over Our Ancient Heritage*. New Jersey: Princeton.

DANCED (2001) Project Completion Report (June 1998–June 2001). DANCED: Capacity Building in SANParks. Pretoria: South African National Parks.

Daniel, J., R. Southall, and J. Lutchman (eds) (2005) *State of the Nation: South Africa 2004–2005*. Cape Town: HSRC Press.

De Jonge, E. (2004) *Spinoza and Deep Ecology: Challenging Traditional Approaches to Environmentalism*. Surrey: Ashgate Publishing.

de Jongh, M. (1994) Mozambican refugee resettlement: Survival strategies of involuntary migrants in South Africa. *Journal of Refugee Studies* 7: 220–38.

De Kok, A. (1998) Cracked heirlooms: Memory on exhibition, in S. Nuttall and C. Coetzee (eds), *Negotiating the Past: The Making of Memory in South Africa*. Cape Town: Oxford University Press, pp. 57–71.

de Villiers, B. (1999) *Land Claims and National Parks: The Makuleke Experience*. Pretoria: Human Sciences Research Council Publishers.

Deacon, H. and C. Foster (2005) *My Heart Stands in the Hill*. Cape Town: Struik.

Deacon, H., S. Mngqolo, and S. Prosalendis (2003) *Protecting Our Cultural Capital: A Research Plan for the Heritage Sector*. Cape Town: HSRC Publishers.

Deacon, H., L. with Dondolo, M. Mrunata, and S. Prosalendis (2004) *The Subtle Power of Intangible Heritage: Legal and Financial Instruments for Safeguarding Intangible Heritage*. Cape Town: Human Sciences Research Council.

DEAT (2000) Mandate to continue with 2000/2001 Annual Workplan (New Environmental Cooperation Programme between RSA and Norway). On file in the Skukuza Archives, Kruger National Park.

Deese, R. S. (2009) The artifact of nature: "Spaceship Earth" and the dawn of global environmentalism. *Endeavour* 33: 70–5.

Delius, P. and M. Hay (2009) *Mpumalanga: An Illustrated History*. Johannesburg: The Highveld Press.

Dladla, Y. (1999) *Cultural Heritage Management Manual*. Social Ecology Department, South African National Parks. On file in the Skukuza Archives, Kruger National Park.

Dladla, Y. (2000) Kruger National Park as a cultural landscape. *The World Heritage Convention and Cultural Landscapes in Africa Tiwi, Kenya, 9–14 March 1999 2000*, pp. 87–91.

Donahue, B. (2001) *Reclaiming the Commons: Community Farms and Forests in a New England Town*. New Haven: Yale University Press.

Dowie, M. (2009) *Conservation Refugees: The Hundred-Year Conflict between Global Conservation and Native Peoples*. Cambridge: MIT Press.

Draper, M. (1998) Zen and the art of garden province maintenance: The soft intimacy of hard men in the wilderness of KwaZulu-Natal, South Africa, 1952–1997. *Journal of Southern African Studies* 24: 801–28.

Draper, M., M. Spierenburg, and H. Wels (2004) African dreams of cohesion: Elite pacting and community development in Transfrontier Conservation Areas in Southern Africa. *Culture and Organization* 10: 341–53.

Droit, R.-P. (2005) *Humanity in the Making: Overview of the Intellectual History of UNESCO 1945–2005*. Paris: UNESCO.

Dubow, S. (1995) *Scientific Racism in Modern South Africa*. Cambridge: Cambridge University Press.

Dubow, S. (2006) *A Commonwealth of Knowledge: Science, Sensibility, and White South Africa 1820–2000*. Oxford: Oxford University Press.

Duffy, R. (1997) The Environmental Challenge to the Nation-State: Superparks and National Parks Policy in Zimbabwe. *Journal of Southern African Studies* 23.

Duffy, R. (2002) *A Trip Too Far: Ecotourism, Politics and Exploitation*. London and Sterling, VA: Earthscan.

Durrant, S. (2004) *Postcolonial Narrative and the Work of Mourning: J.M. Coetzee, Wilson Harris, and Toni Morrison*. Albany: State University of New York Press.

Dyson, L. E., M. A. N. Hendriks, and S. Grant (eds) (2006) *Information Technology and Indigenous People*. London: Information Science Publishing.

Eastwood, E. and G. Blundell (1999) Rediscovering the rock art of the Limpopo–Shashi confluence area, Southern Africa. *Southern African Field Archaeology* 8: 17–27.

Eastwood, E. and W. Fish (1996) Sheep in the rock paintings of the Soutpansberg and Limpopo River valley. *Southern African Field Archaeology* 5: 56–69.

Eastwood, E. and B. W. Smith (2005) Fingerprints of the KhoeKhoen: Geometric and handprinted rock art in the central Limpopo Basin, Southern Africa. *South African Archaeological Society Goodwin Series* 9: 63–76.

Eaton, M. M. (2008) The beauty that requires health, in A. Carlson and S. Lintott (eds), *Nature, Aesthetics, and Environmentalism*. New York: Columbia University Press, pp. 339–62.

Ebron, P. A. (2002) *Performing Africa*. Princeton: Princeton University Press.

Edensor, T. (2001) Performing tourism, staging tourism. *Tourist Studies* 1: 59–81.

Ehret, C. (1998) *An African Classical Age: Eastern and southern Africa in World History, 1000 BC to AD 400*. Oxford: James Curry.

Ellis, S. (1994) Of elephants and men: Politics and nature conservation. *Journal of Southern African Studies* 20: 53–69.

Ellis, S. (1998) The historical significance of South Africa's third force. *Journal of Southern African Studies* 24: 261–99.

Eloff, J. F. (1966) Verslag van werk by Makahane, noord van Punda Milia. University of Pretoria, Pretoria: Unpublished Report.

Eloff, J. F. and J. B. De Vaal (1965) Makahane. *Koedoe* 8: 68–74.

Elton, F. (1873) Journal of an exploration of the Limpopo. *Journal of the Royal Geographical Society* 42: 1–49.

Engelbrecht, W. G. and P. T. van der Walt (1993) Notes on the economic use of the Kruger National Park. *Koedoe* 36: 113–20.

English, M. (1990) Die rotskuns van die Boesmans (San) in die Nasionale Krugerwildtuin, in U. D. V. Pienaar (ed.), *Neem uit die Verleede*. Pretoria: South Africa National Parks, pp. 18–24.

Erasmus, Z. (2008) Race, in N. Shepherd and S. Robins (eds), *South African Keywords*. Johannesburg: Jacana, pp. 169–81.

Ericksen, T. H. (2009) Between universalism and relativism: A critique of the UNESCO concept of culture, in M. Goodale (ed.), *Human Rights: An Anthropological Reader*. Malden: Wiley-Blackwell, pp. 356–71.

Erickson, C. (2003) Agricultural landscapes as world heritage: Raised field agriculture in Bolivia and Peru, in J.-M. Teutonico and F. Matero (eds), *Managing Change: Sustainable Approaches to the Conservation of the Built Environment*. Los Angeles: Getty Conservation Institute, pp. 181–204.

Escobar, A. (1998) Whose knowledge, whose nature? Biodiversity, conservation, and the political ecology of social movements. *Journal of Political Ecology* 5: 53–82.

Escobar, A. (2008) *Territories of Difference: Place, Movements, Life, Redes*. Durham: Duke University Press.

Eskom. (2006) *Due South: Travel Guide to South African Craft Sites*. Erasmuskloof: Eskom.

Esterhuysen, A. (n.d.) *Thulamela: An Educator's Resource*. Johannesburg: ARDP.

Esterhuysen, A. B. (2000) The birth of education archaeology in South Africa. *Antiquity* 74: 159–65.

Fabricius, C. (2001) A Social Ecology Policy for South Africa National Parks. SANParks and DANCED, October 2001. On file in the Skukuza Archives, Kruger National Park.

Fabricius, C. and C. de Wet (2002) The influence of forced removals and land restitution in South Africa, in D. Chatty and M. Colchester (eds), *Conservation and Mobile Indigenous Peoples: Displacement, Forced Settlement and Sustainable Development*. Oxford: Berghan Books, pp. 142–57.

Fanon, F. (1963) *The Wretched of the Earth*. New York: Grove Press, Inc.

Fanon, F. (2008) *Concerning Violence*. London: Penguin.

Farred, G. (2004) The not-yet counterpartisan: A new politics of oppositionality. *The South Atlantic Quarterly Special Issue. After the Thrill is Gone: A Decade of Post-Apartheid South Africa* 103: 589–605.

Ferguson, J. (2006) *Global Shadows: Africa in the Neoliberal World Order.* Durham: Duke University Press.

Ferguson, J. (2007) Formalities of poverty: Thinking about social assistance in neoliberal South Africa. *African Studies Review* 50: 71–86.

Ferguson, J. (2010) The uses of neoliberalism. *Antipode* 41: 166–184.

Ferguson, T. J. and C. Colwell-Chanthaphonh (2006) *History is in the Land: Multivocal Tribal Traditions in Arizona's San Pedro Valley.* Tucson: University of Arizona Press.

Field, S. (2007) Sites of memory in Langa, in S. Field, R. Meyer, and F. Swanson (eds), *Imagining the City: Memories and Cultures in Cape Town.* Cape Town: HSRC Publishers, pp. 21–36.

Fitzpatrick, P. (1907) *Jock of the Bushveld.* London: Longmans, Green and Co.

Fleminger, D. (2008) *Mapungubwe Cultural Landscape.* Johannesburg: 30° South Publishers.

Fontein, J. (2005) *The Silence of Great Zimbabwe: Contested Landscapes and the Power of Heritage.* London: University College London Press.

Fortmann, L. (2005) What we need is a community Bambi: The perils and possibilities of powerful symbols, in J. P. Brosius, A. L. Tsing, and C. Zerner (eds), *Communities and Conservation: Histories and Politics of Community-Based Natural Resource Management.* Walnut Creek: Altamira, pp. 195–205.

Fortwangler, C. (2007) Friends with Money: Private Support for a National Park in the US Virgin Islands. *Conservation & Society* 5: 504–33.

Fourie, J. (1991) The concept of life: On the social role of conservation areas. *Koedoe* 34: 157–65.

Foxcroft, L. C. (2004) An adaptive management framework for linking science and management of invasive alien plants. *Weed Technology* 18: 1275–7.

Foxcroft, L. C. (2009) Developing thresholds of potential concern for invasive alien species: Hypotheses and concepts. *Koedoe* 50: 51–7.

Frandsen, J. (2009) *Kruger National Park Map.* Fourways: Honeyguide Publications.

Galla, A. (1999) Transformation in South Africa: A legacy challenged. *Museum International* 51: 38–43.

Garland, E. (2008) The elephant in the room: Confronting the colonial character of wildlife conservation in Africa. *African Studies Review* 51: 51–74.

Garland, E. and R. J. Gordon (1999) The Authentic (In)Authentic: Bushmen Anthro-Tourism. *Visual Anthropology* 12: 267–87.

Garuba, H. and S. Radithalo (2008) Culture, in N. Shepherd and S. Robins (eds), *South African Keywords.* Johannesburg: Jacana, pp. 35–46.

Gelb, S. (2003) *Inequality in South Africa: Nature, causes and responses.* Bramfontein: The Edge Institute.

Geldenhuys, H. (2004) Shame of San kids on public display. *Sunday Times* (Johannesburg), p. 5.

Gibson, D., A. Ismail, D. Kilian, and M. Matshikiza (2008) The state of our environment: Safeguarding the foundation for development, in P. Kagwanja and K. Kondlo (eds), *State of the Nation: South Africa 2008.* Cape Town: HSRC Press, pp. 178–200.

Giles, K. and J. Finch (eds) (2008) *Estate Landscapes.* Ipswich: Boydell Press.

Gillson, L. and K. I. Duffin (2007) Thresholds of potential concern as benchmarks in the management of African savannahs. *Philosophical Transactions of the Royal Society B: Biological Sciences* 362: 309–19.

Gillson, L. and A. Ekblom (2009) Untangling anthropogenic and climatic influence on riverine forest in the Kruger National Park, South Africa. *Vegetation History and Archaeobotany* 18: 171–85.

Gilroy, P. (2005) *Postcolonial Melancholia.* New York: Columbia University Press.

Goethe, J. W. V. (1998) *Maxims and Reflections.* London: Penguin.

Goldman, M. (2001) Constructing an environmental state: Eco-governmentality and other trans-national practices of a "green" World Bank. *Social Problems* 48: 499–523.

Golliher, J. (1999) Ethical, moral and religious concerns, in D. A. Posey (ed.), *Cultural and Spiritual Values of Biodiversity.* London: UNEP, pp. 437–50.

González-Ruibal, A. (2006) The dream of reason: An archaeology of the failures of modernity in Ethiopia. *Journal of Social Archaeology* 6: 175–201.

González-Ruibal, A. (2009) Vernacular cosmopolitanism: An archaeological critique of universalistic reason, in L. M. Meskell (ed.), *Cosmopolitan Archaeologies.* Durham: Duke University Press, pp. 113–39.

Goodin, R. E. (1991) Utility and the good, in P. Singer (ed.), *A Companion to Ethics.* Oxford: Blackwell, pp. 241–8.

Gordimer, N. (2003) *Jump and Other Stories.* London: Bloomsbury.

Gordon, R. (1992) *The Bushman Myth: The Making of A Namibian Underclass. Conflict and Social Change.* Boulder: Westview Press.

Gordon, R. (2003) Fido: Dog tales of colonialism in Namibia, in W. Beinart and J. McGregor (eds), *Social History and African Environments.* Oxford: James Currey.

Gordon, R. B. (1987) Anthropology and apartheid: The rise of military ethnology in South Africa. *Cultural Survival* 11, www.culturalsurvival.org (accessed May 3, 2011).

Gordon, R. B. and J. H. van der Merwe (1984) Metallographic study of iron artefacts from the Eastern Transvaal, South Africa. *Archaeometry* 26: 108–27.

Gordon, R. J. and S. Sholto-Douglas (2000) *The Bushman myth: The making of a Namibian underclass,* 2nd edn. Boulder: Westview Press.

Gorz, A. (1994) *Capitalism, Socialism, Ecology.* London: Verso.

Graber, D. M. (1994) Resolute biocentrism: The dilemma of wilderness in national parks, in M. E. Soule and G. Lease (eds), *Reinventing Nature? Responses to Postmodern Deconstruction.* Washington, DC: Island Press, pp. 123–35.

Greenberg, R. (2009) Archaeology in Jerusalem 1967–2008. Towards an inclusive archaeology in Jerusalem: The case of Silwan/The City of David. *Public Archaeology* 8: 35–50.

Greenenough, P. and A. Tsing (eds) (2003) *Nature in the Global South: Environmental Projects in South and Southeast Asia.* Durham: Duke University Press.

Grigorova, B. W. Smith, K. Stiilpner, J.A. Tumilty, and D. Miller (1998) Fingerprinting of Gold Artefacts from Mapungubwe, Bosutswe and Thulamela. *Gold Bulletin* 31: 99–102.

Groenewald, Y. (2008) New land Act like apartheid. *Mail & Guardian* (Johannesburg), October 23. http://www.mg.co.za/article/2008-10-23-new-land-act-like-apartheid (accessed October 23, 2009).

Groenewald, Y. (2009a) Kruger headache returns. *Mail & Guardian (Johannesburg)*, July 21. http://www.mg.co.za/article/2009-07-21-kruger-headache-returns (accessed October 23, 2009).

Groenewald, Y. (2009b) SANParks declares war on rhino poachers. *Mail & Guardian (Johannesburg)*, July 23. http://www.mg.co.za/article/2009-07-23-sanparks-declares-war-on-rhino-poachers (accessed October 23, 2009).

Groenewald, Y. and F. Macleod (2005) Land claims "could kill Kruger," in *Mail & Guardian, (Johannesburg)*, February 18, p. 6.

Groenewald, Y. and I. Rawoot (2009) Kruger land claimants furious. *Mail & Guardian (Johannesburg)*, February 6 to 12, p. 4.

Gronenborn, D. (2004) Comparing contact-period archaeologies: The expansion of farming and pastorialist societies to continental temperate Europe and to southern Africa. *Before Farming* 4: 1–35.

Grosz, L. (2005) *Time Travels: Feminism, Nature, Power*. Durham: Duke University Press.

Grove, R. H. (1995) *Green Imperialism: Colonial Expansion, Tropical Island Edens and the Origins of Environmentalism, 1600–1860*. Cambridge: Cambridge University Press.

Grunebaum, H. and Y. Henri (2003) Where the mountain meets its shadow: A conversation on memory, identity, and fragmented belonging in present-day South Africa, in B. Strath and R. Robbins (eds), *Homelands: Poetic power and the Politics of Space*. Brussels: Peter Lang.

Grunebaum-Ralph, H. (2001) Re-Placing Pasts, Forgetting Presents: Narrative, Place, and Memory in the Time of the Truth and Reconciliation Commission. *Research in African Literatures* 32: 198–212.

Guattari, F. (2000) *The Three Ecologies*. London: The Athlone Press.

Gunner, L. (2005) Remapping land and remaking culture: Memory and landscape in 20th-century South Africa. *Journal of Historical Geography* 31: 281–95.

Hall, M. (1984) The burden of tribalism: The social context of southern African Iron Age Studies. *American Antiquity* 49: 455–67.

Hall, M. (1988) Archaeology under apartheid. *Archaeology* 41: 62–4.

Hall, M. (1994) Lifting the veil of popular history: Archaeology and politics in urban Cape Town, in G. C. Bond and A. Gilliam (eds), *Social Construction of the Past*. London and New York: Routledge, pp. 176–84.

Hall, M. (1995) The Legend of the Lost City; Or, the Man with Golden Balls. *Journal of Southern African Studies* 21: 179–99.

Hall, M. (2001) Social archaeology and the theaters of memory. *Journal of Social Archaeology* 1: 50–61.

Hall, M. (2005) Situational ethics and engaged practice: The case of archaeology in Africa, in L. M. Meskell and P. Pels (eds), *Embedding Ethics: Shifting the Boundaries of the Anthropological Profession*. Oxford: Berg, pp. 169–94.

Hall, M. (2006) Identity, memory and countermemory: The archaeology of an urban landscape. *Journal of Material Culture* 11: 189–209.

Hall, M. and P. Bombardella (2005) Las Vegas in Africa. *Journal of Social Archaeology* 5: 5–24.

Hall, S. (2010) Farming communities of the second millennium: Internal frontiers, identity, continuity and change, in C. Hamilton , B. K. Mbenga, and R. Ross (eds), *The

Cambridge History of South Africa, Volume I: From Early Times to 1885. Cambridge: Cambridge University Press, pp. 112–66.

Hall, S., M. Anderson, J. Boeyens, and F. Coetzee (2008) Towards an outline of the oral geography, historical identity and political economy of the late precolonial Tswana in the Rustenburg region, in A. Esterhuysen, N. Swanepoel, and P. Bonner (eds), *500 Years Rediscovered.* Johannesburg: Witwatersrand University Press, pp. 55–86.

Hall, S. and B. W. Smith (2000) Empowering places: Rock shelters and ritual control in farmer–forager interaction in the Northern Province, South Africa. *South African Archaeological Society Goodwin Series* 8: 30–46.

Hamilton, C. (2009) Uncertain citizenship and public deliberation in post-apartheid South Africa. *Social Dynamics: A Journal of African Studies* 35: 355–74.

Hamilton, C. V. Harris, J. Taylor, M. Pickover, G. Reid, and R. Saleh (eds) (2002) *Refiguring the Archive.* Cape Town: David Philip.

Hamin, E. (2002) Western European approaches to landscape protection: A review of the literature. *Journal of Planning Literature* 16: 339–58.

Hammett, D. (2010) Zapiro and Zuma: A symptom of an emerging constitutional crisis in South Africa? *Political Geography* 29: 88–96.

Hampson, J., W. Challis, G. Blundell, and C. de Rosner. (2002) The rock art of Bongani Mountain Lodge and its environs, Mpulmalanga province, South Africa: An introduction to problems of Southern African rock-art regions. *South African Archaeological Bulletin* 57: 15–30.

Hannigan, J. (2006) *Environmental Sociology.* London: Routledge.

Hansen, H. (2008) Community perceptions of a mine recruitment centre in Pafuri and the development of a cultural heritage site in the Greater Limpopo Transfrontier Park. MA thesis, University of the Witwatersrand.

Hardin, G. (1968) The Tragedy of the Commons. *Science* 162: 1243–8.

Harries, P. (1991) Exclusion, classification and internal colonialism: The emergence of ethnicity among the Tsonga-speakers of South Africa, in L. Vail (ed.), *The Creation of Tribalism in Southern Africa.* Berkeley and Los Angeles: University of California Press, pp. 82–117.

Harvey, D. (2003) *The New Imperialism.* Oxford: Oxford University Press.

Hasinoff, E. L. (2009) A Fragment of Kawgun: Curatorial and Interpretive Futures of the AMNH Buddha Tablet. Paper presented at the American Anthropological Association Annual Meeting, December 3, 2009.

Hayashida, F. M. (2005) Archaeology, ecological history, and conservation. *Annual Review of Anthropology* 34: 43–65.

Hayden, C. (2003) *When Nature Goes Public: The Making and Unmaking of Bioprospecting in Mexico.* Princeton: Princeton University Press.

Head, L., J. Atchison and R. Fullagar (2002) Country and garden: Ethnobotany, archaeobotany and Aborginal landscapes near the Keep River, northwestern Australia. *Journal of Social Archaeology* 2: 173–97.

Helmy, E. and C. Cooper (2002) An assessment of sustainable tourism planning for the archaeological heritage: The case of Egypt. *Journal of Sustainable Tourism* 10: 514–35.

Hendricks, H. (2005) Biodiversity conservation – the often missing link. *Go Wild,* vol. June, pp. 4. Pretoria: SANParks.

Henkel, H. and R. Stirrat (2001) Participation as spiritual duty: Empowerment as secular subjection, in B. Cooke and U. Kothari (eds), *Participation: The New Tyranny?* New York: Zed Books, pp. 169–84.

Herzfeld, M. (1991) *A Place in History: Social and Monumental Time in a Cretan Town.* Princeton: Princeton University Press.

Herzfeld, M. (2003) Pom Mahakan: Humanity and order in the historic center of Bangkok. *Thailand Journal of Human Rights* 1: 101–19.

Herzfeld, M. (2006) Spatial cleansing: Monumental vacuity and the idea of the west. *Journal of Material Culture* 11: 127–49.

Herzfeld, M. (2009) *Evicted from Eternity: The Restructuring of Modern Rome.* Chicago: University of Chicago Press.

Hill, M. A. and A. J. Press (1994) Kakadu National Park: An Australian Experience in Comanagement, in D. Western and R. M. Wright (eds), *Natural Connections: Perspectives in Community-based Conservation.* Washington, DC: Island Press.

Hitchcock, R. K. (2002) "We are the First People": Land, natural resources and identity in the central Kalahari, Botswana. *Journal of Southern African Studies* 28: 797–824.

Hodgson, D. L. (2002a) Introduction: Comparative Perspectives on the Indigenous Rights Movement in Africa and the Americas. *American Anthropologist* 104: 1037–49.

Hodgson, D. L. (2002b) Precarious Alliances: The Cultural Politics and Structural Predicaments of the Indigenous Rights Movement in Tanzania. *American Anthropologist* 104: 1086–97.

Hofstätter, S. (2008) "Land claims and conservation," in *FM Campus Online, 30th March, 2008.* 2009. http://www.fmcampus.co.za/Archives/article.aspx?name=23Ft-Kruger 771198 (accessed October 24, 2009).

Holmberg, K. (in press) An inheritance of loss: Archaeology's imagination of disaster, in M. Davis and F. Nkirote (eds), *Humans and the Environment: New Archaeological Perspectives for the 21st Century.* Oxford: Oxford University Press.

Homewood, K., P. Kristjanson, and C. P. Trench (eds) (2009) *Staying Maasai? Livelihoods, Conservation and Development in East African Rangelands.* New York: Springer.

Honey, M. (1999) *Ecotourism and Sustainable Development: Who Owns Paradise?* Washington, DC and Covelo, CA: Island Press.

Huffman, T. N. (1996) Archaeological evidence for climatic change during the last 2000 years in southern Africa. *Quaternary International* 33: 55–60.

Huggan, G. and H. Tiffin (2007) Green postcolonialism. *Interventions: International Journal of Postcolonial Studies* 9: 1–11.

Hughes, H. (2007) Rainbow, renaissance, tribes and townships: Tourism and heritage in South Africa since 1994, *State of the Nation: South Africa 2007.* Cape Town: HSRC Press, pp. 266–88.

Humboldt, A. V. (1850) *Views of Nature: Or Contemplations on the Sublime Phenomena of Creation.* London: Henry G. Bohn.

Humboldt, A. V. (2007) *Jaguars and Electric Eels.* London: Penguin.

Hutton, J., W. Adams, and J. C. Murombedzi (2005) Back to the barriers? Changing narratives in biodiversity. *Forum for Development Studies* 2: 341–70.

Igoe, J. (2004) *Conservation and Globalization: A Study of National Parks and Indigenous Communities from East Africa to South Dakota.* Belmont: Wadsworth/Thomson.

Igoe, J. and D. Brockington (2007) Neoliberal conservation: A brief introduction. *Conservation and Society* 5: 432–49.

Ivison, D. (2002) *Postcolonial Liberalism*. Cambridge: Cambridge University Press.

Ivison, D. (2006) Historical injustice, in J. Dryzek, B. Honnig, and A. Philipps (eds), *Oxford Handbook to Political Theory*. Oxford: Oxford University Press, pp. 507–25.

Ivison, D. (2007) Indigenous rights and the history of colonization, in W. A. Darity (ed.), *International Encyclopedia of the Social Sciences*. Farmington Hills: MacMillan, pp. 614–17.

Ivison, D. (2008) *Rights*. Montreal: McGill Queens University Press.

Jacobs, J. M. (1996) *Edge of Empire: Postcolonialism and the City*. London: Routledge.

Jacobs, N. (2003) *Environment, Power, and Injustice: A South African History*. Cambridge: Cambridge University Press.

James, D. (2009) Burial sites, informal rights and lost kingdoms: Land claims in Mpumalanga, South Africa. *African Studies* 79: 228–51.

Jeppie, S. and S. B. Diagne (eds) (2008) *The Meanings of Timbuktu*. Cape Town: Human Sciences Research Council.

Johnson, M. H. (1996) *An Archaeology of Capitalism*. Oxford: Blackwell.

Johnson, M. H. (2008) *Ideas of Landscape*. Oxford: Blackwell.

Jordan, P. Z. (1996) Thulamela Excavation Proves Black Heritage. Speech delivered in Kruger National Park, September 24, 1996.

Jordan, P. Z. (2004) Keynote address by Minister Z Pallo Jordan, Minister of Arts and Culture, at the Third meeting of the National Heritage Council (NHC), in Mpumalanga, July 31, 2004.

Jordan, P. Z. (2006a) Keynote Address by Minister of Arts and Culture, Z Pallo Jordan at the Launch of the African World Heritage Fund. Maropeng Exhibition Centre, May 5, 2006.

Jordan, P. Z. (2006b) Minister of Arts and Culture, Dr Z. Pallo Jordan, on the Occasion of the Donor's Conference for the African World Heritage Fund. Maropeng, Cradle of Humankind, May 4, 2006.

Jordan, P. Z. (2007) Speech by Minister Z Pallo Jordan Opening of the National Conference on Cultural Legislation, April 21, 2007.

Junod, H. A. (1926) *Life of a South African Tribe*. London: Macmillan and Co..

Kagwanja, P. (2008) Introduction: Uncertain democracy – elite fragmentation and the disintegration of the "nationalist consensus" in South Africa, *State of the Nation South Africa 2008*. Cape Town: HSRC, pp. xv–xlix.

Kaplan, R. M. (2004) Treatment of homosexuality. *British Medical Journal* 329: 1415–16.

Kareiva, P., S. Watts, R. McDonald, and T. Boucher (2007) Domesticated nature: Shaping landscapes and ecosystems for human welfare. *Science* 29: 1866–9.

Keitumetse, S. O. (2009) The eco-tourism of cultural heritage management (ECT-CHM): Linking heritage and "Environment" in the Okavango Delta regions of Botswana. *International Journal of Heritage Studies* 15: 223–44.

Keller, R. and M. Turek (1998) *American Indians and National Parks*. Tucson: University of Arizona Press.

King, B. (2009) Commercializing conservation in South Africa. *Environment and Planning A* 41: 407–27.

King, T. F. (1998) How the archeologists stole culture: A gap in American environmental impact assessment practice and how to fill it. *Environmental Impact Assessment Review* 18: 117.

Kirshenblatt-Gimblett, B. (1998) *Destination Culture: Tourism, Museums, and Heritage*. Berkeley: University of California Press.

Kloppers, J. J. and H. Bornman (2005) *A Dictionary of Kruger National Park Place Names*. Barberton: SA Country Life.

Krüger, K. (1994) *Mahlangeni: Stories of a Game Ranger's Family*. London: Penguin Books.

Krüger, K. (2002) *The Wilderness Family*. London: Bantam.

Kuper, A. (2003) The return of the native. *Current Anthropology* 4: 389–95.

Küsel, U. S. (1992) A preliminary report on settlement layout and gold smelting at Thulamela, a Late Iron Age site in the Kruger National Park. *Koedoe* 35: 55–64.

Lafrenz Samuels, K. (2008) Value and significance in archaeology. *Archaeological Dialogues* 15: 71–97.

Lafrenz Samuels, K. (2009) Trajectories of development: International heritage management of archaeology in the Middle East and North Africa. *Archaeologies* 5: 68–91.

Lafrenz Samuels, K. (2010) Mobilizing heritage in the Maghrib: Rights, development, and transnational archaeologies. PhD thesis, Department of Anthropology, Stanford University, Stanford.

Lane, P. J. (2009) Environmental narratives and the history of soil erosion in Kondoa District, Tanzania: An archaeological perspective. *International Journal of African Historical Studies* 42: 1–24.

Langford, R. (2003) The "wild", nature and the native: Indigenous people face new forms of global colonization, in W. Adams and M. Mulligan (eds), *Decolonizing Nature: Strategies for Conservation in a Post-colonial Era*. London: Earthscan, pp. 79–107.

Latour, B. (2004a) *The Politics of Nature: How to Bring the Sciences into Democracy*. Harvard: Harvard University Press.

Latour, B. (2004b) Whose cosmos, which cosmopolitics? *Common Knowledge* 10: 450–62.

Latour, B. (2007) It's development, stupid! Or how to modernize modernization? http://www.bruno-latour.fr/articles/index.html (accessed January 18, 2010).

Layton, R., P. G. Stone, and J. Thomas (eds) (2001) *Destruction and Conservation of Cultural Property*. London: Routledge.

Lazarus, N. (2004) The South African ideology: The myth of exceptionalism, the idea of renaissance. *The South Atlantic Quarterly Special Issue. After the Thrill is Gone: A Decade of Post-Apartheid South Africa* 103: 606–28.

Leibhammer, N. (2005) Technologies and transformations: Baskets, women and change in twentieth-century KwaZulu Natal, in M. Arnold and B. Schmahmann (eds), *Between Union And Liberation: Women Artists In South Africa 1910–1994*. Aldershot: Ashgate, pp. 111–31.

Leopold, A. (1949) *A Sand County Almanac*. New York: Oxford University Press.

Lepczyk, C. A., O. D. Boyle, T. L. Vargo, P. Gould, R. Jordan, L. Liebenberg, S. Masi, W. P. Mueller, M. D. Prysby, and H. Vaughan (2009) Symposium 18: Citizen science in ecology: The intersection of research and education. *Bulletin of the Ecological Society of America* 90: 308–17.

Levi-Strauss, C. (1963) *Structural Anthropology*. New York: Basic Books.

Libsekal, Y. (2008) Multiplying and sharing heritage values: Planning conservation and site management at the Acheulean sites of Buya, Eritrea. *Conservation and Management of Archaeological Sites* 10: 251–63.

Lilley, I. Editor. (2000a) *Native Title and the Transformation of Archaeology in the Postcolonial World*. Vol. 50. Oceania Monographs. Sydney: University of Sydney.

Lilley, I. (2000b) Professional attitudes to indigenous interests in the native title era: Settler societes compared, in I. Lilley (ed.), *Native Title and the Transformation of Archaeology in the Postcolonial World*. Sydney: Oceania Publications, Monograph 50, pp. 99–119.

Lilley, I. (2006) Archaeology, diaspora and decolonization. *Journal of Social Archaeology* 6: 28–47.

Lilley, I. (2009) Strangers and brothers? Heritage, human rights, and cosmopolitan archaeology in Oceania, in L. M. Meskell (ed.), *Cosmopolitan Archaeologies*. Durham: Duke University Press, pp. 48–67.

Lilley, I. and M. Williams (2005) Archaeological and indigenous significance: A view from Australia, in C. Mathers, T. Darvill, and B. Little (eds), *Heritage of Value, Archaeology of Renown: Reshaping Archaeological Assessment and Significance*. University of Florida Press, pp. 227–47.

Link, T. (2006) Models of Sustainability: Museums, Citizenship, and Common Wealth. *Museums & Social Issues* 1: 173–90.

Litzinger, R. A. (2006) Contested sovereignties and the Critical Ecosystem Partnership Fund. *Political and Legal Anthropology Review* 29: 66–87.

Liverman, D. M. and S. Vilas (2006) Neoliberalism and the environment in Latin America. *Annual Review of Environment and Resources* 31: 327–63.

Lockwood, M. (2006) Values and benefits, in M. Lockwood, G. Worboys, and A. Kothari (eds), *Managing Protected Areas*. London: Earthscan, pp. 101–15.

Logan, W. S. (2008) Closing Pandora's box: Human rights conundrums in cultural heritage protection, in H. Silverman and Fairchild Ruggles (eds), *Cultural Heritage and Human Rights*. New York: Springer, pp. 33–52.

Logan, W. S. and K. Reeves (eds) (2008) *Places of Pain and Shame: Dealing with "Difficult Heritage."* London: Routledge.

Lowenthal, D. (1985) *The Past is a Foreign Country*. Cambridge: Cambridge University Press.

Lowenthal, D. (1997) Environment as heritage, in K. Flint and H. Morphy (eds), *Culture, Landscape, and the Environment: The Linacre Lectures, 1997*. Oxford: Oxford University Press, pp. 197–217.

Lowenthal, D. (2000) Nature and morality from George Perkins Marsh to the millennium. *Journal of Historical Geography* 26: 3–23.

Lowenthal, D. (2006) Natural and cultural heritage, in K. R. Olwig and D. Lowenthal (eds), *The Nature of Cultural Heritage and the Culture of Natural Heritage: Northern Perspectives on a Contested Patrimony*. London: Routledge, pp. 79–90.

Lozny, L. R. (2006) Place, historical ecology and cultural landscape: New directions for Cultural Resource Management, *Landscapes Under Pressure: Theory and Practice of Cultural Heritage Research*. New York: Springer, pp. 15–26.

Lunstrum, E. (2008) Mozambique, neoliberal land reform, and the Limpopo National Park. *Geographical Review* 98: 339–55.

Lydon, J. (2005) Driving by: Visiting Australian colonial monuments. *Journal of Social Archaeology* 5: 108–34.

Mabunda, D. (2009) Response from SANParks to Misleading Reports and Claims about Rhino Sales and Hunting in National Parks. http://www.sanparks.org/about/news/2009/july/rhino_response.php (accessed January 26, 2010).

Mabunda, D., D. Pienaar, and J. Verhoef (2003) The Kruger National Park: A century of management and research, in J. T. Du Toit, K. H. Rogers, and H. C. Biggs (eds), *The Kruger Experience: Ecology and Management of a Savanna Heterogeneity*. Washington: Island Press, pp. 3–21.

MacDonald, M. (2006) *Why Race Matters in South Africa*. Scottsville: KZN Press.

Macleod, F. (2003) Hunt is off in Kruger: A new ecotourism deal will put an end to hunting in the national park. *Mail & Guardian (Johannesburg)* August 29–September 4, p. 10.

Magome, D. T. (2004) Managing protected areas in post-apartheid South Africa: A framework for integrating conservation with rural development. PhD thesis, University of Kent.

Magome, H. and J. Murombedzi (2003) Sharing South African National Parks: Community land and conservation in a democratic South Africa, in W. Adams and M. Mulligan (eds), *Decolonizing Nature: Strategies for Conservation in a Post-colonial Era*. London: Earthscan, pp. 108–34.

Maguranyanga, B. (2009) "Our battles also changed": Transformation and black empowerment in South African National Parks, 1991–2008. PhD thesis, University of Michigan.

Mail & Guardian (2005a) Special Section: Greening the Future. Johannesburg, February 25, pp. 1–11.

Mail & Guardian (2005b) Kruger workers fired for slaughtering impala. Johannesburg, May 20.

Mail & Guardian (2005c) Comment and Analysis: Kruger is our Amazon. Johannesburg, March 4–10, p. 24.

Malan, T. and P. S. Hattingh (1976) *Black Homelands in South Africa*. Pretoria: Africa Institute of South Africa.

Mamdani, M. (1996) *Citizen and Subject: Contemporary Africa and the Legacy of Late Colonialism*. Princeton: Princeton University Press.

Mancotywa, S. (2007) Renaissance of African civilization challenges facing the heritage sector, Eastern Cape Heritage Indaba. Unpublished report. National heritage Council.

Mandela, N. (1994) Statement of the President of the African National Congress, Nelson Mandela, at his Inauguration as President of the Democratic Republic of South Africa, Union Buildings, Pretoria, May 10 1994. Pretoria, South Africa.

Mandela, N. (1996) Speech by President Nelson Mandela at the Unveiling of the Monument to Enoch Sontonga on Heritage Day, September 23, 1996. http://www.info.gov.za/speeches/1996/960925_0x12696.htm.

Mandela, N. (1998) Address at the Launch of the Kruger National Park Centenary Celebrations. Skukuza, Kruger National Park, March 26, 1998.

Marais, T. L. (1986) Snuffels. Unpublished pamphlet produced by the Kruger National Park Commando Unit. On file in the Skukuza Archives, Kruger National Park.

Marschall, S. (2006a) Commemorating "Struggle Heroes": Constructing a genealogy for the new South Africa. *International Journal of Heritage Studies* 12: 176–93.

Marschall, S. (2006b) Visualizing memories: The Hector Pieterson Memorial in Soweto. *Visual Anthropology*. 19: 145–69.

Mason, R. (1962) *Prehistory of the Tranvaal*. Johannesburg: Witwatersrand University Press.

Massad, J. A. (2001) *Colonial Effects*. New York: Columbia University Press.

Masuku Van Damme, L. S. and L. M. Meskell (2009) Producing conservation and community. *Ethics, Place & Environment* 12: 69–89.

Masuku Van Damme, L. S. and E. F. Neluvhalani (2004) Indigenous knowledge in environmental education processes: Perspectives on a growing research arena. *Environmental Education Research* 10: 353–70.

Matthew, E. L. (1915) South African native land laws. *Journal of the Society of Comparative Legislation* 15: 9–16.

Mavhunga, C. (2002) "If they are thirsty let them come down to the pool": Unearthing "Wildlife" history and reconstructing "heritage" in Gonarezhou National Park, from the late nineteenth century to the 1930s. *Historia* 47: 531–8.

Mavhunga, C. (2007) Even the rider and a horse are a partnership: A response to Vermeulen & Sheil. *Oryx* 41: 441–2.

Mavhunga, C. and W. Dressler (2007) On *the local community*: The language of disengagement? *Conservation and Society* 5: 44–59.

Mavhunga, C. and M. Spierenburg (2009) Transfrontier talk, cordon politics: The early history of the Great Limpopo Transfrontier Park in Southern Africa, 1925–1940. *Journal of Southern African Studies* 35: 715–35.

Mbeki, T. (1996) Statement of Deputy President Tabo Mbeki, on behalf of the African National Congress, on the occasion of the adoption by the constitutional assembly of "The Republic of South Africa Constitution Bill 1996." Cape Town, May 8, 1996.

Mbeki, T. (1998) The African Renaissance Statement of Deputy President, Thabo Mbeki. SABC, Gallagher Estate, August 13, 1998.

Mbeki, T. (2004) Remarks of the President of South Africa, Thabo Mbeki, on the occasion of the celebration of National Heritage Day. Galeshewe, Kimberly, September 24, 2004.

Mbembe, A. (2000) At the edge of the world: Boundaries, territoriality, and sovereignty in Africa. *Public Culture* 12: 259–84.

Mbembe, A. (2001) *On the Postcolony*. Berkeley: University of California Press.

Mbembe, A. and S. Nuttall (2004) Writing the world from an African metropolis. *Public Culture* 16: 347–72.

McCann, J. C. (1999) *Green Land, Brown Land, Black Land: An Environmental History of Africa, 1800–1990*. Oxford: James Currey.

McDonald, D. A. Editor. (2002a) *Environmental Justice in South Africa*. Athens: Ohio University Press.

McDonald, D. A. (2002b) What is environmental justice? in D. A. McDonald (ed.), *Environmental Justice in South Africa*. Cape Town: University of Cape Town Press, pp. 1–12.

McEachern, C. (2002) *Narratives of National Media, Memory and Representation in the Making of the New South Africa*. New York: Nova.

McGimsey, C. R. and H. A. Davis (1984) United States of America, in H. Cleere (ed.), *Approaches to the Archaeological Heritage*. Cambridge: Cambridge University Press, pp. 116–24.

McGregor, J. (2005) The social life of ruins: Sites of memory and the politics of a Zimbabwean periphery. *Journal of Historical Geography* 31: 316–37.

McGregor, J. and L. Schumaker (2006) Heritage in Southern Africa: Imagining and marketing public culture and history. *Journal of Southern African Studies* 32: 649–65.

McKinsey Report (2002) *SANParks and McKinsey Final Meeting*. South Africa National Parks, Pretoria.

Meskell, L. M. (2002) Negative heritage and past mastering in archaeology. *Anthropological Quarterly* 75: 557–74.

Meskell, L. M. (2005a) Archaeological ethnography: Conversations around Kruger National Park. *Archaeologies: Journal of the World Archaeology Congress* 1: 83–102.

Meskell, L. M. (2005b) Object orientations, in L. M. Meskell (ed.), *Archaeologies of Materiality*. Oxford: Blackwell, pp. 1–17.

Meskell, L. M. (2005c) Objects in the mirror appear closer than they are, in D. Miller (ed.), *Materiality*. Durham: Duke University Press.

Meskell, L. M. (2005d) Recognition, restitution and the potentials of postcolonial liberalism for South African heritage. *South African Archaeological Bulletin* 60: 72–8.

Meskell, L. M. (2005e) Sites of violence: Terrorism, tourism and heritage in the archaeological present, in L. M. Meskell and P. Pels (eds), *Embedding Ethics*. Oxford: Berg, pp. 123–46.

Meskell, L. M. (2006a) Deep past, divided present: South Africa's heritage at the frontier. *Western Humanities Review* 60: 110–16.

Meskell, L. M. (2006b) Trauma culture: Remembering and forgetting in the new South Africa, in D. Bell (ed.), *Memory, Trauma, and World Politics*. New York: Palgrave Macmillan, pp. 157–74.

Meskell, L. M. (2007a) Falling walls and mending fences: Archaeological ethnography in the Limpopo. *Journal of Southern African Studies* 33: 383–400.

Meskell, L. M. (2007b) Living in the past: Historic futures in double time in N. Murray, M. Hall, and N. Shepherd (eds), *Desire Lines: Space Memory and Identity in the Postapartheid City*. London: Routledge, pp. 165–79.

Meskell, L. M. Editor. (2009a) *Cosmopolitan Archaeologies*. Durham: Duke University Press.

Meskell, L. M. (2009b) Cosmopolitan heritage ethics, in L. M. Meskell (ed.), *Cosmopolitan Archaeologies*. Durham: Duke University Press.

Meskell, L. M. (2009c) The nature of culture in Kruger National Park, in L. M. Meskell (ed.), *Cosmopolitan Archaeologies*. Durham: Duke University Press, pp. 89–112.

Meskell, L. M. and L. S. Masuku Van Damme (2007) Heritage ethics and descendent communities, in C. Colwell-Chanthaphonh and T. J. Ferguson (eds), *The Collaborative Continuum: Archaeological Engagements with Descendent Communities*. Thousand Oaks: Altamira Press, pp. 131–50.

Meskell, L. M. and C. Scheermeyer (2008) Heritage as therapy: Set pieces from the new South Africa. *Journal of Material Culture* 13: 153–73.

Meskell, L. M. and L. W. Weiss (2006) Coetzee on South Africa's past: Remembering in the time of forgetting. *American Anthropologist* 108: 88–99.

Mhlongo, E. S. (1995) Observation Report Thulamela Project. On file in the Skukuza Archives: Kruger National Park, November 30, 1995.

Miller, D. (1996) Letter From Thulamela. *Southern African Review of Books* 45: 19–20.

Miller, D., D. Killick, and N. J. van der Merwe (2001) Metal Working in the Northern Lowveld, South Africa, A.D. 1000–1890. *Journal of Field Archaeology* 28: 401–17.

Miller, S. (1997) *The Archaeological Investigation, the Rebuilding of the Walls and the Public Presentation of the Thulamela Site in the Northern Kruger National Park*. On file in the Skukuza Archives, Kruger National Park.

Mitchell, P. (2002a) *The Archaeology of Southern Africa*. Cambridge: Cambridge University Press.

Mitchell, P. (2004) Some reflections on the spread of food-production in southernmost Africa. *Before Farming* 4: 1–14.

Mitchell, P. and G. Whitelaw (2005) The archaeology of southernmost Africa from c. 2000 BP to the early 1800s: A review of recent research. *The Journal of African History* 46: 209–41.

Mitchell, T. (2000) Making the nation: The politics of heritage in Egypt, in N. A. Sayyad (ed.), *Global Forms/Urban Norms: On the Manufacture and Consumption of Traditions in the Built Environment*. London: E & F Spon/Routledge.

Mitchell, T. (2002b) *Rule of Experts*. Berekely: University of California Press.

Mohan, G. (2001) Beyond participation: Strategies for deeper empowerment, in B. Cooke and U. Kothari (eds), *Participation: The New Tyranny?* New York: Zed Books, pp. 153–67.

Moore, D. S. (1998) Clear waters and muddied histories: Environmental history and the politics of community in Zimbabwe's Eastern Highlands. *Journal of Southern African Studies* 24: 377–403.

Moore, D. S. (2005) *Suffering for Territory: Race, Place, and Power in Zimbabwe*. Durham: Duke University Press.

Moore, D. S., J. Kosek, and A. Pandian (2003) *Race, Nature and the Politics of Difference*. Durham and London: Duke University Press.

Moore, K. and L. S. Masuku Van Damme (2002) The evolution of people-and-parks relationships in South Africa's national conservation organization, in J. Hattingh, H. Lotz-Sisitka, and R. O'Donoghue (eds), *Environmental Education, Ethics and Action in Southern Africa*. Pretoria: Human Sciences Research Council, pp. 61–73.

Morris, D. (2003) Rock art as source and resource: Research and responsibility towards education, heritage and tourism. *South African Historical Journal* 49: 193–206.

Mortensen, L. and J. Hollowell (eds) (2009) *Ethnographies and Archaeologies: Iterations of the Past*. Gainesville: University Press of Florida.

Mosse, D. (2001) People's knowledge, participation and patronage: Operations and representations in rural development, in B. Cooke and U. Kothari (eds), *Participation: The New Tyranny?* New York: Zed Books, pp. 18–35.

Motshekga, M. (2009) Heritage Month 2009. http://www.anc.org.za/caucus/docs/notes/2009/nt0925.html (accessed November 13, 2009).

Mphahlele, M. (2009) The duty of the state to eradicate the legacy of apartheid in South Africa versus resistance to change: Critical analysis of the Chairperson's Association Case. *US–China Law Review* 6: 24–32.

Murray, N., M. Hall, and N. Shepherd (eds) (2007) *Desire Lines: Space Memory and Identity in the Postapartheid City*. London: Routledge.

Nasson, B. (2000) Commemorating the Anglo-Boer War in post-apartheid South Africa. *Radical History Review* 2000: 149–65.

Ndebele, N. (1998) Memory, metaphor, and the triumph of narrative, in S. Nuttall and C. Coetzee (eds), *Negotiating the Past: The Making of Memory in South Africa*. Cape Town: Oxford University Press, pp. 19–28.

Ndlovu, N. (2009) Access to rock art sites: A right or a qualification. *South African Archaeological Bulletin* 64: 61–8.

Ndlovu-Gatsheni, S. J. (2008) Black republican tradition, nativism and populist politics in South Africa. *Transformation* 68: 53–86.

Nelson, F. Editor. (2010) *Community Rights, Conservation and Contested Land: The Politics of Natural Resource Governance in Africa*. London: Earthscan.

Nemaheni, T. I. (2003) A cultural heritage resource management plan for Thulamela Heritage Site. MA thesis, Pretoria University.

Nemaheni, T. I. (2004) The reburial of human remains at Thulamela, Kruger National Park, South Africa, in C. Fforde, J. Hubert, and P. Turnbull (eds), *The Dead and Their Possessions: Repatriation in Principle, Policy and Practice*. London: Routledge, pp. 256–61.

Neumann, R. P. (1997) Primitive ideas: Protected area buffer zones and the politics of land in Africa. *Development and Change* 28: 559–82.

Neumann, R. P. (1998) *Imposing Wilderness: Struggles Over Livelihood and Nature Preservation in Africa*. Berkeley: California University Press.

Nieves, A. D. (2008) Places of pain as tools for social justice in the "new" South Africa: Black heritage preservation in the "rainbow" nation's townships, in W. S. Logan and K. Reeves (eds), *Places of Pain and Shame: Dealing with "Difficult Heritage."* London: Routledge, pp. 198–214.

Norton, B. G. (2005) *Sustainability: A Philosophy of Adaptive Ecosystem Management*. Chicago: Chicago University Press.

Notar, B. E. (2006) *Displacing Desire: Travel and Popular Culture in China*. Honolulu: University of Hawaii Press.

Nuttall, S. (2009) *Entanglement: Literary and Cultural Reflections on Post-Apartheid*. Johannesburg: Wits University Press.

Nuttall, S. and C. Coetzee (eds) (1998) *Negotiating the Past: The Making of Memory in South Africa*. Cape Town: Oxford University Press.

Nyambe, N. (2005) Organizational culture and its underlying basic assumptions as a determinate of response to change: A case study of KwaZulu-Natal's conservation sector. South Africa. PhD thesis, University of KwaZulu-Natal.

Omond, R. (1985) *The Apartheid Handbook: A Guide to South Africa's Everyday Racial Policies*. Harmondsworth: Penguin.

Oomen, B. (2005) *Chiefs in South Africa: Law, Power and Culture in the Post-Apartheid Era*. New York: Palgrave.

Orlove, B. and S. B. Brush (1996) Anthropology and the conservation of biodiversity. *Annual Review of Anthropology* 25: 329–52.

Ouzman, S. (2005) Indigenous archaeologies: Decolonizing theory and practice, in C. Smith and M. Wobst (eds), London: Routledge, pp. 208–24.

Parkington, J. (1999) Clanwillian Living Landscape Project. *Nordisk Museologi* 1: 147–54.

Parr, C., J. Woinarski, and D. Pienaar (2009) Cornerstones of biodiversity conservation? Comparing the management effectiveness of Kruger and Kakadu National Parks, two key savanna reserves. *Biodiversity and Conservation* 18 (13): 3643–62.

Patel, Z. (2009) Environmental justice in South Africa: Tools and trade-offs. *Social Dynamics: A Journal of African Studies* 35: 94–110.

Patterson, T. C. (1999) The political economy of archaeology in the United States. *Annual Review of Anthropology* 28: 155–74.

Pearson, T. (2009) On the trail of living modified organisms: Environmentalism within and against neoliberal order. *Cultural Anthropology* 24: 712–45.

Peluso, N. L. (1993) Coercing conservation? The politics of state resource control. *Global Environmental Change* 3: 199–217.

Pienaar, U. D. V. (1990) *Neem Uit Die Verlede*. Nasionale Parkeraad: Pretoria.

Pikirayi, I. (2007) Ceramics and group identities: Towards a social archaeology in southern African Iron Age ceramic studies. *Journal of Social Archaeology* 7: 286–301.

Plug, I. (1988) Hunters and Herders: An Archaeozoological study of some prehistoric communities in the Kruger National Park. PhD thesis, University of Pretoria.

Plug, I. (1989a) Aspects of Life in the Kruger National Park during the Early Iron Age. *Goodwin Series* 6: 62–8.

Plug, I. (1989b) Notes on the distribution and relative abundance of some animal species, and on climate in the Kruger National Park during prehistoric times. *Koedoe* 32: 101–19.

Plug, I. and J. C. C. Pistorius (1999) Animal remains from industrial Iron Age communities in Phalaborwa, South Africa. *African Archaeological Review* 16: 155–84.

Pollard, S., C. Shackelton, and J. Carruthers (2003) Beyond the fence: People and the Lowveld landscape, in J. T. Du Toit, K. H. Rogers, and H. C. Biggs (eds), *The Kruger Experience: Ecology and Management of a Savanna Heterogeneity*. Washington: Island Press, pp. 422–46.

Posey, D. A. Editor. (1999) *Cultural and Spiritual Values of Biodiversity*. London: UNEP.

Povinelli, E. A. (2002) *The Cunning of Recognition*. Durham: Duke University Press.

Pratt, M. (1992) *Imperial Eyes: Travel Writing and Transculturation*. London: Routledge.

Price, S. V. Editor. (2003) *War and Tropical Forests: Conservation in Areas of Armed Conflict*. Binghamton, NY: Food Products Press.

Prins, F. E. (2009) Secret San of the Drakensberg and their rock art legacy. *Critical Arts: A Journal of South–North Cultural Studies* 23: 190–208.

Proctor, R. (2009) Agnatology: A missing term to describe the cultural production of ignorance (and its study), in R. Proctor and L. Scheibinger (eds), *Agnatology: The Making and Unmaking of Ignorance*. Stanford: Stanford University Press, pp. 1–33.

Punt, W. H. J. (1975) *The First Europeans in Kruger National Park 1725*. Pretoria: National Parks Board of Trustees.

Pwiti, G. and W. Ndoro (1999) The legacy of colonialism: Perceptions of the cultural heritage in Southern Africa, with special reference to Zimbabwe. *African Archaeological Review* 16: 143–53.

Rademan, L. K. (2004) An ecological assessment of the sustainable utilization of the woody vegetation in the Lowveld Bushveld Mpumalanga Province. MSc thesis, Pretoria University.

Raffles, H. (2002) *In Amazonia: A Natural History*. Princeton and Oxford: Princeton University Press.

Raman, P. G. (2007) Narrative shifts in architecture. *South African Journal of Art History* 22: 250–76.

Ramphele, M. (2008) *Laying Ghosts to Rest: Dilemmas of the Transformation in South Africa*. Cape Town: Tafelberg.

Ramutsindela, M. (2003) Land reform in South Africa's national parks: A catalyst for the human–nature nexus. *Land Use Policy* 20: 41–9.

Ramutsindela, M. (2004) *Parks and People in Postcolonial Societies: Experiences in Southern Africa*. Netherlands: Springer.

Ranger, T. (1999) *Voices From the Rocks*. Bloomington: Indiana University Press.

Ranger, T. (2010) The invention of tradition in colonial Africa, in R. R. Grinker, S. C. Lubkemann, and C. B. Steiner (eds), *Perspectives on Africa: A Reader in Culture, History and Representation*. Oxford: Blackwell, pp. 450–61.

Rassool, C. (2000) The rise of heritage and the reconstitution of history in South Africa. *Kronos: Journal of Cape History* 26: 1–21.

Rassool, C. (2007) Memory and the politics of history in the District Six Museum, in N. Murray, N. Shepherd, and M. Hall (eds), *Desire Lines: Space, Memory and Identity in the Post-Apartheid City*. London: Routledge, pp. 113–27.

Rassool, C. and S. Prosalendis (2001) *Recalling Community in Cape Town: Creating and Curating the District Six Museum*. Cape Town: District Six Museum Foundation.

Rassool, C. and L. Witz (1996) South Africa: A World in One Country; Moments in International Tourist Encounters with Wildlife, the Primitive and the Modern. *Cahiers d'études africaines* 143: 335–71.

Redman, C. (2005) Resilience theory in archaeology. *American Anthropologist* 107: 70–7.

Redman, C. L. and A. P. Kinzig (2003) Resilience of past landscapes: Resilience theory, society, and the longue durée. *Conservation Ecology* 7. http://www.ecologyandsociety. org/vol7/iss1/art14/ (accessed May 3, 2011).

Reid, H. (2001) Contractual national parks and the Makuleke. *Human Ecology* 29: 135–55.

Reid, H., D. Fig, H. Magome, and N. Leader-Williams (2004) Co-management of contractual national parks in South Africa: Lessons from Australia. *Conservation & Society* 2: 377–409.

Republic of South Africa (1996) White paper on the development and promotion of tourism in South Africa. Pretoria: Government of South Africa, Department of Environmental Affairs and Tourism.

Republic of South Africa (1999) Preamble: National Heritage Resources Act. Pretoria: Government Printer.

Rico, T. (2007) Archaeology in conflict: Cultural heritage, site management and sustainable development in conflict and post-conflict states in the Middle East, London, November 10–12, 2006. *Conservation and Management of Archaeological Sites* 8: 105–7.

Ritvo, H. (1987) *The Animal Estate*. Cambridge, MA: Harvard University Press.

Roberts, N. (2003) Disturbing nature's harmonies? Pre-modern human impact and the myth of the virgin earth, the *Alexander von Humboldt Lecture*. UCLA.

Robins, S. (2001) NGOs, "Bushmen" and double vision: The ≠khomani San land claim and the cultural politics of "community" and "development" in the Kalahari. *Journal of South African Studies* 27: 833–53.

Robins, S. (2002) Land struggles and the politics and ethics of representing "bushman" history and identity. *Kronos: Journal of Cape History* 26: 56–75.

Robins, S. and K. van der Waal (2008) "Model tribes" and iconic conservationists? The Makuleke restitution case in Kruger National Park. *Development and Change* 39: 53–72.

Robinson, G. A. (1994) Towards a neighbour relations policy and strategy for the National Parks Board. Unpublished report. Pretoria, South Africa.

Rodgers, G. (2009) The faint footprint of man: Representing race, place and conservation on the Mozambique–South Africa borderland. *Journal of Refugee Studies*: 22(3): 1–21.

Romero, C. and G. I. Andrade (2004) International conservation organizations and the fate of local tropical forest conservation initiatives. *Conservation Biology* 18: 578–80.

Rosenfeld, G. D. (2000) *Munich and Memory*. Berkeley: University of California Press.

Rössler, M. (2003) Linking nature and culture: World heritage cultural landscapes, in *Cultural Landscapes: The Challenges of Conservation*. Paris: UNESCO, pp. 10–15.

Saayman, M. and A. Saayman (2006) Estimating the economic contribution of visitor spending in the Kruger National Park to the regional economy. *Journal of Sustainable Tourism* 14: 67–81.

Sachs, A. (2007) *The Humboldt Current: A European Explorer and His American Disciples*. Oxford: Oxford University Press.

Sack, S. (2003) Poverty alleviation, in *Investing in Culture*. Pretoria: Department of Arts and Culture, pp. 4–5.

Sadr, K. (2003) The Neolithic of southern Africa. *Journal of African History* 44: 195–209.

Scham, S. (2009) "Time's wheel runs back": Conversations with the Middle Eastern past, in L. M. Meskell (ed.), *Cosmopolitan Archaeologies*. Durham: Duke University Press, pp. 166–83.

Scheermeyer, C. (2005) A changing and challenging landscape: Heritage resources management in South Africa. *South African Archaeological Bulletin* 60: 121–3.

Schoeman, M. H. (2006a) Clouding power? Rain control, space, landscapes and ideology in Shashe–Limpopo state formation. PhD thesis, University of the Witwatersrand.

Schoeman, M. H. (2006b) Imagining rain-places: Rain-control and changing ritual landscapes in the Shashe–Limpopo confluence area, South Africa. *South African Archaeological Bulletin* 61: 152–65.

Scholze, M. (2008) Arrested heritage: The politics of inscription into the UNESCO World Heritage List: The case of Agadez in Niger. *Journal of Material Culture* 13: 215–31.

Schutte, G. (2003) Tourists and tribes in the "New" South Africa. *Ethnohistory* 50: 473–87.

Scott, J. C. (1999) *Seeing Like a State: How Certain Schemes to Improve the Human Condition Have Failed*. New Haven: Yale University Press.

Secretariat of the Convention on Biological Diversity (2009) *Biodiversity, Development and Poverty Alleviation*. Montreal: Secretariat of the Convention on Biological Diversity.

Seekings, J. and N. Nattrass (2002) Class, distribution and retribution in post-apartheid South Africa. *Transformation* 50: 1–30.

Segadika, P. (2006) Managing Intangible Heritage at Tsodilo. *Museum International* 58: 31–40.

Segobye, A. K. (2005) Weaving fragments of the past for a united Africa: Reflections on the place of African archaeology in the development of the continent in the 21st century. *The South African Archaeological Bulletin* 60: 79–83.

Segobye, A. K. (2006) Divided commons: The political economy of Southern Africa's cultural heritage landscapes—Observations of the central Kalahari game reserve, Botswana. *Archaeologies* 2: 52–72.

Sharp, J. (2006) Corporate social responsibility and development: An anthropological perspective. *Development Southern Africa* 23: 213–22.

Shepherd, N. (2002a) Heading south, looking north: Why we need a post-colonial archaeology. *Archaeological Dialogues* 9: 74–82.

Shepherd, N. (2002b) The politics of archaeology in Africa. *Annual Review of Anthropology* 31: 189–209.

Shepherd, N. (2003) State of the discipline: Science, culture and identity in South African archaeology, 1870–2003. *Journal of Southern African Studies* 29: 823–44.

Shepherd, N. (2005) Who is doing courses in archaeology at South African universities? And what are they studying? *The South African Archaeological Bulletin* 60: 123–6.

Shepherd, N. (2007) Archaeology dreaming: Post-apartheid urban imaginaries and the bones of the Prestwich Street dead. *Journal of Social Archaeology* 7: 3–28.

Shepherd, N. (2008) Heritage, in N. Shepherd and S. Robins (eds), *South African Keywords*. Johannesburg: Jacana, pp. 116–28.

Shepherd, N. and C. Ernsten (2007) The world below: Post-apartheid imaginaries and the bones of the Prestwich Street dead, in N. Murray, N. Shepherd, and M. Hall (eds), *Desire Lines: Space, Memory and Identity in the Post-Apartheid City*. London: Routledge, pp. 215–32.

Shepherd, N. and N. Murray (2007) Introduction, in N. Murray, N. Shepherd, and M. Hall (eds), *Desire Lines: Space, Memory and Identity in the Post-Apartheid City*. London: Routledge, pp. 1–18.

Shetawy, A. A. A. and S. M. El Khateeb (2009) The pyramids plateau: A dream searching for survival. *Tourism Management* 30: 819–27.

Shetler, J. B. (2007) *Imagining Serengeti: A History of Landscape Memory in Tanzania from Earliest Times to the Present*. Athens, OH: Ohio University Press.

Shutt, A. K. (2002) The settlers' cattle complex: The etiquette of culling cattle in colonial Zimbabwe, 1938. *Journal of African History* 43: 263–86.

Skotnes, P. Editor. (1996) *Miscast: Negotiating the Presence of the Bushmen*. Cape Town: University of Cape Town Press.

Smith, B. W. (2009) A transformation charter for South African Archaeology. *South African Archaeological Bulletin* 64: 87–9.

Smith, B. W., J. D. Lewis-Williams, G. Blundell, and C. Chippendale (2000) Archaeology and symbolism in the new South African coat of arms. *Antiquity* 74: 467–8.

Smith, C. (2004) *Country, Kin and Culture: Survival of an Australian Aboriginal Community*. Adelaide: Wakefield Press.

Smith, C. and H. Burke (2007) *Digging it up Down Under: A Practical Guide to Doing Archaeology in Australia*. New York: Springer.

Smith, L. (2000) A history of Aboriginal heritage legislation in south-eastern Australia. *Australian Archaeology* 50: 109–18.

Smith, L. and G. Campbell (1998) Governing material culture, in M. Dean and B. Hindes (eds), *Governing Australia: Studies in Contemporary Rationalities of Government*. Cambridge: Cambridge University Press, pp. 173–91.

Smith, L.-J. (2004) *Archaeological Theory and the Politics of Cultural Heritage*. Routledge: London.

Smith, L. T. (1999) *Decolonizing Methodologies*. London: Zed Books.

Soper, K. (2000) *What is Nature?* Oxford: Blackwell.

Soudien, C. (2008) Emerging discourses around identity in new South African museum exhibitions. *Interventions: International Journal of Postcolonial Studies* 10: 207–21.

Soudien, C. (2009) Emerging multiculturalisms in South African museum practice: Some examples from the Western Cape, in M. H. Ross (ed.), *Culture and Belonging in Divided*

Societies: Contestation and Symbolic Landscapes. Philadelphia: University of Pennsylvania Press, pp. 176–92.

Soundy, S. (2004) *The Establishment of an Effective Public Sector-cum-Private Sector Balanced Scorecard Business Performance Management System for South African National Parks.* Pretoria: South African National Parks.

South African National Parks (2000) Minutes of the meeting between SANP and the Thulamela Board of Trustees. On file in the Skukuza Archives, Kruger National Park.

South African National Parks (2004) Annual Report. Pretoria: SANParks.

South African National Parks (2005a) A Framework for Developing and Implementing Management Plans for South African National Parks. http://www.sanparks.org/parks/kruger/conservation/scientific/key_issues/ (accessed May 3, 2011).

South African National Parks (2005b) Annual Report. Pretoria: SANParks.

South African National Parks (2006) *Go Wild.* April 2006. Pretoria: SANParks.

South African National Parks (2008a) Annual Report. Pretoria: SANParks.

South African National Parks (2008b) SANParks' Biodiversity Custodianship and Management Plan Framework. Pretoria: SANParks.

South African National Parks (2009) Annual Report. Pretoria: SANParks.

Spence, M. (1999) *Dispossessing the Wilderness: Indian Removal and the Making of the National Parks.* Oxford: Oxford University Press.

Spenceley, A. (2003) *Tourism, Local Livelihoods, and the Private Sector in South Africa: Case Studies on the Growing Role of the Private Sector in Natural Resources Management.* Sustainable Livelihoods in Southern Africa: Institutions, Governance and Policy Processes. http://www.ids.ac.uk/slsa (accessed May 3, 2011).

Spierenburg, M., C. Steenkamp, and H. Wels (2008) Enclosing the local for the global commons: Community land rights in the Great Limpopo Transfrontier conservation area. *Conservation and Society* 6: 87–97.

Spinage, C. A. (2003) *Cattle Plague: A History.* New York: Springer.

Stanley, L. (2005) Aftermaths: Post/memory, commemoration and the concentration camps of the South African War 1899–1902. *European Review of History* 12: 91–119.

Steinberg, J. (2008) Crime, in N. Shepherd and S. Robins (eds), *South African Keywords.* Johannesburg: Jacana, pp. 25–34.

Steinhart, E. I. (2006) *Black Poachers, White Hunters: A Social History of Hunting in Colonial Kenya.* Oxford: James Currey.

Stevenson-Hamilton, J. (1929) *The Low-Veld: Its Wild Life and Its People.* London: Cassell.

Stevenson-Hamilton, J. (1993) *South African Eden: The Kruger National Park, 1902–1946.* Cape Town: Struik Publishing.

Steyn, M., S. Miller, W. C. Neinaber, and M. Loots (1998) Late Iron Age gold burials from Thulamela (Parfuri region, Kruger National Park). *South African Archaeological Bulletin* 53: 73–85.

Stoler, A. (1995) *Race and the Education of Desire.* Durham: Duke University Press.

Stoler, A. L. (2008) *Reading Along the Archival Grain: Epistemic Anxieties and Colonial Common Sense.* Princeton: Princeton University Press.

Stronza, A. (2001) Anthropology of tourism: Forging new ground for ecotourism and other alternatives. *Annual Review of Anthropology* 30: 261–83.

Swyngedouw, E. (1999) Modernity and hybridity: Nature, regeneracionismo, and the production of the Spanish waterscape, 1890–1930. *Annals of the Association of American Geographers* 89: 443–65.

Sylvain, R. (2002) Land, Water, and Truth: San identity and global indigenism. *American Anthropologist* 104: 1074–85.

Tapela, B. N., L. Maluleke, and C. Mavhunga (2007) New architecture, old agendas: Perspectives on social research in rural communities neighbouring the Kruger National Park. *Conservation and Society* 5: 60–87.

Tapela, B. N. and P. H. Omara-Ojungu (1999) Towards bridging the gap between wildlife conservation and rural development in post-apartheid South Africa: The case of the Makuleke community and the Kruger National Park. *South African Geographical Journal* 81: 148–55.

Taussig, M. (2004) *My Cocaine Museum*. Chicago: University of Chicago.

Terreblanche, S. (2003) *A History of Inequality in South Africa 1652–2002*. Pietermaritzburg: University of Natal Press.

Terreblanche, S. (2008) The developmental state in South Africa: The difficult road ahead, in P. Kagwanja and K. Kondlo (eds), *State of the Nation: South Africa 2008*. Cape Town: HSRC Press, pp. 107–30.

Thomas, J. (2004) *Archaeology and Modernity*. London: Routledge.

Thomas, M. (2001) *A Multicultural Landscape: National Parks and the Macedonian Experience*. Sydney: NSW Department of Environment, Climate Change & Water.

Thomas, N. (1994) *Colonialism's Culture: Anthropology, Travel and Government*. Princeton: Princeton University Press.

Thompson, J. (2008) Aesthetics and the value of nature, in A. Carlson and S. Lintott (eds), *Nature, Aesthetics, and Environmentalism*. New York: Columbia University Press, pp. 254–67.

Thys-Senocak, L. (2010) Divided spaces, contested pasts: The Gallipoli Peninsula historical national park, in E. Carr, S. Eyring, and R. G. Wilson (eds), *Public Nature: Scenery, History, and Park Design*. Charlottesville: University of Virginia Press.

Tomalin, D. J., P. Simpson, and J. M. Bingeman (2000) Excavation versus sustainability in situ: A conclusion on 25 years of archaeological investigations at Goose Rock, a designated historic wreck-site at the Needles, Isle of Wight, England. *International Journal of Nautical Archaeology* 29: 3–42.

Trigger, B. G. (1989) *A History of Archaeological Thought*. Cambridge: University of Cambridge Press.

Tropp, J. (2002) Dogs, poison and the meaning of colonial intervention in the Transkei, South Africa. *Journal of African History* 43: 451–72.

Tsing, A. (2005) *Friction: An Ethnography of Global Connection*. Princeton: Princeton University Press.

UNESCO (1972) Convention Concerning the Protection of the World Cultural and Natural Heritage. Adopted by the General Conference at its seventeenth session. Paris, November 16, 1972. http://whc.unesco.org/en/conventiontext (accessed May 3, 2011).

UNESCO (2005) The Convention on the Protection and Promotion of the Diversity of Cultural Expressions. Adopted by the General Conference at its seventeenth session. Paris, October 20, 2005.

UNESCO (2009) *Case Studies on Climate Change and World Heritage*. Paris: UNESCO World Heritage Center.

UNESCO & UNEP (2002) *Cultural diversity and biodiversity for sustainable development*. World Summit on Sustainable Development, Johannesburg, September 3, 2002: UNEP, Nairobi.

van Amerom, M. and B. Büscher (2005) Peace parks in Southern Africa: Bringers of an African renaissance? *Journal of Modern African Studies* 43: 159–82.

van der Merwe, N. J. and R. T. K. Skully (2003) The Phalaborwa story: Archaeological and ethnographic investigation of a South African Iron Age group. *World Archaeology* 3: 178–96.

van der Spek, K. (1998) Dead mountain versus living community: The Theban necropolis as cultural landscape, in W. S. Logan, C. Long, and J. Martin (eds), Proceedings of the 3rd International Seminar Forum UNESCO: University and Heritage. Melbourne: Deakin University, pp. 176–82.

van der Waal, K. (2008) Development, in N. Shepherd and S. Robins (eds), *South African Keywords*. Johannesburg: Jacana, pp. 58–68.

van Noort, E. (2005a) Cull Kruger's elephants, say wildlife groups. *Mail & Guardian (Johannesburg)*, December 2.

van Noort, E. (2005b) Plan to cull Kruger elephants is "deeply flawed." *Mail & Guardian (Johannesburg)*, November 28.

van Rensburg, E. J. (1995) Thulamela Report and Recommendations (ZA 398). Report prepared for the World Wildlife Fund South Africa. Kruger National Park, September, 10 1995. On file in the Skukuza Archives, Kruger National Park.

Van Sittert, L. (2002) Holding the line: The rural enclosure movement in the Cape Colony, c.1965–1910. *Journal of African History* 43: 95–118.

van Vollenhoven, A. C., A. J. Pelser, and J. W. van den Bos (1998) A historical–archaeological investigation of an Anglo-Boer war outpost in the Kruger National Park. *Koedoe* 4: 113–20.

van Warmelo, N. J. (1961) *Place Names of the Kruger National Park/Plekname van die Kruger Nasionale Park*. Pretoria: Departement van Bantoe-Administrasie.

Van Wyk, L. (2010) Xingwana: Homophobic claims "baseless, insulting." *Mail & Guardian (Johannesburg)*, March 5. http://www.mg.co.za/article/2010-03-05-xingwana-homophobic-claims-baseless-insulting (accessed May 3, 2011).

Van Zyl, M., J. De Gruchy, S. Lapinsky, and S. Lewin (1999) *The Aversion Project: Human Rights Abuses of Gays and Lesbians in the SADF by Health Workers During the Apartheid Era*. Cape Town: Simply Said and Done.

Varty, D. (2008) *The Full Circle*. Johannesburg: Penguin.

Vasudevan, A., C. McFarlane, and A. Jeffrey (2008) Spaces of enclosure. *Geoforum* 39: 1641–6.

Verhoef, J. (1986) Notes on archaeology and prehistoric mining in the Kruger National Park. *Koedoe* 29: 149–56.

Verhoef, J. (1995) The Gold Fields Thulamela Project (ZA 398). On file in the Skukuza Archives, Kruger National Park.

Verschuuren, B. (2007) *Believing is Seeing: Integrating Cultural and Spiritual Values in Conservation Management*. Gland, Switzerland: Foundation for Sustainable Development, The Netherlands and the IUCN.

Vogel, J. C. (2000) Radiocarbon dating of the Iron Age Sequence in the Limpopo Valley. *Goodwin Series: African Naissance: The Limpopo Valley 1000 Years Ago* 8: 51–7.

Wainaina, B. (2005) How to write about Africa. *Granta* 92: The View from Africa: 92–5.

Wainaina, B. (2006) The power of love. *Mail & Guardian (Johannesburg)*, July 14 to 20, p. 21.

Walker, C. (2006) Delivery and disarray: The multiple meanings of land restitution, in S. Buhlungu, J. Daniel, R. Southall, and J. Lutchman (eds), *State of the Nation: South Africa 2005–2006*. Pretoria: Human Sciences Research Council, pp. 67–92.

Walker, C. (2008) *Landmarked: Land Claims and Restitution in South Africa*. Athens: Ohio University Press.

Weisman, A. (2007) *The World Without Us*. New York: Thomas Dunne Books.

Weiss, L. M. (2005) The social life of rock art: Materiality, consumption and power in South African heritage, in L. M. Meskell (ed.), *Archaeologies of Materiality*. Oxford: Blackwell, pp. 46–70.

Weiss, L. M. (2007) Heritage making and political identity. *Journal of Social Archaeology* 7: 413–31.

Weiss, L. M. (2009) Fictive capital and economies of desire: A case study of illegal diamond buying and apartheid landscapes in 19th century Southern Africa. PhD thesis, Department of Anthropology, Columbia University.

West, P. (2006) *Conservation is our Government Now: The Politics of Ecology in Papua New Guinea*. Durham: Duke University Press.

West, P., J. Igoe, and D. Brockington (2006) Parks and people: The social impacts of protected areas. *Annual Review of Anthropology* 35: 251–77.

Whyte, I., R. J. van Aarde, and S. L. Pimm (2003) Kruger's elephant population: Its size and consequences for ecosystem heterogeneity, in J. T. Du Toit, K. H. Rogers, and H. C. Biggs (eds), *The Kruger Experience: Ecology and Management of a Savanna Heterogeneity*. Washington: Island Press, pp. 332–48.

Williams, G. (2004) Evaluating participatory development: Tyranny, power and (re)politicisation. *Third World Quarterly* 25: 557–78.

Winstanley, G. (1945) The True Levellers Standard Advanced, in G. H. Sabine (ed.), *The Works of Gerrard Winstanley*. New York: Russell & Russell, pp. 247–66.

Witz, L. (2003) *Apartheid's Festival: Contesting South Africa's National Pasts*. Bloomingdale: Indiana University Press.

Witz, L. (2007) Museums on Cape Town's township tours, in N. Murray, M. Hall, and N. Shepherd (eds), *Desire Lines: Space Memory and Identity in the Postapartheid City*. London: Routledge, pp. 259–75.

Witz, L., C. Rassool, and G. Minkley (2001) Repackaging the past for South African Tourism. *Daedalus* 130: 277–96.

Wolhuter, H. (1948) *Memories of a Game Ranger*. Johannesburg: Wild Life Protection and Conservation Society of South Africa.

Wolmer, W. (2003) Transboundary conservation: The politics of ecological integrity in the Great Limpopo Transfrontier Park. *Journal of Southern African Studies* 29: 261–78.

Wolmer, W. (2005) Wilderness gained, wilderness lost: Wildlife management and land occupations in Zimbabwe's southeast lowveld. *Journal of Historical Geography* 31: 260–80.

Woodward, W. (2008) *The Animal Gaze: Animal Subjectivities in Southern African Narratives*. Johannesburg: Wits University Press.

Wordie, J. R. (1983) The chronology of English Enclosure, 1500–1914. *The Economic History Review* 36: 483–505.

Wurz, S. and J. H. van der Merwe (2005) Gauging Site sensitivity for sustainable archaeo-tourism in the Western Cape Province of South Africa. *The South African Archaeological Bulletin* 60: 10–19.

Wynn, L. L. (2008) Shape shifting lizard people, Israelite slaves, and other theories of pyramid building: Notes on labor, nationalism, and archaeology in Egypt. *Journal of Social Archaeology* 8: 272–95.

Zerner, C. (2003) Dividing lines: Nature, culture, and commerce in Indonesia's Aru Islands, 1856–1997, in P. Greenenough and A. Tsing (eds), *Nature in the Global South: Environmental Projects in South and Southeast Asia*. Durham: Duke University Press, pp. 47–78.

Zhou, L. (2009) Tourism policy, biodiversity conservation and management: a case study of the Kruger National Park, South Africa. PhD thesis, Department of Geography, University of Fort Hare, South Africa.

Zimmerer, K. and T. J. Bassett (2003) *Political Ecology: An Integrative Approach to Geography and Environment–Development Studies*. New York: Guildford Press.

Zizek, S. (2010) *Living in the End of Times*. New York: Verso.

Index

adaptive management   5, 10
affirmative action   121, 173
Africa Foundation   178, 193, 194
African National Congress (ANC)
  and commercialization   167
  and employment   5
  and heritage   10–11, 57, 212
  and inequality   7
  and land reform   108
  and Rainbow Nation   44
  and SANParks   61
  and tribalism   42
  approach to culture   52
  neoliberalism of   9, 38, 46
  post-apartheid legacy   37
African Renaissance   44, 46, 48, 89, 206
African World Heritage Fund   51
Afrikaners
  and archaeology   155
  and the Kruger National Park   77,
    211
  culture   55, 184
  nationalism   2, 5, 65, 77, 89
  victimhood   77
AndBeyond   11, 178, 181, 191–6
  See also Conservation Corporation
    Africa

apartheid
  and archaeology   7, 132, 206
  and false consciousness   52
  and heritage   46, 209
  and past mastering   6
  and the environment   104, 109
  and tourism   143
  ecological   109
  economic   67
appropriation   17, 34, 64, 117, 158, 193
archaeological heritage   3, 9, 14, 27, 30,
    31, 67, 126, 128, 146
archaeology
  and apartheid   7, 132, 206
  and conservation   14–15
  and development   168
  and land claims   134
  and racial tension   172
  and restitution projects   61
  and SANParks   95, 96, 136, 140, 142,
    151
  and the People and Conservation Unit
    10, 135, 136, 140, 212
  as therapy   8, 95
  funding   7, 132, 151
  in Australia   145, 170
  in South Africa   169–73

The Nature of Heritage: The New South Africa, First Editon. Lynn Meskell.
© 2012 John Wiley & Sons, Inc. Published 2012 by Blackwell Publishing Ltd.

in the Kruger National Park   10, 96,
     147, 171–3
indigenous   20
influence of Resilience Alliance/
     Panarchy   115
Iron Age   35, 65, 127, 171, 206
low status of   7
students of   7, 170, 172
Thumalela as first collaborative project
     161
Association of Private Nature Reserves
     188
Association of South African Professional
     Archaeologists (ASAPA)   173
Australia   34, 35, 40, 142–5, 170, 210

benefit sharing   187, 189, 201, 210
Bernstein, Alan   195
Bill and Melinda Gates Foundation   180
biocentric ethics   23
biodiversity   98–124
     and culture   4, 9, 26, 27, 29, 98–124,
          140, 167, 208
     and ecological apartheid   109
     and heritage   6, 27, 95, 140, 141, 146,
          167
     and neoliberalism   10, 107, 110, 123,
          140
     and poverty   101, 109
     and SANParks   61, 95, 100, 108, 110,
          111, 112, 113, 115, 128, 141, 146, 157,
          182, 210
     and *terra nullius* discourse   116, 117,
          146
     and the Kruger National Park   10, 96,
          99, 100, 101, 103, 106, 108, 109, 111,
          112, 122, 124, 126, 128, 166, 167, 185,
          210
     and UNESCO's work   25, 26, 210
     as an elitist concern   28, 94, 108
     benefits   108, 109, 110
     conservation of   4, 5, 6, 10, 28, 61,
          71, 100, 102, 103, 106, 109, 110, 111,
          114, 117, 118, 121, 136, 140, 141, 166,
          174, 182, 183, 184, 192, 202, 209, 210,
          214
     definition   99, 100, 101, 107

global   26–7, 29, 106, 107, 108, 212
hegemonic nature of   26, 122
management   28, 95, 110, 111, 121,
     146, 165, 183, 213
bioprospecting   110
black history   10, 63, 66, 76, 84, 98, 119,
     168, 169
black poverty   37, 127, 139
     see also poverty
boundary policing   191
burning   99, 100, 129, 130, 146
     see also firing

capacity building   10, 12, 37, 57, 139, 163,
     184, 189, 196, 209, 216
capitalism   110, 152
carbon credits   182
carbon trading   110
carcass model   180
Carlisle, Les   194–5
Carruthers, Jane   77, 96
casino capitalism   152
cattle killing   80–2, 205, 213
     see also culling
charitable organizations   180
child slavery   76
Clanwilliam Living Landscape Project
     206
class   84, 197
Clean Up Kruger campaign   140
climate change   26, 214
collaborative projects   20
colonialism   4, 40, 66, 75, 87, 100
co-management   145, 178, 202
command-and-control management
     structure   186
commodification   11, 23, 24, 61, 93, 202,
     207, 210
     of communities   55
     of culture   181, 192
     of ethnicity   39
     of local life   57
     of nature   110, 181, 192
     of Zulu past   19
communal tenure   106
Community Based Natural Resource
     Management (CBNRM)   162, 215

community development   10, 61, 94, 131,
    132, 142, 167, 182, 194
community involvement   106, 135, 152,
    165, 181, 196
community projects   183, 189, 202
compensation   6, 80–1, 106, 121, 185,
    201, 207
competitive tender   47
conservation   4, 61, 102, 121, 181, 184,
    194, 201, 202
  and archaeology   14–15
  and development   14
  and ecological apartheid   109
  and farming   111
  and global goods   109
  and heritage   3, 6, 8, 10, 11, 12, 14, 18,
    20, 39, 48, 60, 114, 125, 139, 142, 178,
    185, 215
  and public–private management   94
  and sustainability   14
  and *terra nullius* discourse   117
  and tourism   210
  coercive nature of   107
  community-based   14
  corporatization of   210
  fortress   15, 16–21
  in Australia   142
  of biodiversity   4, 5, 6, 10, 28, 61, 71,
    100, 102, 103, 106, 109, 110, 111,
    114, 117, 118, 121, 136, 140, 141,
    166, 174, 182, 183, 184, 192, 202,
    209, 210, 214
conservation agencies   181
Conservation Corporation Africa (CCA)
    192
  see also AndBeyond
conservation enforcement   84
Conservation International   25, 30
consultancy culture   49, 61, 94, 96
Convention on Biological Diversity (CBD)
    107
Convention on International Trade in
    Endangered Species of Wild Flora
    and Fauna (CITES)   117
Convention on the Protection of the
    World Cultural and Natural Heritage
    215

corporate social responsibility (CSR)
    182, 209
corruption   7, 182, 206
Crocodile Bridge   104
Crooks Corner   87
culling   100, 112, 116, 138, 189, 194,
    213
  see also cattle killing
cultural assets   179
cultural diversity   27, 28, 29, 59
cultural heritage   25, 93, 123, 135,
    140
  alternative vision of   142–6
  and capacity building   12
  and development   12, 128
  and engagement   214–15
  and natural heritage   4, 9, 13–15, 20,
    27, 35, 142–6, 204, 209, 213
  and neoliberalism   46
  and restitution projects   61
  and SANParks   95
  and sustainability   12, 34
  and the People and Conservation unit
    128
  as politicized undertaking   10–11,
    15
  in Australia   144
  racialized   127
  roles of   215–16
culturalism   9, 41, 42, 207
cultural management   132
cultural mapping   132
cultural villages   6, 39, 55, 57, 60
culture
  ANC approach to   52
  and biodiversity   4, 9, 26, 27, 29,
    98–124, 140, 167, 208
  and nature   4, 100, 101, 124, 214–16
  and race   206
  capitalization of   11–12, 38, 120, 207,
    208
  employment through   2
  of sustainability   27
  pan-African   208
  struggles around   40
  tribal   29, 55, 205
cybertrackers   132

damage-causing animals (DCAs) 106

Danish Cooperation for Environment and Tourism (DANCED) 183

De Cuiper expedition 74

deep ecology 213

Department of Environment and Tourism (DEAT) 48, 103, 153, 208

Department of Environment, Climate Change and Water (DECWW) (Australia) 144

designer vegetation communities 111

deurlopers 86, 113

development 122, 140, 178–83, 206, 207, 215
 agencies 61
 and archaeology 168
 and conservation 14
 and cultural heritage 12, 128
 and dislocation 21
 and neoliberalism 210
 and sustainability 6
 community 61, 94
 destructive 26
 of heritage 43–7, 55
 sustainable development 6, 32, 49, 102

dislocation 20, 21

diversity 12, 14, 15, 30, 123
 and future generations 26–33
 and sustainability 32
 and universality 28
 biological 59
 cultural 27, 28, 29, 59
 loss of 30
 UNESCO on 27

Dladla, Yvonne 137

dog cemeteries 64, 212

donors 31, 122, 142, 151, 152, 160, 164, 180, 181, 182, 194, 208

ecological health 31

ecological salvage politics 204

ecology 136–42, 213

ecosystem resilience 115

ecosystem services 24

ecotherapy 101

ecotourism 30, 35, 120, 174, 181, 192, 193, 201, 207, 211
 see also tourism

education 7, 61, 120, 183, 194, 208
 and heritage 39
 deficits 54
 environmental 110, 113, 123, 136, 137, 140, 141, 152, 153, 167, 168, 182, 209, 212
 programs 122, 123, 167

elites 136, 161, 198, 199

Emerson, Ralph Waldo 23

employment 2, 24, 106, 109, 130, 134, 136, 164, 184, 189, 194, 197, 201, 209, 215
 black 5, 170
 in the Kruger National Park 6, 106, 140, 163, 196
 projects creating 7

empowerment 4, 10, 37, 60, 61, 102, 128, 133, 153, 182, 184, 194, 201

enclosure 14, 15, 16–21, 211
 see also fencing

Endangered Wildlife Trust 193

environmental degradation 102

Environmental Investigation Agency 87

environmentality 6, 113

ethical stakeholding 170

ethnic craft initiatives 39

ethnic tension 8, 9, 84, 205, 209

evictions 5, 14, 64, 77, 104, 106, 129, 163, 177, 211
 Native American 20
 see also forced removals

excavations 73, 138, 170, 173, 174, 214

exhumation of burials 151

false consciousness 52

farming 17, 18, 73, 76, 111, 194

fencing 18, 19, 66, 100, 189, 211
 see also enclosure

firing 107, 111
 see also burning

First Peoples 40, 53, 55

forced labor 85, 177

forced removals 42, 104, 205
 see also evictions

forgetting   1, 10, 46, 47, 75
fortress conservation   15, 16–21
Foucault, Michel   113
funding   100, 109, 134, 179, 180, 182–4,
    200, 207, 208
  for archaeology   7, 132, 151
  for cultural heritage institutions   128
  for natural heritage   46
  for the Kruger National Park   75, 122
  for the National Parks Board   94
  for Thulamela   151, 152–5, 167
funding agencies   200
future generations   26–33

game   29, 76, 194
  culling   189
gentrification   19
Global Diversity Strategy   107
Global Environment Facility   181
global heritage   8, 30, 31, 116
Global Heritage Fund (GHF)   30
graves   19, 38, 45, 72, 82, 104, 106, 186,
    188, 200, 201
Great Limpopo Transfrontier Peace Park
    (GLTP)   18, 89, 201
green consumerism   109
greenhouse emissions   101
green politics   33
Green Scorpions   103
green theory of value   23
Growth, Employment and Redistribution
    (GEAR)   61, 178, 179
gun running   87
  see also weapons smuggling

Hazyview Forum   188
healing   182, 189
heritage
  and apartheid   46, 209
  and biodiversity   6, 27, 95, 140, 141,
    146, 167
  and conservation   3, 6, 8, 10, 11, 12,
    14, 18, 20, 39, 48, 60, 114, 125, 139,
    142, 178, 185, 215
  and ecology   136–42, 213
  and economic growth   46
  and education   39

  and empowerment   10, 37, 128
  and neoliberalism   9, 11, 47, 96, 204,
    205
  and poverty   38
  and social ecology   212
  and the ANC   10–11, 57, 212
  archaeological   3, 9, 14, 27, 30, 31, 67,
    126, 128, 146
  as production of arts and crafts   95
  as therapy   4, 38, 39, 151
  black   122, 158, 168
  capitalizing on   37–62, 172, 203
  cultural, *see* cultural heritage
  development of   43–7, 55
  global   8, 30, 31, 116
  in post-apartheid South Africa   204
  in the Kruger National Park   60–2
  legislation   46, 171
  liberal   9, 61
  management   19, 35, 136, 142, 143,
    144
  markers   64, 65
  natural, *see* natural heritage
  naturalization of   9
  negative   1, 2
  rock art   134, 206
heritage agencies   34, 47, 142, 181, 172
heritage sector   47
heritage trails   146
housing   7, 32, 67, 127, 167, 176, 196,
    198, 199
Hoxani forum   177
human rights   12, 29, 32, 47, 107, 216
Humboldt, Alexander von   15, 22, 26,
    205, 213, 215
hunting   70, 76, 99, 111, 115, 116

identity claims   185
identity politics   39, 49
ignorance   67, 75
immigrants   72, 85, 86, 90, 96, 118
  see also migrants
immigration   85, 89, 92
indigenous knowledge   8, 35, 53, 61, 95,
    117, 140, 141, 164, 171, 188, 211, 215
indigenous rights   216
indigenous stewardship   95

intellectual property   185, 188
International Centre for the Preservation
    and Restoration of Cultural Property
    (ICCROM)   25
International Council on Monuments and
    Sites (ICOMOS)   25
International Union for the Conservation
    of Nature and Natural Resources
    (IUCN)   25, 30, 117, 180, 215
Iron Age   35, 65, 127, 171, 206
    research   138
    settlements   71
    sites   3, 68, 70, 72, 73, 119, 128
    trade   72
ivory   72, 74, 76, 87, 89, 112

Jock of the Bushveld   65, 66, 213
Jordan, Z. Pallo   29, 48, 51, 172, 183, 206

Kalahari Picnic   126
Keep Kruger Clean Campaign   113, 114
Khayelitsha   196, 197
Kruger, Paul   5, 64, 77, 157, 174
Kruger Millions   156, 174
Kruger National Park
    access to   10, 11, 104, 112, 128, 139,
        151, 186, 189, 193
    and biodiversity   10, 96, 99, 100, 101,
        103, 106, 108, 109, 111, 112, 122, 124,
        126, 128, 166, 167, 185, 210
    animal distributions in   71
    archaeology in   10, 96, 147, 171–3
    as a transfrontier peace park   6, 89
    as fortress reserve   18
    as parastatal agency   5, 103, 196
    as symbol of Afrikaner nationalism   5,
        77
    black perceptions of   106
    colonial period   75–9
    commercialization strategy   94
    early trade in   74
    employment in   6, 106, 140, 163, 196
    evictions in   5, 64, 77, 83, 106, 129, 177
    farming in   73
    funding   75, 122
    heritage in   60–2
    history   3, 5, 10, 68–93, 96

influence of Yosemite model   20
    making heritage pay in   60–2
    management policies   5, 10, 100, 111
    Mandela's views on   38
    past mastering in   146
    planning   188–91
    post-apartheid   86, 93–6
    poverty in adjacent areas   6, 181, 182
    prehistory   65, 96
    relationship between nature and culture
        in   4–9, 35, 204
    SADF activities in   87–92
Kruger Park Commando Unit   90

land acquisition   181
land alienation   205
land claims   5, 62, 71, 80–1, 83, 108, 109,
        128, 129, 140, 147, 185, 195, 201, 207,
        209, 212
land reform   108
land resources   211
land restitution   201
land transfers   92
legacy projects   54
Levi-Strauss, Claude   28
Locke, John   117

Mabo court decision   143
Mabunda, David   64, 92, 95, 183, 185
Manifest Destiny   22, 44, 215
Mapungubwe Cultural Landscape   25
Mapungubwe Interpretive Centre   172
Mapungubwe National Park   3, 42, 48,
        49, 51, 85, 122, 138, 162, 170, 173,
        185, 210
Maropeng   48, 49, 50, 51, 208
Masorini   68, 73, 74, 128–32, 141, 146,
        147, 168, 212
Masterplanning Kruger meeting   189
Matopos   118
memorials   63
memory   185, 203
Mfecane   75
Mhlongo, Elizabeth   162, 163
migrants   113
    see also immigrants
Miller, Duncan   150, 151

Miller, Sidney   149, 154, 158, 163, 168
monuments   7, 21, 65, 66, 209
Mopani Plan   153–4
Mpumalanga Parks Board   167, 194

nagana (animal African trypanosomiasis)
    71, 74, 76
National Heritage Council (NHC)   171,
    172
National Parks Board   66, 137, 183, 195
National Parks Trust   195
National Peace Accord Trust   101
National Science Foundation   154
natural heritage
    alternative vision   142–6
    and apartheid   46
    and cultural heritage   4, 9, 13–15, 20,
        27, 35, 142–6, 204, 209, 213
    global imperatives surrounding   14
    in Australia   142
    roles of   215–16
natural resources   200
nature
    and biodiversity   100
    and culture   4, 100, 101, 124, 214–16
    and neoliberalism   110
    as healing force   110
    decolonization of   107
    exploitation by capital   109, 110
    presentation of   100
    privatization of   181, 210
    protection of   4, 108, 215
Nature Conservancy   31
neoliberalism
    and biodiversity   10, 107, 110, 123,
        140
    and commodification of ethnicity
        39
    and cultural heritage   46
    and heritage   11, 47, 96, 204, 205
    and nature   110
    and poverty   38
    and SANParks   61
    and the ANC   9, 38, 46
    development   210
New Partnership for Africa's Development
    (NEPAD)   46, 48

Norwegian Agency for Development
    Co-operation (NORAD)   153
Numbi Gate   82, 91, 92, 121

Operation Prevail   180, 209
Origins Centre (University of the
    Witwatersrand)   7, 48, 53, 169, 208
outsourcing   7, 94, 182

Pafuri, land exchange   92
Paleolithic research   138
Panarchy   115
parastatals   5, 47–8, 101–7, 182
Paris Declaration on Biodiversity   108
past mastering   1, 2, 3, 6, 146–7, 202, 203,
    205
People and Conservation unit (of
    SANParks)
    and archaeology   10, 135, 136, 140, 212
    and black poverty   127
    and cultural heritage   128
    and rock art project   135
    and Scientific Services unit   138
    and social ecology   212
    core business   141
    rationale for establishing   182
    resistance to   168
    Social Science Research unit   138–9,
        142
people-centred participatory approach
    151
performance measurement   94
Platfontein   56
Plug, Ina   70
Poacher's Corner   86
poaching   18, 87, 111, 116, 127, 163, 181,
    194
poverty   6, 7, 16, 50, 61, 85, 86, 136, 164,
    198, 207
    and biodiversity   101, 109
    and environmental degradation   102
    and heritage   38
    and macroeconomic policy   179
    and neoliberalism   38
    and race   9
    black   37, 127, 139
    failure to combat   9

near the Kruger National Park   6, 181, 182

relief   48, 53, 95, 128, 182, 198, 216

Pretoria University   42, 68, 73, 154, 167–8, 169, 170

Pretoriuskop Camp   91

primitivism   55, 95

prison labor   85

private conservation companies   11

private game reserves   115, 180, 211

private lodges   3, 61, 93, 188, 189, 196

private–public partnerships   8, 14, 39, 49, 94, 179, 180, 181, 200

private sector   3, 4, 61, 132, 181

privatization   9, 61, 181, 183, 187, 209, 210, 211

property rights   117, 179, 185

prospecting   106, 174

protected areas

  and alleviation of poverty   109

  and capitalism   110

  and community building   140

  and corporate conservation   192

  and developers   30

  and dispossesion   19

  and human rights   107

  and international organizations   25, 117

  and land reform   185

  and restitution   84

  and rhetoric of stakeholding   106

  and social justice   107

  and the security of nature   108

  anthropogenic aspect   96

  as percentage of South African land surface   102

  during apartheid   41

  expansion of   19

  impact on local population   169

  influence of *terra nullius* discourse   18, 117

  management of   107, 110

  private sector investment in   181

public–private venues   208

racial mapping   42, 205

racial profiling   127

Rainbow Nation   8, 44–6, 53, 158, 206

reburial   170, 207

recognition   40, 71, 121

reconciliation   19, 51, 61, 63

Reconstruction and Development Programme   178

refugees   20, 86, 87, 91, 92, 198

remembering   1, 10, 46, 47, 71

reparations   10, 84, 121, 182, 200, 211

Resilience Alliance   115

restitution   40, 61, 71, 109, 117, 121, 140, 185, 187

restructuring programs   209

risk registers   30

rock art

  and restitution   61

  funding   151

  geometric   70

  heritage   134, 206

  iconology   206

  mapping   133

  San   127, 188

  sites   3, 29, 35, 65, 70, 72, 126, 132

  walking trails   133, 134

Rock Art Research Institute (RARI)   3, 133, 134, 192

Rural Development Plan   102

Sandenbergh, J. A. B.   82, 83

Savannah Networking Meeting   138

Scientific Services Unit (of SANParks)   138

segregation   9, 17, 18, 57, 121, 126

Shangaan community   57, 59, 149, 158, 159

Shark Island   86

Skukuza (individual), *see* Stevenson-Hamilton, James (Col.)

Skukuza (place)   6, 64, 75, 103, 104, 127, 196, 198, 199

social ecology   136–42, 152, 157, 162, 168, 183, 185, 188, 212

social justice   185

Social Science Research Unit   138–9, 142

social sciences   124, 125, 142

social transformation   5, 46–7

socionature   213

South African Defence Force (SADF)   42,
    87–92
South African Heritage Resources Agency
    (SAHRA)   65
South African National Parks (SANParks)
    achievements   211
    and ANC policies   61
    and archaeology   95, 96, 136, 140, 142,
        151
    and biodiversity   61, 95, 100, 108, 110,
        111, 112, 113, 115, 128, 141, 146, 157,
        182, 210
    and cultural heritage   95
    and neoliberalism   61
    and sustainability   10
    and Thulamela   3, 150–4, 157, 160,
        163–5, 167–70, 173–4
    and tourism   210
    as healing institution   95
    contract with the Makulele   201
    corporate structure   140
    liberalization   182
    marketing campaigns   110
    meetings with stakeholders   188
    mission   122, 210, 211
    public–private management system
        94
    restructuring   180, 183
Southern African Development
    Community (SADC)   46
Spatial Development Initiative (SDI)
    179
squatters   18, 79, 80, 83, 85
Statement of Reconciliation (Australia)
    145
Stevenson-Hamilton, James (Col.)
    ("Skukuza")   63, 75, 77, 79, 81, 85,
        93, 103, 119, 123, 146
sustainability
    and conservation   14
    and cultural heritage   12, 34
    and diversity   32
    and economic development   102
    and future generations   26–33
    and human rights   32
    and SANParks management   10
    and UNESCO's work   26

    at Maropeng   41
    culture of   27
    role of museums   32
Sustainability Index   103
sustainable development   6, 32, 49,
    102
Sustainable Preservation Initiative   32

tendering   47, 164, 172, 189, 207, 208
terra nullius   18, 20, 116–21, 127, 143, 146,
    187, 212, 215
threshold of potential concern (TPC)
    141, 142
Thulamela   11, 149–75
    and South African National Parks   3,
        150–4, 157, 160, 163–5, 167–70,
        173–4
    and Z. Pallo Jordan   48–9
    as a Venda site   158
    as neglected archaeological heritage
        67, 212
    condition of site   141, 147, 166, 168
    development   183
    early history   72, 73
    Environment Education Center   153
    excavation   68
    first collaborative archaeological project
        161
    funding   151, 152–5, 167, 208
    management   153
    political uses   51
    reburials   157–60
tourism
    and apartheid   143
    and conservation   210
    and public–private management   94
    and SANParks   210
    community-based   48
    cultural   114, 163, 164, 179
    development   179
    employment through   2
    environmental   46, 114
    exclusive   195, 196
    heritage   7, 20, 179, 207
    international   48, 57, 58, 115, 193,
        209
    nature-based   61, 179

people-centred   61
safari   35, 120, 210
tradeoff with conservation   61
trauma   39, 101
see also ecotourism
tourist levies   186
trade   35, 50, 61, 66, 72, 74, 76, 79, 87, 94, 117, 178, 179, 184, 212
Transformation Charter   173
Transformation Task Team   173
trekpas   75, 79–84, 213
tribal authority   106
tribal culture   29, 55, 205
tribalism   9, 38, 41–3, 52, 55, 208
tribal lands   187
tribal villages   28, 208
Truth and Reconciliation Commission   2, 46

unemployment   7, 50, 57, 86, 89
United Nations Environment Program (UNEP)   27, 109
United States Agency for International Development (USAID)   208

Van de Capelle, Jan   74
Van Riebeeck celebrations   44
Varty, Dave   195
Vergangenheitsbewältung   1

violence   5, 9, 34, 40, 89, 94, 199, 209
visitation   5, 26, 34

wages   116, 179
walking trails   133, 134
watershed protection   110
weapons smuggling   89
see also gun running
Welverdiend   165, 176–8, 179, 191; 193, 195
West Coast National Park   138
Wildebeest Kuil Rock Art Centre   7, 206, 208
wilderness   9, 10, 12, 13, 16, 18, 21, 35, 63, 111, 146, 157, 197, 208, 211
workshop culture   8, 172
World Heritage Fund   31
World Heritage List   25
world heritage sites   47, 208
World Wildlife Fund (WWF)   25, 31, 89, 117, 152, 180, 193, 195, 215

xenophobia   8, 9, 47, 113, 205

Yellowstone model   85
Yosemite National Park   23

Zuid Afrikaansche Republiek (ZAR)   76
Zuma, Jacob   8, 49, 206, 207